FREAKS AND GEEKS.

FREAKS AND GEEKS®

The Complete Scripts
Volume 2
Episodes 10-18

Introduction by Judd Apatow

NEWMARKET PRESS • NEW YORK

This book is published in the United States of America.

Freaks and Geeks Created by Paul Feig
Executive Produced by Judd Apatow
Pilot Episode Directed by Jake Kasdan

Book Edited by Andrew Jay Cohen, Paul Feig, and Judd Apatow

Episodes Written by Judd Apatow, Steve Bannos, Paul Feig, Jeff Judah, Jon Kasdan, Rebecca Kirshner, Patty Lin, Bob Nickman, Gabe Sachs, J. Elvis Weinstein, and Mike White

Scrapbook Design by Andrew Jay Cohen

Photography by Saeed Adyani, Mike Ansell, Byron Cohen, Paul Drinkwater, Chris Haston, Ethan Hill, Kurt Iswarienko, Gabe Sachs, Sam Urdank, and Scott Wolf

Scripts Prepared by Jeff Warrington

Book Production by Paul Sugarman

Project Assistance by Keith Hollaman, Shannon Berning, and Kristy Cox

Special thanks to Esther Margolis, Publisher of Newmarket Press

www.freaksandgeeks.com

Cover Design by Timothy Shaner

First Edition

10 9 8 7 6 5 4 3 2 1

Library of Congress Cataloging-in-Publication Data available upon request.

ISBN 1-55704-646-8

QUANTITY PURCHASES

Companies, professional groups, clubs, and other organizations may qualify for special terms when ordering quantities of this title. For information, write Special Sales Department, Newmarket Press, 18 East 48th Street, New York, NY 10017; call (212) 832-3575; fax (212) 832-3629; or e-mail mailbox@newmarketpress.com.

www.newmarketpress.com

Manufactured in the United States of America.

CONTENTS

INTRODUCTION

When first asked to write the introduction to this book, I hesitated because I have spoken so often and so extensively on the subject of *Freaks and Geeks* that I thought I had nothing else to say. But Paul had written four pages for the first book, and the publisher wanted me to do the same. It wouldn't be easy, because I personally did more than a dozen DVD commentaries and literally hundreds of interviews. What haven't I said on the subject? So, I sat and thought—what else is there?

Hmmmm.

Uh.

Hmmm.

Well...

Hmmmm.

Oh, here's something. Recently I was talking to J. J. Abrams, the guy who created *Alias* and co-created *Felicity*. I recommended a writer to him, and a few days later I sent him a copy of the *Freaks and Geeks* DVD. He sent me a letter saying thank you. So...that's something. What else? Once when we were shooting the Disney film *Heavyweights*, Paul Feig and I took one of the kids who was in the film to a Minor League Baseball game. That kid's name is Kenan Thompson and now he is on *Saturday Night Live*. He is also going to play Fat Albert in a new movie. That's kind of interesting, but I guess it isn't about *Freaks and Geeks*. He read for *Undeclared*. But I guess that still isn't about *Freaks and Geeks*. Oh, once I was yelling at the editor because whatever I asked him to do, he would edit it just a little bit differently. It was like he wasn't listening. I was on pills for my back and had a short fuse, so I said, "What is the matter with you today? You are driving me out of my mind!" He replied, "One of my best friends just died," and began to cry. I felt bad. That's not a fun story. Maybe I shouldn't have told that one. Once I had dinner with Ben Stiller and Mick Jagger. We were talking about making a film. I was so scared that I barely spoke. At one point, I tried to say I related to what it is like for Jagger to be on the road, because I used to go on the road as a stand-up comedian. He didn't really respond. I couldn't tell if he didn't care or was annoyed that I compared my life to his. We also met Keith Richards. When we pitched the film to him, Ben said he wanted to shoot it in the same style as their concert film *Gimme Shelter*. Keith Richards replied, "But this time, let's do it without the murder," then laughed his ass off. Now we are on a roll here. This intro is going well. When I was in seventh grade, my parents said I could go to rock concerts, so I bought tickets to see Jethro Tull on Monday and Styx on Friday, both at Nassau Coliseum. The night before the Tull concert, my appendix was killing me, but I didn't want to tell my parents because I knew that meant I wouldn't be able to go to the concerts. After several hours of vomiting, I relented and had an appendectomy. My friends Ron and Kevin went to the show and rubbed in my face that I missed the sight of the people sitting in front of them doing coke. Appendixes suck! Other concerts I saw as a kid: Billy Squire, Bob Seger, The Doobie Brothers,

Foreigner (with Michael Bolton opening up), Queen, The Who, and Kool and the Gang. My musical taste cannot be denied. About fifteen years ago, I took mushrooms and went to see Frank Sinatra. I sat right behind his teleprompter, and every time he looked up from reading the lyrics, he had to look at me and my friends losing our minds. The whole show, I had two thoughts which I thought were very insightful. One was, "Frank has really lived these songs. I understand Frank." The other was, "Every guy here tonight is gonna get laid." The first time I had sex, when it was over, I said as a joke, "So, was it good for you, too?" She replied, "I guess it will get better." I just want to go on record and say THAT WAS SO UNCOOL. Do we have time for the story where I went to third base against my will? No. Okay, maybe next time. This turned out to be fun. Enjoy the book. And remember, we turned suffering into comedy and so can you.

—Judd Apatow, Executive Producer

FREAKS AND GEEKS

"THE DIARY"

Episode #10

Story by Judd Apatow & Rebecca Kirshner

Teleplay by Rebecca Kirshner

Directed by Ken Olin

Freaks and Geeks was my first real job & 'The Diary' was the 1st episode of TV I ever wrote. The weird magic of watching something you made up in your head become real is the most amazing thing. I learned how to re-write and how to tell a better joke and what 'craft services' are during the making of this show. I'm really grateful to Judd + Paul for letting me participate in the whole process -- casting, filming, editing, etc -- without ever making me feel like the ignorant rookie I was. I'm really proud of this script. REBECCA

CASTING NOTES

at Freaks + Geeks office

NO
Ich
Great
wild hair with freckles
Maybe
tall 21+8
very dirty...
but very cool looking
Red hair - slitty e...

KIRSHNER "THE DIARY"
Rough draft

FADE IN:

EXT. ROADSIDE - AFTERNOON

Four or five cars whiz past, the residue of a Michigan winter clinging to their rusty chassis. Across the street is a Hardee's restaurant and a bleak strip mall.

LINDSAY and KIM stand at the curb hitchhiking.

KIM
(to passing car)
Nice muffler!

Road salt still litters the curb but spring is in the air. Lindsay takes off her coat and ties it around her waist. She opens her face up to the sunlight.

LINDSAY
This is beautiful.

KIM
You don't get out much do you?

LINDSAY
Not enough; not like this.

KIM
Oh yeah, this is living. Pass the fish eggs.

LINDSAY
I just feel like, you know. It's the open road. Possibilities unfurling before us.

Kim ignores Lindsay, scanning the horizon for an approaching car.

KIM
We should be getting a ride here. Right here's the best spot.

LINDSAY
It's like, this is what it means to be an American. Who knows where we're going or what we'll see. Who knows--

KIM
--What? What the hell are you talking about?

(CONTINUED)

JUDD'S NOTES
- Jeep for new thing
- Julie handled ...
- Maybe Kim adds...
- How has Kid watching
- More believable
- Not worth her getting mad.
- looking for diary is too long, doesn't have to be hidden

INT. ENGLISH CLASS - DAY

...in the back row, chec...
Lindsay tries to catch Kim's e...

MS. LEWIS
Very good Mr. Lewis.
H.B. Lawrence a bit.
...Soar with an "O-A-R"
notswith an "-O-R-E".

She laughs by herself.

MS. LEWIS
Anyway. Who haven't...
Kelly. Would you do...

KIM
I'll go later.

MS. LEWIS
Oh, but I insist. I...
have to say for your...

Kim snaps her gum and begrudgi...
tries to give her an encouragi...

KIM
Fine.

Kim takes the podium. She's tr...
pretty nervous.

KIM (cont'...
Okay. So I read um...

She looks at the book's cover.

KIM (cont'...
Jack Kerouac. And so...
important book in my...
who wrote it. the wr...
say about. um, freedo...
being on the road.

CONTINUED: (2)   13.

LINDSAY
They were like, 'Kim Kelly is a bad ... going to go anywhere ...ag you down.' Like

...the locker room. Lindsay...

...want to work on our...

...turns to face Lindsay...

can't.

...to help each other.

...ling you'll get by ...'t want to drag you...the locker room. After a beat...

...giving...

LINDSAY
What does that mean?

KIM
NO, Lindsay.

L
I guess ... like a bad influence. They and you.

KIM
What else did they say?

L
I don't know! They said you didn't have a future and that you would drag me down. okay?

CUT TO:

K   Huh.

(CONTINUED)

FREAKS AND GEEKS

"THE DIARY"

CAST LIST

LINDSAY WEIR
SAM WEIR
HAROLD WEIR
JEAN WEIR
DANIEL DESARIO
NICK ANDOPOLIS
BILL HAVERCHUCK
NEAL SCHWEIBER
KIM KELLY
MR. FREDRICKS
MR. ROSSO
ALAN WHITE
MR. CASPER
GORDON CRISP
COOKIE KELLY
CHIP KELLY
DR. SCHWEIBER
MISS RUTH
ALBY PEAKEM
MIKE STEVENS
RICK PHILLIPS
SENOR O'HARA
KOBIE PILGRIM

FREAKS AND GEEKS

"THE DIARY"

SET LIST

INTERIORS:

MCKINLEY HIGH SCHOOL
    /LOCKER ROOM
    /FREDRICKS' OFFICE
    /OUTSIDE FREDRICKS' OFFICE
    /ENGLISH CLASSROOM
    /HALLWAY
    /CAFETERIA
    /MR. ROSSO'S OFFICE
WEIR HOUSE
    /DINING ROOM
    /LIVING ROOM
    /KITCHEN
    /LINDSAY'S BEDROOM
    /PARENT'S BEDROOM
ALBY'S CAR
NEAL SCHWEIBER'S HOUSE
    /LIVING ROOM
KIM KELLY'S HOUSE
    /LIVING ROOM
FREDRICKS' HOUSE
    /LIVING ROOM

EXTERIORS:

MCKINLEY HIGH SCHOOL
    /BASEBALL DIAMOND
ROADSIDE
WEIR HOUSE
    /FRONT PORCH
WOODED PATH

<u>TEASER</u>

FADE IN:

EXT. ROADSIDE - AFTERNOON

Four or five cars whiz past. LINDSAY and KIM stand at the
side of the road hitchhiking.

> KIM
> (to passing car)
> Nice muffler!

Kim scans the horizon for an approaching car.

> KIM (CONT'D)
> We should be getting a ride here.
> Right here's the best spot.

Lindsay basks in the sunlight.

> LINDSAY
> This is cool. Hitchhiking. Just
> like in Kerouac, you know?

> KIM
> Kerouac?

> LINDSAY
> Jack Kerouac. He wrote *On the Road*.
> Kim, we've been reading it in
> English for the last two weeks.
> Where've you been?

> KIM
> God. All we ever do in that class
> is read. Stick out your thumb,
> would ya?

> LINDSAY
> (getting worked up)
> We're so sheltered, you know? But
> there's this whole other America
> out there. The person who picks us
> up could be like an artist or a
> psychic or an escaped felon. It's
> so exciting.

> KIM
> Hey, Linds. One thing that helps -
> point your boobs toward the road.

Lindsay sticks out her tongue at Kim.

(CONTINUED)

CONTINUED:

A wood-paneled station wagon with a gun rack approaches slowly but passes them.

>   KIM (CONT'D)
>   (to Lindsay)
>   Dumb redneck.

The station wagon slams on its brakes and stops up the road. Lindsay and Kim bound over.

>   KIM (CONT'D)
>   Oops. I mean, cool guy.

INT. ALBY'S CAR - CONTINUOUS

They slide into the backseat. The driver, ALBY PEAKEM, is a hulking older man with a hairy neck. He grunts a hello and starts driving.

>   KIM
>   What's up? Drop us as close to the
>   corner of Wilson and Elm as you
>   can.

Kim settles back, content that they've gotten their ride. Lindsay's excited. She rolls down her window and lets the wind blow through her hair. Lindsay leans forward.

>   LINDSAY
>   I'm Lindsay. This is Kim.

Kim rolls her eyes, embarrassed at Lindsay's friendliness. The driver gives no response.

>   LINDSAY (CONT'D)
>   So, you from around these parts?

>   ALBY
>   1210 Lilac Terrace.

>   LINDSAY
>   (disappointed)
>   Oh. So, what do you do?

No response. Lindsay's getting a little anxious.

>   LINDSAY (CONT'D)
>   You pick up hitchers a lot?

The car stops at a stop sign. Alby Peakem turns to face Lindsay.

>   (CONTINUED)

CONTINUED:

>   ALBY
> Listen. I know you. I buy gear from
> your dad's store. I don't think you
> girls should be doing this and I
> feel obliged to tell him what
> you're up to.

He turns around. Kim gives Lindsay a wicked glare. Lindsay
buckles her seatbelt in defeat. Off her glum face, we...

>   CUT TO:

MAIN TITLES

ACT ONE

FADE IN:

INT. WEIR KITCHEN - EVENING

Lindsay sits at the kitchen table. Jean feverishly peppers
the meatloaf. Harold waves his thumb in Lindsay's face.

>   HAROLD
> This? The thumb? You think I don't
> know what this means? I know,
> Lindsay. It means: "Hey stranger.
> Please lock me in your car, drive
> me God knows where, and murder me!"

>   LINDSAY
> Dad. You're overreacting.

>   HAROLD
> Lindsay, I will not have my
> daughter hopping in cars like some
> woman of the night. You could have
> been picked up by Ted Bundy.

>   LINDSAY
> It was your friend, Dad.

>   HAROLD
> Alby Peakem is not my friend. He's
> a hunter who buys guns at my store.
> I don't trust that guy as far as I
> can throw him.

>   JEAN
> He seemed like a very conscientious
> man.

>   (CONTINUED)

CONTINUED:

Harold shoots her a look. Jean recovers with:

> JEAN (CONT'D)
> Lindsay. Your father and I don't
> want you to hitchhike ever again.

> LINDSAY
> Fine. It's not like it's my hobby.
> I did it once.

> HAROLD
> And once is one time too many.
> You're lucky you're alive right
> now.

> LINDSAY
> Dad, Kim does it all the time.
> Don't be so overdramatic.

> JEAN
> Her parents let her hitchhike?

> LINDSAY
> I don't know.

> HAROLD
> I'll bet she doesn't even have
> parents.

> LINDSAY
> Of course she does. Or at least she
> has a mom.

> JEAN
> Maybe we should meet her. We used
> to know all your friends' parents.

> LINDSAY
> Mom, that's 'cause I'm not in
> Brownies anymore and you don't pick
> me up from slumber parties.

> JEAN
> You know, I think we should have
> her over for dinner. Get
> acquainted.

> LINDSAY
> Mom, no. Please. Mrs. Kelly is
> really...
>   (MORE)

(CONTINUED)

CONTINUED: (2)

> LINDSAY (CONT'D)
> (struggles for the right
> word)
> ...busy.

> HAROLD
> Well, I think she ought to know
> what a bad influence her daughter
> is, don't you?

Lindsay eases out of her seat and begins to exit.

> LINDSAY
> Can we deal with this later? I've
> got homework.

> HAROLD
> You just cool your jets young lady.
> I'm not through talking to you. You
> know, I picked up a hitchhiker
> once. And you know where that
> hitchhiker is now?

Lindsay slumps back in her chair. Off her sullen look, we:

> CUT TO:

EXT. BASEBALL DIAMOND - DAY

Sam, BILL, NEAL, and GORDON CRISP are standing in a line with
all the other students (including ALAN) in gym class against
the backstop. Standing across from them on the field is COACH
FREDRICKS who is flanked by two big jocks, MIKE STEVENS and
RICK PHILLIPS.

> FREDRICKS
> All right, guys. Let's play a
> little softball.
> (slapping the two jocks on
> their backs)
> Pick your teams, gents.

Bill, Sam and Neal all heave a collective sigh. However, Bill
looks extremely distressed.

> BILL
> Oh, man, here we go.

ANGLE ON: BILL - looking pained. We PUSH IN ON HIS FACE.
Everything starts to go to SLOW MOTION as he heaves another
sigh. We hear nothing except his breathing. The SIGH is very
loud.

BILL'S POV: All in SLOW MOTION, he sees:

> (CONTINUED)

CONTINUED:

ANGLE ON: STEVENS

> STEVENS
> (slo-mo voice)
> Okay, I've got Lewis.

ANGLE ON: ATHLETIC KID as he jogs over to Stevens.

ANGLE ON: ANOTHER ATHLETIC KID jogging to Phillips.

ANGLE ON: RICK PHILLIPS pointing and waving for another guy to join his team.

ANGLE ON: FREDRICKS giving another athletic kid a slap on the back as he runs up next to Stevens' team. The slap sounds like a cannon going off.

ANGLE ON: THE GEEKS staring at the captains impassively, resigned to their fate. Gordon is digging something out of his ear. The digging sounds like somebody crushing a bag of potato chips.

ANGLE ON: ALAN WHITE realizing he is picked. He throws his fist in the air, then turns and looks at the geeks. He laughs and gives them a mocking "see ya" wave. His laugh sounds deep and demonic.

ANGLE ON: Bill closing his eyes and shaking his head. Then he turns and sees...

BILL'S POV: Some CUTE GIRLS from the girl's gym class are stretching. They stare at the good looking kids and laugh at the geeks.

ANGLE ON: BILL looking even more depressed. We hear his BREATHING GET LOUDER. He looks back out at the teams.

ANGLE ON: THE TWO TEAMS almost full as another jock kid jogs out. His footsteps echo loudly as he runs up to his team. All the athletic kids are out there.

ANGLE ON: PHILLIPS AND STEVENS with their arms crossed, brows furrowed, not pleased with their final options.

ANGLE ON: FREDRICKS smiling and shaking his head good-naturedly.

> FREDRICKS
> (his voice slowed down)
> Divvy them up. Let's go.

ANGLE ON: THE GEEKS, Bill, Sam, Neal and Gordon. They are the only ones left.

(CONTINUED)

CONTINUED: (2)

ANGLE ON: BILL, his eyes go wide as he waits for the final judgment.

We HEAR HIS HEARTBEATS. They slowly speed up.

ANGLE ON: STEVENS pointing to Sam weir.

ANGLE ON: SAM shrugging his shoulders to Bill then jogging out.

ANGLE ON: PHILLIPS who gives his teammates a look that says "who the hell should I pick?" Then he shrugs and points.

ANGLE ON: BILL, his eyes go wide in disbelief and his jaw drops. He looks over.

ANGLE ON: GORDON CRISP walking out to his team.

ANGLE ON: BILL, who can't believe it. Then he looks at Neal, standing next to him. BILL'S HEARTBEATS SPEED UP.

ANGLE ON: NEAL who gives Bill a look like "here we go again." Neal looks at Stevens with confidence, selling himself as a potential player.

ANGLE ON: BILL looking back out at the captains, nervous.

> BILL
> (slow-mo voice; to
> himself)
> Pick me. Pick me. Pick me.

ANGLE ON: STEVENS, who studies them both. He's really deliberating. BILL'S HEARTBEAT IS NOW GOING A MILE A MINUTE. Stevens nods his head and slowly points.

> STEVENS
> (slo-mo voice)
> We'll take HIM.

ANGLE ON: NEAL, who jumps in the air like he's just won a gold medal.

> NEAL
> (slowed down)
> YYYYYYEEEEEEAAAAAAYYYYYYYY!!!

Bill's face drops. His eyes close in pain. He looks like he's just been shot.

(CONTINUED)

CONTINUED: (3)

>   BILL
>   (slowed way down)
>   Oh, no.

He smacks his hand against his forehead. THE SLAP SOUNDS
GIGANTIC.

SUDDENLY, WE'RE BACK IN REAL TIME. Fredricks claps his hands
and whistles.

>   FREDRICKS
>   All right. Let's play ball!

>   PHILLIPS
>   Haverchuck, you and Crisp head out
>   to left field.

>   BILL
>   Left field. Wow. I've never played
>   <u>left</u> field. I'm always in right.

>   PHILLIPS
>   No... back up left. There's a big
>   puddle way out there. Stand in
>   front of it and make sure the ball
>   doesn't get all muddy.

Bill sighs and slogs out to the field.

>   CUT TO:

INT. ENGLISH CLASS - DAY

Students are congregating before class. NICK is at his desk.
Lindsay searches for a place to sit. She sits down at the
desk in front of Nick, looks at him and smiles lamely.

>   LINDSAY
>   Hey. How's it going?

>   NICK
>   It's going.

There is an awkward silence. Nick won't give her eye contact.

>   LINDSAY
>   So. What have you been doing?

>   NICK
>   (mumbling)
>   Stuff. Drumming.

>   (CONTINUED)

CONTINUED:

> LINDSAY
> Great.

> NICK
> Yeah. It's really great. Never been
> greater.

Kim interrupts them. She takes the seat next to Lindsay.

> KIM
> So, what happened with your parents
> last night? You grounded?

> LINDSAY
> Not exactly.

Lindsay laughs a little, sort of nervously.

> LINDSAY (CONT'D)
> My parents want to meet your mom.

> KIM
> What?

> LINDSAY
> They want to get to know her.

> KIM
> (disturbed)
> Shut up.

> LINDSAY
> I'm serious. They're inviting her
> over for dinner.

> NICK
> Could you please be quiet? Class is
> starting.

The English teacher, MR. CASPER, calls the class to order.

> MR. CASPER
> I hope you all brought your books
> to class. Because today, we're not
> in a classroom, we're in a coffee
> house. And you're not students,
> you're all beat poets. And we're
> gonna be reading aloud.

He waves his copy of <u>On the Road</u>.

(CONTINUED)

CONTINUED: (2)

> KIM
> Lindsay, my mom's not like that.
> She can't just have dinner with
> other people. She's crazy.

Mr. Casper barks out to them.

> MR. CASPER
> Ladies.

> KIM
> Tell your parents I'm an orphan. I
> raised myself.

> MR. CASPER
> Ms. Kelly, could I please have your
> attention up here?

> KIM
> Yes, Ms. Casper.

The class chuckles at Kim's dig. Mr. Casper is not amused.

> MR. CASPER
> I guess we know who's reading out
> loud first.

CUT TO:

EXT. BASEBALL DIAMOND - SAME TIME

Gordon sits in front of a puddle in deep left field. Bill
stands, trying to get into the game.

> BILL
> (hopelessly)
> Hey, batta-batta-batta.

> GORDON
> Could you be quiet, please?

A beat.

> BILL
> I'm really a shortstop.

> GORDON
> Is that right?

They stare off into the distance.

(CONTINUED)

CONTINUED:

>   BILL
>   (wistful)
>   A meeting on the mound. I wonder
>   what they're talking about.

>   GORDON
>   Yeah.

Another beat.

>   BILL
>   (venomous)
>   I really hate this. This is so
>   unfair. You know, maybe I'm good.
>   They have no idea. Maybe I'm
>   unbelievably good. But are they
>   ever going to find out? No. Because
>   they never put me in a position
>   where I can catch a ball. I hate
>   them.

>   GORDON
>   Maybe they're scared of you.

>   BILL
>   Maybe.

ANGLE ON: Bill and Gordon from behind, revealing how very far
they are from the infield. Play continues in the BG, the
players as small as ants.

>   FREDRICKS
>   (yelling from the infield)
>   Hey, Haverchuck, look alive out
>   there.

Bill's eyes narrow into dangerous-looking slits.

>   CUT TO:

INT. MCKINLEY HIGH SCHOOL HALLWAY - DAY

Bill stands outside the door marked "GUIDANCE". He looks both
ways and eases open the door.

INT. ROSSO'S OFFICE - CONTINUOUS

Bill enters. He scans the deserted office nervously. He makes
his way to a corkboard where a hot pink colored packet is
pinned. He's about to snatch it when MR. ROSSO enters.

>   (CONTINUED)

CONTINUED:

> MR. ROSSO
> Hey, what a surprise. What are you
> doing here Mr. Bill?

> BILL
> (caught off guard)
> Um, I need some help?

Bill sits down.

> MR. ROSSO
> What's going on?

> BILL
> (grasping at straws)
> Uh. My grandpa died.

Rosso's casual demeanor changes. He is genuinely sympathetic.

> MR. ROSSO
> I am so sorry. When did he pass on?

> BILL
> Um, three years ago?

Rosso nods.

> MR. ROSSO
> And it's still getting you down,
> huh? Well, you're not alone, Bill.
> Losing someone like a grandpa can
> be pretty tough.

> BILL
> Yeah.

> MR. ROSSO
> I'm really glad you came to talk to
> me. I've got this great little
> pamphlet about grieving that I
> think we should take a look at.
> Does that sound like a plan?

> BILL
> Yeah, I guess.

> MR. ROSSO
> I'll just poke around here for a
> minute and find it.
> (rifling through his desk)
> Darn. I think it might be in the
> back room. Hang tight, Kiddo.

(CONTINUED)

13.

CONTINUED: (2)

Rosso disappears into the back room. Bill approaches the corkboard on tip-toe. He swiftly tears down the pink packet.

> MR. ROSSO (O.S.) (CONT'D)
> O-kay. What have we here? Yes indeed, the pamphlet in question.

Rosso returns. Bill hides the pink packet behind his back and sits down. Rosso pulls around his chair to sit next to Bill. He hands Bill the pamphlet which is titled 'DEALING WITH GRIEF' and features a cartoon kid crying on its cover.

> MR. ROSSO (CONT'D)
> Here we go.
> (reading)
> People are like flowers. When a flower is plucked, the garden mourns, but the flower itself is in a vase somewhere bringing great joy to others...

Off Bill's look of dread, we:

CUT TO:

INT. WEIR PARENTS BEDROOM - EARLY EVENING

Bill, Sam and Neal look at the teachers' phone list.

CLOSE-UP: Bill's dirty fingernail traces under the name 'COACH FREDRICKS' across to a phone number.

> SAM
> So are we going to send him a pizza? That could be really funny.

> NEAL
> Aw, that's only funny if we could watch him get it.

Neal lies on the Weirs' bed.

> SAM
> Don't lay on my parents' bed.

> BILL
> No. No pizzas. I know what I'm doing.

(CONTINUED)

CONTINUED:

> NEAL
> Wait, all the teachers' numbers are
> in here? Ooh, Mrs. Garcia. Up for a
> date with an older woman, Sam?

> SAM
> Mrs. Garcia? You're sick.

Bill takes a big swig of his Faygo Pop for courage.

> BILL
> Hand me the phone.

Bill dials the number in the directory.

> SAM
> Can you get arrested for making
> prank phone calls?

> NEAL
> (sarcastic)
> Yeah, you go to telephone jail.

> BILL
> (in a monotonous baritone)
> Hello, Coach Fredricks?

> FREDRICKS
> Yes.

INTERCUT AS NEEDED WITH:

INT. FREDRICKS' LIVING ROOM - SAME TIME

Fredricks lies on his couch, wearing underwear and knee-high
tube socks. He is eating directly from a carton of ice cream.

> BILL
> Yes, this is Mr. Crisp, Gordon
> Crisp's father.

> FREDRICKS
> Yes, Mr. Crisp. How are you?

> BILL
> Not good. I want to give you a
> piece of my mind. I think it's
> really unfair how you run baseball
> in gym class. You always let the
> jock kids run the game.
> (MORE)

(CONTINUED)

CONTINUED:

> BILL (CONT'D)
> Some kids, like Gordon, my son,
> might be really good ball players
> but you never give them a chance.
> They might want to play shortstop
> for instance. But you assume
> they're bad without ever giving
> them a shot.

> FREDRICKS
> I'm sorry, Mr. Crisp. I just always
> assumed Gordon didn't have an
> interest in sports.

> BILL
> Well, he does. Don't judge a book
> by its cover.

> FREDRICKS
> I apologize. I'll rectify the
> situation immediately.

> BILL
> Okay, then. Thank you for your
> time. Goodbye now.

Bill hangs up the phone. The geeks crack up.

> BILL (CONT'D)
> I did it!

> SAM
> What did he say?

> BILL
> He totally bought it. He called me
> Mr. Crisp! Man, I can't wait till
> tomorrow.

> SAM
> (sarcastic)
> Yeah. Now we're really gonna have
> to play baseball. Good work, Bill.

> BILL
> Fellas, I just changed our lives.

Neal and Sam look worried. Bill smiles, pleased with himself.

> FADE OUT.

END OF ACT ONE

<u>ACT TWO</u>

FADE IN:

INT. KIM KELLY'S LIVING ROOM - EARLY EVENING

An anxious Kim sits in the living room, in front of the TV.
Her brother CHIP is passed out on the couch. COOKIE KELLY
runs into the room, frantic.

            COOKIE
    Kim, I can't find my earrings.

            KIM
    What earrings?

            COOKIE
    The gold hoops...

Cookie realizes Kim is wearing the earrings.

            COOKIE (CONT'D)
    The ones in your ears. Hand them
    over.

Kim takes off the earrings. Cookie puts on the earrings.

            COOKIE (CONT'D)
    Are these Weirs gonna spring
    something on me? Did they find
    drugs on you? You steal from them?

            KIM
    No! It's just the hitchhiking.

            COOKIE
    It better be. I don't want any
    surprises.

            KIM
    Look, they're uptight. So, please -
    try to act normal.

            COOKIE
    Oh, you think I'm going to
    embarrass you?

            KIM
    Just don't get wasted, okay?

            COOKIE
    How do I look?

                                 (CONTINUED)

CONTINUED:

>   KIM
>   (genuine)
>   Nice.

>   COOKIE
>   Thanks. Jeez, I'm nervous.

Cookie gives herself one last look-over.

                                        CUT TO:

INT. WEIR DINING ROOM - SOON AFTER

Harold, Jean, and Cookie are in the middle of dinner. Cookie is on her best behavior.

>   COOKIE
>   You have such a lovely house.

>   JEAN
>   Thank you.

>   COOKIE
>   I had a beautiful house once. Over
>   on Maple. But then Kim's father
>   left me with two kids and a huge
>   mortgage and... well, that's life.

Cookie lets out a sad sigh. Jean gives a sympathetic smile.

>   JEAN
>   I can't imagine how difficult it
>   must be to raise children all by
>   yourself.

>   COOKIE
>   It's not easy. Chip, my oldest,
>   he's a doll. He's got water in his
>   brain, but he's a sweet kid. Kim's
>   another story.

IN THE HALLWAY

Lindsay is spying in the hall, trying to eavesdrop. As she peers around to get a better look, she accidentally knocks a knickknack off a countertop.

Lindsay retreats back towards her room.

                                        (CONTINUED)

CONTINUED:

BACK AT TABLE

> HAROLD
> Tell us about Kim.

> COOKIE
> Well, she ain't the sharpest crayon
> in the box. She's a real pain in
> the neck. And I know she hates me
> for being strict but I get worried.

> JEAN
> Of course.

> COOKIE
> Because I don't know what she's out
> there doing. She lies. These girls -
> they all lie.

Harold and Jean look suitably distressed.

> COOKIE (CONT'D)
> Kim tells me she's gonna study at
> the library - she goes to a party
> and gets loaded. She tells me she's
> seeing a movie - she's fooling
> around with some guy in the back of
> a van.

> JEAN
> Oh, my.

> COOKIE
> And you know how I find out?

> HAROLD
> How?

> COOKIE
> (quietly)
> I read her diary. I sneak into her
> room and I read it. She won't do
> her homework, but she's got a
> freakin' novel in there. I have to.
> It's the only way I can get the
> truth. And you want to know
> something? The truth is very scary
> because times have changed. These
> girls today - they run wild.

(CONTINUED

CONTINUED: (2)

Cookie gives them an alarming look. Harold and Jean are profoundly troubled.

                                                    CUT TO:

INT. LINDSAY'S ROOM - SOON AFTER

Lindsay is doing homework on her bed. Harold and Jean enter.

                    LINDSAY
          So... how was dinner?

                    HAROLD
          Lindsay, your mother and I don't
          want you spending any more time
          with Kim Kelly. Do you understand?

                    LINDSAY
          Just because her mother's insane
          doesn't mean--

                    JEAN
          She's not insane. She's practically
          a saint.

                    HAROLD
          Cookie Kelly is a hard working
          single mother who is doing her best
          with a selfish, delinquent teenage
          daughter. Let's just say I
          sympathize.

                    LINDSAY
          What?! Kim's mother is totally
          nuts.

                    HAROLD
          Lindsay, you know what happens when
          you put a rotten banana in a fruit
          bowl? All the other bananas go
          rotten. And that's what Kim Kelly
          is - a bad banana.

                    LINDSAY
          She's my friend. I mean, yeah,
          she's not like Millie.

                                              (CONTINUED)

CONTINUED:

                    HAROLD
          Oh, she's not like Millie, all
          right. She's as dumb as a crayon.
          Even her own mother says so.

                    JEAN
          Mrs. Kelly told us some very
          alarming things about Kim.

                    LINDSAY
          Like what?

                    HAROLD
          She experiments with drugs. And
          boys.

                    JEAN
          Is that true?

Lindsay hesitates, struggling for a diplomatic answer.

                    HAROLD
          Enough said. That girl is going to
          hell in a handbasket and I won't
          have you in it. No more Kim Kelly.

                    LINDSAY
          You can't tell me who I can be
          friends with!

                    HAROLD
          Well, I think I just did. And don't
          raise your voice to me.

Harold and Jean exit.

                                        CUT TO:

INT. WEIR PARENTS BEDROOM - NIGHT

Harold sits up in bed, struggling with the cap of an antacid
bottle. Jean emerges from the bathroom with a glass of water
and carries it to Harold.

                    HAROLD
          Maybe she needs her head shrunk.

                    JEAN
          Harold.

Jean hands Harold the glass of water. In exchange, he hands
her the pill bottle which she opens easily.

                                        (CONTINUED)

CONTINUED:

She hands him two antacid tablets which he swallows with the
water. They do this without comment; this is their routine.

>   HAROLD
>   It's about trust. And frankly, I
>   don't trust her anymore.

>   JEAN
>   Oh. Lindsay's always been very
>   honest with us.

>   HAROLD
>   Yeah, well, she told us she didn't
>   cheat. We believed her and we ended
>   up with egg on our faces.

Harold lifts up the covers and Jean slides into bed.

>   HAROLD (CONT'D)
>   Does Lindsay have a diary?

>   JEAN
>   (nods)
>   I've seen her writing in it.

Harold gives Jean an insinuating look.

>   JEAN (CONT'D)
>   Harold, that's her private
>   property.

>   HAROLD
>   Well, I want to know what's going
>   on.

>   JEAN
>   I had a diary when I was a girl. If
>   my parents had read it, I would
>   have been furious. It's such a
>   violation.

>   HAROLD
>   Spooning with a stranger in the
>   back of a van: that's a violation.

>   JEAN
>   She hasn't done that.

>   HAROLD
>   Yeah? Well, there's only one way to
>   know for sure. Goodnight, dear.

(CONTINUED)

CONTINUED: (2)

> JEAN
> Goodnight.

They peck and reach to turn off their respective reading lamps. It's completely dark.

> HAROLD
> I have the worst gas.

> JEAN
> Sweetheart, please don't.

CUT TO:

EXT. BASEBALL DIAMOND - DAY

Sam, Bill, Neal, and Gordon Crisp shiver along the backstop with the other unathletic kids. Bill shakes his head in disbelief; obviously their plan was a bust. Bill watches Fredricks joke around with the jocks who have already been picked. Phillips and Stevens keep choosing kids, as before.

Fredricks whispers something in Stevens' ear. Stevens shrugs good-naturedly.

> STEVENS
> All right, I want Crisp.

At the backstop, Gordon Crisp looks over his shoulder as if Stevens might be talking about someone else.

> FREDRICKS
> You heard him, Crisp. Join your
> team.

He hesitantly jogs out to join Stevens' team. Fredricks slaps Gordon on the back, nearly knocking the poor kid prostrate.

> FREDRICKS (CONT'D)
> You want to play shortstop?

> GORDON
> (terrified)
> No! Back-up right.

> BILL
> I can play shortstop.

> FREDRICKS
> Yeah, and I'm married to Raquel
> Welch, in my dreams.

(CONTINUED)

CONTINUED:

The jocks laugh. Bill stews.

>   FREDRICKS (CONT'D)
>   Okay Phillips, your pick.

>   PHILLIPS
>   Okay, I'll take... not Haverchuck.

Everyone laughs again.

>   CUT TO:

INT. MCKINLEY HIGH SCHOOL HALLWAY - DAY

Lindsay walks through the crowded hallway. Kim catches up
with her.

>   KIM
>   Hey.

>   LINDSAY
>   (awkward)
>   Hey, Kim.

>   KIM
>   So my mom like loves your parents.
>   I guess it went all right.

>   LINDSAY
>   Yeah. I guess.

>   KIM
>   What'd your parents say?

>   LINDSAY
>   Oh, they really liked your mom.

>   KIM
>   Cool.

>   LINDSAY
>   They also said...
>   (beat)
>   They're such dorks. Get this: I'm
>   not allowed to hang out with you.

Kim stares at Lindsay.

>   LINDSAY (CONT'D)
>   Look, it'll blow over. We just have
>   to wait it out awhile.

>   (CONTINUED)

CONTINUED:

> KIM
> What did they say about me?

> LINDSAY
> Oh, I don't know.

> KIM
> No. What? I'm interested.

> LINDSAY
> (thinks it's funny)
> Well, they said you're a bad
> banana. Aren't they queer?

> KIM
> What does that mean?

> LINDSAY
> I guess like a bad influence; I
> don't know.

> KIM
> What else did they say?
> (long beat)
> Tell me.

> LINDSAY
> Ki-im! I don't know. You're not
> smart, you do drugs; you have sex.
> Stupid stuff like that.

Kim is silent. They reach Lindsay's Spanish class.

> LINDSAY (CONT'D)
> I'm telling you, they're morons,
> Kim.

> KIM
> Wait. Do you think I care what your
> parents think of me?

> LINDSAY
> No. Of course not.

The second BELL rings. SENOR O'HARA, the bearded Irishman who teaches Spanish, waves Lindsay into the classroom.

> SENOR O'HARA
> Lindsay. Que te mueves el culo.

(CONTINUED)

CONTINUED: (2)

>   LINDSAY
> Lo siento Senor O'Hara. Estoy
> hablando con mi amiga. Es
> importante.

>   SENOR O'HARA
> La clase es importante, tambien.

>   LINDSAY
> Yo se, pero puede esterar un
> momento por favor?

Kim splits.

>   LINDSAY (CONT'D)
> Kim! Kim!

>   SENOR O'HARA
>   (to Lindsay; warning)
> Senorita, ahora.

Kim turns around.

>   KIM
> What?

>   LINDSAY
> I'll see you later, right?

>   KIM
> Yeah.

A confused Lindsay is shepherded inside by the Senor.

>   CUT TO:

INT. LINDSAY'S ROOM - DAY

Early afternoon light slants through the window. It's quiet.

>   JEAN (O.S.)
> Lindsay?

A RAP at the door. It opens a crack; Jean pokes her head in.

>   JEAN (CONT'D)
> Lindsay?

The door is pushed open revealing Harold and Jean.

>   (CONTINUED)

CONTINUED:

>   HAROLD
>   Why do you keep calling her name?
>   She's at school, for God's sake.

They enter. Jean puts her fingers to her throat.

>   JEAN
>   My heart is racing. Honey, maybe we
>   shouldn't do this.

>   HAROLD
>   Jean. We have to know what's going
>   on in our daughter's life, don't
>   we? For all we know, she could
>   become a junkie. Or a hooker.

>   JEAN
>   Harold, she's not going to become a
>   hooker.

>   HAROLD
>   Everybody's got parents, Jean. Even
>   hookers. Remember that TV movie we
>   saw.

Silently, they begin to prowl through Lindsay's belongings.
There is an illicit tension in the air. Harold sits at
Lindsay's under-sized desk and eases open a drawer. Jean
watches, her hand on his shoulder. The drawer contains odds
and ends. No diary.

Jean looks through the bookcase. She pulls out a volume.
Reading its cover:

>   JEAN
>   Are You There God? It's Me,
>   Margaret.

>   HAROLD
>   What?

>   JEAN
>   Just the name of a book.

Jean scans the rest of the covers. Nothing. She goes to the
dresser and opens the top drawer. There, nestled among the
underwear, bras, and socks, is Lindsay's diary. Jean holds it
to her chest.

>   JEAN (CONT'D)
>   Harold. Here it is.

>   (CONTINUED)

CONTINUED: (2)

> HAROLD
> Bring it here.

Jean doesn't budge.

> JEAN
> Maybe we should read it later.

> HAROLD
> Jean. Come on. My lunch hour's
> almost over. The store's not gonna
> run itself.

Jean opens the diary.

> JEAN
> (reading)
> "Warning to all snoops! Do not read
> beyond this page. If you read on
> it's because you have no life and
> have nothing better to do than pry
> into mine. Anyone who keeps reading
> on is cursed and will suffer until
> they die a slow and painful death.
> This means you Sam!"

Harold raises his eyebrows and smiles at Jean. She doesn't
smile.

> HAROLD
> Read on!

> FADE OUT.

<u>END OF ACT TWO</u>

<u>ACT THREE</u>

FADE IN:

INT. LINDSAY'S ROOM - DAY

Harold lies back with his feet kicked up on Lindsay's bed.
Jean paces, flipping through the diary.

> HAROLD
> What does it say about Kim Kelly?

> JEAN
> Nothing. Just that she thinks Kim
> Kelly has...

(CONTINUED)

CONTINUED:

Jean trails off, embarrassed.

                    HAROLD
          Has what?

                    JEAN
          ...a different word for courage?

                    HAROLD
               (grimacing)
          Anything about drugs? Pot? Acid?

                    JEAN
          I don't think so.

                    HAROLD
          Well, what does it say?

                    JEAN
               (reading)
          "I'm so sick of living in this
          claustrophobic suburban world--"

                    HAROLD
          --Get used to it.

                    JEAN
          "Where everyone is trying to fit
          in. I feel like I live in a world
          of scared robots. Honestly, and
          this is terrible, but two of the
          worst ones are Mom and Dad."

                    HAROLD
          What? What does that mean?

This starts to hit home for Jean; she is truly distressed.

                    JEAN
               (reading)
          "They are the most boring,
          repressed people on the face of the
          entire earth."

                    HAROLD
          Repressed? I'll repress her. Go on.

Harold sits next to Jean.

(CONTINUED)

CONTINUED: (2)

                    JEAN
              (reading)
    "They say they love each other but
    who knows, it's probably just part
    of their routine. Anyway can robots
    really be in love?"
              (beat)
    Harold, I don't think we should be
    doing this.

                    HAROLD
    Keep reading.

                    JEAN
    Let's see.
              (reading)
    "Their whole life is this
    monotonous routine. She cooks
    dinner - practically the same meal
    every night. He comes home, barking
    at everyone, like a fascist
    dictator who's scared his, ah...
    who's scared his penis will fall
    off if he ever helped clear the
    table. "

Harold sits up on the bed, looking disturbed.

                    JEAN (CONT'D)
    "And she lets him walk all over
    her. I love them. But it's not the
    life for me. No, thank you--"

                    HAROLD
    --Stop. Stop. That's enough.

Jean closes the diary. They look at each other, stricken.

The phone RINGS and Harold and Jean jump a mile. Harold
shoves the diary back into Lindsay's sock drawer. Again, the
phone RINGS. Harold looks at Jean. She looks away, awkward.
Her voice comes out funny:

                    JEAN
    I'll get it.

She runs out of the room.

                                        CUT TO:

INT. CAFETERIA - DAY

DANIEL, Nick and Kim are eating lunch.

                    NICK
        I think the worst would be getting
        eaten alive by wolves. No question.

                    DANIEL
        No way. Falling into a grain
        thresher is so much worse. It's
        like embarrassing to die in a piece
        of farm equipment.

                    KIM
        You know what I think? I think
        you're all really morbid.

                    NICK
        Hey, you asked the question.

                    KIM
        Yeah, but you answered it.

Lindsay joins them at the table with her tray.

                    LINDSAY
        Hey, guys.

The tension is palpable. Kim and Nick don't even acknowledge
her. Suddenly, Nick stands.

                    NICK
        I gotta go. I told Ken I'd help him
        in the auto shop.

He exits.

                    KIM
            (glaring at Lindsay)
        I should get going, too. I've gotta
        go do some drugs. Oh yeah, and have
        sex.

                    DANIEL
        What?

                    KIM
        Lindsay knows what I'm talking
        about.

                                  (CONTINUED)

CONTINUED:

> LINDSAY
> No, I don't.

> DANIEL
> Somebody want to fill me in?

Kim shakes her head in disgust and starts to get up.

> LINDSAY
> Wait, you mean what my parents
> said?

Kim looms over Lindsay.

> KIM
> I told you. I don't care what your
> parents say about me.

> LINDSAY
> So why are you pissed?

> KIM
> Well, I do happen to care what my
> friends say about me.

> LINDSAY
> I didn't say anything.

And with that Kim exits. Daniel smiles at Lindsay.

> DANIEL
> You sure know how to clear a room.

And off Lindsay's distressed look, we...

> CUT TO:

INT. SCHWEIBER LIVING ROOM - RIGHT AFTER SCHOOL

A fancier living room than any we've seen yet. Wall-to-wall carpeting, lots of leather and lucite. Sam sits on the white leather couch eating straight from a box of bran cereal. Bill looks bored. Neal pokes around, looking for something.

> BILL
> Sam's spilling cereal.

> SAM
> Is this the best cereal you've got?

> (CONTINUED)

CONTINUED:

> NEAL
> I don't know. I never eat
> breakfast. I just have my coffee.

Sam holds up the box of bran cereal.

> SAM
> Don't you have any sugar cereals?

DR. RICHARD SCHWEIBER enters the room. Knotting his necktie, full of good cheer.

> DR. SCHWEIBER
> Not in this house. Rots the
> choppers.

> NEAL
> Hey, Dad. Why are you home?

Dr. Schweiber just ruffles his son's hair; Neal squirms.

> SAM
> Hi, Dr. Schweiber.

> DR. SCHWEIBER
> Sam, Bill. How we doin'? You guys
> got big plans for this afternoon?

> NEAL
> Not really.

> BILL
> We're gonna make some, ah, phone
> calls.

> NEAL
> (staring BILL down)
> Ix-nay ig-bay outh-may.

> DR. SCHWEIBER
> (jovial)
> Hey, I speak Pig Latin too, you
> know. Who are you calling?

Bill shrugs.

> BILL
> Mean people.

> DR. SCHWEIBER
> Oh, prank calls, huh? Well, boys
> will be boys I guess.

(CONTINUED)

CONTINUED: (2)

Dr. Schweiber puts on his jacket.

> DR. SCHWEIBER (CONT'D)
> I could tell you guys some great
> prank call stories.

> SAM
> Yeah?

> DR. SCHWEIBER
> Okay, just one. My freshman year in
> college there was a pay phone on
> the street that we could see from
> our dorm room. So we get the number
> right?

> SAM
> Right.

> DR. SCHWEIBER
> And we'd wait until there was some
> real big guy standing near it,
> wearing a green hat, say. Then I'd
> call the number and tell whoever
> answered that I was calling for my
> father. I'd describe my father: big
> guy, green hat. Yeah, that was some
> pretty funny stuff.

Dr. Schweiber ruffles Neal's hair. He picks up his briefcase
and checks his watch. He makes a 'telephone' with his
fingers.

> DR. SCHWEIBER (CONT'D)
> Just keep it clean, all right? No
> heavy breathing.
>   (to Neal)
> See you at dinner, Short-stuff.

Dr. Schweiber exits; the geeks ad-lib good-byes. Neal watches
his father go, perplexed: why was his father home?

> BILL
> Heavy breathing, that's a good
> idea.

> SAM
> Doesn't your dad work during the
> day?

(CONTINUED)

CONTINUED: (3)

> NEAL
> Sometimes he comes home to change
> his shirt. Root canals make him
> sweaty.

Bill has already picked up the phone and dialed.

> BILL
> Listen to this. This is gonna be
> good.
> (into phone; super-low
> voice)
> Fredricks? You're a turd. A stinky,
> fat turd. Go sniff a jock strap,
> you poop-head...

INTERCUT AS NEEDED WITH:

INT. FREDRICKS' LIVING ROOM - SAME TIME

Fredricks is standing with the young woman gym teacher, MISS
RUTH, when the phone rings. His face remains blank as he
listens.

INT. SCHWEIBER LIVING ROOM - SAME TIME

> BILL
> You love patting boys' butts. You
> love patting boys' butts. Butt
> butt, butt patter! You're a perv
> and a loser and a turd.

Bill hangs up the phone, very pleased with himself.

> SAM
> You better hope he never finds you
> out.

> NEAL
> Yeah. If the cops trace that call
> you are so dead.

> BILL
> You mean if the cops trace that
> call, you are dead.

Neal cringes.

INT. FREDRICKS' LIVING ROOM - SAME TIME

> MISS RUTH
> Who was that?

(CONTINUED)

CONTINUED:

After a beat.

> FREDRICKS
> An old friend.

CUT TO:

EXT. WOODED PATH - AFTERNOON

Kim and Daniel are walking and talking. By the look on
Daniel's bored face we can tell that Kim has been ranting
about Lindsay for quite a while.

> KIM
> I mean, who the hell does she think
> she is?

> DANIEL
> (disinterested)
> I don't know. Let's talk about it
> for four more hours and try to find
> out.

> KIM
> Oh, you should have seen her
> speaking Spanish. Uno moment. Uno
> moment. Oh, god.

> DANIEL
> Sounds terrible.

> KIM
> She thinks she's the Queen of
> England.

Kim steps in dog doodie.

> KIM (CONT'D)
> I'll kill that dog. Daniel, get me
> a stick.

Daniel hands her a stick. Kim sits down and picks out the
poo from the bottom of her shoe.

> KIM (CONT'D)
> Who are they, the great Weirs, to
> call me a whore and a drug addict?

> DANIEL
> They didn't actually call you a
> whore and a drug addict.

(CONTINUED)

CONTINUED:

> KIM
> Basically! I'm not some whore. They
> just can't take it that I have sex.
> They're terrified that some bad man
> will soil their perfect little
> daughter.

> DANIEL
> You do have sex.

> KIM
> Yeah, with you.

> DANIEL
> But I'm a guy.

> KIM
> What the hell does that mean?

> DANIEL
> I don't know, if I had a daughter
> in high school I wouldn't want some
> guy climbing all over her.

> KIM
> What the hell are you talking
> about?

> DANIEL
> I'm just saying, it's not like they
> don't have a point. Who wants their
> kid to have sex and do drugs?
> Nobody.

Kim gets up.

> KIM
> You are such a jerk.

> DANIEL
> Don't get mad at me. I'm just
> trying to be rational.

> KIM
> Are you calling me irrational? I'll
> tear your face off right now. I'll
> tear it off and throw it over the
> fence.

They start walking.

(CONTINUED)

CONTINUED: (2)

> DANIEL
> I'm not saying I don't love you. I
> like the way you are. But you
> probably scare the hell out of
> them.

> KIM
> Oh, and how am I?

> DANIEL
> You're a sex crazed drug addict.

> KIM
> Screw you Daniel.

She exits.

> DANIEL
> I didn't mean anything. I'm just
> trying to spice up the
> conversation.

CUT TO:

INT. WEIR DINING ROOM - EVENING

Harold, Lindsay, and Sam sit at the table. Candles light the
room, the light flickering eerily. Sam dips his fingers in
the candle wax.

> HAROLD
> Sam, are you getting a kick-back
> from the fire department?

> SAM
> No. Mom's the one who put candles
> on the table.

> JEAN (O.S.)
> Okay, I've got something special
> for us tonight.

She carries two plates into the dining room and sets them
before Harold and Lindsay. On each plate is a tiny and
delicate bird dripping with a purple sauce.

> JEAN (CONT'D)
> Ta-da!

> HAROLD
> What the hell?

(CONTINUED)

CONTINUED:

Jean fetches two more plates, for herself and Sam. Jean steps behind Harold and puts her hands on his shoulders. She is full of nervous energy; teetering on the edge.

> JEAN
> Aren't they fantastic? They're
> Cornish game hens with a plum wine
> sauce.

> HAROLD
> What did you do, put poison in the
> birdfeeder?

Jean absorbs this blow. Sam giggles.

> JEAN
> They're exotic.

> SAM
> Is it a pigeon?

> JEAN
> It's not a pigeon; It's a kind of
> chicken.

> HAROLD
> You know, we can afford to buy
> fully grown chickens, Jean.

Sam giggles again. Lindsay gingerly cuts herself a bite.

> JEAN
> That a girl, Lindsay. It's good to
> try new things.

The bird slips around on Lindsay's plate.

> HAROLD
> Watch out, that miniature bird is
> trying to escape.

Harold holds up the little bird on his plate and makes its minute wings flap. He plays to Lindsay.

> HAROLD (CONT'D)
> "Hey, why don't you pick on someone
> your own size."

Sam cracks up. Catching his mother's expression, he tries to contain himself. Lindsay just rolls her eyes.

(CONTINUED)

CONTINUED: (2)

                    SAM
              (laughing)
        Mom, Dad's playing with his food.

                    HAROLD
        It's better than eating it.

                    JEAN
              (growing really
               frustrated)
        Just try a bite, they're delicious.

                    HAROLD
        Then help yourself to mine. I'm
        going to go make a sandwich.

                    SAM
        Me, too.

                    JEAN
        Harold, if you're not going to eat,
        then help me clear the table.

                    HAROLD
        What? That's not my job.

                    JEAN
        Oh, but it's mine?

Harold stands up.

                    HAROLD
        Yes. You don't run a store for
        twelve hours a day.

Harold walks into the kitchen.

                    SAM
        Can I be excused, too?

                    JEAN
        Lindsay, wouldn't it be nice if
        your father helped clear the table?

                    LINDSAY
              (weirded-out)
        I don't care. I'll clear my own
        plate. C'mon, Sam.

Sam and Lindsay escape. Harold and Jean face off through the
go-between.

                                        (CONTINUED)

CONTINUED: (3)

> HAROLD
> What was that all about?

> JEAN
> What do you think?

CUT TO:

INT. LOCKER ROOM - MORNING

Fredricks stands before the gym class.

> FREDRICKS
> Settle down. Don't bother changing
> yet.

GROANS from the jocks. Excited looks from the geeks.

> PHILLIPS
> Aw, scoliosis testing again.

> FREDRICKS
> Shut it. I've got something serious
> to say here. I've been getting
> prank phone calls at my house. Now,
> I know I got some jokers in here -
> some real funny guys. But what
> you're doing isn't funny. It's
> annoying. And more importantly,
> it's illegal.

Fredricks's eyes scan the crowd.

> FREDRICKS (CONT'D)
> I want to see each and every one of
> you comedians in my office. One at
> a time.

All our geeks look worried. Sam glares at Bill.

> NEAL
> Smooth move, Alexander Graham Bell.

CUT TO:

INT. OUTSIDE FREDRICKS' OFFICE - MOMENTS LATER

The line of boys trails back from Fredricks's door. Our geeks
have split up. There is one SKINNY FRESHMAN between Sam and
the door.

(CONTINUED)

CONTINUED:

Gordon Crisp exits the office, white as a ghost. As he passes Sam:

> SAM
> What happened in there?

Gordon just shakes his head, in shock.

> SAM (CONT'D)
> Did he beat you?

> GORDON
> I can't tell you. Ever.

The Skinny Freshman in front of Sam pushes him ahead.

> CUT TO:

INT. FREDRICKS' OFFICE - MOMENTS LATER

Sam sits. Fredricks hands Sam a piece of paper. Sam looks at it and looks back to Fredricks, with an exaggerated look of ignorance: what's this?

> FREDRICKS
> Read it.

Fredricks turns his head away and closes his eyes to listen.

> SAM
> (reading)
> You are a turd. A stinky, fat turd.

Sam stops. Fredricks opens his eyes.

> FREDRICKS
> Keep going.

> SAM
> Go sniff a jock strap.

> FREDRICKS
> Go on. Make your voice lower.

> SAM
> (low voice)
> You poop-head. Hey, Fredricks. You
> love patting boys' butts. You love--

> FREDRICKS
> I've heard enough.

(CONTINUED)

CONTINUED:

                  SAM
      Sorry.

                                   DISSOLVE TO:

Mike Stevens reads to Fredricks.

                STEVENS
          (low voice)
      Go sniff a jock strap, you poop-
      head. Hey, Fredricks. You love
      patting boys' butts.
         (to Fredricks)
      Geez, Coach. This is harsh.

                                     DISSOLVE TO:

Alan White sits in front of Fredricks.

                ALAN
      Butt, butt, butt patter.

He CRACKS UP, laughing until tears run down his face.

                                     DISSOLVE TO:

Neal reads to Fredricks. He clears his throat and reads very
dramatically, like he's auditioning for a play

                NEAL
          (low voice)
      You are a turd. A stinky, fat turd.
      Go sniff a jock strap. You poop-
      head. You are a dim-wit and an
      imbecile. I blow my nose in your
      general direction.

                FREDRICKS
      Hey! That's not in there!

Fredricks snatches the script away from Neal.

                NEAL
      It isn't?

                                     DISSOLVE TO:

Bill reads to Fredricks. His hands are shaking.

                                    (CONTINUED

CONTINUED: (2)

>   BILL
>   (soft voice)
>   Hey, Fredricks. You love patting
>   boys' butts--

>   FREDRICKS
>   Not softer; lower!

>   BILL
>   (reading; low voice)
>   You love patting boys' butts. You
>   love patting boys' butts. Butt,
>   butt, butt patter!

Fredricks listens carefully with his eyes still closed.

>   CUT TO:

INT. LOCKER ROOM - SOON AFTER

Fredricks stands before the class. He looks stern.

>   FREDRICKS
>   Just what I suspected. One of my
>   own men has been pranking me. It's
>   a sad day, let me tell you. But I'm
>   glad the culprit has been
>   identified.

The geeks go white with dread. Curious looks from all.

>   FREDRICKS (CONT'D)
>   Sam Weir, will you join me on a
>   stroll to the principal's office?

All eyes on Sam. He looks panicked. Bill bites his lip, as
we:

>   FADE OUT.

END OF ACT THREE

ACT FOUR

FADE IN:

INT. LOCKER ROOM - CONTINUOUS

All eyes on Sam. He looks like he's about to explode.

>   SAM
>   But... but... I didn't do it!

>   (CONTINUED)

CONTINUED:

>   FREDRICKS
>   You, young man are facing
>   suspension, possibly expulsion.
>   (to the others)
>   Not to mention, making obscene
>   phone calls is a felony in the
>   state of Michigan. My bet is they
>   give him the full five years in
>   juvenile detention...

Bill can't take it anymore.

>   BILL
>   No! It wasn't Sam! It was me! I did
>   it! I called you a butt-patter.

Fredricks smiles at Bill, not surprised.

>   FREDRICKS
>   I knew that would work. Okay, suit
>   up everybody. Haverchuck, you, me,
>   my office; now.

Fredricks walks into his office. Neal and Sam both turn to
Bill. He is quivering, terrified.

>   NEAL
>   Maybe you should call a lawyer.

>   SAM
>   It's gonna be okay, Bill.

>   BILL
>   I don't want to go to juvey hall.

Bill takes a deep breath, then exits into the office.

>   CUT TO:

INT. FREDRICKS' OFFICE - SOON AFTER

Fredricks leans back in his chair. Bill, distraught, sits
opposite.

>   FREDRICKS
>   So you think you're a comedian,
>   huh? Why don't you tell me a joke?

He smiles at Bill, expectantly. Bill's eyes go wide; his mind
blank.

>   (CONTINUED)

CONTINUED:

> > > BILL
>
> A joke?

> > > FREDRICKS
>
> C'mon, give me something to laugh
> about.

> > > BILL
> > > (really uncomfortable)
>
> I don't know. Um, there's the one
> about the guy ringing the doorbell--

> > > FREDRICKS
>
> Stifle. You see, I don't think we
> share a similar sense of humor.

> > > BILL
>
> It wasn't supposed to be funny.

> > > FREDRICKS
>
> Yeah? It was supposed to be what?
> Educational?

> > > BILL
> > > (emotional)
>
> It's not fair. You don't
> understand. It's not like anyone
> forgets who gets picked last.
> Everybody knows. Girls know. And
> the thing is, maybe I'm not bad. I
> never get better 'cause I never get
> a chance. I could be good. I know I
> could be good.

> > > FREDRICKS
>
> It's not my fault you get picked
> last.

> > > BILL
>
> Yes, it is. You've got the power.
> You could change everything.

> > > FREDRICKS
>
> And how would I do that?

> > > BILL
>
> Let me pick the teams.

Fredricks smiles, an almost-wicked sparkle in his eye.

> > > > > > CUT TO:

INT. MCKINLEY HIGH SCHOOL HALLWAY - DAY

Daniel approaches Lindsay.

                    DANIEL
          Lindsay, I can't take it anymore.
          You gotta go talk to Kim.

                    LINDSAY
          Why? Does she want to talk to me?

                    DANIEL
          No. She's trying to avoid you.

                    LINDSAY
          Well, then, how am I supposed to
          talk to her?

                    DANIEL
          I don't know. But you've just
          gotta do something. She's been
          bitchin' non-stop about her mother,
          you, your parents. I'm dying.

                    LINDSAY
          Why is she so mad at me?

                    DANIEL
              (shrugs)
          She says you didn't stick up for
          her.

                    LINDSAY
          I tried. Is she crazy mad?

                    DANIEL
          Yeah, but it's mostly like her
          feelings are hurt.

                    LINDSAY
          Oh. That's weird. I thought Kim was
          too tough to get her feelings hurt.

                    DANIEL
          Yeah, right. She's like the rawest
          nerve there is. She's like a body
          without skin.

                    LINDSAY
          Okay, I get it.

                                        (CONTINUED)

CONTINUED:

>   DANIEL
> Great. And listen? Could you make
> up with her soon? She's really
> being a big pain in my ass.

>   LINDSAY
>   (distracted)
> Okay, yeah sure.

>   DANIEL
> Thanks, Linds.

CUT TO:

EXT. BASEBALL DIAMOND - DAY

The whole class stands along the backstop. Fredricks stands
with Bill on the mound.

>   FREDRICKS
>   (over-the-top nice)
> Haverchuck here is one of our
> captains today.

The jocks let out a collective groan.

>   PHILLIPS
> Hey, shouldn't the captains
> actually know how to play baseball?

>   FREDRICKS
> Don't question me, people.
>   (to Bill)
> Who's the other captain?

>   BILL
> Gordon Crisp.

Fredricks smiles, extravagantly sweet.

>   FREDRICKS
> Gordon Crisp, it is.

CLOSE UP: Bill's hand clutches a bat; Gordon's hand grips
above his; then Bill's; then Gordon's; then Bill cups the end
of the bat. Bill has won the right to pick first.

Bill scans the backstop. Sam and Neal look eager.

>   BILL
> Who should I pick first? Let me
> see.
>   (MORE)

(CONTINUED)

CONTINUED: (2)

> BILL (CONT'D)
> I need a power hitter who really
> knows how to hustle in the field.
> (beat)
> Give me Weir.

Sam grins, trots out and high-fives Bill. The jocks sneer.

> GORDON
> Okay, I'll take...

Gordon's eyes scan the muscular jocks. Bill pulls him aside.

> BILL
> (to Gordon; under his
> breath)
> Gordon, don't pick the jocks.

> GORDON
> But I want to win.

> BILL
> Well, then you're a big fat
> hypocrite.

> GORDON
> (offended)
> I'm no hypocrite.

Gordon looks at the backstop.

> GORDON (CONT'D)
> Okay, gimme Lewis.

A geek smiles shyly and jogs out.

> BILL
> I'm going need some speed on the
> "Basepaths." I'll take Schweiber.

> NEAL
> (pumping his arm)
> Yes!

The geeks are elated. The jocks are confused.

DISSOLVE TO:

EXT. BASEBALL DIAMOND - SOON AFTER

The backstop. Only jocks remain, disgruntled, waiting to be
picked.

(CONTINUED)

CONTINUED:

Bill and Gordon adopt the derisive tone the jocks used
before. The geeks GROAN as Alan White jogs out to join
Gordon's team.

> BILL
> Man, I guess I'm stuck with
> Stevens.

Bill's squad GROANS emphatically as Stevens walks out.

> GORDON
> Aw, I don't know. Gimme Phillips, I
> guess.

ANGLE ON: Bill talking to Stevens.

> BILL
> Listen. I want you to play back-up
> left. Way deep. Keep going till
> you're up to your knees in mud.
> Now, let's hustle.

Stevens grimaces. As he saunters to the outfield, a grinning
Bill shouts to him.

> BILL (CONT'D)
> I said, hustle!

> STEVENS
> Don't push it, Haverchuck.

> BILL
> Sorry.

ANGLE ON: Gordon in the dugout. He addresses his team.

> GORDON
> Okay, I guess we've got to figure
> out who's batting when.

> PHILLIPS
> You're batting ninth.

> GORDON
> Okay. That's good. I'm comfortable
> there.

> PHILLIPS
> I'm batting clean up.

> GORDON
> Great, great.

(CONTINUED)

CONTINUED: (2)

ANGLE ON: Neal buckling himself into the catcher's equipment. It's way too big for him.

> NEAL
> What is this made for, a giant?

ANGLE ON: Bill's geek infielders warming each other up. Balls flying everywhere.

> STEVENS
> (from deep left)
> Hey can we get a ball out here?

> BILL
> Never you mind a ball, just go
> deeper Stevens, much deeper.

Stevens shakes his head in disgust.

ANGLE ON: Fredricks, leaning against a fence, smirking.

> FREDRICKS
> All right, balls in.

Balls thrown from the infield bombard the bench. Gordon's geek teammates SQUEAL as if they're under attack.

ANGLE ON: Sam on the mound, looks to Bill at short. Bill winks and nods.

> FREDRICKS (CONT'D)
> Play ball!

> CUT TO:

INT. ENGLISH CLASS - DAY

The blackboard at the front of the class reads: "Howl = redeeming social importance" "Kerouac: 1922-1969". Mr. Casper now writes: "What is a Beat? Who is a Beat?"

Lindsay watches Mr. Casper's butt wave back and forth as he writes on the board. Mr. Casper finishes writing and turns around, breaking Lindsay's hypnotic trance.

> MR. CASPER
> Today we will continue our
> discussion of *On the Road*. I
> thought Ms. Proetzel's comments
> last time about pioneer symbolism
> were particularly interesting. I
> think you really got Kerouac.

(CONTINUED)

CONTINUED:

A nerdy girl beams. Kim can't help but SNORT.

>   MR. CASPER (CONT'D)
>   Ms. Kelly. I'm sure you have some
>   original insights. Tell me, what,
>   in your opinion, is the theme of *On
>   the Road*?

The entire class looks at Kim. She stands, holding the book,
her hands shaking slightly.

>   KIM
>   Ummm... the theme is... the theme
>   is...

>   MR. CASPER
>   (to Kim; patronizing)
>   Take a deep breath.

A few GIGGLES from the class. Kim looks embarrassed.

>   KIM
>   The theme is America and... and,
>   umm, being on the road.

>   MR. CASPER
>   (sarcastic as hell)
>   *On the Road* is about being on the
>   road. That's good, that's good. Do
>   go on!

More laughter. Kim blushes. Cornered, she lashes out.

>   KIM
>   Look, I hated the book, all right?
>   I have no idea what it's about and
>   the writer was clearly on drugs
>   when he wrote it. It just went on
>   and on like it was totally written
>   in a hurry. If I handed in
>   something like this, there's no way
>   I'd get a good grade. It's boring
>   and "unorganized" and I only read
>   thirty pages of it anyway.

With that, she collapses into her seat. The class is silent.
Nick looks embarrassed for her.

(CONTINUED)

CONTINUED: (2)

>   MR. CASPER
>   Well, that was certainly
>   passionate, albeit entirely
>   misinformed. Who dares follow Ms.
>   Kelly's lucid analysis?

Lindsay raises her hand.

>   MR. CASPER (CONT'D)
>   Yes?

Lindsay stands; Kim gives her the evil eye.

>   LINDSAY
>   I think Kim is right. Kerouac was
>   high on Benzadrine during the three
>   weeks he took to write *On the Road*.
>   The structure of the story isn't
>   strong and his experiments with
>   prose style are tedious. In fact,
>   Truman Capote said about *On the
>   Road*, "That isn't writing; it's
>   typing."

The class erupts into conversation. Lindsay looks to Kim. Kim
looks away.

>   MR. CASPER
>   (pained)
>   Pearls before swine.

>   CUT TO:

EXT. BASEBALL DIAMOND - DAY

The game is underway.

KOBIE PILGRIM, a black geek, is up to bat. From behind the
plate:

>   NEAL
>   Hey, man. I sure had fun with your
>   wife last night.

Pilgrim looks at Neal like he's insane.

>   PILGRIM
>   My what?

The ball comes bouncing over the plate.

>   (CONTINUED)

CONTINUED:

> FREDRICKS
> Ball four. Take your base.

> NEAL
> (yelling after)
> I mean a lot of fun!

Pilgrim trots to first. The bases are loaded with geeks from Gordon's team. At the mound, Sam looks nervous, disheartened.

Bill waves his hands at Fredricks in what appears to be a football sign.

> FREDRICKS
> What's wrong with you? Are you hurt?

> BILL
> Ump. Time.

Fredricks rolls his eyes.

ANGLE ON: Sam and Bill on the mound.

> SAM
> What? I never said I could pitch.

> BILL
> It's not about your pitching.

> SAM
> Then what are you doing out here?

> BILL
> (shrugs)
> I always wanted to have a meeting on the mound.
> (he looks around)
> This is cool.

Neal jogs over to them.

> NEAL
> Hey! A meeting on the mound, cool.

> SAM
> Look Bill, I've got nothing left. Why don't you let a jock pitch?

> BILL
> What are you talking about? This is our game. We can't give up.
> (MORE)

(CONTINUED)

CONTINUED: (2)

                    BILL (CONT'D)
         We can do this. I don't want them
         to think they were right for
         sticking me in deep right field for
         eleven years.

Sam looks at him, nodding slowly. Bill pats him on the ass
and runs out to shortstop. Neal raises an eyebrow.

                    NEAL
         He's the butt patter.

ANGLE ON: Out in deep left field, Stevens picks at a weed,
bored out of his mind.

ANGLE ON: Home plate as Neal crouches back in place.

Phillips steps up to the plate. He takes a dangerous-looking
practice swing. Glares at the geeks in the field.

ANGLE ON: Bill, hands on his knees, intense.

ANGLE ON: Neal crouched behind the plate. A bead of sweat
collects behind his mask and rolls down his face. He flashes
Sam a signal, two fingers. Sam shakes his head. He flashes
one finger. Sam nods.

ANGLE ON: Phillips spitting. Kicking up the dirt as he
settles behind the plate.

ANGLE ON: Bill smacking his glove: ready.

                    BILL
         This is it! This is it!

ANGLE ON: Sam at the mound. He wipes his brow. He fingers the
stitches of the ball, concentrating. He looks over his
shoulder at Bill.

ANGLE ON: Bill nods. Winks.

SLOW MOTION: The pitch...

Phillips swings, and hits the ball!

The ball is popped up. Behind the pitcher's head. To short
left field. Bill is there, shifting, left, right.

                    BILL (CONT'D)
          I... got... it!

                                        (CONTINUED)

CONTINUED: (3)

Bill twists and reaches over his shoulder. And the ball goes right into Bill's glove. He looks at it, amazed. Holds it up, triumphant!

Sam and Neal run over and hug Bill. Neal and his catcher's equipment give Bill a giant hug. Bill is lifted onto their shoulders.

REAL TIME: In reality, Bill just made a routine catch.

                    PHILLIPS
              (to his teammates on base)
          Tag up!

The runners tag up and start running around the bases. The three geeks run off the field. Bill holds the ball over his head, ecstatic.

                    ALAN
              (from the dugout)
          That was the first out, you morons.

The three geeks do an about-face and jog back onto the field.

                    NEAL
          Well, eight and two-thirds innings
          to go.

                                        CUT TO:

INT. MCKINLEY HIGH SCHOOL HALLWAY - AFTERNOON

The end of school. Everyone is getting ready to go home. Kim, Daniel and Nick and a few other FREAKS are walking down the hall as Lindsay approaches, looking determined.

                    NICK
          I hate that crap, "only boring
          people get bored." That's so
          freakin' dumb.

                    DANIEL
          Yeah, that's like saying only scary
          people get scared.

                    NICK
          Uh, actually, not really.

Lindsay squeezes in next to Kim.

                    LINDSAY
          Hey, Kim.

                                        (CONTINUED)

CONTINUED:

Kim slows up, letting Daniel and the others go ahead.

> KIM
> Yeah? What do you want?

> LINDSAY
> Can I talk to you for a minute?

> KIM
> Obviously you already are.

> LINDSAY
> What are you doing now?

> KIM
> Nothing.

> LINDSAY
> You wanna come over to my house?

> KIM
> Why would I want to?

> LINDSAY
> I was thinking we could hang out.

> KIM
> What about your parents?

> LINDSAY
> What about them?

> KIM
> You think I'll just forgive you
> like that?

> LINDSAY
> (almost giving up)
> I don't know.

Kim thinks for a beat, then yells to Daniel and the others.

> KIM
> Daniel, I'll see you later. I'm
> going over to Lindsay's.

> DANIEL
> Later.

As Lindsay and Kim start to walk in another direction, Daniel pumps his fist, happy to be free of Kim for an afternoon.

(CONTINUED)

CONTINUED: (2)

> KIM
> This is good. I swear, another day
> hanging out with Daniel and I'd
> puke my guts out.

CUT TO:

INT. WEIR KITCHEN - LATE AFTERNOON

Exotic groceries on the counter. Jean attempts to flambe
something. Harold is home and they are already fighting.

> HAROLD
> Is the grocery store out of normal
> food; is that the problem?

> JEAN
> This is normal food.

Foot-high FLAMES shoot off the pan. Jean douses it with
baking soda, trying to act casual.

> HAROLD
> Normal food is pot roast. Normal
> food is meat loaf. It is a dead
> animal and it is not on fire.

> JEAN
> Maybe some of us are up for
> something different around here.
> Don't you want to live life,
> Harold? Or maybe you've turned into
> a mean old man.

Jean runs into the bedroom. Harold turns off the burner and
watches the smoking pan.

CUT TO:

INT. WEIR PARENTS BEDROOM - MOMENTS LATER

Jean is sniffling on the bed, when Harold enters.

> HAROLD
> Don't you run away from me.

> JEAN
> What's wrong with us Harold? What's
> happened to us? We need change,
> don't we? Things need to change. I
> don't want us to be robots.

(CONTINUED)

CONTINUED:

> HAROLD
> (yelling)
> We are not robots and things do not
> need to change. I like how things
> are. I like to eat the same things.
> Do you know why? Because those are
> the things I like. I like chicken.
> I like pot roast. That's how I feel
> about you, Jean--

> JEAN
> Oh, please! You like me like you
> like a pot roast?

> HAROLD
> Yes! I <u>love</u> pot roast!

> JEAN
> You know what, you don't get it. I
> give up. I quit.

> HAROLD
> Is that right?

> JEAN
> You don't appreciate me. Maybe I'll
> go back to school, what about that?

> HAROLD
> (yelling; passionate)
> You think I don't appreciate you? I
> do. And everything I do, I do to
> serve you.
> (starting to break down)
> I think of you when I stock fishing
> poles, Jean. I think of you when
> I'm answering questions about cross-
> country ski wax. My whole life is
> about serving you. And I love you,
> Jean. Thank you.

Jean turns to face him, wiping at her tears.

> JEAN
> You mean it?

Harold shuts her mouth with a kiss.

He pushes her back onto the bed. She giggles. The stuff on
Harold's bedside table, including the antacid bottle, spills
to the floor.

(CONTINUED)

CONTINUED: (2)

>   HAROLD
>   (sexy)
>   C'mere my little pot roast.

CUT TO:

INT. KITCHEN - MOMENTS LATER

Sam, Neal, and Bill enter.

>   SAM
>   Mom, Dad! We're home!

No response. Bill pokes at the burnt food still sitting on
the stove.

>   BILL
>   Is this what's for dinner?

>   SAM
>   Mom!

We FOLLOW Sam as he walks down the hallway to his parents'
bedroom, Bill and Neal in tow.

He stands outside his parents bedroom. He can HEAR odd noises
coming from inside.

>   SAM (CONT'D)
>   (a whisper)
>   Mom? Dad?

He tries the knob: it's locked. The geeks look at each other,
realizing.

>   BILL
>   Eeeeww!!!

>   SAM
>   (stunned)
>   Let's get out of here.

Bill and Sam head off, but Neal lingers at the door.

>   SAM (CONT'D)
>   NEAL! That's my parents.

>   NEAL
>   Okay, okay.

(CONTINUED)

CONTINUED:

                  SAM
        God, you're gross.

                              CUT TO:

EXT. WEIR FRONT PORCH - SOON AFTER

Kim and Lindsay open the front door. Lindsay steels herself
for the confrontation. Kim notices Lindsay's anxiety.

                  KIM
        Lindsay. Look, I know what you're
        trying to do. But we don't have to
        do this.

                LINDSAY
        No, I want to.

                  KIM
        All right. But if they call the
        cops on me, I'm out of here.

                              CUT TO:

INT. WEIR LIVING ROOM - CONTINUOUS

Kim and Lindsay enter the house and spot Sam, Neal and Bill,
watching TV.

                  NEAL
        Hey, Lindsay. I was the catcher in
        gym today.

                LINDSAY
           (distracted)
        Great, Neal. Where are Mom and Dad?

                  SAM
        In their room.

                  BILL
        They've been in there for an hour.

                LINDSAY
        Are they fighting?

                  NEAL
           (slowly raised eyebrows)
        No.

Lindsay is weirded out.

                             (CONTINUED)

CONTINUED:

Suddenly, Jean enters the living room. She's flushed, her clothes askew. She is grinning.

>   LINDSAY
>   (determined)
>   Hi, Mom.

>   JEAN
>   Sweetheart, I think we're gonna
>   order food in tonight. So why don't
>   you call a pizza place and have
>   them deliver?

>   HAROLD (O.S.)
>   Jean!

>   LINDSAY
>   (bewildered)
>   Dad, Kim's here! She drove me home
>   from school!

Harold appears at the corner of the room, his hair looking odd.

>   KIM
>   Hi, Mr. Weir.

>   HAROLD
>   (blithe)
>   Nice to see you, Kim. Thanks for
>   giving Lindsay a ride home. Jean,
>   could I have a word with you?

>   JEAN
>   Your father and I will be in our
>   room. Tell us when the food gets
>   here. You kids play nice, now.

Lindsay nods, as Harold and Jean walk back to their room. We can HEAR Jean giggling...

>   JEAN (O.S.) (CONT'D)
>   Harold, stop. That tickles.

ANGLE ON: The parents' bedroom door closing.

>   KIM
>   Oh my god. Your parents are like...
>   swingers.

(CONTINUED)

CONTINUED: (2)   62.

And off Lindsay's frozen reaction, we...

                                                  FADE OUT.

THE END

FREAKS AND GEEKS

"LOOKS AND BOOKS"

Episode #11

Written by Paul Feig

Directed by Ken Kwapis

This episode is all about clothes. Sam tries to change his image by hitting the disco clothing store at the mall, and Lindsay decides to go back to her old self, which includes wearing all her old conservative clothes to school. There's other stuff that happens in here that I'm very proud I wrote, but it's all about the clothes, as far as I'm concerned.

I was really into clothes back in high school. But before you judge me too harshly for being so superficial, you have to realize that back in the late 1970s, *everybody* was into clothes. And their hair. Even some of the freaks had fallen for it. The disco revolution was omnipresent, and it affected the way everybody dressed and groomed, whether they wanted to admit it or not. Silk shirts were in (even though none of ours were actually made out of silk—they were mostly shiny polyester). Tight-fitting, bell-bottomed Angels Flight dress pants were in. Platform shoes were in. Puca shell necklaces were in. Vests were in. Three-piece suits were in. Yes, friends, even silk scarves were in (although, once again, not usually made out of silk). Disco was king, queen, prince, princess, and in my case, court jester.

I fell for it hook, line, and sinker. I spent more time worrying about my clothes and my hair than I ever spent worrying about my homework or grades. I had my mother take me to Silverman's men's clothing store at Lakeside mall once a week to see what new disco fashions they had received from their supplier. I started wearing jewelry for the first time in my life (a silver necklace with a big isosceles triangle made out of different pieces of polished stone that used to practically crack my solar plexus in half whenever I had to run to catch the bus in the morning). I once spent several months' wages from working at my dad's store on a pair of disco boots that were white leather and that had what one of my non–disco-dressing sci-fi friends called "cow fur" on the top. I even bought a white three-piece suit that allowed me to straddle my two favorite worlds—John Travolta in *Saturday Night Fever* wore a white suit (I didn't like the movie but still wanted to look like him), and Steve Martin wore a white suit (and I wanted more than anything back then to be Steve Martin). It was amazingly convenient for my fantasy life since:

- If I wanted to be John Travolta, I just had to slip on a black "silk" shirt and put the collar out over the suit collar, and I was ready for the discotheque; and

- If I wanted to be Steve Martin, I simply had to put on a white dress shirt and a black tie, slip a rubber fish inside my jacket and put on a fake arrow-through-the-head, and I was ready to play his "Let's Get Small" album and pretend to be Steve Martin in the sad solitude of my bedroom.

And, just like Sam Weir in this episode, I did indeed buy a disco jumpsuit. In fact, the one that Sam wears in the episode is a carbon copy of the one I wore. I had the costume department make an exact replica from my description of it (alas, the original is lost to history and the Goodwill), and then I made poor John Francis Daley wear it on camera. The only difference is that in the episode, Sam Weir is a clueless freshman, and in real life, I was a junior who should have known better when I wore it to school on a day that became one of the most embarrassing of my entire life. There's nothing like being stuck at school knowing you've made a serious fashion blunder and yet you can't escape or change your clothes.

And so, "Looks and Books" is all about clothes and how they change your appearance and your attitude. It's about how the way you dress affects what you want the world to think about you. It's about how our clothes are our uniforms, and how we use them to attract the people we want to be like. *And* it's also about Mathletes and old friends and car accidents and getting in trouble with your parents and growing up and growing away from people you thought you'd be friends with forever. So, I guess it's about a lot of stuff.

But mostly it's about clothes. Enjoy!

—Paul Feig

```
                  FREAKS AND GEEKS

                 "LOOKS AND BOOKS"

                    CAST LIST


       LINDSAY WEIR
       SAM WEIR
       HAROLD WEIR
       JEAN WEIR
       DANIEL DESARIO
       NICK ANDOPOLIS
       BILL HAVERCHUCK
       NEAL SCHWEIBER
       KEN MILLER
       KIM KELLY
       MILLIE KENTNER
       CINDY SANDERS
       MR. ROSSO
       MR. KOWCHEVSKI
       ALAN WHITE
       HARRIS
       SEIDELMAN
       GORDON CRISP
       DOLORES
       TODD SCHELLINGER
       MS. YEATS
       JOCK #1
       JOCK #2
       HOUSEWIFE
       CAREY
       ERIN
       SHELLY WEAVER
       SALESMAN
       BULLY #1
       JUDGE
       LINCOLN MATHLETE #1
       LINCOLN MATHLETE #2
```

FREAKS AND GEEKS

"LOOKS AND BOOKS"

SET LIST

INTERIORS:

MCKINLEY HIGH SCHOOL
    /HALLWAY
    /CAFETERIA
    /UNDER THE STAIRS
    /STAIRWELL
    /KOWCHEVSKI'S CLASSROOM
    /KOWCHEVSKI'S OFFICE
    /ENGLISH CLASSROOM
WEIR HOUSE
    /FRONT DOOR
    /DINING ROOM
    /LIVING ROOM
    /KITCHEN
    /LINDSAY'S ROOM
    /SAM'S ROOM
MILLIE'S HOUSE
    /MILLIE'S BEDROOM
    /HALLWAY
WEIR FAMILY STATION WAGON
SILVERMAN'S MENS FASHION STORE

EXTERIORS:

MCKINLEY HIGH SCHOOL
    /QUAD
NEIGHBORHOOD STREET
WEIR HOUSE
SALVATORE'S ITALIAN DELI

<u>TEASER</u>

FADE IN:

INT. MCKINLEY HIGH SCHOOL HALLWAY - DAY

LINDSAY is at the drinking fountain taking a drink. When she stands up and turns, she finds herself face to face with TWO JOCKS who are trying to keep straight faces.

                    JOCK #1
               (mock serious)
          Hey... um... my friend was
          wondering... uh...

                    JOCK #2
          If I gave you a joint, would you
          have sex with me?

                    LINDSAY
          What?

The jocks crack up and take off, slapping each other five.

                    JOCK #1
               (to Jock #2)
          I can't believe you did it.

They keep laughing as they disappear into the crowd. Lindsay stares after them, disgusted. Behind her, THE FREAKS appear around the corner.

                    KEN
          Lindsay!

                    LINDSAY
               (still thrown from jocks)
          Oh... hey.

                    DANIEL
          Hey, guess what? We got a gig.

                    NICK
          Stroker's throwing a party and
          we're gonna play. His brother's
          even gonna lend us a Marshall stack
          and a Peavey bass cabinet. Total
          pro equipment.

                    KEN
          We're gonna blow the roof off his
          garage in a most rock-tagious way.

                                        (CONTINUED)

CONTINUED:

The guys slap each other five.

>   LINDSAY
>   Wow, that's great, you guys.

>   DANIEL
>   Yeah, so we need your folks'
>   station wagon to pick the amps up.

>   LINDSAY
>   What? We can't use their car.
>   They're insane about it. My dad
>   even calls it Betty.

>   KEN
>   Your dad nicknamed a station wagon?
>   That's kinda sad.

>   LINDSAY
>   Yeah, I know. It's really
>   embarrassing when we get the oil
>   changed. He calls it a
>   "transfusion."

>   DANIEL
>   Lindsay, please. We've gotta get
>   those amps. Don't be lame.

>   LINDSAY
>   (with a laugh)
>   Daniel, I'm not being lame. They're
>   just never gonna let me borrow the
>   station wagon.

>   KIM
>   I thought your mom plays bridge or
>   something on Tuesdays.

>   LINDSAY
>   Yeah, so?

>   DANIEL
>   So, she's not even gonna know the
>   car's gone. Grab her keys. We'll
>   have it back before she finishes
>   one hand.

>   LINDSAY
>   Well... I don't know. I mean, I
>   guess I could...

(CONTINUED)

CONTINUED: (2)

The freaks give her pleased smiles.

CUT TO:

INT. STATION WAGON - DAY

MUSIC UP: JOE JACKSON'S "I'M THE MAN"

The music is loud. Lindsay is gripping the wheel, looking nervous and tense but excited as she drives.

She's definitely invigorated by driving. Daniel is in the front seat, Kim, Nick and Ken in the back, Kim leaning up between Daniel and Lindsay, backseat driving. Everybody's amped up. Lindsay jerks the wheel to the side.

> LINDSAY
> Squirrel, look out!

The freaks get tossed around.

> KIM
> Ow, my neck! Just run over the
> stupid squirrel.

> LINDSAY
> Awwwww.

> DANIEL
> God, you're a terrible driver,
> Lindsay.

> LINDSAY
> (laughing)
> Shut up. How far away is this place
> anyway? Japan?

> DANIEL
> We're almost there, all right? It's
> on the next block.

> KIM
> No, Daniel, it's not on Hancock.
> It's on Warren.

> DANIEL
> It's on Hancock. I was just there.

> KEN
> Could you put on some real music? I
> hate this new wave crap.

(CONTINUED)

CONTINUED:

> NICK
> Hey, shut up, man. Joe Jackson's
> cool. His bass player rules.

Kim sees something.

> KIM
> Daniel, we just passed Valerie's
> house. I told you, we're going the
> wrong way!

Lindsay looks back at the house Kim pointed to. The car
swerves a bit.

> DANIEL
> No, we're not. Lindsay, drive like
> a normal person, would you?

> KEN
> You better roll down the windows
> 'cause I've got a big one brewing.

> NICK
> (laughing)
> Oh, man! Don't do it. Don't do it!

> LINDSAY
> Ken, you better not.

Lindsay looks back at him and laughs. Nick is cracking up in
anticipation. Just then...

> KIM
> OVER THERE! THERE'S THE HOUSE!

Kim points over at a house they're about to pass. Lindsay
jumps and jerks the wheel quickly to turn. SMASH! The
station wagon clips the back fender of a Plymouth Aspen that
was backing out of a driveway. That sickening dull thud of a
traffic accident. The freaks looks stunned.

                                                    CUT TO:

EXT. NEIGHBORHOOD STREET - CONTINUOUS

All is quiet. The Aspen and the station wagon sit in post-
accident silence. The station wagon's front fender is torn
off. SSSSSS. Steam rises from the hood of Lindsay's car.
The Aspen's back end is crushed.

                                                    CUT TO:

                                               (CONTINUED)

CONTINUED:

INT. STATION WAGON - CONTINUOUS

Lindsay sits stunned, still gripping the wheel. The freaks look stunned and surprised too. Nobody speaks.

>   LINDSAY
>   ...oh, my god...

                                              CUT TO:

                    MAIN TITLES

                     ACT ONE

FADE IN:

INT. MCKINLEY HIGH SCHOOL HALLWAY - DAY

THE GEEKS are by Sam's locker. He's digging around inside. The halls are empty.

>   SAM
>   I can't believe I lost my math
>   book.

>   NEAL
>   I hate being in school after it's
>   out. It makes me feel like a
>   janitor.

>   BILL
>   Janitors are cool. I'd like to be a
>   janitor.

>   NEAL
>   Why? So you can show up with the
>   red saw dust after a kid throws up?

>   BILL
>   No, 'cause janitors make way more
>   than teachers. It makes up for all
>   the gross stuff they have to do.

Sam pulls out his math book, then shuts his locker. They turn and see...

GEEKS' POV: CINDY and TODD are at the other end of the hallway. Cindy has her back against the wall and Todd is facing her with his hand on the wall above her head, talking nose to nose in hushed tones.

Sam deflates when he sees them.

                                          (CONTINUED)

CONTINUED:

>   BILL (CONT'D)
>   Geez, get a room.

>   SAM
>   No, shut up. <u>Don't</u> get a room.

Just then, Cindy reaches up and touches Todd's perfectly
feathered hair, straightening it and cooing over it. Sam
looks like he's in pain. He and the geeks start off down the
hall, Cindy and Todd in the background.

>   SAM (CONT'D)
>   What's so great about him anyway?

>   NEAL
>   It's the hair.

>   SAM
>   (disbelieving)
>   C'mon. She likes him for his hair?

>   NEAL
>   Of course. He's got the feathered
>   thing going. Girls love that.

>   BILL
>   Yeah, all the guys my mom dates
>   have feathered hair. I heard her
>   tell one of her friends that any
>   guy with feathered hair is foxy.

>   SAM
>   (frustrated)
>   It's just hair. Why do girls care
>   how you comb it?

>   NEAL
>   Women are weird, Sam. They get
>   turned on by weird things.

>   BILL
>   Do they get turned on by glasses?

>   NEAL
>   Not thick ones.

The geeks exit around a corner. After a beat, Sam peeks back
around the corner down the hall at Cindy and Todd.

SAM'S POV: CINDY TRIES TO RUN HER FINGERS THROUGH TODD'S
hair.

                                        (CONTINUED)

CONTINUED: (2)

He gently stops her and pulls out a large comb with a handle out of his back pocket. He combs his hair as Cindy watches, in love.

Off Sam's preoccupied look, we...

CUT TO:

EXT. NEIGHBORHOOD STREET - DAY

Lindsay and the freaks are standing at the accident scene. The HOUSEWIFE who was driving the Aspen is staring at her wrecked car in shock. Lindsay looks sick.

> HOUSEWIFE
> My car. Look at my car.
> (turning on Lindsay)
> What were you doing? What were you
> thinking?!

> LINDSAY
> Ma'am, I am so, so sorry.

> HOUSEWIFE
> What is wrong with you? You were
> driving like a crazy person!

> KIM
> Hey, lady, she said she was sorry.
> Don't have a hairy. We're all
> upset.

> LINDSAY
> Kim...

Lindsay gives Kim a glare. A resident comes out of the house the cars are in front of.

> HOUSEWIFE
> Don't talk to me, any of you.
> (to resident)
> Call the police!

The resident nods yes and heads back into the house. The freaks make worried faces to each other. Lindsay looks completely flipped out.

> KIM
> Hey, lady, calm the hell down. God!

> LINDSAY
> Kim, shut up! This is all your
> fault.

(CONTINUED)

CONTINUED:

> KIM
> What? Screw you.

> DANIEL
> C'mon, you guys. Take it easy. It
> was both of your faults.

> LINDSAY
> This isn't my fault! You're the one
> who talked me into this, Daniel!

> DANIEL
> I didn't talk you into anything.

> LINDSAY
> What?! Do you have any idea how
> much trouble I'm gonna be in? Do
> you know how many stupid lectures
> I'm gonna have to sit through now?!

> HOUSEWIFE
> You're gonna pay for every cent of
> damage on my car.

> DANIEL
> Hey, lady, here's something you
> might not have heard of. It's
> called insurance.

Ken stifles a laugh. Lindsay tries to ignore him.

> LINDSAY
> Ma'am, please let me help you. I
> can get my dad to drive you home.

> HOUSEWIFE
> Stay away from me! All of you!

> DANIEL
> Who wants to be near you anyway,
> sexy?

The housewife glares at Daniel as if he were a murderer.
Lindsay also glares at Daniel, in total anger and disbelief.

> CUT TO:

EXT. WEIR HOUSE - NIGHT

Quiet. CRICKETS CHIRP. The smashed station wagon sits in the
driveway. The front fender is gone, but the car's still
drivable.

CUT TO:

INT. WEIR DINING ROOM - NIGHT

Silence. Harold, Jean and Lindsay are sitting around the dinner table. Tick tick tick tick. The kitchen clock ticks loudly. Lindsay looks shell-shocked. JEAN looks mad. HAROLD looks beyond furious.

> HAROLD
> (quiet; scary serious)
> You know I could call the police, don't you? I could call the police and report this as grand theft auto. I could send my own daughter to jail. Do you know that?

> LINDSAY
> (quietly)
> I know.

> HAROLD
> I really don't know why I shouldn't. I'm serious, Lindsay. I'd like to hear one good reason why I shouldn't.

> LINDSAY
> I'm so sorry, daddy.

> HAROLD
> You know what? I don't think I believe anything you say anymore. Why should I? There's this strange girl at my table and I don't know who she is. I know she's not the daughter I raised, I'll tell you that much.

Jean just glares at Lindsay, not saying a word. Lindsay's completely drained.

> HAROLD (CONT'D)
> You're grounded. I can't even tell you for how long. You're coming right home from school every day and you're sitting in your room. No stereo, no radio, no TV, no telephone. Nothing.
> (then, very serious)
> (MORE)

(CONTINUED)

CONTINUED:

> HAROLD (CONT'D)
> <u>And</u> you are <u>not</u> to hang out with
> those burn-out friends of yours
> ever again. <u>Ever</u>. Do you hear me?

Lindsay finally looks up at her dad. Looks him right in the eye. Dead serious.

> LINDSAY
> Don't worry. I won't.

Harold stares back. Lindsay's serious. They stare at each other for several beats.

> HAROLD
> You'd better not.

Jean sighs wearily and shakes her head to herself. The silence continues.

> CUT TO:

INT. LINDSAY'S BEDROOM - NIGHT

Lindsay is sitting on her bed, staring at the floor. She's like stone. Not moving a muscle. TAP TAP TAP. The door cracks open. It's Millie. She peeks in cautiously.

> MILLIE
> Hey, Lindsay. Your mom said I could
> come in. I saw the smashed car in
> your driveway and wanted to make
> sure everything was all right.

Lindsay looks up at Millie. Lindsay looks damaged. Millie gives her a very concerned look.

> MILLIE (CONT'D)
> (very sincere)
> Are you okay, Lindsay?

Lindsay stares at her a couple of beats, then she finally cracks. Her eyes well up and she starts to cry.

> LINDSAY
> No.

Millie comes over and sits next to Lindsay as she talks.

> (CONTINUED)

CONTINUED: (2)

> LINDSAY (CONT'D)
> It was terrible, Millie. It was so
> terrible. It didn't sound anything
> like car accidents on TV. It was
> just a thud. It was so scary.

> MILLIE
> Who was in the car with you?

> LINDSAY
> Who do you think?

> MILLIE
> I'm sorry, Lindsay.
> (beat)
> If you want, I can bring over my
> Uno deck.

> LINDSAY
> No, I'm fine.

They sit in silence, Lindsay wiping her eyes, composing
herself. Millie keeps looking at Lindsay, trying to figure
out what to say. Then she gets a smile.

> MILLIE
> Did you hear what happened at our
> Mathletes scrimmage against North
> Lake? Sheila was so nervous when
> she was doing her round that she
> got a bloody nose. But she didn't
> know she had it and then she
> sneezed and she blew blood all over
> the place. When she looked down and
> saw it on her shirt, she fainted.

Millie really laughs at this.

> LINDSAY
> (amused)
> No, she didn't.

> MILLIE
> Well, no, but she looked like she
> was gonna. It was pretty funny.

Millie laughs again. Lindsay can't help but smile.

> LINDSAY
> You guys been having fun this year?

(CONTINUED)

CONTINUED: (3)

> MILLIE
> Oh, yeah, it's been cool. But not
> as fun as last year. I really miss
> having you there, Lindsay. All the
> Mathletes do.

Lindsay and Millie share a nice moment. Lindsay looks happy
to have Millie there.

> LINDSAY
> (after a beat)
> You wanna go get your Uno deck?

> MILLIE
> (trying to be cool)
> Really? Sure. That'd be great.

Millie gets up. She's about to go out the door, then turns
back.

> MILLIE (CONT'D)
> Don't go away.

> LINDSAY
> (a smile)
> I won't. I can't.

Millie leaves the room looking extremely happy. Lindsay sighs
and smiles. She looks almost relieved.

CUT TO:

INT. SAM'S BEDROOM - MORNING

MUSIC: RICK JAMES' "SUPER FREAK"

Sam is blow-drying his hair in front of his bedroom mirror,
wearing his pants but no shirt. His hair is feathered back,
but his haircut doesn't quite make it look right.

He puts down the blow-dryer and studies himself. He uses his
hand to put a few stray hairs in place, then smiles. He's
pleased with what he sees.

Sam picks up his pullover shirt and looks at it.

> SAM
> Oh, man. How am I gonna get this on
> without messing up my hair?

Sam sighs at his dilemma, then pulls the neck of his shirt
open very wide, then slowly eases it over his head.

(CONTINUED)

CONTINUED:

As he pulls the neck wider, RIIIIP! Sam gets a pained look, then eases the ripped shirt back off his head.

CUT TO:

INT. LINDSAY'S BEDROOM - MORNING

Lindsay is in her pajamas, getting her clothes out of her closet. She pulls out her jeans, freak shirt and army jacket. She stops and looks at them. Studies them. Frowns.

She puts them back in the closet, then pulls a bunch of hanging clothes to the side to get at the clothes at the far end of the closet.

She pulls out a nice but conservative looking blouse and skirt. She holds them up. Studies them.

Then, she puts them on the bed so she can get undressed and change into them.

CUT TO:

INT. WEIR KITCHEN - MORNING

Jean is cooking bacon. Harold is at the kitchen table eating a plate of scrambled eggs. He's still in a bad mood.

> HAROLD
> You'll have to follow me to the body shop this morning. Boy, I can only imagine how much those pirates are gonna charge me for a new fender.

> JEAN
> Just pretend you know a lot about cars.

> HAROLD
> But I don't. And they can smell it, the bloodsuckers.

Lindsay enters in her blouse and skirt. Jean sees her first and lets out a little gasp. Harold sees this.

> HAROLD (CONT'D)
> What's the matter... ?

He turns and sees Lindsay. Harold and Jean exchange surprised looks. Harold looks like he wants to say something but Jean makes a "don't say a word" face at him.

(CONTINUED)

14.

CONTINUED:

> JEAN
> Lindsay... you want some bacon?

> LINDSAY
> No thanks, mom. I'll just have
> some orange juice.

Lindsay pours a small glass as Harold and Jean continue to have a whole dialogue with each other through puzzled facial expressions.

Just then, Sam enters with his fancy feathered hair. Harold sees him and looks completely perplexed.

> HAROLD
> Sam?

> SAM
> Hey, dad.

> JEAN
> Sam, you're so handsome. You look
> just like one of the Hardy Boys.

> SAM
> Thanks.

Sam starts to head out the back door. Lindsay downs her orange juice.

> LINDSAY
> Sam, wait up.
> (to Harold & Jean)
> Bye, mom. Bye, dad.

> HAROLD/JEAN
> Bye.

Lindsay puts down her glass and heads out the door with Sam.

When they shut the door behind them, Harold and Jean stare after them for a beat, then look at each other. They break into huge smiles.

> HAROLD
> If I thought that it was only going
> to take one trip to the body shop
> to get her back to normal, I would
> have let her bust up my car months
> ago.

(CONTINUED)

CONTINUED: (2)

They both look beyond happy.

                                                    CUT TO:

INT. MCKINLEY HIGH SCHOOL HALLWAY - MORNING

Sam and Lindsay enter the school and walk down the hall in
silence. Sam with his feathered hair, Lindsay in her blouse
and dress pants, both in their own worlds.

They walk past Mr. Rosso, who's heading to his office.

                    MR. ROSSO
          My goodness. Don't the Weirs look
          nice today?

                    LINDSAY/SAM
          Thank you.

They both force a smile at him and keep on walking as he
watches after them, pleasantly surprised. At the stairs, they
part ways.

                    SAM
          See you later.

                    LINDSAY
          See you, Sam.

Sam heads up the stairs as Lindsay continues down the
hallway. Daniel, Kim and Ken come around the corner and see
her. Kim starts laughing. Daniel's wearing his knit cap.

                    KIM
          What, did you just come from
          church?

Lindsay just glares at her.

                    KEN
          So, how'd things go with your dad?
          Was he pissed?

                    LINDSAY
          No, not at all. He was really happy
          that I stole his car and smashed
          it.

Lindsay pushes past the freaks. They exchange a look and
watch her go.

                                              (CONTINUED)

CONTINUED:

> DANIEL
> Hey, if it makes you feel any
> better, the party got pushed 'til
> tonight so you can come.

> LINDSAY
> You know what? That doesn't make me
> feel any better 'cause now I'm
> grounded. So I can't go to your
> stupid party. Ever.

> DANIEL
> (cool guy smile)
> Why don't you just sneak out?

> LINDSAY
> Why don't you go to Hell?

> KIM
> (laughs)
> Whoa. God, Lindsay.

> LINDSAY
> Shut up, Kim. I'm sick of you guys
> getting me in trouble all the time.
> I'm sick of you guys period.

> DANIEL
> Maybe you're just on your period.

The freaks laugh. Something snaps in Lindsay.

> LINDSAY
> Yeah, Daniel. That's exactly it.
> I'm on my period. You've figured it
> out. You're the smartest man in the
> world.

> DANIEL
> Uh, I was joking.

> LINDSAY
> Oh, I'm sorry. It was hard to pick
> up the subtlety of your wit.

> DANIEL
> What's up your butt?

> LINDSAY
> You are, Daniel. I'm tired of you
> using me all the time.

(CONTINUED)

CONTINUED: (2)

> KIM
> Lindsay, c'mon.

> LINDSAY
> No, you c'mon. You guys all used
> me. You're the most selfish people
> I ever met in my life. I know you
> don't give a crap about school or
> being smart or anything else, but
> just because your lives are such a
> lost cause, don't keep assuming
> that mine is.

She turns and heads off down the hall. The freaks watch after
her, completely surprised. Daniel looks stunned.

> DANIEL
> What the hell was that all about?

> KEN
> I don't know but it was pretty
> funny.

> KIM
> (punches Ken on arm)
> Shut up.

Daniel stares after her, looking angry and stunned.

> FADE OUT.

<u>END OF ACT ONE</u>

<u>ACT TWO</u>

FADE IN:

INT. CAFETERIA - DAY

The freaks are sitting around a table eating junk food. Nick
sits with them, looking lost in thought. Daniel's stewing.

> DANIEL
> You know, who asked her to hang out
> with us, anyway? Like we need her
> little judgments.

> KIM
> My life ain't a lost cause, man.
> Hers is. It's such a stupid thing
> to say.

> (CONTINUED)

CONTINUED:

                    KEN
          She's just a big baby. I've told
          you guys that from day one. It's
          like hanging out with my grandma.

                    DANIEL
          Yeah, well, Little Miss Perfect
          doesn't know what I'm gonna do with
          my life. She don't know what my
          plans are.

                    KEN
               (after a beat)
          What the hell are your plans?

                    DANIEL
          I got a lot of plans. I've got a
          ton of stuff I'm gonna do.

                    KIM
          Yeah, me too.

                    KEN
          Like?

                    DANIEL
          Who are you, my guidance counselor?
          What are you gonna do?

                    KEN
          I'm just waiting for my dad to die
          so I can inherit his company. Then
          I'm gonna sell it and move to
          Hawaii.

                    DANIEL
          Great plan.

                    KEN
          I don't hear anything better comin'
          out of you.

                    DANIEL
          There's so many things I'm gonna do
          I can't even name them all.

                    KEN
          Name one.

                    KIM
          I'm gonna be like a lawyer or
          something, you know.
               (MORE)

(CONTINUED)

CONTINUED: (2)

> KIM (CONT'D)
> I'm gonna put like the police on trial or like get guys out of jail, you know?

> KEN
> Yeah? Maybe you can break Daniel out of there.

> DANIEL
> I ain't going to jail, man. Screw you.

> KEN
> Yeah? Then what will you be doing?

> DANIEL
> Plenty. Now if you're finished grilling me, gimme a dollar. I wanna get some Sno-Balls, Mr. Rosso.

Ken digs out a dollar and hands it to Daniel, who takes it and stalks off. Kim watches him go, unsure.

> NICK
> I'm telling you guys. This isn't about the accident. Lindsay's just still really depressed that I broke up with her. But she's gotta get over it, you know?

> KIM
> Yeah, Nick. So, I guess you're gonna be a psychiatrist, right?

> NICK
> Nah, I'm gonna be a deejay, man. And maybe a lumberjack.

Kim and Ken look at Nick as if he's insane. He just nods to himself, convinced.

CUT TO:

INT. ANOTHER PART OF THE CAFETERIA - SAME TIME

Lindsay is walking with her hot lunch tray. She looks lost, unsure. Her eyes scan the cafeteria.

LINDSAY'S POV: Mille, Carey, and Erin are sitting at a table having lunch. They're all looking at a large calculator.

(CONTINUED)

CONTINUED:

>   MILLIE
>   (joking)
>   The name of the company is Texas
>   Instruments but it's made in
>   Taiwan.

The girls laugh. Lindsay watches them a beat, thinks about
it, then walks over to the table.

>   LINDSAY
>   Hey. Is it okay if I sit here?

The girls look up. Carey and Erin are very surprised. Millie
looks happy.

>   MILLIE
>   Yeah. Sit down, Lindsay.

Lindsay sits and sets down her tray. Carey and Erin stare at
her, completely thrown.

>   LINDSAY
>   Hi, Carey. Hi, Erin.

>   CAREY/ERIN
>   Hi, Lindsay.

Carey and Erin exchange surprised looks with Millie as
Lindsay busies herself opening her milk. Millie makes a "be
cool" face at them.

>   MILLIE
>   Look. Erin got a new calculator. It
>   graphs and everything.

>   ERIN
>   I got it for my birthday. That and
>   a Kenny Rogers greatest hits album.

>   LINDSAY
>   (re: calculator)
>   Cool. Can I see it?

Lindsay takes the calculator and starts punching numbers into
it. She looks like she really knows what she's doing.

>   MILLIE
>   Do you have a calculator, Lindsay?

>   (CONTINUED)

CONTINUED: (2)

>   LINDSAY
> No, my dad wouldn't buy me one. He
> said that Einstein did fine without
> one and so would I.

>   ERIN
> You don't need one, Lindsay.

>   CAREY
> Yeah, remember that judge at the
> intradistricts last year? He called
> you the "Human Calculator."

>   MILLIE
> I think he had a crush on you.

>   CAREY
> Eww, he was like forty years old.

>   ERIN
> Gross!

The girls all laugh. Lindsay looks a little embarrassed but
seems to be enjoying the attention.

>   MILLIE
> Hey, Lindsay, I'm having a slumber
> party Friday night. All the
> Mathletes are gonna be there. You
> wanna come?

>   LINDSAY
> I would but I'm grounded.

>   MILLIE
> Oh, yeah. Well, you should ask your
> dad. It's just across the street,
> it's gonna be a lot of fun.

>   LINDSAY
> Yeah. Maybe. Okay.

>   MILLIE
> Great.

Millie beams. Carey and Erin look happy to have Lindsay back.
Lindsay gives them all a smile. She looks happy to be back
too.

INT. CAFETERIA - OVER AT THE GEEK TABLE

The geek table is crowded today with Sam, Neal, Bill, HARRIS
and GORDON CRISP. They are all staring at Sam's hair. Sam
looks uncomfortable about this. Gordon's eating a SnakPak
chocolate pudding.

                    HARRIS
          Well, Sam, it's an interesting
          look.

                    NEAL
          Your hair's not long enough to be
          feathered.

                    BILL
          I think it looks weird. Like you're
          trying to be all fancy or
          something.

                    GORDON
          I don't think you should worry
          about how you look, Sam. My mom
          always says you should be happy
          with whatever the good Lord gave
          you.

                    BILL
          Well, the good Lord gave you a lot,
          Gordon.

The geeks all give Bill a disapproving look. Gordon shrugs.

                    GORDON
              (a mouthful of pudding)
          My whole family's big-boned. It's
          genetic.

                    HARRIS
          Besides, the world loves jolly fat
          guys. Burl Ives, Jackie Gleason,
          Lou Costello...

                    GORDON
              (counting on his fingers)
          Santa Claus, Curly, Raymond Burr.

                    NEAL
          Raymond Burr's not jolly.

                                        (CONTINUED)

CONTINUED:

>   GORDON
>   Well, he was extremely nice to me
>   at the Auto Show last year.

Cindy walks up to the table.

>   CINDY
>   Hi, guys. Any one of you have a
>   pencil I can borrow?

The geeks all scramble for pencils. However, Sam self-
consciously poses for Cindy, trying to get her to notice his
hair.

>   SAM
>   Hey, Cindy. Uh... how's it going?

>   CINDY
>   It's okay. I sat on a piece of
>   chocolate in chemistry and had to
>   go home and change my pants.

She looks at Sam oddly, studying him. Sam goes a little wide-
eyed, waiting for a compliment.

>   CINDY (CONT'D)
>   Did you wear a hat today, Sam? Your
>   hair's all flat.

Sam's face falls.

>   GORDON
>   Got one!

Gordon hands Cindy a chewed up pencil. Cindy looks a little
grossed out but quickly recovers.

>   CINDY
>   Thanks. I'll bring it right back.

>   GORDON
>   You better.

Cindy takes off. Sam deflates.

>   SAM
>   Oh, man...

(CONTINUED)

CONTINUED: (2)

>   NEAL
>   What'd you expect? You can't just
>   comb your hair different and expect
>   Cindy to start liking you. You've
>   gotta change your clothes too.

>   SAM
>   I dress okay.

>   NEAL
>   Sam, you look like your mother
>   dresses you.

>   SAM
>   Hey, at least I don't dress like a
>   ventriloquist's dummy.

>   NEAL
>   Sam, don't kill the messenger. I
>   know I look good. I dress well and
>   I groom myself properly. Look
>   around. The whole school dresses
>   better than you do.

Neal points. The geeks all look.

GEEKS POV: Most of the students in the cafeteria seem to be
dressed well at this moment. Four guys in nice shirts,
wearing dress pants or new looking jeans are talking, three
girls in cowl neck sweaters and skirts are standing and
laughing. A disco-looking couple are walking hand in hand.

Sam stares at them all. He sees that Neal's right. Sam sighs
as Neal pats him on the back.

>   NEAL (CONT'D)
>   Change your clothes, change your
>   life.

>   CUT TO:

INT. MCKINLEY HIGH SCHOOL HALLWAY - DAY

The bell rings. Students come out of their classes. A happy
looking Lindsay comes out and starts down the hall. Kim walks
up next to her, as if she's been waiting for Lindsay. Lindsay
gets an icy look.

>   KIM
>   What's up?

>   (CONTINUED)

CONTINUED:

> LINDSAY
> (cold)
> Nothing. Just going to my next
> class.

> KIM
> Look, I'm sorry you got in trouble.

> LINDSAY
> Yeah, so am I.

> KIM
> But I gotta tell you, I don't think
> you should take all this out on us.
> It's kinda bogus of you.

Lindsay stops. Turns to Kim. Sighs. Seems to soften.

> LINDSAY
> You know what, Kim? I'm sorry.

> KIM
> That's okay.

> LINDSAY
> (apologetic)
> No. Look, I mean I'm sorry I was
> expecting so much out of you. I
> was messed up after my grandma died
> and I thought you guys could help
> me. And you sorta did. But you're
> not really making my life any
> better now. You're kinda making it
> a lot worse.
> (feels bad)
> I gotta get to class.

Lindsay turns and heads off, leaving Kim staring after her,
not sure what to say or do.

> CUT TO:

INT. LINDSAY'S BEDROOM - DAY

Lindsay and Millie are sitting on Lindsay's bed cross-legged,
playing Uno. As Lindsay draws a card...

> (CONTINUED)

CONTINUED:

> MILLIE
> Lindsay... did you ever take acid?
> 'Cause there's a rumor around the
> school that you became a freak
> because you were at a party and
> somebody put acid in your punch and
> you went crazy.

> LINDSAY
> Yeah, I heard that one. I think
> they got it from an After School
> Special.

> MILLIE
> (Laughs)
> Yeah, there's a bunch of weird
> rumors around, like Nick is a
> junkie and that Ken guy killed his
> teacher when he was in third grade
> and that Kim and Daniel had a baby
> but one night they got high and
> thought it was a turkey and
> accidently put it in the oven and
> cooked it.

> LINDSAY
> God, that stupid school's filled
> with such gossipy idiots. You don't
> believe any of it, do you?

> MILLIE
> C'mon, Lindsay. Of course not.

> LINDSAY
> (suddenly very serious)
> Well, you know what? You should.
> 'Cause it's true.

> MILLIE
> (her face dropping)
> It is?

> LINDSAY
> Yes...

Lindsay nods ominously, then puts down her cards.

> LINDSAY (CONT'D)
> It's true that I have Uno.

Millie looks down, then quickly recovers.

(CONTINUED)

CONTINUED: (2)

>   MILLIE
>   (laughing)
>   Oh, Lindsay. Man...

>   LINDSAY
>   Are the Mathletes ready for the
>   scrimmage against Lincoln?

>   MILLIE
>   I guess so. We've been practicing
>   pretty hard. And Shelly's doing
>   great this year. She broke your
>   algebra record by four points last
>   week.

Lindsay stops. Looks at Millie, surprised.

>   LINDSAY
>   Four points? Really?

>   MILLIE
>   Oh, yeah. Mr. Kowchevski called her
>   "Lindsay Two" once but she got
>   really mad. She said she's not
>   number two at anything.

>   LINDSAY
>   Huh.

Lindsay thinks about this as Millie starts to deal another
hand of Uno.

>   CUT TO:

INT. WEIR DINING ROOM - NIGHT

The Weirs are sitting around the dinner table. Lindsay is
still deep in thought, poking at her food.

>   HAROLD
>   Pirates! We live right outside
>   Detroit and they can't find a
>   <u>fender</u>? Now I get two weeks of
>   driving around town looking like
>   some kind of hillbilly.

>   LINDSAY
>   Dad, I think I'm gonna go back to
>   the Mathletes. But I'll have to
>   stay after school for practices. Is
>   that okay?

>   (CONTINUED)

CONTINUED:

Harold and Jean's jaws drop. They look at each other, trying
to be cool again. They're a little speechless.

                    LINDSAY (CONT'D)
          Dad?

Harold and Jean exchange a dialogue of eye communications.
Jean makes faces that say "yes, do it," while Harold's eyes
seem to say "I don't know if she's lying or not."

                    HAROLD
          Well, I guess that'd be okay. But
          you are to come directly home after
          practice is over. And if this is
          some kind of ploy, then heaven help
          you.

                    LINDSAY
          Dad, it's not a ploy. And thanks.

                    HAROLD
          Well... okay.

Harold looks at Jean. Jean is beaming. Lindsay gives her
parents a smile and goes back to her food.

                    SAM
          Hey, dad, can I borrow some money?
          I wanna go buy new clothes
          tomorrow.

                    JEAN
          Oh, Sammy, I'll take you to the
          mall. We'll use my credit card.
          Then we can go to the Magic Pan and
          get crepes like we always do.

                    SAM
          No, you always make me get
          Garanimals or something dumb
          looking like that. I wanna go buy
          my own clothes.

Jean looks to Harold for support.

                    HAROLD
          I think it's a good idea, Sam. A
          man has to learn to dress himself.
          Gotta cut those apron strings
          sometime.

                                        (CONTINUED)

CONTINUED: (2)

Harold gives Jean another smile. This time, it's met by her sad face. She throws a look at Sam.

>   JEAN
> Well .... I think I dress you very
> nicely.

>   SAM
> Cindy doesn't.

>   JEAN
> Well, what does Cindy know? I dress
> your brother nice, don't I,
> Lindsay?

Lindsay looks at Sam's clothes, then she and Sam exchange a look.

>   LINDSAY
> Give him the cash, dad.

Sam gives Lindsay a grateful smile as Jean looks upset and studies Sam's shirt as Sam goes back to his food.

                                              CUT TO:

INT. MCKINLEY HIGH SCHOOL HALLWAY - DAY

Lindsay and Mr. Kowchevski are walking down the hall. Mr. Kowchevski looks suspicious.

>   MR. KOWCHEVSKI
> So what's the gag?

>   LINDSAY
> There's no gag. I thought you
> wanted me back on the team.

>   MR. KOWCHEVSKI
> I'd love to have you back on the
> team if you're serious.

>   LINDSAY
> I'm serious.

>   MR. KOWCHEVSKI
> Well, great. But the problem is
> I've gotta put you in the reserves.

>   LINDSAY
> The reserves? Really? There aren't
> any blocks open?

                                         (CONTINUED)

CONTINUED:

> MR. KOWCHEVSKI
> No, we've got a big team this year.
> It's a good group but we really do
> need you. Look, just start coming
> to practices and get caught up and
> after a few weeks we'll see what we
> can do. Okay?

> LINDSAY
> Yeah, okay. That's fine.

But we can see from her face that she's not very happy about
this. She and Kowchevski go into his classroom just as Sam
passes the door. As Sam walks, he scans the crowd.

SAM'S POV: A lot of people seem to be nicely dressed. Lots of
dress shirts, guys wearing open vests, girls in dress pants,
puca shell necklaces.

Sam looks down at his goofy striped shirt and makes a face to
himself. He's suddenly self-conscious.

Just then, Bill enters from around the corner. If anybody
ever looked goofier and worse-dressed than Sam, it's Bill.
He's wearing a sloppy pullover, odd colored pants and his
multi-colored tennis shoes.

Sam sees him and heads over.

> SAM
> Bill, you wanna go to the mall with
> me after school today? I'm gonna
> buy some new clothes.

> BILL
> Really? Can we go to Lakeside? They
> have those giant pretzels.

> SAM
> Yeah, okay.
> (looks Bill up and down)
> Maybe you should get some new
> clothes, too.

> BILL
> Hey, back off. This is about you,
> not me.

Sam and Bill head off just as the bell rings.

CUT TO:

INT. UNDER THE STAIRS/HALLWAY - CONTINUOUS

Daniel and Kim are hanging out. Daniel has his arms around
Kim and is kissing her neck. She looks depressed and
preoccupied. She looks up when she hears the bell.

                    KIM
        I gotta get to class.

                    DANIEL
        No, c'mon. Let's get outta here.
        Dez gave me the keys to his place.
        Let's go earn some extra credit.

He tightens his grip and kisses her on the ear playfully. She
pulls away.

                    DANIEL (CONT'D)
        What's your problem?

                    KIM
            (impatient)
        I told you. I gotta get to class.

                    DANIEL
        Oh, okay, Lindsay.

                    KIM
        Shut up, man. I thought you were
        the guy who had all the big plans.

                    DANIEL
        Hey, I went to all my classes
        yesterday, okay? I could barely
        stay awake.

                    KIM
        Then drink a cup of coffee. I'm
        outta here.

Kim storms away. Daniel watches after her, then gets up and
walks into the hall. Students are running to their classes.

Daniel walks into the middle of the hallway just as the final
students go into their classes or disappear down the hall.
Daniel is left standing all alone in the empty hall. He looks
around, not sure what to do.

                                        FADE OUT.

            <u>END OF ACT TWO</u>

                                        (CONTINUED)

105

CONTINUED:

ACT THREE

FADE IN:

INT. KOWCHEVSKI'S CLASSROOM - DAY

Kowchevski is at his desk grading papers. A shadow falls across him. He looks up to see Daniel standing before him.

                    KOWCHEVSKI
                (startled)
          Desario, never sneak up on an ex-
          Marine.

                    DANIEL
          Oh, sorry.

Daniel stands staring at him for a beat with an earnest smile on his face. Kowchevski's confused and suspicious.

                    KOWCHEVSKI
          What do you want?

                    DANIEL
          Well, I'm really crappy at math,
          you know. So, I was wondering...
          uh... you wanna tutor me?

Kowchevski stares at Daniel for a beat. Then...

                    KOWCHEVSKI
          You wanna get out of my face?

                    DANIEL
          Hey, I'm serious.

Kowchevski studies him some more. He's very skeptical.

                    KOWCHEVSKI
          Yeah? Well, great. I hold a
          tutoring session for you everyday.
          It's called your math class. Drop
          by sometime.

Kowchevski gives him a look that says "we're done talking." Daniel looks surprised at the cool reception.

                                  CUT TO:

INT. CAFETERIA - DAY

Lunchtime at the Mathlete table. Lindsay and Millie are
there, along with Carey and Erin and several other girls.
They are all pretty conservative looking.

> LINDSAY
> So Carl Sagan says, "That's not a
> cosine. You don't know your
> asymptote from a hole in the
> ground."

The Mathletes all crack up. Just then, SHELLY WEAVER walks up
with her lunch tray. She's a Mathlete with an ego.

> SHELLY
> Oh, hi, Lindsay. I heard you have
> to be in the reserves. That's too
> bad. It'd be great if there was a
> block open for you on the team.

> LINDSAY
> Yeah, well, that's okay.

> MILLIE
> Shelly, if you give up First Block,
> then Lindsay can be back on the
> team.

> LINDSAY
> Millie...

> MILLIE
> I'm just kidding.

> SHELLY
> Don't kid about First Block.

> MILLIE
> (laughing)
> Sorry.

> CAREY
> You know, M.I.T. looks at your
> application way more carefully if
> you've been a First Block.

(CONTINUED)

CONTINUED:

>   ERIN
> It's true. My cousin knew this guy
> who worked in admissions there and
> he said that they give the biggest
> points for First Block Mathletes,
> and if you represented Norway in
> Student United Nations.

>   CAREY
> What? That's stupid. Why Norway?

>   ERIN
> M.I.T.'s owned by Norwegians.

>   SHELLY
> No, it's not, Erin. Don't be dumb.
>   (to Lindsay)
> I just can't believe you gave up
> being First Block just to hang out
> with freaks.

>   CAREY/ERIN
> God, Shelly!/Jeez.

>   SHELLY
> Well, it's true. She did. I'm not
> putting her down. They're the ones
> who made her get into that
> accident. I bet they were all high.

>   LINDSAY
> Nobody was high.

>   SHELLY
> Oh. Was that Kim girl with you?
> She's pregnant, you know.
>   (to the Mathletes,
>   gossipy)
> My neighbor works at the Free
> Clinic and he said that she was in
> there the other day.

>   LINDSAY
>   (trying to stay calm)
> Shelly, she's not pregnant. You
> know, just because a girl lives her
> life different than you doesn't
> automatically mean she's barefoot
> and pregnant.

(CONTINUED)

CONTINUED: (2)

> SHELLY
> (trying to joke)
> I didn't say she was barefoot.
> Anyway, you know her better than I
> do. Don't get all mad.
> (then, to the Mathletes)
> Hey, you guys. The Dean of the
> business department at U of M is
> gonna come talk to my dad's Kiwanis
> club. Anybody want to come?

Lindsay stares at Shelly, thinking.

SMASH CUT TO:

INT. KOWCHEVSKI'S OFFICE - DAY

Lindsay is standing before Mr. Kowchevski, who is seated at
his desk.

> LINDSAY
> Mr. Kowchevski, I want you to make
> me First Block.

> MR. KOWCHEVSKI
> Well, I remember you being First
> Block. You know, before you quit to
> hang out with the potheads?

> LINDSAY
> Look, you've gotta put me back on
> the team. I'm the best person at
> math in this school.

> MR. KOWCHEVSKI
> Actually, I think that I'm the best
> person at math in this school.

> LINDSAY
> Mr. K, I'm not joking. You know I'm
> your best Mathlete and I've got a
> bedroom full of trophies to prove
> it.

> MR. KOWCHEVSKI
> (amused)
> Lindsay, look, you're right. The
> team needs you desperately. If it
> wasn't for Shelly, we'd be in the
> toilet. The two of you would make a
> strong front.

(CONTINUED)

CONTINUED:

Lindsay grimaces at this reference to Shelly.

> MR. KOWCHEVSKI (CONT'D)
> But I can't bump anybody out.
> They've been coming every day.
> It wouldn't be fair. This is the
> Mathletes, not the football team.

> LINDSAY
> What's the difference? It's still
> a team, so you might as well have a
> winning team. Otherwise, what the
> hell's the point of competing?

Lindsay stares at Kowchevski with fire in her eyes. He stares
at her, not sure what to say.

> CUT TO:

INT. SILVERMAN'S MENS FASHION STORE - DAY

A fashion store at a mall. It's a very disco-oriented place,
with lots of chrome racks, white shelves and black walls.
Nightclub-style lighting. DISCO MUSIC PLAYS.

Sam and Bill wander in. Bill's munching on half of a huge
soft pretzel.

> BILL
> It looks like a disco.

> SAM
> The radio said this is where all
> the cool guys shop.

A sleepy-eyed SALESMAN approaches the geeks. He's dressed in
a slightly ill-fitting fashion suit.

> SALESMAN
> Hey, kid, you can't eat in here.

> BILL
> I'm not done. I can't throw it
> away.

> SALESMAN
> Well, I can't let you get mustard
> all over the clothes.

> SAM
> You wanna wait outside?

> (CONTINUED)

CONTINUED:

> BILL
> No. Just a minute.

Bill shoves the entire pretzel in his mouth, making his cheeks bulge out.

> BILL (CONT'D)
> (incomprehensible through
> the mouthful of pretzel)
> There. All gone.

> SALESMAN
> Anything I can help you gents out with today?

> SAM
> Well, I'm... uh... I want to get some new clothes. Something that'll make me the best dressed guy in school.

> SALESMAN
> Oh, I get it. You wanna make an impression with the ladies, huh?

> BILL
> (mouth still full)
> Yes, that's what he wants.

> SALESMAN
> Well then, let me ask you a question. Do you want to be a stud... or do you want to be a super stud?

> BILL
> Super stud, Sam. Go for super stud.

> SAM
> Uh, yeah, sure.

> SALESMAN
> Then walk this way, my man.

The salesman heads to a rack. Sam and Bill exchange a look, then follow after. The salesman reaches into a rack and extracts a powder blue denim disco jumpsuit, complete with huge bell bottoms and a giant collar.

(CONTINUED)

CONTINUED: (2)

                    SALESMAN (CONT'D)
Check it out. This just came in.
The hottest thing going in Europe
right now.

                    SAM
What is it?

                    SALESMAN
It's a Parisian nightsuit. I'm
telling you, a month from now every
man of distinction in town is gonna
have one of these on. You would
look like such a trendsetter that
the girls would go nuts. You'd be
fighting them off with a stick.

                    BILL
Wow.

                    SAM
        (unsure)
Really?

                    SALESMAN
I don't lie about stuff like that.

                    BILL
<u>Parisian</u> nightsuit, Sam. Girls
love French stuff. Think about it.

Sam does, then turns to the salesman.

                    SAM
How much is it?

                    SALESMAN
Ninety dollars.

Sam looks at Bill again, then pulls his money out of his
pocket and looks at it. Thinks a second, then gets a big
smile.

                    SAM
Okay. I'll take it.

                                        CUT TO:

INT. KOWCHEVSKI'S CLASSROOM - LATER

Kowchevski is standing in front of the Mathletes. Sighs.

                                        (CONTINUED)

CONTINUED:

> MR. KOWCHEVSKI
> I've had to make some tough
> decisions about who's gonna be
> competing tomorrow and some of you
> aren't going to like them, but we
> need to do something to get the
> season off on the right foot.
> (turns to Lindsay)
> Lindsay... you're on the team.

Lindsay smiles. Shelly doesn't look pleased.

> SHELLY
> She rejoins and gets into
> competition in one day? That's not
> fair.

> MR. KOWCHEVSKI
> You're right, Shelly, but if we
> lose against Lincoln, we blow our
> home advantage for the rest of the
> season. This is just a little
> insurance.

> SHELLY
> Well, then who's getting bumped?

Mr. Kowchevski looks down at his clipboard. The Mathletes
look at each other, bracing for bad news. Kowchevski lingers
on his clipboard a beat, then walks toward the Mathletes.

> MR. KOWCHEVSKI
> This is strictly a decision based
> on the last few practices. Millie,
> would you mind sitting tomorrow
> out?

Lindsay looks surprised. Shelly and the Mathletes' eyes all
go wide. Millie looks a little shocked but quickly recovers.

> MILLIE
> Oh... no, Mr. Kowchevski. That's
> fine. I don't mind.

> LINDSAY
> Mr. K, I don't think that Millie
> should have to--

> MILLIE
> No, it's cool, Lindsay. The team
> really needs you.

(CONTINUED)

CONTINUED: (2)

                    SHELLY
          No, we don't. This is completely
          unfair to you, Millie. It's unfair
          to all of us.

                    LINDSAY
                 (taking offense)
          Shelly, I don't think--

                    MR. KOWCHEVSKI
          Ladies, look, this is only for
          tomorrow's scrimmage. It's not the
          last chopper out of Saigon, so
          let's try to crank down the drama a
          notch, okay?

Lindsay throws Millie an apologetic look. This isn't the way
she was expecting to get back on the team. Millie just
smiles and waves Lindsay off. Shelly, however, glares at
Lindsay.

                                              CUT TO:

INT. SAM'S BEDROOM - DAY

MUSIC UP: THE J. GEILS BAND "FLAMETHROWER"

Sam is standing in front of his bedroom mirror. He holds up a
plastic hanging bag with the words "SILVERMAN'S FASHIONS" on
the front. He excitedly pulls off the bag, revealing the
jumpsuit.

Sam holds the jumpsuit up in front of himself and poses.

                    SAM
                 (to himself)
          Oh, hi, Cindy. You know what? Let's
          you and me get outta here.

Sam dances around like a nut with the jumpsuit in front of
him, then takes the jumpsuit and hangs it on the back of his
door so he can stare at it. He looks quite happy with his
purchase.

                                              CUT TO:

INT. MILLIE'S BEDROOM - DAY

Millie's room is a disaster area. Dirty clothes are flung all
over the room, books and games are piled everywhere and the
bed is unmade.

(CONTINUED)

CONTINUED:

Lindsay and Millie are sitting on the floor, surrounded by junk. They have math books spread out in front of them. Lindsay is hunched over one. She shifts and flinches in pain.

> LINDSAY
> Ow!

She reaches behind her and pulls a set of Clacker Balls (Kerbangers) out from under her butt.

> LINDSAY (CONT'D)
> Millie, don't you ever clean your room?

> MILLIE
> I just did. Lindsay, I'm really happy Mr. Kowchevski kicked me off the team so that you can be on it.

> LINDSAY
> Millie, you're not kicked off the team. You're in the reserves.

> MILLIE
> Yeah, I know. But it's cool. I'm better at Biology anyway. Too bad they don't have Bio-letes.

> LINDSAY
> Yeah. But I never wanted to get back on the team this way.
> You know that, don't you?

> MILLIE
> I know, Lindsay. Don't worry.

Millie gives Lindsay a reassuring smile. Lindsay gives her a smile back, then dives back into her books, intense again.

> LINDSAY
> How much does Shelly know about trig? Is she good at it?

> MILLIE
> I think so. We don't get that many trig questions.

> LINDSAY
> But when you do, does she get them right?

(CONTINUED)

CONTINUED: (2)

> MILLIE
> I forget.

> LINDSAY
> ..Millie! C'mon, think. I wanna
> make sure I can blow Shelly out of
> the water. I need to know this
> stuff.

> MILLIE
> You think Mr. Kowchevski'll move
> you to First Block?

> LINDSAY
> He'd better. If I'm gonna be a
> Mathlete, I'm gonna be number one
> or I'm not gonna do it.

> MILLIE
> (a huge smile)
> Oh, man. That's the old Lindsay!

                                    CUT TO :

EXT. WEIR HOUSE - DUSK

The fenderless station wagon sits in the Weir driveway. We
hear a rumble. Daniel's car pulls up.

INSIDE DANIEL'S CAR

Daniel sits, staring at Lindsay's house. He lights a
cigarette. He stares at the station wagon.

DANIEL'S POV: The front of the car with the fender missing.

Daniel sighs, depressed and confused, takes a drag, then
looks at the just-lit cigarette. Furrows his brow.

He puts out the cigarette on his car door and tosses it out
the window. He puts his car into gear and slowly pulls away.

                                    CUT TO:

INT. WEIR KITCHEN - EVENING

Lindsay enters the kitchen with her huge stack of books.
Jean is preparing dinner.

> LINDSAY
> Mom, I'm gonna eat in my room.
> I've gotta cram for the scrimmage.

                                    (CONTINUED)

CONTINUED:

> JEAN
> Honey, you've been studying non-
> stop. Why don't you take a little
> break?

> LINDSAY
> Mom, I can't. Not if I wanna win.

> JEAN
> Lindsay, there's more to life than
> competition.

> LINDSAY
> Not if you're trying to wipe out
> Shelly Weaver.

> JEAN
> Oh, is she from Lincoln?

> LINDSAY
> No, she's on our team.

> JEAN
> Oh. Hey, your dad and I thought we
> might come down and watch you
> tomorrow.

> LINDSAY
> Okay. You can watch me destroy
> Shelly. But don't embarrass me.

Lindsay starts out of the kitchen.

> JEAN
> Honey?
> (when Lindsay turns)
> Are you having fun?

The question stops Lindsay for a second. Is she?

> LINDSAY
> (not convincing)
> Yeah. Of course I am.

But the question has unnerved her a bit. She turns and heads
to her room.

CUT TO:

INT. MCKINLEY HIGH SCHOOL HALLWAY - MORNING

MUSIC UP: JOE JACKSON'S "LOOK SHARP"

(CONTINUED)

CONTINUED:

A very confident Sam strides in through the front doors, standing out in his jumpsuit. People behind him stare, giving him strange looks. Sam walks with supreme confidence.

An oblivious Sam wades into the crowded hallways, looking around for his first compliment. He smiles at people. Winks. Gives the ladies little waves.

SAM'S POV: Students are walking in a morning haze. However, the minute they see him, their faces go blank. They stare at him oddly.

Sam starts looking around and notices how many people are now staring at him. He keeps smiling and nodding to them but he starts to see that they're looking at him like he's an alien. He becomes a little unnerved at all the attention.

A couple of students approach, look surprised and then stifle their laughter. Sam's confidence starts to erode. Everybody in the hall is staring at him and whispering to each other. He's definitely the center of attention.

Two JOCKS, a normal sized one and a huge farmer boy, are walking down the hall. They see Sam and really stare at him.

> SEIDELMAN
> What the hell is that?

The jocks come up to Sam and really look him up and down, perplexed. Then they see a bunch of jocks down the hallway. The huge jock reaches out and picks up Sam by his waist.

He holds Sam up in the air for the jocks down the hall to see. Sam squirms a bit but tries to retain his dignity.

> SEIDELMAN (CONT'D)
> Hey, Henson, check it out. It's the
> new Disco Ken doll.

> JOCK #1
> (calling out from other
> end)
> Pull the string and make him talk!

The jocks all crack up as the huge jock sets Sam down. Sam hustles off down the hall and around the corner, knowing he has officially made a fashion mistake.

IN ANOTHER PART OF THE HALLWAY

Neal, Bill and Gordon are walking to class.

(CONTINUED)

118

CONTINUED: (2)

> NEAL
> I'm telling you, you can light
> them. It's methane.

> BILL
> What if the flame goes back inside
> you? Do you explode?

Sam runs up behind them. They turn and see him in his
jumpsuit.

> NEAL
> Oh my God. I guess Elvis <u>hasn't</u>
> left the building.

> BILL
> Hey, don't make fun of him. That's
> a Parisian nightsuit, in case you
> didn't know.

> GORDON
> Parisian? Ooo la la.

> NEAL
> No, it's not. It's a jumpsuit. My
> grandpa in Fort Lauderdale wears
> them all the time because he's too
> lazy to put on pants.

> SAM
> Just head for the front door. I'm
> getting out of here.

Sam slips into the middle of them and they form a triangle
formation around him as they walk, obscuring him from view.

> NEAL
> Why did you buy that?

> SAM
> You're the one who said I had to
> dress better.

> NEAL
> Yeah, but I didn't tell you to
> dress like Evel Knievel.

They all move down the hall in formation, shielding Sam from
sight. However, they look so odd that everybody stares at
them.

(CONTINUED)

CONTINUED: (3)

> BILL
> I think we're drawing more
> attention by doing this.

> GORDON
> This is cool. I feel like I'm in
> the Secret Service.

> SAM
> Just get me to the front door.

Just then, the BELL RINGS. The guys suddenly all step away to
head to class, leaving Sam exposed.

> SAM (CONT'D)
> Hey!

> NEAL
> We've gotta get to class. We've got
> a pop quiz in Whitman's class,
> remember?

> SAM
> Oh, man. Look, just tell Whitman I
> missed the bus, okay?

The geeks shrug and hurry off. Sam walks quickly to the front
doors to escape. As his hand touches the door...

> DOLORES (O.C.)
> Excuse me. Where you going?

Sam looks to see that DOLORES, the office receptionist, is
standing at the office window watching him.

> SAM
> Oh, uh, I need to get something
> from outside.

> DOLORES
> Yeah? Well, unless you're going out
> to drive a bus, you'd better turn
> around and get your butt to class.

Sam gives her a helpless look. She makes a mocking face back
at him and signals "move it" with her thumb. Sam SIGHS and
heads back up the hallway.

FADE OUT.

<u>END OF ACT THREE</u>

(CONTINUED)

CONTINUED: (4)

ACT FOUR

FADE IN:

INT. STAIRWELL - DAY

Kim is coming down the stairs, looking a little sad. As she's halfway down, she sees Lindsay and the Mathletes walk past on their way down the hall.

                    LINDSAY
          You guys, let's get to the
          cafeteria a half hour early so we
          can run a few logarithms.

                    SHELLY
          Lindsay, we usually get there an
          <u>hour</u> early before a scrimmage. But
          feel free to show up when you like.

The Mathletes laugh at Shelly's joke/dig (an uncomfortable laugh that shows they side with Lindsay). Lindsay forces a terse smile.

Kim keeps coming down, watching Lindsay and the Mathletes as they head to Mr. Kowchevski's class. Kim walks into the hall and watches them. She looks depressed -- she misses Lindsay. Then Kim turns and heads off.

Just as the Mathletes are entering Kowchevski's room, Lindsay looks down the hall and sees Kim walking away by herself. Lindsay stares for a brief moment, looks uncertain, then heads into the room.

                                        CUT TO:

INT. ENGLISH CLASSROOM - DAY

Ms. Yeats is in front of her class, writing a long sentence on the chalkboard. Sam is sitting toward the back of the class, slumped down. WE HEAR A COUPLE OF VOICES MAKING DISCO DRUM SOUNDS. Sam looks over.

ANGLE ON: The two jocks are looking over at him, making the disco sounds. They make faces at Sam and do a finger version of John Travolta's dance in "Saturday Night Fever."

Sam gives them a pained look and they snicker to themselves.

                                        (CONTINUED)

CONTINUED:

>   MS. YEATS
>   Okay, now, who wants to take a
>   crack at identifying all the
>   prepositional phrases in this
>   sentence?

No one raises their hands. Ms. Yeats scans the room.

>   MS. YEATS (CONT'D)
>   No takers? Okaaay... Sam. You want
>   to come up here and give it a shot?

Sam's eyes go wide in dread. He looks around at the class.

>   SAM
>   Um... I, uh... I...

>   MS. YEATS
>   C'mon, Sam. Make me proud.

She holds up the piece of chalk and gives Sam a friendly
smile. Sam's face falls. He slowly gets up and starts the
long walk to the front of the class. If everybody hadn't seen
his outfit before, they all have now.

The students stare at Sam and exchange looks. A couple stifle
laughter. Sam gets to the front and takes the chalk from Ms.
Yeats.

>   MS. YEATS (CONT'D)
>   My, don't you look nice.

The jocks do a hand over the mouth "HOMO" cough. Scattered
laughter. Sam's dying. Ms. Yeats gives the jocks an angry
look.

>   MS. YEATS (CONT'D)
>   Hey, if Sam wearing something
>   different to show off his
>   individuality makes him a "homo,"
>   then we should all be proud to be
>   "homos." Go on, Sam.

Sam looks like he wants to crawl under a rock as he turns
toward the chalkboard.

>   CUT TO:

EXT. MCKINLEY HIGH SCHOOL QUAD - DAY

Harris is sitting on a bench, reading a Dungeons and Dragons
manual entitled "The Monstrous Compendium." Daniel is
walking past. He glances at Harris strangely, then walks
past.

After a beat, Daniel comes back. He walks over and sits on
the bench next to Harris. Harris' eyes shift over to Daniel,
confused, then back to his book. Daniel shifts himself to
read the cover. After a beat...

                    HARRIS
          You're not going to beat me up, are
          you?

                    DANIEL
          No, man. What're you reading?

                    HARRIS
          "The Monstrous Compendium." It's a
          Dungeons and Dragons handbook. Do
          you play?

                    DANIEL
          Uh... no.

                    HARRIS
          You should. You'd make a great
          dungeon master. I can tell.

                    DANIEL
          Yeah? Thanks. Let me ask you
          something. What do you make of me?

                    HARRIS
          Excuse me?

                    DANIEL
          I mean, if someone said to you
          "what do you think of Daniel
          Desario?" What would you say?

                    HARRIS
          Well... um...

                    DANIEL
          Would you say he's a loser?

                    HARRIS
          Well, you're not a loser 'cause you
          have sex.
                    (MORE)

(CONTINUED)

CONTINUED:

> HARRIS (CONT'D)
> But if you weren't having sex, we
> definitely could debate the issue.

Daniel stares at him, then nods.

> DANIEL
> You get good grades, right?

> HARRIS
> Oh, yeah. Don't you?

> DANIEL
> Nah, I get terrible grades. Man, I
> don't even like thinking about
> school 'cause then I think about
> how bad I'm really doing. I was
> even left back once.

> HARRIS
> Well, today is the first day of the
> rest of your life. Someone sent my
> dad a card with that on it for his
> 65th birthday.

> DANIEL
> Your dad's sixty-five?

> HARRIS
> He's seventy now. When I'm forty-
> five, he'll be a hundred.

Daniel laughs. Harris smiles, pleased at the approval of
Daniel.

> DANIEL
> You're an interesting guy, Harris.
> You do your own thing. You're
> comfortable with yourself. You've
> really got it wired, huh?

> HARRIS
> Yeah, I guess. But I'm not having
> sex, though.

They laugh again.

                                        CUT TO:

INT. CAFETERIA - DAY

All the tables in the cafeteria have been pushed to the
sides. There's a small audience of chairs in the middle. A
few parents and students sit in them.

                                        (CONTINUED)

CONTINUED:

At the front are two tables, one for each Mathlete team. This isn't what you'd call a big ticket event.

The Lincoln High School Mathlete team is having a pow-wow by one wall. There are about ten Mathletes and their coach.

Mr. Kowchevski is with the McKinley Mathletes against the wall. They're going through a final prep.

>   MR. KOWCHEVSKI
>   All right. You all know your stuff,
>   so just stay clear-headed and we'll
>   blaze through this. Now, let's go
>   kick some Lincoln butt.

The Mathletes all give nervous laughs.

>   LINDSAY
>   Good luck, everybody.
>   (then)
>   Good luck, Shelly.

>   SHELLY
>   Thanks. Same to you.

Shelly and Lindsay give each other the most insincere smiles imaginable. A very excited Millie comes up to Lindsay.

>   MILLIE
>   Good luck, Lindsay, although I know
>   you don't need it.
>   (whispers)
>   Go, First Block!

Millie gives Lindsay a big hug, surprising Lindsay.

IN THE AUDIENCE

Harold and Jean settle in to watch the competition. They look happy.

IN THE BACK OF THE CAFETERIA

The door opens. Kim enters. She looks around tentatively, then walks over to a seat on the edge of the audience. She settles in, then sees something off to the side.

PULL BACK TO REVEAL

Nick is sitting at the other far edge of the chairs, waiting for the scrimmage to begin.

(CONTINUED)

CONTINUED: (2)

> KIM
> (loud whisper)
> Nick!

> NICK
> (turns; surprised)
> Oh, hey, uh... what are you doing
> here?

> KIM
> What are <u>you</u> doing here?

> NICK
> Oh, I was, uh, just killing time.

Nick forces an uncomfortable smile at Kim, then looks around
the cafeteria.

> NICK (CONT'D)
> It's pretty wild in here without
> the tables, huh? I feel this weird
> vibe of people chewing.
> (after a beat)
> Well, I better get going.

Nick gets up and slinks out, looking embarrassed at having
been caught.

CUT TO:

INT. MCKINLEY HIGH SCHOOL HALLWAY - DAY

Sam is on the payphone. Students keep walking by and staring
at him.

> SAM
> (into phone)
> Mrs. Amendella? My mom's not at
> home. Do you know where she went?
> (then)
> Oh. Well, could you come to
> McKinley and pick me up? I forgot
> my homework. No, I need to get it
> myself.

A hand comes in, takes the phone from Sam and hangs it up.
It's Alan. He's got a couple of his buddies with him.

> ALAN
> Excuse me. Aren't you Deney Terrio
> from "Dance Fever?"

(CONTINUED)

CONTINUED:

                    BULLY #1
          No, I told you. He's Chrissy from
          "Three's Company."

The bullies crack up.

                    SAM
          What do you want?

                    ALAN
          I just need to know something.
          Exactly how queer are you?

                    SAM
          Shut up.

                    ALAN
          No, really, I'm serious. See, every
          time I think you're as queer as you
          can be, you go and do something
          even queerer.

Sam snaps. He rushes at Alan, pushing Alan back. Alan's
caught completely off-guard and stumbles back against a
locker.

                    SAM
               (yelling at Alan)
          Why don't you just leave me alone!
          I'm sick of you!

                    ALAN
          Oh, man. Now it's go time.

Alan's about to charge back at Sam when Mr. Rosso jumps in
between them.

                    MR. ROSSO
          Hey, Alan, how many times a day do
          I have to tell you to be cool?

                    ALAN
          I'm just talking to Sam.

                    MR. ROSSO
          Yeah, it looked like you guys were
          having a regular meeting of the
          minds. What's this all about, Sam?

                    SAM
          Mr. Rosso... I need a ride home.

                                        (CONTINUED)

CONTINUED: (2)

Sam gives Rosso an "I'm not kidding" look. Rosso nods.

CUT TO:

INT. CAFETERIA - DAY

The intradistrict scrimmage is under way. A Lincoln Mathlete is competing against Erin. A JUDGE is feeding the questions as the Mathletes scribble on pads in front of them.

                    JUDGE
          If the hour hand of a clock moves k
          radians in forty-eight minutes,
          then k equals...

The Lincoln Mathlete throws her hand up immediately.

                    LINCOLN MATHLETE #1
          Zero point four.

                    JUDGE
          Correct.

Sitting off to the side are the Mathletes. Lindsay and Shelly are sitting next to each other. They're both in psych-out mode and dripping with insincerity.

                    LINDSAY
          They're a tough team. Are you
          nervous?

                    SHELLY
          No, I don't get nervous.

                    LINDSAY
          Wow, that's great. I wish I was
          that confident.

                    SHELLY
          Well, it comes with being First
          Block.

                    LINDSAY
              (pointedly)
          Yeah, I remember.
              (looks over)
          I guess I'm up. Wish me luck.

Lindsay gives Shelly an "I'm gonna beat you" smile and gets up. Shelly watches her go, a little unnerved.

                                        (CONTINUED)

CONTINUED:

Lindsay walks to the table. When she gets there, she hears APPLAUSE. She looks out at the audience. Her face goes blank.

LINDSAY'S POV: She sees her parents smiling at her but then she sees Kim behind them. She is now sitting with Daniel and Ken, a fender for Harold's station wagon at their feet, clapping.

Harold and Jean turn around and see the freaks. The freaks wave to the Weirs. The Weirs give them suspicious looks. The freaks then lift the fender up and show it to Harold.

Harold looks at the fender, then the freaks. He doesn't know what to think. Daniel gives him a look that kinda says everything's cool. Harold turns back around, completely confused. The freaks throw Lindsay a pleased look.

Lindsay stares at them, completely thrown.

> JUDGE
> First question: If the longer
> diagonal of the rhombus is ten and
> the large angle is one-hundred
> degrees, what is the area of the
> rhombus?

Lindsay snaps herself back to reality. Raises her hand.

> LINDSAY
> Forty-two.

> JUDGE
> Correct.

The freaks all clap. Lindsay still looks thrown.

                                                        CUT TO:

INT. WEIR HOUSE FRONT DOOR/LIVING ROOM - DAY

Mr. Rosso is standing by the front door with his arms crossed. Sam is slumped on the couch in his jumpsuit, completely depressed. A few seconds pass. Finally ...

> MR. ROSSO
> You gonna change, Sam?

> SAM
> Do I have to go back to school? I'm
> tired of having people laugh at me.
> It's not like they're gonna forget
> I was wearing this.

                                                    (CONTINUED)

CONTINUED:

> MR. ROSSO
> So let them laugh. Who cares?

Sam gives Rosso a "you've gotta be kidding" look. Rosso sees this. He thinks a minute, then starts walking around the living room with his arms crossed, telling his story.

> MR. ROSSO (CONT'D)
> Sam, when I was about twenty, I was hanging out in this honky tonk down south when a big bunch of rednecks surrounded me. They started making jokes about my fringe vest, my hair, calling me a hippie, a woman. They dragged me into an alley, made me dance, told me to bark like a dog.

> SAM
> Did you do it?

> MR. ROSSO
> Yeah. Pretty much had to. There was ten of them.

> SAM
> What happened?

> MR. ROSSO
> (after a beat)
> It doesn't matter. What matters is that I never lost pride in who I am.

> SAM
> (confused)
> Mr. Rosso, I was just trying to dress up to impress Cindy Sanders.

> MR. ROSSO
> Sam, some of my friends are the dirtiest, stinkiest guys you'll ever meet. But those guys date more women than you or I could ever hope for.
> (off Sam's skeptical look)
> It's all about <u>confidence</u>.

Sam gives Rosso a disbelieving look.

(CONTINUED)

CONTINUED: (2)

> MR. ROSSO (CONT'D)
> It's true. If I say I'm the coolest
> guy in the world and I <u>believe</u> I'm
> the coolest guy in the world, then
> suddenly, I <u>become</u> the coolest guy
> in the world. I'm telling you, it
> sounds weird but it works. The only
> hard part is convincing yourself of
> it.

> SAM
> But I'm not cool.

Rosso gives Sam a look, then stops in front of the goofy
charcoal portrait of Sam hanging on the wall. He looks at it
a second, then back at Sam.

> MR. ROSSO
> You're not? Hmmm. Well, then take a
> look at this kid.
> > (pointing to portrait of
> > Sam)
> Because that's a cool kid.

Sam stares at Mr. Rosso, who has a very sincere look on his
face. He gives Sam a smile. Sam is unsure but slowly he gets
a small smile.

> CUT TO:

INT. CAFETERIA - DAY

Lindsay raises her hand. She's on a roll.

> LINDSAY
> One horizontal and one vertical
> asymptote.

> JUDGE
> Correct. Well done, McKinley.

Millie claps loudly, as do the other Mathletes on the
sideline.

INT. MCKINLEY HIGH SCHOOL HALLWAY - LATER THAT AFTERNOON

Sam re-enters the school. He's back in his normal school
clothes, with his same old hair. He steps in and looks
around. He breathes a sigh of relief.

SAM'S POV: Cindy is standing with a couple of cheerleader
friends, talking and laughing.

(CONTINUED)

CONTINUED:

Sam looks at her, then takes a deep breath and heads over to her and her friends.

>   SAM
>   (super-confident)
>   Hello, ladies. Hello, Cindy.

He points a cool guy finger at them, winks and continues off down the hallway. Cindy and the cheerleaders all stare after him, not sure what to think.

Sam keeps walking down the hall with a confident gait. Mr. Rosso comes around the corner. He and Sam see each other.

As soon as they pass each other, Sam holds out his hand. Mr. Rosso holds out his and they slap each other a low five.

As each continues on his way, we...

>   CUT TO:

INT. CAFETERIA - DAY

Kowchevski looks beyond happy. Shelly is watching Lindsay, more unnerved. She looks upset that Lindsay's doing so well.

>   JUDGE (CONT'D)
>   If Arcsin X equals two Arccos X,
>   then x equals...

ANGLE ON: THE FREAKS are trying to follow what the judge is saying.

>   KIM
>   Damn, I've never felt so stupid in
>   my life.

Lindsay raises her hand quickly.

>   LINDSAY
>   Zero point nine.

>   JUDGE
>   Correct. Perfect round to McKinley.

The Mathletes jump up and cheer. Mr. Kowchevski runs up and hugs Lindsay. Lindsay looks happy but a little unsure. She looks at Shelly, who looks rather freaked out by Lindsay's perfect score.

>   (CONTINUED)

CONTINUED:

> MR. KOWCHEVSKI
> You were great, Lindsay. You were
> so great. You're a born Mathlete.

Lindsay's not sure how to take this comment. She looks out at the audience.

LINDSAY'S POV: The freaks are standing in the audience. Ken gives her a nod. Daniel smiles at her and gestures that he'll take the fender to her house. As they head out, Kim mouths "congratulations" to Lindsay, then gives a sad little wave and heads out of the cafeteria.

> MR. KOWCHEVSKI (CONT'D)
> All right, Shelly, you're up. Let's
> give 'em the ol' McKinley one two
> punch.

Shelly looks at Mr. Kowchevski and forces a smile. She tries to get a determined look, gets up and heads for the table.

> LINDSAY
> (sincere)
> Good luck, Shelly.

But Shelly looks too nervous to answer. She stands at the table and takes a deep breath. She has the look of someone who's about to try way too hard.

Lindsay sees this. She looks a little guilty.

> JUDGE
> A sphere is inscribed in a cube.
> The ratio of the volume of the
> sphere to the volume of the cube
> is...

Shelly looks very out of sorts. She scribbles on a pad of note paper as the LINCOLN MATHLETE #2 thinks.

> MR. KOWCHEVSKI
> (quietly, to Lindsay)
> C'mon, Shelly. We just went over
> this last week.

The Lincoln Mathlete throws her hand in the air.

> LINCOLN MATHLETE #2
> Zero point fifty two to one.

The McKinley Mathletes roll their eyes. Lindsay sees them. She looks back at Shelly.

(CONTINUED)

CONTINUED: (2)

Shelly doesn't look well at all. In fact, she's about to fall apart. She takes another deep breath.

Lindsay watches this, then looks out at Millie. Millie looks very concerned about Shelly. Lindsay just continues to watch the scene, looking guilty. She's not enjoying this at all.

CUT TO:

INT. MILLIE'S BEDROOM - NIGHT

A bunch of the Mathlete girls, including Carey and Erin, are laying around in Millie's bedroom in their sleeping bags.

Lindsay is in the middle of them in a camping sleeping bag, looking completely out of place. The girls are all in pajamas or nightgowns. Lindsay is wearing a T-shirt and pajama bottoms. She doesn't look like she's having fun.

> CAREY
> Did you see when she missed that
> square root problem? She started
> sweating like a pig.

> ERIN
> Millie, now maybe Kowchevski'll
> kick Shelly off the team so you can
> get your block back.

> MILLIE
> Yeah, I guess. I hope so. I kinda
> feel bad for Shelly, though.

> CAREY
> Forget her. She had it coming.

The girls all laugh. Lindsay and Millie exchange a look. Lindsay's not enjoying this.

> ERIN
> Hey, you guys, I got the new M.I.T.
> catalogue. You've gotta see their
> dorms.

As the girls excited gather around, the sound of their voices FADES as we PUSH IN ON LINDSAY.

Lindsay watches the girls strangely, then slowly lays back in her sleeping bag and goes into her own world. She looks depressed and lonely.

CUT TO:

INT. SAM'S BEDROOM - NIGHT

Sam is in bed. Neal and Bill are on the ground in their
sleeping bags. The lights are out but they're in talk-all-
night mode.

>   NEAL
>   If I think I'm cool, then people
>   will think I'm cool, too?

>   SAM
>   That's what Mr. Rosso says.

>   BILL
>   Yeah, and he's pretty cool.

>   NEAL
>   Well, I think I'm cool but nobody
>   else does.

>   BILL
>   That's because you're not.

>   NEAL
>   Hey, shut up! I am so.

>   SAM
>   So am I. I'm really cool.

Bill looks over at Sam. Thinks a beat.

>   BILL
>   You know what, Sam? You actually do
>   seem cooler to me all of a sudden.
>   I think it's working.
>   (thinks)
>   It's weird. Mr. Rosso's like some
>   kind of genius.

>   NEAL
>   If he can make Sam seem cool to
>   you, he must be Einstein.

Sam just gives Neal a look that says "you're just jealous."

                                        CUT TO:

INT. MILLIE'S BEDROOM - LATER

It's dark. The girls are all asleep. Lindsay is wide awake.
She sits up and looks at Millie's clock radio. The time reads
11:04pm.

                                        (CONTINUED)

CONTINUED:

Lindsay looks over at Millie, who's asleep in her bed. Millie looks like a little kid, hugging her pillow, wearing a high-necked flannel night gown.

Lindsay looks at her sadly. She gets a small, sad smile. Then she gets up and quietly picks up her clothes and starts to get dressed.

                                                    CUT TO:

INT. MILLIE'S HALLWAY - NIGHT

Lindsay quietly slips out of Millie's bedroom in her clothes and very gently closes the door, not making a sound. She starts to walk down the hall.

                    MILLIE (O.C.)
                (loud whisper)
            Lindsay?

Lindsay stops and turns back. Millie is standing in the open doorway in her nightgown, looking at Lindsay.

                    MILLIE (CONT'D)
            Where are you going?

                    LINDSAY
            Um...Millie. I...I'm gonna go home.

                    MILLIE
            What's the matter? Are you gonna go
            use your own bathroom?

                    LINDSAY
            No, Millie. It's just...I can't do
            this.

                    MILLIE
            Really?

                    LINDSAY
            Yeah. I don't know. I mean, it's
            been really great hanging with you
            but...this isn't where I'm at
            anymore. You know?

Millie stares at her, then SIGHS.

                    MILLIE
            Yeah, I know. I didn't think you
            were having very much fun.

                                            (CONTINUED)

63.

CONTINUED:

>   LINDSAY
>   I was, Millie. But...I don't know.
>   It's just me. Things are different
>   now. I really thought I wanted to
>   win, but I don't think I want to
>   win anymore.
>
>   MILLIE
>   What do you want to do?
>
>   LINDSAY
>   (after a beat)
>   I don't know. But I don't think I
>   want to be a Mathlete.
>
>   MILLIE
>   That's okay. I understand.
>   (beat)
>   But can we still play Uno
>   sometimes? I mean, when you've got
>   nothing else to do?
>
>   LINDSAY
>   (after a beat; a small
>   smile)
>   Yeah. We can always do that. We'll
>   always be friends, Millie.

Lindsay and Millie exchange a small, sad smile. Then, Lindsay
starts to back away.

>   LINDSAY (CONT'D)
>   I'll see you around tomorrow.
>
>   MILLIE
>   Yeah. Okay. I'll see you then.

They give each other a small wave, then Lindsay heads off.
Millie watches her, gives a sad SIGH and goes back into her
room. Shuts the door behind her.

>   CUT TO:

EXT. SALVATORE'S ITALIAN DELI-NIGHT

MUSIC UP: SUPERTRAMP'S "TAKE THE LONG WAY HOME"

The freaks are all hanging out in the parking lot of
Salvatore's. They are sitting on the hoods of Daniel and
Nick's cars, looking bored.

>   (CONTINUED)

CONTINUED:

>   KIM
>   Any of you guys wanna go see a
>   midnight movie? There's some
>   foreign film playing at the State
>   Theater.

>   NICK
>   A foreign film? Like, the kind you
>   have to read?

>   KEN
>   Uh...what's the point?

>   KIM
>   The point is trying to not be a
>   dumb ass for once in your life,
>   that's what.

>   DANIEL
>   I'm up for it.

Ken and Nick look at each other and shrug.

>   KEN
>   It better not be about a guy who
>   talks a lot.

Just then, Lindsay walks up.

>   LINDSAY
>   Hey.

The freaks all look very surprised to see her. Nick gets up.

>   KIM
>   Hey. What's up?

>   LINDSAY
>   Nothing. What're you guys up to?

>   KEN
>   Nothing.

>   KIM
>   Uh, actually, we were just about to
>   go to see a foreign film. You know,
>   just because.

>   LINDSAY
>   Cool. Is it okay if I come with
>   you?

(CONTINUED)

CONTINUED: (2)

They all exchange looks.

                    KEN
          Sure, can we borrow your dad's car?

                    DANIEL
          Shut up, man. C'mon, Linds. I'll
          give you a ride.

Lindsay gives them a smile and they all start to get into
their cars. Nick pulls Lindsay aside, uncomfortable.

                    NICK
          Hey, I just wanted you to
          know...I'm really glad that you're
          feeling better about our break-up.
          You know, I think you're handling
          it really well.

                    LINDSAY
               (after a beat)
          Thanks, Nick. I think I'll be okay.

She gives him a friendly smile and they get into the car.

                                        FADE TO BLACK.

                    THE END

FREAKS AND GEEKS

"THE GARAGE DOOR"

Episode #12

Written by Gabe Sachs & Jeff Judah & Patty Lin

Directed by Bryan Gordon

I had a great time writing this episode with Gabe Sachs and Jeff Judah. They pitched a story for the geeks that was based on a personal experience of Jeff's. So I was left to write the freak story, in which Lindsay and Nick dealt with the fallout of their breakup and Ken fell in love with a band geek. That was the most fun for me—to show the vulnerable, romantic side of the usually sarcastic Ken. In the process, we got to make a lot of jokes about Seth Rogen's mannerisms and appearance. He was a great sport about it. My favorite contribution to the script was the scene where Amy makes fun of Ken's "mutton chops," and as she walks off, he touches his sideburns, in love. We did a callback to that comment at the end, when Amy strokes Ken's sideburns while they make out.

The unconventional love story between Amy and Ken took a sharp turn in a later episode when Amy turned out to be a hermaphrodite—but in this episode, we were just trying to show the attraction between two unlikely people. The scene in the Laser Dome where Amy and Ken bond over a series of wisecracks was toned down after Judd Apatow told us it sounded like a comedy routine. We kept some of the jokes, but tried to make the conversation feel sweet and awkward in a real way.

A final note about the Laser Dome scene: The southern rock motif was inspired by a laser program that Laserium put together for this episode. Daniel's line, "I think it's a cactus taking off his hat," was a direct reference to one of the laser effects we used. That line still cracks me up.

—Patty Lin

FREAKS AND GEEKS

"THE GARAGE DOOR"

CAST LIST

LINDSAY WEIR
SAM WEIR
HAROLD WEIR
JEAN WEIR
DANIEL DESARIO
NICK ANDOPOLIS
BILL HAVERCHUCK
NEAL SCHWEIBER
KEN MILLER
KIM KELLY
DR. SCHWEIBER
MRS. SCHWEIBER
AMY ANDREWS
WALTER
SALESMAN
CAROL
HYGIENIST
COWBOY

FREAKS AND GEEKS

"THE GARAGE DOOR"

SET LIST

INTERIORS:

MCKINLEY HIGH SCHOOL
    /HALLWAY
    /CAFETERIA
    /CLASSROOM
WEIR HOUSE
    /DINING ROOM
    /FRONT DOOR
    /LIVING ROOM
    /KITCHEN
    /SAM'S BEDROOM
SCHWEIBER HOUSE
    /LIVING ROOM
    /DINING ROOM
    /GARAGE
APPLIANCE STORE
COFFEE SHOP
DR. SCHWEIBER'S OFFICE
LASER DOME

EXTERIORS:

MCKINLEY HIGH SCHOOL
    /FOOTBALL FIELD
    /ON THE BLEACHERS
    /UNDER THE BLEACHERS
RESIDENTIAL STREET
SCHWEIBER HOUSE
    /DOORWAY

FADE IN:

INT. SCHWEIBER LIVING ROOM - LATE NIGHT

TIGHT ON A TV AIRING AN EPISODE OF "SATURDAY NIGHT LIVE."

               V.O.
      Live from New York, it's Saturday
      Night.

We reveal SAM, who is fighting to stay awake, and NEAL, who is wide awake, sitting on the floor watching. BILL is fast asleep, breathing heavily through his mouth.

Neal is placing various items, such as SOCKS, PAPER, and PENCILS, etc., on top of Bill.

               NEAL
      Bill. Wake up. It's on.

Bill is still asleep. Neal turns and sees Sam drifting off.

             NEAL (CONT'D)
      Sam. Come on. Up and at 'em.

Sam opens his eyes.

             SAM
        (sleepily)
      Why is it on so late?

             NEAL
      Because you can't say, "Jane, you
      ignorant slut" at eight o'clock.

DR. SCHWEIBER, Neal's dad, enters carrying a tray with four bowls of ICE CREAM, SPRINKLES, MARASCHINO CHERRIES, CHOCOLATE AND BUTTERSCOTCH SYRUP, NUTS, ETC.

             DR. SCHWEIBER
        (like a ballpark barker)
      Ice cream. Ice cream. Get your ice
      cream.

             NEAL
      Two down front, dad.

             DR. SCHWEIBER
        (a la Groucho)
      Certainly.

(CONTINUED)

CONTINUED:

Sam and Neal start putting the various toppings on the mounds of ice cream. Dr. Schweiber turns and sees that Bill is asleep.

> DR. SCHWEIBER (CONT'D)
> Bill?

The boys laugh when they see Dr. Schweiber's reaction to Bill covered with the various items. Dr. Schweiber lifts a sock to see Bill's face.

> DR. SCHWEIBER (CONT'D)
> Bill. You want some ice cream?

Bill, talking in his sleep, mutters unintelligibly. Sam's eyes blink heavily.

> DR. SCHWEIBER (CONT'D)
> (energetically)
> Come on, everybody wake up. We got
> ice cream and Saturday Night Live.

ANGLE ON TV: JOE PISCOPO "I'm from Jersey" sketch is playing,

> NEAL
> I miss Bill Murray.

> SAM
> Eddie Murphy's kinda funny.

> NEAL
> Yeah, but he's no Bill Murray.

> DR. SCHWEIBER
> Piscopo cracks me up.

> SAM
> (laughing)
> "I'm from Jersey! Are you from
> Jersey?"

> NEAL
> Dad. Can I have Bill's ice cream if
> he's not going to eat it?

> DR. SCHWEIBER
> (determined)
> He'll eat it.
> (to Bill)
> Hey, Bill. Live from New York, it's
> Saturday Night!

(CONTINUED)

CONTINUED: (2)

Bill stirs and all of the items fall off his head and onto
the floor. Sam and Neal laugh.

> BILL
> (still out of it)
> What? What? Why do you guys always
> stack stuff on me?

All laugh.

> DR. SCHWEIBER
> I'm going to get you some pop.
> That'll keep you up.

Dr. Schweiber exits into the kitchen, Sam turns to Neal.

> SAM
> You have the coolest dad.

> NEAL
> Yeah. I know.

CUT TO:

MAIN TITLES

ACT ONE

FADE IN:

EXT. FOOTBALL FIELD - DAY

The MARCHING BAND is practicing after school. They're playing
a cheesy version of CHICAGO'S "25 OR 6 TO 4."

CUT TO:

EXT. ON THE BLEACHERS - CONTINUOUS

We find LINDSAY, DANIEL, NICK, KEN, and KIM. Daniel, Nick and
Ken are sitting on the bleachers, laughing at the band kids.

> NICK
> I can't believe what they're doing
> to this song.

> DANIEL
> What the hell is it?

(CONTINUED)

CONTINUED:

>   NICK
> It's Chicago. "25 or 6 to 4."
>   (yells out)
> And they're butchering it.

>   KEN
> Why do you even know that song?

Kim laughs and goes over to join the guys. Lindsay follows. She and Nick exchange an awkward glance.

>   KIM
> Oh my God. Look at that Pizza-face
> dork with the trombone. Why doesn't
> he just pop those things?

ON THE FIELD - We see a skinny, pimply TROMBONE PLAYER.

>   DANIEL
> I think that kid's in my typing
> class. Tim Waterson or something.

>   LINDSAY
> His name is Jim Petersen.

>   KEN
>   (to Lindsay)
> Good friend of yours?

The freaks laugh. Lindsay looks embarrassed. Ken spots someone else on the field.

>   KEN (CONT'D)
> Oh. Here we go. It's tuba girl.

The freaks turn their attention to AMY ANDREWS, a cute tomboy. She plays her tuba very seriously. We can tell that Lindsay recognizes her.

>   KEN (CONT'D)
>   (yelling to Amy)
> Your tuba is so sexy. It gets me
> hot. Play me some Billy Joel.

The freaks laugh.

>   LINDSAY
> At least she knows how to play an
> instrument.

Everyone laughs at Lindsay's burn.

>   (CONTINUED)

CONTINUED: (2)

> KEN
> It's not an instrument. It's like
> playing a toilet.

> LINDSAY
> It sounds better than your singing.

> KEN
> Hey, Lindsay. Why don't you break
> up our band again so you can make
> out with Nick?

Daniel and Kim can't help but laugh. Lindsay's mortified.
Nick kicks Ken in the leg.

> NICK
> (angry)
> Shut up. Jerk.

Nick tugs Lindsay aside.

> NICK (CONT'D)
> I'm really, really sorry he said
> that. Really. He didn't mean it.

Lindsay smiles awkwardly. Nick looks happy to be sharing a
moment with her. Daniel notices this and shakes his head.

> CUT TO:

INT. WEIR DINING ROOM - DUSK

Neal is having dinner with the Weirs. There is the quiet
clinking of dinnerware. Lindsay looks bored.

> JEAN
> So Harold, Neal's father is
> performing emergency dental surgery
> tonight.

> HAROLD
> Good for him.

> NEAL
> Yeah. Last week, my dad told me
> about this lady who slipped on the
> ice and fell face-first and cracked
> her teeth on the sidewalk.
> (everyone winces)
> She was allergic to anesthetics so
> she had to be awake for the whole
> thing.
> (MORE)

> (CONTINUED)

CONTINUED:

> NEAL (CONT'D)
> A tooth was imbedded in the roof of
> her mouth and my dad had to suction
> out like a gallon of blood.

Harold drops his fork. All look like they're going to be
sick.

> HAROLD
> Well, what a charming story.

> NEAL
> So Lindsay, have you seen "Ordinary
> People"? Robert Redford's first
> foray behind the camera. Pretty
> impressive.

> LINDSAY
> No, I haven't seen it.

> NEAL
> Oh, well, you've got to. I cried.
> And...
> (hinting)
> I'm going to see it again.

> LINDSAY
> Cool. You and Sam will have a
> really good time.

Neal deflates.

> SAM
> I'm not going to see that. It's
> not funny.

After an awkward moment..

> JEAN
> Would you like some more meatballs,
> Neal?

> NEAL
> No, thank you. My dad says too much
> red meat can lead to heart disease.

Harold examines his meatball before he bites it. An awkward
beat passes. Then...

> SAM
> Dad. Can I have an Atari for my
> birthday?

(CONTINUED)

CONTINUED: (2)

> HAROLD
> An A-what-ee?

> SAM
> An Atari.

> HAROLD
> What the heck is that?

> JEAN
> That's one of those expensive video
> games, isn't it?

> SAM
> It's not that expensive.

> HAROLD
> Well, whatever it costs, it's a
> waste of money. And time. The
> welfare rolls are full of video
> game players.

> LINDSAY
> No, they're not.

> HAROLD
> Well, they're gonna be. Trust me.

Sam, mortified, exchanges a look with Lindsay. She rolls her
eyes.

> SAM
> But Dr. Schweiber told Neal he was
> gonna get him an Atari for his
> birthday.

Harold shoots a look at Neal. Neal doesn't want to be on the
spot.

> NEAL
> (nervously)
> Hey. I asked for it. That doesn't
> mean I'll get it.

Lindsay gets up.

> LINDSAY
> I'm outta here.

> HAROLD
> Whoa whoa. Wait a minute there.
> Where are you going?

(CONTINUED)

CONTINUED: (3)

> LINDSAY
> To the library. I have to do some
> research for my history paper on
> The Panama Canal.

> HAROLD
> Well, could you at least finish
> your dinner first?

> LINDSAY
> Okay.

Lindsay reaches down to her plate without sitting and stuffs
a huge meatball into her mouth. She looks like a chipmunk.
She smiles at Sam who smiles back and laughs.

> LINDSAY
> (mouth full)
> See ya.

> NEAL
> Bye, Linds.

Lindsay exits, ignoring Harold's disapproving look. Sam and
Neal both start to stuff meatballs in their mouths.

> HAROLD
> Don't even try it.

CUT TO:

INT. COFFEE SHOP - DUSK

Daniel, Nick, Ken and Kim are sitting in a booth, eating junk
food. Lindsay enters and joins them, out of breath.

> LINDSAY
> Hey, guys. Sorry I'm late.

> KEN
> Yeah, well, thanks to you, we had
> to cancel our dinner reservations.

All the freaks laugh, except Nick. Lindsay shoots Ken a
peeved look.

> NICK
> Can you ever not be sarcastic?

> KEN
> I'm sarcastic?

(CONTINUED)

CONTINUED:

Nick gives Lindsay a sympathetic look. Lindsay forces a
smile. Daniel rolls his eyes at this exchange.

                    DANIEL
          Andopolis. I got the joneses for
          some more chili fries. C'mon.

Daniel wolfs down his last fries and heads for the counter.
Nick follows after him. Ken sits with the girls for an
awkward beat.

                    KEN
          I think I'm gonna go pee.

Ken gets up and heads for the bathroom, leaving Kim and
Lindsay alone. Kim waits until he's out of earshot.

                    KIM
          So, Linds. What's the deal with you
          two? Do you still like Nick?

                    LINDSAY
          No. I'm just trying to be friends
          again.

                    KIM
          Forget it. You'll never be friends.
          I mean, maybe like in two years.
          And you can't really be friends
          again until he has another
          girlfriend. But then you'll just
          want him back and the whole thing
          will start over again.

                    LINDSAY
          I'm not gonna want him back.

                    KIM
             (knowingly)
          Yeah, okay. Sure.
             (beat)
          Look, just don't lead him on.
          'Cause he's obviously still in love
          with you.

                    LINDSAY
          No he's not. Nick broke up with <u>me</u>.
          Remember?

                    KIM
          Yeah, like that really fooled
          anybody.
             (MORE)

                                        (CONTINUED)

CONTINUED: (2)

        KIM (CONT'D)
Lindsay, you're being way too nice.
He's gonna get the wrong idea.

        LINDSAY
So I'm supposed to be mean?

        KIM
No, don't be mean. Just be a bitch.

        LINDSAY
I don't know...

        KIM
It's for his own good. He'd thank
you if he knew what you were doing.

Lindsay takes this in.

ANGLE ON: Daniel, Nick and Ken are standing at the counter,
waiting for their order.

        NICK
I can't help it, man. I'm just so
in love with her.

        DANIEL
Yeah, no kidding. You gotta stop
being so nice to her. That's how
you blew it the first time.

        NICK
You're the expert? Gimme a break.
You and Kim fight all the time.

        DANIEL
Not anymore. Check out my new
strategy. She can flap her lips all
she wants, but I ain't fighting
back. Sooner or later, she's gonna
run out of gas.

        KEN
    (sarcastic)
Brilliant plan. It took you two
years to figure that out?

        DANIEL
It's like the tortoise and the
hare. That little rabbit gets
tired, and guess who wins?

Nick and Ken exchange a confused look.

               (CONTINUED)

CONTINUED: (3)

> KEN
> Are we still talking about the same
> thing?

> DANIEL
> Never mind, pea brain. Listen,
> Nick. If you want to get Lindsay
> back, you gotta give her the cold
> shoulder.

> NICK
> That doesn't sound right.

> DANIEL
> Trust me. Don't call her, don't
> write her notes, and don't sing to
> her.
>   (emphatic)
> No more Styx songs. We barely want
> to be friends with you after
> hearing about that one.

> KEN
> Yeah, Nick. We need our space.

Daniel and Ken crack up.

                                                      CUT TO:

INT. WEIR HOUSE - NIGHT

Jean is talking to MRS. SCHWEIBER, who is dressed in a FANCY
TENNIS OUTFIT and looking very upscale.

> MRS. SCHWEIBER
> You cut your hair. It looks nice.

> JEAN
> Thanks.

> MRS. SCHWEIBER
> It's shorter.

> JEAN
>   (calls out)
> Neal! Your mom's here.
>   (to Mrs. Schweiber)
> So how was your tennis game,
> Lillian?

                                              (CONTINUED)

CONTINUED:

> MRS. SCHWEIBER
> Uh. Don't ask. My serve was in the
> crapper. I'm telling you, I'm
> getting too old for this. I swing
> that racket and everything jiggles.

> JEAN
> Well, maybe it will be better next
> time.

> MRS. SCHWEIBER
> I'd spend more time on the court,
> but I've got a full-time job.

> JEAN
> (surprised)
> Oh, really?

> MRS. SCHWEIBER
> Yeah, being Neal' s chauffeur. I
> swear, the only thing I'm missing
> is the little hat and a wet bar in
> the back of the Buick.

> JEAN
> (laughs)
> I know that feeling.

Sam and Neal come up.

> MRS. SCHWEIBER
> (to Neal)
> Hello, Baby Angel.

Mrs. Schweiber gives Neal a big kiss. Neal squirms away. Sam
laughs.

> SAM
> (to Neal)
> Baby Angel.

> JEAN
> Well, anyway. Sam and I need to get
> to the mall before they close,
> so...

> MRS. SCHWEIBER
> Then I won't keep you. And thanks
> again for letting Neal eat at your
> house.

(CONTINUED)

CONTINUED: (2)

>   JEAN
>   He's welcome anytime.

>   MRS. SCHWEIBER
>   Okay, well... ciao.

Neal and Sam exchange good-byes. The Schweibers exit.

>   SAM
>   How come you and dad don't play
>   tennis?

>   JEAN
>   Have you seen your father's legs?

Sam looks at her quizzically.

>   JEAN (CONT'D)
>   Never mind.

>   CUT TO:

INT. COFFEE SHOP - NIGHT

As the freaks begin to exit, they run into AMY ANDREWS, the
tuba player from marching band, in uniform.

>   LINDSAY
>   Hey Amy.

>   AMY
>   Hey, Lindsay.

Ken can't control the urge to make fun of her.

>   KEN
>   Nice threads.

To everyone's surprise, Amy turns to Ken, unfazed.

>   AMY
>   (imitating Ken)
>   Nice voice.

The freaks laugh. Especially Lindsay. Ken is taken aback, but
quickly recovers.

>   KEN
>   Where'd you leave your tuba? Geek
>   headquarters?

>   (CONTINUED)

CONTINUED:

> AMY
> Yeah. Your bedroom.

> DANIEL
> Nobody's been in his bedroom.
> Except his mom.

The freaks laugh again.

> KEN
> Hey, Sergeant Pepper. Where's the
> rest of the Lonely Hearts Club
> Band?

Amy reaches over and pats his belly.

> AMY
> Looks like you ate them.

> KIM
> Yeah, Ken. When are the twins due?

The freaks crack up. For once, Ken is stumped.

> AMY
> Lindsay.
> (points to Ken)
> Is this bonehead a friend of yours?

> LINDSAY
> No, he's just a pain in my ass.

Everyone laughs, except Ken. Amy turns to him.

> AMY
> See ya later, Elvis. Good luck with
> those mutton chops.

The freaks explode into laughter. Amy disappears into the
coffee shop. Ken watches her go, his hand unconsciously going
up to touch his sideburns.

MUSIC UP: CHICAGO'S "25 Or 6 To 4"

We STAY ON Ken's face. He's in love.

CUT TO:

INT. APPLIANCE STORE - NIGHT

Sam is slowly tagging along as Jean, carrying a bag full of
socks and underwear, longingly admires the new CERAMIC-TOP
STOVES.

Jean notices a display of MICROWAVE OVENS. A SALESMAN
approaches her.

                    SALESMAN
          I see you're admiring our new
          microwaves.

                    JEAN
          Oh... I'm just browsing, thank you.

                    SALESMAN
          Would you care to see a
          demonstration? It'll just take a
          minute - literally.

                    JEAN
          Oh, I don't know. My husband says
          anything cooked that fast can't be
          good for you.

                    SALESMAN
          He wouldn't say that if he was the
          one doing the cooking.

Jean laughs. The salesman whips out an enormous FROZEN STEAK.
He tries to stab it with a fork.

                    SALESMAN (CONT'D)
          Moo! Just kidding. See? Frozen
          solid. Now watch this.

The salesman puts the steak into the microwave and sets the
timer with a flourish.

                    SALESMAN (CONT'D)
          Think about how much free time
          you'll have to play tennis.

Sam's bored out of his mind.

                    SAM
          Mom. I'm going to go look at the
          Atari's, okay?

                    JEAN
          Okay.

                                        (CONTINUED)

CONTINUED:

Sam walks off towards the TV department. He's mesmerized by an ATARI DISPLAY. Then he thinks he sees Dr. Schweiber cross the aisle. He walks quickly and excitedly towards him.

> SAM
>
> Dr. Schweiber.

Sam turns the corner and enters the TV department. He sees Dr. Schweiber with his arm around an ATTRACTIVE BLONDE WOMAN in her late 20's. Confused, Sam stops frozen in his tracks.

The woman gives Dr. Schweiber a hug as a stock boy brings them a cardboard box containing a new TV.

Dr. Schweiber turns and sees Sam. He immediately untangles himself from the woman. He's momentarily stunned, but recovers quickly if not awkwardly.

> DR. SCHWEIBER
>
> Hey... Sam I Am. What are you doing
> here?

> SAM
>
> Uh... looking at microwaves with my
> mom.

Sam keeps staring at the woman. This kicks Dr. Schweiber into overdrive.

> DR. SCHWEIBER
> (as Captain Kirk)
>
> Well Scottie, I hope you're not
> planning to cook a tribble. I think
> they'd taste better on the
> barbeque.

They all share a nervous laugh. Dr. Schweiber looks around for a moment to see if Jean is in the area.

> DR. SCHWEIBER (CONT'D)
>
> Hey, where are my manners. Sam,
> this is an old high school friend
> of mine... from high school. Kind
> of like you and Neal are now. And
> Carol, this is a friend of my
> son's.

Carol takes Sam's hand and shakes it.

Her fake ivory-and-bamboo bracelets jingle loudly.

(CONTINUED)

CONTINUED: (2)

>   CAROL
>   Nice to meet you, Sam.

>   DR. SCHWEIBER
>   Carol and I just ran into each
>   other. Isn't that something?

>   SAM
>   Yeah. I guess.

Sam looks around for his mom, uncomfortable.

>   DR. SCHWEIBER
>   Sam. Can I talk to you in private
>   for a moment?

>   SAM
>   Uh, sure.

Dr. Schweiber leans down to Sam's level.

>   DR. SCHWEIBER
>   Please don't tell Neal you saw me
>   here. I'm buying him an Atari, but
>   it's a surprise. You can keep that
>   secret for good ole Dr. S. Right?

>   SAM
>   Uh... yeah.

>   DR. SCHWEIBER
>   Thanks, buddy.
>   (to Carol)
>   Well, Carol. It sure was good
>   seeing you again.

Dr. Schweiber shakes her hand, very formal. She's confused at
first, then catches on.

>   DR. SCHWEIBER
>   Maybe we can catch up on old times
>   another day. Hey, you know what?
>   You should have dinner with me and
>   my wife sometime.

>   CAROL
>   That sounds great.
>   (to Sam)
>   It was nice meeting you, Sam. Good
>   bye... Dr. Schweiber.

Carol struggles to lift up the cardboard box.

>   (CONTINUED)

CONTINUED: (3)

>   DR. SCHWEIBER
>   Uh, that TV looks pretty heavy. Can
>   I help you carry that to your car?

>   CAROL
>   Sure. Thank you so much.

Carol smiles as Dr. Schweiber lifts the box. She starts to
lead the way. Dr. Schweiber pauses, turns to Sam.

>   DR. SCHWEIBER
>   See you later, alligator. And
>   remember... shhh on that Atari.

Dr. Schweiber catches up to Carol and they exit together. Sam
watches, confused and unnerved as they disappear.

OFF Sam's confusion we...

>   FADE OUT.

                          END OF ACT ONE

                            ACT TWO

FADE IN:

INT. SCHOOL HALLWAY - DAY

It's lunchtime. Daniel, Nick and Ken enter the building and
head down the hall.

>   NICK
>   (excited)
>   Hey. They're doing Laser Floyd at
>   the Laser Dome tomorrow night.

>   KEN
>   I heard. It was in all the
>   newspapers.

>   NICK
>   What, you're too cool for a laser
>   show?

>   KEN
>   Why do I need a laser show when I
>   can make my own... in my mind.

>   NICK
>   C'mon. It's Floyd.
>   (British accent)
>   (MORE)

>   (CONTINUED)

CONTINUED:

                  NICK (CONT'D)
    "If you don't eat your meat, you
    can't have any pudding! "
        (beat)
    They're not gonna do Laser Floyd
    forever, you know.

                  DANIEL
    All right, Nick. Shut up. Please.
    We'll go, okay?

Nick smiles, psyched. Just then, Kim and Lindsay come out of
a classroom and join the guys. Nick's demeanor immediately
changes. He and Lindsay both try to seem aloof.

                  KIM
        (overhearing)
  Go where?

                  DANIEL
    Laser Dome.

                  KIM
        (flabbergasted)
    You're taking me to Laser Dome?

Daniel ignores her.

                  LINDSAY
    Isn't Laser Dome just a bunch of
    squiggly lights on a ceiling?

                  NICK
        (pissy)
    No. It's not just squiggly lights.
    What's wrong with you people? It's
    a metaphysical experience.

                  KIM
        (directed at Daniel)
    Yeah. Especially if you've got your
    hand up Wendy Franklin's shirt.

Again, Daniel doesn't respond. Nick and Ken exchange a look.
Flustered, Kim turns to Lindsay.

                  KIM (CONT'D)
        (to Lindsay)
    So, you want to go or not?

Lindsay clumsily avoids making eye contact with Nick.

                  LINDSAY
    I don't know. Maybe.

                        (CONTINUED)

CONTINUED: (2)

> NICK
> (overly casual)
> Yeah, well. We'll be there. So you
> know, if you go, maybe we'll run
> into you.

An awkward silence passes.

> KEN
> Is it just me, or did it suddenly
> get chilly in here?

Lindsay, feeling uncomfortable, starts to head toward the
cafeteria.

> LINDSAY
> I'm going to get something to eat.

> NICK
> (fast, loud)
> Yeah, whatever.
> (to everyone else)
> You guys want to go hit Stackey's?

The guys nod. Lindsay walks off, self-conscious and unhappy.
Kim shoots an annoyed look at Daniel, then follows after
Lindsay.

> KIM
> Linds, wait up.

The guys start to head off. Daniel smiles, watching Kim.

> DANIEL
> Did I tell you? Look at her run.
> Like a little rabbit. I am the
> tortoise.

Ken notices some BAND KIDS walking past. Amy is among them.
Ken's mesmerized by her.

> CUT TO:

INT. MCKINLEY HIGH SCHOOL CAFETERIA - DAY

Kim and Lindsay enter the cafeteria and head toward the food
line.

> LINDSAY
> Was I too mean?

(CONTINUED)

CONTINUED:

          KIM
No, that was perfect. I think Nick
got the message.

          LINDSAY
     (unsure)
Yeah. So who's Wendy Franklin?

          KIM
Long story. Let's just say she's a
cheap little slut Daniel made out
with when we were broken up.

          LINDSAY
But it's over with her, right?

          KIM
That's not the point. He did it
with her at the Laser Dome. And now
he wants to go there with me?

          LINDSAY
So, are you going?

          KIM
Yeah. What else am I going to do?

As they get in line they pass...SAM, NEAL AND BILL eating
lunch. Sam is unusually quiet, still wigged out by what he
saw last night.

          NEAL
So I wake up this morning and guess
what is sitting on the end of my
bed?

          BILL
A turd?

          NEAL
Yes. Exactly.

          BILL
Gross.

          NEAL
No. An Atari Video Set. Is my dad
the coolest or what?

Neal looks right at Sam. Sam somehow manages a smile.

          (CONTINUED)

CONTINUED: (2)

> NEAL (CONT'D)
> So, shall we say Asteroids, my
> place, three-thirty?

> BILL
> Yeah, if that's when you want to
> get your butt kicked.

Neal and Bill both turn to Sam.

> SAM
> (after a beat)
> Yeah. Three-thirty's... great.

> NEAL
> And now if you gentlemen excuse me,
> I'm off to get another delicious
> serving of Ben Franklin beans.

Neal gets up and leaves.

> BILL
> Remind me not to sit next to him on
> the bus.

Sam looks like he's going to barf from the pressure of his
secret.

> BILL (CONT'D)
> What's with you?

Sam looks to make sure Neal is gone. Then he pauses, not sure
if he can trust Bill's big mouth.

> SAM
> I'm gonna tell you a secret. But
> you can't tell anyone. Swear?

> BILL
> Okay.

> SAM
> No, really, Bill.

> BILL
> I said okay.

> SAM
> (leans in)
> Last night... I saw Dr. Schweiber
> at the mall. He told me he was
> buying Neal the Atari.

(CONTINUED)

CONTINUED: (3)

> BILL
> So?

> SAM
> He was with a woman.

> BILL
> Really? What did she look like?

> SAM
> I don't know... She was skinny,
> with blonde hair... Dr. Schweiber
> said she was an old friend from
> high school. But it looked weird.
> He was hugging her.

> BILL
> Hugging? Like how?

> SAM
> I don't know.

> BILL
> Well, there's a lot of different
> hugs. Was he slapping her on the
> back while he did it, like guys do?

> SAM
> I don't know, Bill. It was a hug.

> BILL
> Well, show me. Do it to me.

> SAM
> No. I'm not gonna hug you.

> BILL
> Why? I'm comfortable in my
> manliness. It's okay to hug your
> friends, Sam.

Sam looks around to make sure no one's watching, then
reluctantly leans over and hugs Bill. After a beat, Bill
looks uncomfortable and pushes Sam off.

> BILL
> Okay, I get it. Get off me.
>   (beat)
> So, have you told Neal?

> SAM
> No. And I'm not going to.

(CONTINUED)

CONTINUED: (4)

                    BILL
          You have to.

                    SAM
          But he'll freak out.

                    BILL
          I know, but there are no secrets
          between us. That's our code.

                    SAM
          That's easy for you to say. You
          don't have any secrets.

                    BILL
          I do, too. What about the time in
          Science when I tried to sneak out a
          fart but it came out a poop and I
          had to flush my undies down the
          toilet? You think I enjoyed telling
          you that? No, but I did. 'Cause we
          tell each other everything.

                    SAM
          It's not the same thing.

                    BILL
          Yes, it is. It's exactly the same
          thing.

                    SAM
          We can't tell him.

                                        CUT TO:

INT. SCHOOL HALLWAY - DAY

It's after school. The halls are empty. We FIND Ken staring
through the closed door of a classroom.

KEN'S POV: Inside the classroom, Amy and a few other band
kids practice their instruments.

Ken gazes at Amy, smitten. Suddenly, Daniel comes up to him.

                    DANIEL
          Hey. Whatcha doing?

                    KEN
               (quickly)
          Nothing.

                                        (CONTINUED)

CONTINUED:

Ken spins around, blocking the door. But Daniel pushes him aside and peers into the classroom, curious.

> DANIEL
> Who're you looking at?

> KEN
> I was just, uh, making fun of the band geeks.

> DANIEL
> To yourself?

Ken's caught. Daniel looks back into the classroom.

DANIEL'S POV: Amy is jamming out on her tuba, playing "WHEN THE SAINTS COME MARCHING IN" as the other band kids clap and stomp their feet to the beat.

Daniel turns away from the door and faces Ken.

> DANIEL
> Is that who you're looking at?
> Tuba girl?

Ken's face starts to turn red. Daniel cracks up.

> DANIEL (CONT'D)
> Oh, man. You like tuba girl?

> KEN
> Shut up. Just forget it.

Ken quickly walks off down the hall. Daniel follows him.

> DANIEL
> (trying to be serious)
> Nah. I'm just, you know, happy for
> you. We've been waiting since the
> third grade for you to like
> somebody.

Ken studies Daniel for a beat, realizes he's sincere.

> KEN
> You think she has a boyfriend?

> DANIEL
> No way. She's a tuba player.

> KEN
> Hey, screw you.

(CONTINUED)

CONTINUED: (2)

                    DANIEL
          I'm just joking, man. Relax. She's
          cute. Look, Lindsay's friends with
          her. You want me to talk to
          Lindsay?

                    KEN
          Yes. That is what I want you to do.

                    DANIEL
          Okay.

Daniel's amused at Ken's seriousness.

                    KEN
          Hey. Um... thanks.

                    DANIEL
          No problem.

                    KEN
          Tell anybody about this and you're
          dead.

Daniel smiles and exits. Ken returns to watching Amy.

                                        CUT TO:

INT. SCHWEIBER LIVING ROOM - AFTERNOON

TIGHT on a TV showing the video portion of the game
ASTEROIDS.

Sam, Neal and Bill are sitting in front of the TV. SAM'S
taking his turn at the controller.

                    BILL
          You should hit hyperspace.
          Hyperspace. Hyperspace.

                    SAM
          Bill! Shut up. I'm doing it.

Sam hits the hyper-space button. His ship is destroyed.

                    BILL
          Oh. Maybe you shouldn't have hit
          hyperspace.

                    NEAL
              (excited)
          My turn.

                                    (CONTINUED)

CONTINUED:

>   SAM
> I have to go to the bathroom.

Sam heads off to the bathroom. Bill watches him go.

>   NEAL
> Don't forget to lift the seat or my
> mom will kill you.

Neal picks up the controller and resets the game.

>   BILL
>   (this is his chance)
> So, remember when we said we'd
> always tell each other everything?

>   NEAL
> Yeah.

>   BILL
> Did you mean it?

>   NEAL
> Of course.

>   BILL
> Even if it's something really,
> really horrible? I mean, it might
> not be horrible, 'cause it might
> not be true. But if it is true, it
> could be pretty horrible.

This only makes Neal more curious.

He puts down the Atari controller and turns to Bill.

>   NEAL
> Bill. You're killing me here. Now
> you gotta tell me.

Sam comes out of the bathroom.

>   BILL
> Okay, but you might not want to
> know this.

>   SAM
>   (alarmed)
> Bill. You didn't tell him, did you?

(CONTINUED)

CONTINUED: (2)

> NEAL
> Wait. You told Sam and you didn't
> tell me? This isn't fair. If both
> of you guys know, then I get to
> know.

Sam stares at Bill. Bill stares back, torn. Then he finally
turns to Neal.

> BILL
> Sam saw your dad hugging a woman at
> the mall last night.

> NEAL
> What?

> BILL
> (pushing Sam toward Neal)
> Sam, show him.

> NEAL
> That's impossible. My dad was at
> the office performing an emergency
> root canal. So that wasn't my dad.

> SAM
> (quietly)
> It was your dad. I talked to him,
> Neal.

> NEAL
> (pissed)
> You're lying. You're just jealous
> that my dad is cooler than your
> dad.

> SAM
> (stung)
> I'm not jealous.

> BILL
> Neal... we just thought you should
> know. 'Cause we tell each other
> everything.

> NEAL
> (to Bill)
> Oh, shut up. You don't even have a
> dad.

(CONTINUED)

CONTINUED: (3)

> BILL
> Yes, I do. I talked to him three
> months ago.

Bill looks really hurt. The boys go silent, unsure of what
the next move should be. Just then, Dr. Schweiber enters.

> DR. SCHWEIBER
> Hey, boys.

No one responds. Dr. Schweiber senses the tension.

> DR. SCHWEIBER (CONT'D)
> So how's the game? How about
> letting me fly one of those rocket
> ships?

Sam nervously picks up his jacket and starts to exit.

> SAM
> I gotta go home.

> BILL
> Me, too.

Sam and Bill go to the door.

> CUT TO:

EXT. SCHWEIBER HOUSE/DRIVEWAY - LATE AFTERNOON

Sam and Bill exit the Schweiber house and walk by Dr.
Schweiber's BRIGHT RED SPORTS CAR with license plates reading
"I FLOSS EM. "

Dr. Schweiber follows them out.

> DR. SCHWEIBER
> Sam, Bill... You guys want to go
> out for some ice cream?

> SAM
> (weakly)
> No thanks.

Sam and Bill climb on their bikes and head off.

Just then, Mrs. Schweiber pulls up in the driveway with the
radio blaring. She honks the horn. Dr. Schweiber waves to
her, preoccupied.

> (CONTINUED)

CONTINUED:

In the background, Neal looks at his father a little closer than he ever has. Dr. Schweiber turns and looks at Neal. Neal quickly disappears into the house.

Mrs. Schweiber approaches.

> MRS. SCHWEIBER
> Chinese or pizza? I'm famished.

> DR. SCHWEIBER
> Yeah... sure. You pick.

CUT TO:

INT. CLASSROOM - LATE AFTERNOON

Kim and Daniel are sitting in detention. The crying kid from Episode #105, WALTER, is between them. An apathetic TEACHER sits at the front of the classroom, reading a newspaper.

Kim and Daniel are talking to Walter, but it's obviously for each other's benefit.

> KIM
> If you had a boyfriend who humped a slut like Wendy Franklin in a certain place - like a Laser Dome - would you want to hang out there?

Walter doesn't respond. He just looks back and forth nervously.

> DANIEL
> She's got a good point.

> KIM
> I mean, wouldn't you be wigged out by the idea that your boyfriend did <u>things</u> with this slut in the very same seat you might be sitting in?

Walter raises his hand.

> WALTER
> Um, can I go to the bathroom?

The teacher nods. Walter quickly gets up and exits.

Daniel turns to Kim.

> DANIEL
> Look, I regret it.

(CONTINUED)

CONTINUED:

> KIM
> You're so full of crap.

> DANIEL
> What if I'm not?

> KIM
> Well, are you?

> DANIEL
> I don't think so.

Kim stares at Daniel, confused and frustrated. He smiles calmly.

CUT TO:

INT. WEIR KITCHEN - EVENING

Sam enters the house just as Jean is hanging up the phone in the kitchen. He starts to head for his bedroom.

> JEAN (O.S.)
> Sam. Is that you?

> SAM
> Yes.

Jean comes out of the kitchen as Sam heads down the hallway.

> JEAN
> Hey. Hold it right there, Buster.

Sam stops and turns to face his mom.

> JEAN
> Now you know I don't mind if you
> don't come home right away after
> school, but you need to call and
> let me know where you are. I was
> starting to get worried.

> SAM
> Sorry. I was at Neal's playing
> Atari and we lost track of time.

> JEAN
> They got him that TV game? I
> thought they were waiting for his
> birthday.

(CONTINUED)

CONTINUED:

Sam shrugs his shoulders. Jean feels a twinge of parental guilt.

>   JEAN (CONT'D)
>   They certainly spoil that boy, I'll
>   tell you that.

Sam just wants to be alone.

>   SAM
>   I have to do some homework.

>   JEAN
>   Okay. Dinner will be ready in about
>   an hour.

Sam heads to his room. Jean walks to the kitchen, then stops and calls to Sam.

>   JEAN (CONT'D)
>   Oh, and you have to get to bed
>   early tonight. You have a dental
>   appointment at seven tomorrow
>   morning.
>   SAM
>   What?

>   JEAN
>   Dr. Schweiber just called. He said
>   he could fit you in early for your
>   six-month checkup.

Sam's reacts to this like a punch in the gut.

>   SAM
>   Do I have to go?

>   JEAN
>   Yes. You don't get a vote on this.

>   SAM
>   But... can't I do it next week?

>   JEAN
>   No. It was very nice of Dr.
>   Schweiber to fit us in. I think you
>   should show him a little respect.

                                              (CONTINUED)

CONTINUED: (2)

Jean turns and heads for the kitchen. Sam trudges toward his room, his face full of dread.

                                                      CUT TO:

INT. SCHWEIBER DINING ROOM - NIGHT

Neal enters quietly. He looks around, then spots his dad's SUIT JACKET hanging on the back of a chair. He quickly looks through the pockets and pulls out a set of keys, some loose change and his dad's WALLET.

Neal searches the wallet for incriminating evidence. He doesn't find anything. He puts the wallet back, thinking.

                                                      CUT TO:

INT. SCHWEIBER GARAGE - NIGHT

Neal, breathing heavily, slides into his dad's car. He quickly opens the glove compartment. Nothing unusual. Then he checks under the seats and finds a GARAGE DOOR CLICKER.

Confused, Neal pulls down the driver's side sun-visor. Their own garage door clicker is clipped to it. He compares the two clickers -- THEY LOOK VERY DIFFERENT.

Neal points the mystery clicker at the garage door of his house, and presses the button. Nothing happens.

Neal holds the mystery clicker in his hand, his mind racing.

                                                      CUT TO:

INT. SAM'S BEDROOM - NIGHT

Sam's sitting on his bed, doing homework. He's having a hard time concentrating. Lindsay enters.

                    LINDSAY
          Sam. Did you take my Pink Floyd
          album?

                    SAM
          No.

Lindsay notices that Sam looks upset.

                    LINDSAY
          What's the matter?

                                                 (CONTINUED)

CONTINUED:

>   SAM
>   (after a beat)
>   Why do people have affairs?

>   LINDSAY
>   I don't know. I guess they meet
>   somebody else that they like
>   better.

>   SAM
>   Do you think Dr. Schweiber would
>   have an affair?

>   LINDSAY
>   I never thought about it.

>   SAM
>   Do you think <u>Dad</u> would ever have an
>   affair?

>   LINDSAY
>   (incredulous)
>   Dad?!

Just then, Harold is walking in the hallway. He enters Sam's
room, wearing BOXERS and BLACK SOCKS.

>   HAROLD
>   Did somebody call me?

Lindsay and Sam stare at their father, then look at each
other and burst out LAUGHING.

>   CUT TO:

INT. DR. SCHWEIBER'S OFFICE - MORNING

A DENTAL HYGIENIST leads a nervous Sam into Dr. Schweiber's
office. We hear the ominous BUZZING of the dental chair being
lowered. The hygienist spins the chair toward Sam.

>   HYGIENIST
>   Have a seat.

Sam reluctantly slides into the chair, staring at the scary-
looking dental equipment in front of his face. MUZAK plays in
the background.

>   HYGIENIST (CONT'D)
>   Dr. Schweiber will be with you in a
>   minute.

>   (CONTINUED)

CONTINUED:

The hygienist exits. Sam leans back in the chair, his heart pounding with anticipation and fear.

                                              FADE OUT.

                       END OF ACT TWO

                         ACT THREE

FADE IN:

INT. DR. SCHWEIBER'S OFFICE - MORNING

Sam sits in the dental chair, looking nervous. Finally, Dr. Schweiber enters. He shuts the door. He takes the X-rays out of a folder on the wall.

                    DR. SCHWEIBER
                 (curt)
          Hello, Sam.

                       SAM
                 (softly)
          Hi.

Dr. Schweiber goes over to the counter and takes a few tools out of the drawer. He then sits next to Sam, places the tools on the cart and examines the X-rays in silence for a beat. He puts the X-rays down and picks up a scraping tool.

                    DR. SCHWEIBER
          Open up.

Sam opens his mouth.

                    DR. SCHWEIBER (CONT'D)
          A little wider.

Dr. Schweiber takes a dental scraper and starts to slowly scrape at some plaque on Sam's teeth without saying a word. Dr. Schweiber turns his head for a moment to cough. Then starts to hum.

Dr. Schweiber presses the button that returns Sam's chair to the upright position. Sam looks terrified.

Dr. Schweiber continues scraping and flossing Sam.

                    DR. SCHWEIBER (CONT'D)
          Sam, my friend. I think we may need
          to talk.

                                         (CONTINUED)

CONTINUED:

> SAM
> (hesitating)
> What about?

> DR. SCHWEIBER
> Well, for starters, you were acting
> a little different around me
> yesterday. And I have to say I'm a
> little hurt by it. I thought we
> were buddies.

> SAM
> Oh... uh... I just didn't feel
> well.

> DR. SCHWEIBER
> You know what I think? I think you
> may have thought you saw something
> the other night that you really
> didn't see.

> SAM
> Uh... I didn't see anything.

> DR. SCHWEIBER
> (immediately)
> Spit.

Sam leans up to rinse and spit.

> DR. SCHWEIBER (CONT'D)
> You didn't mention anything to Neal
> or anyone else about meeting my
> friend, did you?

Sam is too afraid to tell the truth.

> SAM
> No.

Dr. Schweiber places CHEEK EXTRACTORS in Sam's mouth to make
it easier to get at his back teeth.

> DR. SCHWEIBER
> Good. Because I just wanted to make
> sure there wasn't a mix-up. People
> like nothing more than to gossip if
> they think someone is spending time
> with another woman who isn't their
> wife.

(CONTINUED)

CONTINUED: (2)

Sam sits there in stunned silence. Dr. Schweiber thinks, then sighs, deeply perturbed.

> DR. SCHWEIBER (CONT'D)
> But you should rest assured, Sam, that nothing happened between me and my friend. I'm not saying I wasn't tempted, because I was. You believe me, don't you?

Sam struggles emotionally. He can barely talk with the cheek extractors in his mouth.

> SAM
> I believe you.

Dr. Schweiber is scraping a particularly difficult piece of plaque.

> DR. SCHWEIBER
> Good. You see, Sam, I didn't have many dates when I was younger. Mrs. Schweiber and I met way back in college, and...well, she's a lovely woman who keeps a wonderful house, but as you get older you get bored. Do you understand?

> SAM
> (still struggling)
> Not really.

Dr. Schweiber pauses, takes a shaky breath, then begins to weep. Sam is paralyzed by this inappropriate display.

> DR. SCHWEIBER
> It's just so hard Sam. I feel like I've been missing something in my life, you know? And I think I deserve a chance to see what that something is. Don't you?

> SAM
> I don't know.

Dr. Schweiber tries to compose himself.

> DR. SCHWEIBER
> I promise you, things'll get back to normal. I just need a little time.
> (MORE)

(CONTINUED)

CONTINUED: (3)
                        DR. SCHWEIBER (CONT'D)
                And we'll keep this just between
                you and me, right? Can I count on
                you?

Dr. Schweiber places his hand on Sam's shoulder. Sam flinches
from the contact, scared and confused.

                        SAM
                Uh... sure.

OFF Sam, completely freaked out...

                                                    CUT TO:

INT. MCKINLEY HIGH SCHOOL HALLWAY - MORNING

Lindsay is walking toward her locker. She sees Nick and
Daniel approaching. She starts to smile, then remembers to be
a bitch and puts on an apathetic expression.

                        DANIEL
                Hey, Linds.

                        LINDSAY
                Hey, Daniel.

Nick ignores Lindsay's presence.

                        NICK
                    (to Daniel)
                So anyway, tell that scalper I'm
                gonna need four tickets to Yes.
                See you later, Daniel.

Nick walks away. Daniel hangs back.

                        DANIEL
                Yeah, so... Ken likes your friend
                Amy. Can you hook him up?

                        LINDSAY
                Wait. What?

                        DANIEL
                Ken wants to go out with Amy.

Lindsay takes this in, shocked.

                        LINDSAY
                You're kidding, right? He thinks
                she's a geek. He was ragging on her
                the other night.

                                                (CONTINUED)

CONTINUED:

> DANIEL
> That's what Ken does. So can you
> talk to her?

> LINDSAY
> We're not really friends anymore.

> DANIEL
> How come?

> LINDSAY
> (shrugs)
> I don't know. She just got really
> into band.

> DANIEL
> (sarcastic)
> Yeah, she's really good. Look, why
> don't you just ask her to go out
> with us tonight.

> LINDSAY
> I'm not setting her up with Ken.
> He's always on my case. I'm tired
> of him slamming me with that stupid
> voice of his.

Just then, Ken walks up. He pauses for a moment, then
realizes the deal is going down and walks away. Lindsay
flinches, mortified.

> LINDSAY
> Do you think he heard me?

> DANIEL
> Ken's a sweet guy. He's just got a
> sick sense of humor. The meaner he
> is to you, the more he likes you.

> LINDSAY
> Then he must love me.

> DANIEL
> Would you just ask Amy? Please?

> LINDSAY
> Fine. I'll ask. She'll just say no
> anyway.

> DANIEL
> Thank you.

(CONTINUED)

CONTINUED: (2)

Lindsay walks off.

CUT TO:

INT. CLASSROOM - MORNING

Sam and Bill enter. They both look completely shaken up.
They pause at the doorway as they see Neal sitting at a desk
near the back.

                    SAM
          Have you talked to him yet?

                    BILL
          No. He wasn't on the bus this
          morning.

                    SAM
          I feel really bad, you know?

                    BILL
          Yeah, me too. I knew we shouldn't
          have told him.

Sam shoots Bill a look. They slowly approach Neal.

                    SAM
          Hey.

                    NEAL
          Hey.

An awkward beat.

                    BILL
          So... are... are we... are you
          still mad at us?

                    NEAL
          No. Actually, I'm glad you guys
          told me.

                    SAM
          Neal. I was wrong about your dad.
          He cleaned my teeth this morning.
          I'm sure nothing happened.

                    NEAL
              (full of doubt)
          Well, I don't know. After what you
          guys said, I went through a bunch
          of his things and found this.

                                        (CONTINUED)

CONTINUED:

Neal pulls the GARAGE DOOR CLICKER out of his pocket and shows it to them.

>   BILL
>   So what?

>   NEAL
>   This clicker isn't for our garage.
>   I tested it. Why would he have it?
>   Maybe it belongs to that woman.

>   SAM
>   It could just belong to a friend of
>   his who left it there.

>   NEAL
>   Yeah, a female friend.

>   BILL
>   I saw a Donahue once about husbands
>   who cheat. They couldn't do it in
>   the house, right? So they all had
>   secret love nests. Maybe your dad
>   has a secret love nest.

>   NEAL
>   There's only one way to find out.

>   CUT TO:

EXT. UNDER BLEACHERS - DAY

Ken is peering through the bleachers, watching the band practice their marching. And more specifically, watching Amy. Lindsay approaches.

>   LINDSAY
>   Hey, Ken.

>   KEN
>   (caught off-guard)
>   Oh. Lindsay. Hey.

>   LINDSAY
>   So I talked to Daniel...

>   KEN
>   And he told you I wanted to nail
>   Amy and you're here to tell me
>   it'll never happen. Thanks for
>   dropping by.

>   (CONTINUED)

CONTINUED:

Lindsay stands in stunned silence for a beat.

> LINDSAY
> No. He didn't say you wanted to
> "nail" her. He told me you liked
> her. He wanted me to ask her to
> come to the Laser Dome with us
> tonight.

> KEN
> Oh.

> LINDSAY
> So you want me to do it? 'Cause I
> want to make sure you want me to do
> it before I do it.

> KEN
> (sincere, appreciative)
> I want you to do it.

> LINDSAY
> Are you gonna be nice to her?
> 'Cause I'm not gonna do it if
> you're gonna be a jerk.

> KEN
> Of course I'll be nice to her.
> I'll be an angel.

> LINDSAY
> Forget it.

> KEN
> Lindsay, I'm serious.

Lindsay studies him. She can tell he's sincere.

> LINDSAY
> Okay.

> KEN
> (vulnerable)
> So... do you think there's any
> chance this is really gonna happen?

> LINDSAY
> Oh my God.

> KEN
> What?

(CONTINUED)

CONTINUED: (2)

> LINDSAY
> You really like her, don't you?

> KEN
> (after a beat)
> I feel odd.

CUT TO:

EXT. FOOTBALL FIELD - DAY

Lindsay sits on the bleachers, as the band finishes practice and the band kids start to exit. As Amy passes by...

> LINDSAY
> (calls out)
> Amy!

Amy turns to see Lindsay. She heads over, surprised.

> AMY
> Hey, Lindsay. What're you doing
> here?

> LINDSAY
> Just wanted to say hi.

Amy nods, not sure what to make of this. Lindsay motions toward the field.

> LINDSAY (CONT'D)
> That was great. Makes me wish I
> played an instrument.

> AMY
> You should join band.

> LINDSAY
> I've been sort of taking a break
> from activities. I quit the
> Mathletes. Twice.

> AMY
> Yeah, Millie told me.

Lindsay can't help but smile.

> LINDSAY
> So, anyway. I know this is kinda
> out of the blue, but... there's
> this guy I know. Ken. He's got a
> crush on you.

(CONTINUED)

CONTINUED:

> AMY
> Do I know him?

> LINDSAY
> You kinda met him the other night.

> AMY
> Was it the guy who made fun of me?

Lindsay braces herself, dreading the idea of selling Ken.

> LINDSAY
> (quickly)
> Yeah. He's a total wise-ass, but
> that's his way of showing he likes
> you. He's just got a weird sense of
> humor, I don't know... so if
> you're not doing anything tonight,
> we're all going to the Laser
> Dome...

> AMY
> Laser Dome sucks.

> LINDSAY
> (defeated)
> That's what I thought you'd say. I
> totally understand.

> AMY
> But I'll go.

> LINDSAY
> Really?

> AMY
> Yeah, why not? Ken's cute, don't
> you think?

Lindsay tries to hide her shock.

> LINDSAY
> (forced)
> Uh-huh.

> AMY
> I love those funky sideburns. Don't
> you just want to reach out and
> touch them?

> LINDSAY
> Uh... do I?

(CONTINUED)

CONTINUED: (2)

Lindsay's in pain. She doesn't want to think about touching any part of Ken.

                                        CUT TO:

EXT. NEIGHBORHOOD STREET - AFTERNOON

Sam, Neal and Bill are slowly riding their bikes up a steep road. Bill is lagging a little behind.

                    SAM
                (to Neal)
            I told my mom that I was eating
            over at your house. And Bill told
            his mom he was eating at my house.
            So that should buy us some time.

                    NEAL
            Good. I told my mom I was eating at
            Bill's house. Technically, it's
            all true. We just don't say what
            day we're eating over. My brother
            used to do it all the time.

                    BILL
            Yeah, but when do we really eat?
            I'm hungry.

Sam and Neal ignore Bill.

                    SAM
            Do you really think we're going to
            find this house?

                    BILL
            If we do, I hope she has something
            to eat. I'm starving.

                    NEAL
                (ignoring Bill)
            We'll never know if we don't try.

                    SAM
            But what are you gonna do if we
            find her?

                    NEAL
                (cocky)
            I'm gonna say... "Hey lady, you
            want to mess with the Schweiber
            family? Is that what you want?
            Okay!" BOOM!

                                        (CONTINUED)

CONTINUED:

Neal pantomimes HEAD-BUTTING. Then he looks down at the
ground and says:

> NEAL (CONT'D)
> "You happy now? You glad you messed
> with my dad?"

Sam and Bill laugh.

As the boys ride past the first house, Neal takes out the
clicker, points it at the garage door, and presses the
button. Sam and Bill watch nervously.

FADE OUT.

END OF ACT THREE

ACT FOUR

FADE IN:

EXT. NEIGHBORHOOD STREET - DUSK

MUSIC UP: "TAKE THE LONG WAY HOME" BY SUPERTRAMP

We see a MONTAGE of Neal pressing the clicker (2) garage
doors that don't open (3) the boys looking tired (4) Neal's
face, full of nervous anticipation.

Sam, Neal and Bill ride into a cul-de-sac. They climb off
their bikes. Neal begins to click at each garage door.

> NEAL
> I'll tell you one thing. When I
> get married, I'm never gonna cheat.
> Even if my wife gets old and fat.

> BILL
> Yeah. I'd be happy just to get a
> wife. But I don't think I want the
> kind that's going to get old and
> fat.

> NEAL
> I think they all get old and fat.
> You hardly ever see skinny
> grandmas.

> SAM
> I don't even know how you get one
> girl. How does anyone get two?

(CONTINUED)

CONTINUED:

> BILL
> You know what would be cool? To
> find a girl in a bottle like "I
> Dream of Jeannie." I'd like to make
> out with her on that little couch.

> SAM
> You know, Cindy would look really
> good in those puffy pants.

> BILL
> If I was Major Nelson, I would let
> Jeannie do magic all day long. I
> mean, why would you stop her? I'd
> be like, "Jeannie, I want a
> Corvette and a pastrami sandwich."

Bill folds his arms, blinks his eyes and nods his head a la
Jeannie.

> NEAL
> You think your dad has ever cheated
> on your mom?

> SAM
> I don't think so. He's too old to
> want to make out with anybody.

> NEAL
> (a beat)
> You know, I'm starting to wish my
> dad was as old as yours.

Neal aims the clicker at a house and presses the button. To
his surprise, the GARAGE DOOR begins to OPEN. The geeks all
stare at the door, frozen in shock.

Then a HONK startles them. They turn to see a STATION WAGON
pulling up behind them. The boys quickly scramble out of the
way. The station wagon pulls into the garage.

Neal exhales, relieved.

> NEAL (CONT'D)
> Oh, man. I almost had a heart
> attack.

Bill clutches his chest, a la Fred Sanford.

(CONTINUED)

CONTINUED: (2)

>   BILL
>   (imitating Fred Sanford)
>   "It's the big one! Elizabeth, I'm
>   coming to join you!"

The geeks laugh, then walk in silence for a moment.

>   SAM
>   Should we go home? This isn't
>   working.

>   NEAL
>   We just started.

>   BILL
>   (mumbles)
>   Yeah, three hours ago.

Neal ignores him and keeps walking. Sam and Bill exchange a look, then follow after him.

>   CUT TO:

INT. LASER DOME - NIGHT

The audience is waiting for the show to begin. The seats are arranged in a circle around a projector. The domed ceiling, now in "planetarium mode," displays a projection of the galaxy. It looks like a starry night sky.

In the background, we hear cheesy ROCKIN' SPACE MUSIC (like the theme on the Space Mountain ride at Disneyland).

Lindsay, Nick, Daniel, Kim, Ken, and Amy are seated together.

Ken and Amy are sitting next to each other. There's the usual first date awkwardness. Ken's incredibly nervous. He sits in his chair, stiff as a board.

Amy nervously steals glances at Ken while looking up at the "stars." Finally...

>   AMY
>   (sarcastic)
>   Boy, this is exciting. I could've
>   seen this outside for free.

Ken hesitates, not sure how to respond. Is he supposed to be a wise-ass on a date? After a cautious beat...

>   (CONTINUED)

CONTINUED:

>   KEN
>   You <u>are</u> seeing it for free. I paid
>   for your ticket.

>   AMY
>   Thank you so much. How are you ever
>   gonna live without those two
>   dollars?

They both laugh. The ice is broken.

>   KEN
>   Can I get you a pop?

>   AMY
>   No thanks.

>   KEN
>   How about a lemonade?

>   AMY
>   No, that's okay.

>   KEN
>   Chocolate shake?

>   AMY
>   I'm really not thirsty.

>   KEN
>   Oh, okay.
>   (beat)
>   Are you hungry?

Amy smiles at Ken's effort. She thinks he's sweet.

>   AMY
>   I could go for a hot dog. You want
>   one? It's on me.

>   KEN
>   Uh, sure.

Amy gets up. She points to the ceiling, shaking her head at
the "space music."

>   AMY
>   This song really rocks.

>   KEN
>   Maybe next time you could bring
>   your tuba and jam.

(CONTINUED)

CONTINUED: (2)

Ken watches, in awe, as Amy heads off. He can't believe how cool she is. We PAN OVER to...

DANIEL AND KIM

Kim seems mellow. She looks up at the ceiling.

> KIM
> Man. I haven't been here since my
> fifth grade field trip.

> DANIEL
> You must've been cute in fifth
> grade. With your little blonde
> pigtails...

Daniel smiles. Kim rubs her neck, pained.

> KIM
> Ow. I've already got a crick in my
> neck.

> DANIEL
> Here. Lean your head back.

Daniel gently helps Kim put her head on the headrest.

> DANIEL (CONT'D)
> Better?

Kim nods. All is calm until...

> KIM
> (quietly)
> Did you lean your head back with
> that slut?

Daniel forces himself to stay cool. He looks up at the ceiling.

> DANIEL
> Hey, isn't that the Big Dipper?

This gets Kim even more worked up.

> KIM
> What is with you? You're acting so
> weird!

> DANIEL
> (innocently)
> I am?

(CONTINUED)

CONTINUED: (3)

> KIM
> Uhh! You're driving me crazy!

Kim gets up and storms off. Daniel laughs to himself. He looks over at...

NICK AND LINDSAY

who are sitting with an empty seat between them. They're completely ignoring one another. Neither is enjoying it.

Daniel leans forward and whispers in Nick's ear.

> DANIEL
> No touching. No talking. <u>No</u>
> <u>singing</u>.

Nick nods. Just then, the LIGHTS GO DOWN and the audience starts to APPLAUD. Nick raises his fists and yells out:

> NICK
> Floyd Rules, "Comfortably Numb!"

MUSIC UP: CHARLIE DANIELS BAND'S "THE DEVIL WENT DOWN TO GEORGIA"

Nick looks around, confused. The audience starts clapping and stomping to the music.

> NICK (CONT'D)
> What the hell? What happened to
> Floyd?

A guy in a COWBOY hat turns around.

> COWBOY
> That's next week, man. Tonight's
> Southern Rock Night. Woooo!!!

Nick slumps down in his seat, stunned. He can't believe it. His night is ruined. Lindsay looks up at the ceiling.

ANGLE ON: The laser show features a line drawing of a "cactus man" wearing a cowboy hat and playing a guitar. We also see horses, cowboy boots, lassoes, banjos, etc., to go with the "southern motif."

ANGLE ON: Daniel and Ken as each of them reacts to the music, surprised and annoyed.

(CONTINUED)

CONTINUED: (4)

> DANIEL
> Hey, Nick. You were right. Laser
> Floyd rocks.

Nick is too upset to talk back. Lindsay glances at him,
wondering if he's going to flip out. Finally, Nick looks over
at her. And after a beat, they both CRACK UP.

ANGLE ON: DANIEL AND KEN

Ken is waiting for Amy to return. He's in a good mood,
tapping his foot to the music. Daniel leans over to him.

> DANIEL (CONT'D)
> How's it going with Amy?

> KEN
> Good.

> DANIEL
> You kiss her yet?

Ken tries to hide his embarrassment.

> KEN
> Lay off, man.

> DANIEL
> If you're waiting for her to jump
> your bones, you might as well
> forget it.

> KEN
>   (defensive)
> I'm not.
>   (beat)
> Why?

> DANIEL
> She's a band chick. You're gonna
> have to make the first move.

Ken considers this, getting worried.

> KEN
> So, um... Do I just... I don't
> know... Should I just say,
>   (deep voice)
> "Can I kiss you?"

(CONTINUED)

CONTINUED: (5)

> DANIEL
> No way. What are you, a 'mo? Look,
> it's easy. You just stare at her.
> Don't look away, just keep staring.
> Sooner or later, you'll have to
> kiss 'cause there won't be nothing
> else to do. You got it?

> KEN
> Yeah, yeah.

Ken takes this in, very serious. Daniel sees Amy approaching
with a cardboard tray of snacks.

> DANIEL
> Okay. Here she comes. Do it.

Daniel slaps Ken on the back and leans back in his seat. As
Amy returns, Ken begins to look at her.

CUT TO:

EXT. A DIFFERENT NEIGHBORHOOD - NIGHT

It is now very dark. Sam, Neal and Bill are slowly walking
their bikes down the street. They are exhausted, both
physically and emotionally.

> BILL
> We've been to a million houses,
> Neal. How many houses are we gonna
> do, anyway?

> NEAL
> As many as it takes.

> SAM
> I don't think we're gonna find it.

> NEAL
> (looking straight ahead)
> Then go home.

> SAM
> It could be way on the other side
> of town.

> NEAL
> Then we'll find it there. Right now
> we're looking here.

(CONTINUED)

CONTINUED:

                    SAM
               (cautiously)
          Neal. I have to go. My parents are
          gonna be worried.

                    BILL
          Yeah. Me, too. My mom doesn't like
          to watch "Dallas" alone.

Neal stops walking, looks at Sam and Bill.

                    NEAL
          I can't believe you guys are gonna
          bail on me.

                    SAM
          We'll look tomorrow, I promise. But
          if I don't go home now, I'm gonna
          get in trouble and -

                    NEAL
               (interrupting)
          Well, I'm looking now. You know,
          if this was your dad, you wouldn't
          be in such a hurry to get home. I'd
          be there for you.

Neal's face hardens. He gets on his bike and promptly rides
off, leaving Sam and Bill behind, helpless and spent. OFF
Sam's mixture of emotions, we...

                                             CUT TO:

INT. LASER DOME - NIGHT

MUSIC UP: "AMIE" BY PURE PRAIRIE LEAGUE

Nick and Lindsay are still sitting a seat apart. But the ice
has been broken. Lindsay turns to Nick.

                    LINDSAY
          Sorry about the music.

                    NICK
          It's actually not that bad.
               (points to ceiling)
          Those horses are pretty cool.

                    LINDSAY
          Yeah. Nick...

                    NICK
          Yeah?

                                        (CONTINUED)

CONTINUED: (2)

>   LINDSAY
>   (gathering her courage)
> I know I've been sort of a bitch
> lately. But it's just 'cause I
> didn't want to lead you on or
> anything. I know it's stupid... but
> I was afraid that maybe you still
> liked me.

>   NICK
>   (covering his hurt)
> Wow. You are really conceited.

They share a laugh. Lindsay is relieved. Nick is crushed, but doing his best to hide it. We find ....

AMY AND KEN

MUSIC UP: "FREE BIRD" BY LYNYRD SKYNYRD

Amy's leaning back in her seat, watching the show. Ken is still staring at her. He doesn't blink. After several beats, Amy notices him staring.

>   AMY
> What are you doing?

>   KEN
>   (still staring)
> Nothing.

>   AMY
> Why are you staring at me?

>   KEN
> Oh, am I staring at you?

>   AMY
> Yeah. What's the deal?

>   KEN
>   (flustered)
> Well, I just... want to kiss you.

>   AMY
>   (nervous)
> Oh... Okay.

Amy leans toward Ken and kisses him sweetly.

(CONTINUED)

CONTINUED: (3)

At first, they're both a little stiff, their eyes wide open. Then their instincts kick in. They close their eyes and get into it. And as they begin to make out, we see:

ANGLES ON: Daniel, Lindsay, and Nick, as each of them reacts to Ken and Amy kissing. They're all loving it. We find...

KIM sitting by herself, brooding. Curious, she peers over at the freaks, spots Ken and Amy making out. Kim does a double-take and SMILES. Then she looks over at Daniel.

ANGLE ON: Daniel is leaning back in his seat, gazing up at the ceiling, his mouth ajar. The light is hitting him just right. He looks amazing.

Kim watches Daniel, her anger quickly fading. She gets up and approaches him. Daniel smiles knowingly.

>   DANIEL
>   What?

Kim doesn't answer. She just pulls Daniel toward her and kisses him. As they begin to make out...

>   CUT TO:

INT. WEIR HOUSE - NIGHT

Sam walks into the house. He's shell-shocked from the day's experiences. Harold and Jean get up and sternly approach him.

>   HAROLD
>   Well, it's about time you got home,
>   young man. Your mother and I have
>   something to tell you.

Sam's had enough surprises for one day.

>   SAM
>   What?

Harold and Jean both break into smiles.

>   JEAN
>   That maybe sometimes it's okay to
>   spend a little extra money on such
>   a good kid.

Harold reaches down behind the chair and presents Sam with his very own Atari Video set.

>   (CONTINUED)

CONTINUED:

>   HAROLD
>   Yeah. And maybe you can teach me
>   about those spaced invaders.

Sam wells up with tears and runs into their arms, sobbing.
He hugs both of them for dear life.

>   HAROLD (CONT'D)
>   (to Jean)
>   Boy. He must have really wanted
>   that game.

>   CUT TO:

EXT. A DARKENED STREET - NIGHT

MUSIC: "FREE BIRD" CARRIES OVER

It's very dark. We're following a set of bicycle wheels. We
SLOWLY CRANE UP to reveal the emotionally and physically
burnt Neal.

He is slowly circling a dead end street of townhouses. Each
push of the pedal is like moving 1000 miles. He continues to
wearily press the button on the clicker. As he looks off to
the left, he hears a noise.

He stops his bike, turns to his right and sees a GARAGE DOOR
slowly starting to RISE. He just stares in disbelief.

Neal sees his father's BRIGHT RED SPORTS CAR slowly revealed,
with the license plate that reads "I FLOSS EM."

Neal, about to burst into tears, throws the clicker as hard
as he can at the townhouse. He gets on his bike and
hurriedly rides off.

>   CUT TO:

INT. LASER DOME - NIGHT

MUSIC: "FREE BIRD" CARRIES OVER

Daniel and Kim are still making out. Kim pulls away.

>   KIM
>   Sometimes I just... I don't know.
>   When I think about you with someone
>   else, I get crazy...

>   (CONTINUED)

CONTINUED:

> DANIEL
> I know.
> (beat)
> Can we take back the Laser Dome?

Kim nods and kisses Daniel again. After a beat...

> KIM
> (points to ceiling)
> What the hell is that?

> DANIEL
> I think it's a cactus taking off
> his hat.

Daniel and Kim go back to kissing. And we PULL BACK on the audience. Many couples are making out. It's as if the LASER DOME has a magical effect on everyone. Except...

LINDSAY AND NICK who are still a seat apart. They can't help but see the other couples making out around them. An uncomfortable silence passes.

> NICK
> I'd be lying if I didn't say this
> was painful.

Nick and Lindsay share a laugh, then go back to watching the show. After a beat...

Lindsay steals a glance at Nick, wondering "what if." Then she turns back to the ceiling. A beat later, Nick glances at Lindsay with his own twinge of longing. Neither is aware of the other's bittersweet moment of regret. We PAN OVER to KEN AND AMY kissing passionately. Amy is cradling Ken's face in her hands. Her fingers slowly move up to caress Ken's sideburns.

And we TILT UP to the stars on the ceiling and...

FADE OUT.

THE END

FREAKS AND GEEKS

"CHOKIN' AND TOKIN'"

Episode #13

Written by Judd Apatow

Directed by Miguel Arteta

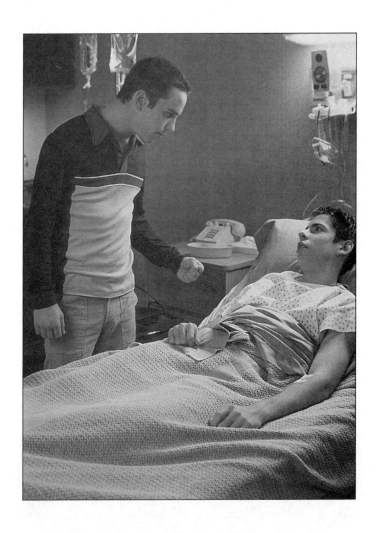

We always wanted to do an episode in which Lindsay does drugs and freaks out. Our first thought was that she should do mushrooms or acid. I knew it would be difficult to get this approved, so I mentioned the idea to the NBC standards and practices person well before we started writing it. She said we couldn't do it, but then suggested she could freak out on pot. Since I have a history of bad pot experiences, I was all for this.

I am not a fan of pot. I have many friends who are fans—big fans. I have seen many of them have problems as a result: depression, panic attacks, loss of their senses of humor. Nothing good comes from it. But I say that as someone who, the second he gets stoned, freaks out and wishes he weren't stoned or falls asleep. Maybe if I loved it I would feel differently.

The first time I smoked pot, I was with my two best friends, and we tried it at a construction site at night. A security guard saw us and pointed a flashlight in our direction. We ran for about fifteen minutes then hid in my friend's room, staring out the window for a few hours. I am sure the security guard did not chase us. All of my pot experiences went downhill from there.

That summer, the summer before seventh grade, I was very concerned that my friends would become potheads, and I never wanted to do it again. I had a nervous stomach as summer camp ended, and my return to my friends loomed. When junior high started, I instantly dropped my friends for new friends who did not smoke pot. We had a blast and rode dirt bikes. Within two years, they became the "Freaks" of our school, so I left them and returned to my original best friends, who in fact never got into smoking pot. One might refer to me as a pussy, if one used that type of language.

During college I smoked pot and drank Southern Comfort. Right before passing out on a couch in a common room, a friend of mine interviewed me with a tape recorder. He said, "How do you feel?" I replied, "I feel like a falafel." When I threw up, twenty lightbulbs popped, and the next day I was shown photos of what looked like an octopus jumping out of my mouth. I begged them not to make copies and pass them around. If that happened today, it surely would have been on the Internet, and I would be known as the octopus guy. When I woke up the next day, I saw that they wrote all over my body with a permanent marker. I remember "asshole" was one of their witty markings.

So at heart, I wanted to make an episode that would be very funny but would let the audience know that smoking pot was destroying Nick's life, and it would do the same to Lindsay if she got into it. I thought it was a good message for America. I was proud of the show. When I watched it air, I thought it seemed quite shocking for American TV. It is rare to see a sixteen-year-old high school girl roll joints at eight o'clock. It is even rarer to see her babysit a four-year-old while high, suffer a panic attack, and then later think she is living in a dog's dream.

The day after the show aired, we were canceled. Jake thinks someone at the highest level of NBC's parent company happened to turn it on and made a call ending our run. That's probably not how it went down, but it's fun to think that's what happened.

I haven't smoked pot in years, but I must admit that when I get the flu, I might enjoy my NyQuil a little more than I should.

—Judd Apatow

FREAKS AND GEEKS

"CHOKIN' AND TOKIN'"

CAST LIST

LINDSAY WEIR
SAM WEIR
HAROLD WEIR
JEAN WEIR
DANIEL DESARIO
NICK ANDOPOLIS
BILL HAVERCHUCK
NEAL SCHWEIBER
KEN MILLER
MILLIE KENTNER
MR. ROSSO
MR. KOWCHEVSKI
ALAN WHITE
MARK
GORDON CRISP
VICKI APPLEBY
MAUREEN SAMPSON
LUNCH LADY
MS. FOOTE
GLORIA HAVERCHUCK
MR. JOHNSON
MRS. JOHNSON
RONNIE JOHNSON
DOCTOR
BEN WHITE
ERNIE HAHUTH
FRANK

FREAKS AND GEEKS

"CHOKIN' AND TOKIN'"

SET LIST

INTERIORS:

MCKINLEY HIGH SCHOOL
    /HALLWAY
    /CAFETERIA
    /SOCIAL STUDIES CLASS
    /MR. ROSSO'S OFFICE
WEIR HOUSE
    /LIVING ROOM
    /KITCHEN
    /LINDSAY'S BEDROOM
NICK'S HOUSE
    /BASEMENT
HOSPITAL
    /HALLWAY
    /BILL'S ROOM
MILLIE'S HOUSE
    /KITCHEN
JOHNSON HOUSE
    /MASTER BEDROOM
    /LIVING ROOM
    /BATHROOM
    /HALLWAY

EXTERIORS:

BASKETBALL COURT
WEIR HOUSE

<u>TEASER</u>

FADE IN:

INT. CAFETERIA - DAY

NICK and DANIEL are making their way through the lunch line. Nick is in the front. He looks at all the food, very carefully. He is clearly high on pot.

>   NICK
>   What's that?

>   LUNCH LADY
>   Creamed spinach.

>   NICK
>   Oooh. What's that?

>   LUNCH LADY
>   That's salisbury steak.

>   NICK
>   What makes it different from a
>   regular steak?

>   LUNCH LADY
>   I don't know. The salisbury sauce,
>   I suppose. You want some?

>   NICK
>   Hmm.

Nick just stares at it for a long time.

>   DANIEL
>   Hey, space cadet! I'm hungry here.

>   NICK
>   (quickly)
>   I always notice that after
>   salisbury steak, we always have
>   hamburgers the next day. Then the
>   next day we have meatball heroes
>   and then a few days later...
>   meatloaf. Is that the same meat?
>   Are you recycling the meat?

>   LUNCH LADY
>   It's different meat.

>   NICK
>   I guess you have to say that.

                                              (CONTINUED)

                         211

CONTINUED:

>   DANIEL
> We all know the food sucks; it's
> school, let's go!

>   NICK
> I guess I'll have the... salisbury
> steak.

>   LUNCH LADY
> Excellent choice sir.

LINDSAY walks over to Nick.

>   LINDSAY
> Where have you been? You told me we
> were going to Denny's. I've been
> waiting in the parking lot.

The lunch lady hands him his lunch.

>   NICK
> Oh, did I say that?

>   LINDSAY
> Yes, after third period.

He pays for his lunch.

>   NICK
> Third period?

>   LINDSAY
> In the hallway. By my locker.

>   NICK
> Oh, yeah.

He sits down. Lindsay joins him. Nick begins to eat.

>   NICK
> I'm sorry. You still want to go?

>   LINDSAY
> You're already eating.

>   NICK
> Oh. I can eat again. I'm kind of
> hungry.

>   LINDSAY
> You're kind of stoned.

(CONTINUED)

CONTINUED: (2)

> NICK
> I'm very stoned. Report cards are
> coming out. I figured I might as
> well have some fun before the whip
> comes down.

> LINDSAY
> Forget it.

She walks away. He watches her go, then begins eating. Daniel
joins him.

> NICK
> What's with Lindsay?

> DANIEL
> (sarcastic)
> I don't know. She's crazy.

Nick sees MARK. He jumps up and walks over to him.

> NICK
> So?

> MARK
> I haven't gotten any in yet.

> NICK
> Well, when?

> MARK
> I told you, I won't know 'til the
> guy calls me.

> NICK
> Well, when will he call?

> MARK
> He calls when he gets some pot.
> What can I do?

> NICK
> How can this town be totally dry?
> It's sick.

> MARK
> It happens. Don't worry. I'll get
> some.

> NICK
> Don't you grow your own, too?

(CONTINUED)

CONTINUED: (3)

                    MARK
          No.

                    NICK
          You are so full of it. I know you
          grow your own. Tommy Genaro said it
          was amazing.

                    MARK
          That's a lie. My dad found the
          lamps and ran over them with his
          car.

                    NICK
          He better have. Don't hold out on
          me. Call me as soon as...that guy
          calls you.

Nick walks away.

                    MARK
          I will...
               (under his breath, trying
                to convince himself)
          The customer is king. The customer
          is king.

Nick exits. Mark looks and sees MILLIE staring at him.

                    MARK (CONT'D)
          What?

                    MILLIE
          You know what.

                                        CUT TO:

                    OPENING TITLES

                      ACT ONE

FADE IN:

INT. WEIR LIVING ROOM - NIGHT

The entire WEIR FAMILY is watching television. Sam stands by
the television, changing channels for his dad.

                    HAROLD
          Try seven.

Sam changes the channel.

                                    (CONTINUED)

CONTINUED:

> HAROLD (CONT'D)
> Try four.

Sam changes the channel.

> HAROLD (CONT'D)
> Try two. That's it. Thanks, Sam.

MUSIC UP: 'CHARLIE'S ANGELS' THEME

> JEAN
> Lindsay, the Johnson's want you to
> baby-sit on Thursday.

> LINDSAY
> What do they pay?

> JEAN
> A dollar fifty an hour.

> LINDSAY
> That's all? They're so cheap.

> HAROLD
> (sarcastic)
> Yes, Lindsay, they should pay you a
> king's ransom to lay around
> drinking pop and watching TV on
> their couch.

> LINDSAY
> So I have to work for slave wages?
> I guess keeping their kid safe and
> secure isn't worth much to them.

> HAROLD
> Enough already, everybody be quiet.
> I'm trying to watch Charlie's
> Angels.
> (to Sam)
> So Sam, who's your favorite Angel?

> SAM
> I like Bosley.

> HAROLD
> Bosley! Nobody watches this show
> for Bosley.

> SAM
> He's funny.

(CONTINUED)

CONTINUED: (2)

> HAROLD
> He's no Kate Jackson, I'll tell you
> that much.

> LINDSAY
> He doesn't care. He's in love with
> Cindy Sanders.

> SAM
> Not anymore. She's going out with
> Todd Schellinger.

> JEAN
> Well, that's her loss. She's the
> one who's missing out.

> HAROLD
> Is anybody else catching your
> fancy?

> SAM
> Dad!

> JEAN
> Harold, stop. You're embarrassing
> him.

> HAROLD
> I just think there's a time in a
> young man's life when he should
> begin testing the waters.

> LINDSAY
> How about me testing the waters?

> HAROLD
> You can test the waters, too --
> after you get married.

> LINDSAY
> (mocking him)
> Ha-ha-ha, Dad. You're so funny.

> HAROLD
> (deadly serious)
> Don't you mock me.

> LINDSAY
> (scared)
> Sorry, Dad.

CUT TO:

(CONTINUED)

INT. SCHOOL HALLWAY - DAY

Sam, NEAL and BILL are walking down the hall, talking.

>   NEAL
>   Hey, Sam, did you hear? The
>   freshmen student government voted
>   Cindy and Todd "Cutest Couple."

>   SAM
>   Is she ever gonna break up with
>   him? I thought jocks were always
>   dumping their girlfriends.

>   NEAL
>   Sam, it may very well be time to
>   admit to yourself that the Cindy
>   ship has sailed. It's time to board
>   another vessel.

>   BILL
>   Board a what?

Just then, the geeks round the corner. Neal crashes right
into VICKI, who is walking with MAUREEN. Vicki's binder goes
crashing to the floor.

>   VICKI
>   Oh, no, my new binder.

Neal immediately dives for it. He picks up Vicki's new
binder, a pristine three-fold Mead Organizer.

>   NEAL
>   The Mead Tri-Fold Organizer. I'm
>   impressed. I have one of these
>   babies myself.

>   VICKI
>   (coldly)
>   Thank you. Could you watch where
>   you're going?

>   NEAL
>   It would be my pleasure. (or "as
>   you wish")

Vicki takes the binder back from Neal.

>   MAUREEN
>   Hey, Sam. Hey, guys.

                                              (CONTINUED)

CONTINUED:

                        SAM
            Hey, Maureen.

                        MAUREEN
            Did you do the reading for social
            studies?

                        VICKI
            Maureen. Come on. Let's go.

                        MAUREEN
            Okay. I'll see you guys in class.

Vicki and Maureen head quickly off. Neal watches them go,
confidently. We reveal that Alan has been watching them.

                        NEAL
            That Vicki Appleby is a real woman.

                        BILL
            She doesn't know you're alive.

                        NEAL
            For now. Sam, those are the kind of
            women that we should be going for.
            The Cindy Sanders of this world are
            hors d'oeuvres. Vicki is a five
            course meal.

                        BILL
            "Hor" what?

ALAN walks up to Bill.

                        ALAN
            Hey Bill, you want some crushed
            nuts with your sundae?
ALTERNATE LINE

                        ALAN (CONT'D)
            Hey Bill, what's the capital of
            Thailand?

                        BILL
            Bangkok.

                        ALAN
            Okay.

Alan smacks Bill in the crotch, then laughs and walks into
class.

                                        (CONTINUED)

CONTINUED: (2)

> BILL
> That guy needs to get a new joke.
> (or)
> How did I not see that coming?

CUT TO:

INT. SOCIAL STUDIES CLASSROOM - MOMENTS LATER

Class is in session. Neal is looking over at Vicki, who is sitting a few desks away. Vicki looks over and sees him staring. Neal gives her a "hello there" look. She looks away, bugged. Neal throws a "she digs me" look to Sam.

The social studies teacher is the beautiful MS. FOOTE. We can tell by the look on his face that Bill is smitten.

> MS. FOOTE
> For the next week we are going to be talking about the civil rights movement. Most people think about Martin Luther King, Jr. when they talk about this time, but the movement was sparked by one woman who refused to give up her seat on a public bus. Does anyone know her name?

Bill raises his hand instantly. He studies hard so he can look good to his favorite teacher.

> BILL
> Rosa Parks.

> MS. FOOTE
> That's right, Bill. Very good.

The geeks give Bill a puzzled look. Bill gives them a look that says "yeah, I'm cool." Ms. Foote sneezes several times.

> BILL
> God bless you, Ms. Foote.

> MS. FOOTE
> Thank you. My allergies are really acting up today.

> BILL
> Mine, too. You want me to close the window, Ms. Foote?

(CONTINUED)

CONTINUED:

She nods as she wipes her nose. Bill promptly closes the classroom window, then takes his seat.

As he passes Alan, Alan mutters, under his breath...

> ALAN
> Kiss butt.

> MS. FOOTE
> It's my hay fever. What are you allergic to, Bill?

> BILL
> A lot of things. Bees, air, cats, but not dogs. Well, some dogs. And if I eat a peanut, I could die.

> MS. FOOTE
> Really?

> BILL
> Yeah, it happened to me once in summer camp. I was taken away in an ambulance.

> ALAN
> So, don't eat 'em, dork.

Kids laugh.

> BILL
> I don't. If I did, I could die.

> MS. FOOTE
> That's very unusual.

> BILL
> Not really. A lot of people have ailments like that. Neal has psoriasis. It's like lizard skin. And Sam passes out if he even thinks about blood.

The class laughs. Sam and Neal look enraged at Bill. Vicki and Maureen laugh.

> BILL
> It's not that unusual.

CUT TO:

INT. SCHOOL HALLWAY - LATER

Sam and Neal have cornered Bill.

> NEAL
> I can't believe you!

> BILL
> What?

> NEAL
> We are finally beginning to get
> some respect around here and you
> have to go and ruin it.

> SAM
> How are we going to get in with
> Maureen and her friends if you tell
> the whole class about me fainting
> and your dumb allergies and Neal's
> lizard skin?

> NEAL
> Hey, it's called psoriasis! Ten
> percent of the population will
> suffer from it at some point in
> their life.

> BILL
> What's the big deal? It's nothing
> to be ashamed of.

> NEAL
> You're too busy flirting with Ms.
> Foote to know you're making fools
> of us.

> BILL
> I was not flirting with her.

> SAM
>   (mocking)
> "It's not that unusual. I could die
> if I eat a peanut."

> NEAL
> You're killing my chances with
> Vicki.

> BILL
> You don't have a chance with Vicki.

(CONTINUED)

CONTINUED:

>   NEAL
> You don't have a chance with Ms.
> Foote.

>   BILL
> I have a better chance with Ms.
> Foote than you have with Vicki...
> and I don't have any chance at all.

>   SAM
> Fine, Bill. Be a geek your whole
> life. I'm sick of it.

Sam and Neal exit, leaving Bill all alone.

CUT TO:

INT. CAFETERIA - DAY

Nick, KEN, Lindsay, and Daniel are eating.

>   NICK
> Do you guys have any pot?

>   DANIEL
> No.

>   KEN
> The cupboard is bare.

>   NICK
> I am running out quick. I've been
> rationing all week, but I'm down to
> scraping the resin out of my bong.
> What am I gonna do?

>   DANIEL
> Uh... not be stoned.

>   NICK
> Ha-ha. I'm serious. I can't believe
> you guys don't have any pot.

>   KEN
> Maybe Lindsay has some.

>   LINDSAY
> I...don't.

>   KEN
> I was making a jest.

(CONTINUED)

CONTINUED: (2)

                    NICK
                 (thinks)
           Daniel, you have pot. I know it.
           Don't be a cheap bastard. I always
           hook you up.

                    DANIEL
           I don't have any. Ease up, Cheech
           and Chong.

                    NICK
           It's just so uncool if you guys are
           holding out on me.

There is a long silence. Suddenly Nick jumps to his feet.

                    NICK
           I'm gonna kill Mark.

He exits.

                    DANIEL
           That guy is turning into such a
           waste case. Do I act like that when
           I'm high?

                    KEN
           Do you really want to know?

                    DANIEL
           Yeah.

                    KEN
                 (long pause)
           Uh... no?

                                              CUT TO:

INT. SCHOOL HALLWAY - DAY

Daniel and Ken are standing by Daniel's locker.

                    DANIEL
           If I look like Nick when I'm
           wasted, then I don't want to do it
           anymore.

                    KEN
           Really?

Daniel goes through his locker.

                                      (CONTINUED)

CONTINUED:

> DANIEL
> Yeah. That stuff eats your brain.
> Look at him. He's a mess.

> KEN
> So, you're gonna get rid of all
> your pot?

> DANIEL
> That's right.

Daniel finds some pot.

> DANIEL
> This stuff is no good. I've got to
> stay sharp if I wanna, you know...

> KEN
> Stay sharp?

> DANIEL
> Yeah.

> KEN
> Well, here's a plan. Instead of
> letting it go to waste, why don't
> you donate it to a worthy cause?
> Me.

> DANIEL
> I'm not giving it to you.

> KEN
> Why not?

> DANIEL
> Because it amuses me not to.

> KEN
> Oh, come on. Just give it to me!

MR. ROSSO appears behind them.

> MR. ROSSO
> Why don't you give it to me?

Daniel and Ken are busted.

FADE OUT.

<u>END OF ACT ONE</u>

ACT TWO

FADE IN:

INT. SCHOOL HALLWAY - DAY

Nick is walking down the hallway. Lindsay walks up to him.

                    LINDSAY
          Nick. How are you holding up?

                    NICK
          Five days with no pot. I almost
          smoked my mom's ferns last night.

                    LINDSAY
          You look good. Your eyes are all
          clear.

                    NICK
               (sarcastic)
          Well, at least I'm saving money on
          eye drops.

                    LINDSAY
          Oh, come on. It's not that big a
          deal, is it?

                    NICK
          No. It's just a bummer.

                    LINDSAY
          Then let's do something fun.

                    NICK
          Yeah?

                    LINDSAY
          Yeah. I'll meet you at lunch.

                    NICK
          Okay.

Millie comes walking from the other direction.

                    MILLIE
          Hey, Lindsay.

                    LINDSAY
               (without stopping)
          Hey.

                                        (CONTINUED)

CONTINUED:

Millie looks hurt as Lindsay just keeps walking.

>   LINDSAY (CONT'D)
>   (to Nick)
>   Did you do your English homework?

>   NICK
>   Yeah. I was so bored I did <u>all</u> my
>   homework.

                                             CUT TO:

INT. SOCIAL STUDIES CLASSROOM - DAY

Ms. Foote is speaking to the class.

>   MS. FOOTE
>   George Washington Carver had many
>   accomplishments, but he is best
>   known for his work with the peanut.
>   (beat)
>   And for being Bill's mortal enemy.

Everyone laughs, except Bill, Sam and Neal.

>   MS. FOOTE (CONT'D)
>   Get it, Bill? Because you're
>   allergic to peanuts.

Sam and Neal look annoyed that this has been brought up
again.

>   BILL
>   (embarrassed)
>   Yeah. That was a good one.

Ms. Foote looks confused. They had such a nice repartee
yesterday.

SFX: The bell rings.

Everyone begins to exit.

>   MS. FOOTE
>   Anyway...don't forget your reading
>   assignments. And your essays are
>   due Monday.

Ms. Foote walks over to Bill.

>   MS. FOOTE (CONT'D)
>   Are you all right, Bill?

                                        (CONTINUED)

CONTINUED:

                    BILL
          I'm fine. I just... don't like you
          mentioning my allergies so much. It
          makes me look like a geek.

                    MS. FOOTE
          Oh, I'm sorry.

                    BILL
          It's all right.

                    MS. FOOTE
          You know, you're not a geek, Bill.
          You're unique. That's nothing to be
          ashamed of.

                    BILL
          Tell that to everyone else.

He quickly exits. Ms. Foote looks sad.

                                             CUT TO:

EXT. BASKETBALL COURT - DAY

Lindsay and Nick are playing HORSE.

                    NICK
          Okay. If you can't make this,
          that's horse.

                    LINDSAY
          Okay, do an easy one.

                    NICK
          Fine.

Nick runs and dunks the ball.

                    LINDSAY
          Oh, come on!

                    NICK
          What? That was easy...for me.

They laugh.

                    NICK (CONT'D)
          Okay. Here's an easy one.

Nick dribbles, then does a sky hook. It goes in.

                                        (CONTINUED)

CONTINUED:

> LINDSAY
> Nick. That's not fair.

> NICK
> That one's easy, too. For me and
> Kareem Abdul-Jabbar.

Mark walks over.

> MARK
> Hey, Nick. The eagle has landed.

> NICK
> Oh, man! I love that eagle.

He runs over to Mark. Lindsay look concerned.

> MARK
> You know how there was a drought?
> Now there's a flood. Tell your
> friends we're having a harvest
> sale.

He takes out a baggie and covertly hands it to Nick, who
stuffs it in his pocket.

> MARK (CONT'D)
> That's forty.

Nick hands him the money.

> MARK (CONT'D)
> Well, enjoy. Go easy, this is
> strong stuff. It's hydroponic.

> LINDSAY
> Like the lettuce?

> MARK
> Yeah, like the lettuce. I'll see
> ya' later.

Mark exits.

> NICK
> You want to go to my house and
> smoke some of this?

> LINDSAY
> Uh...no.

(CONTINUED)

CONTINUED: (2)

> NICK
> Oh, come on. It'll be so much fun.

> LINDSAY
> I don't smoke pot.

> NICK
> Really? I couldn't tell.
> (laughs)
> What's the big deal? It's from the
> Earth. It's natural. Why would it
> be here if we weren't supposed to
> smoke it?

> LINDSAY
> Dog crap is here. We don't smoke
> that.

> NICK
> Fine Lindsay, be that way. You're
> too good for pot. I'm the low life.

> LINDSAY
> I'm not saying that.

> NICK
> Everyone smokes pot. The Beatles.
> Dylan. Think of all the great art
> and poetry that was written under
> the influence.

He makes a long jump shot.

> NICK
> It opens your mind. Why do you want
> your mind closed?

> LINDSAY
> Well...maybe just a little. Just to
> see what it's like.

> NICK
> Oh my God, we are going to have so
> much fun.

CUT TO:

INT. SCHOOL HALLWAY - MOMENTS LATER

Bill walks over to Sam and Neal.

(CONTINUED)

CONTINUED:

> BILL
> Now I have no chance with Ms.
> Foote.

> NEAL
> As opposed to before.

> BILL
> So, whose mom's gonna drive us to
> the science fiction fair on
> Saturday?

> NEAL
> Actually, we can't go. We're going
> to go to a cheerleading competition
> to see Vicki and Maureen compete.

> SAM
> Maureen invited us.

> BILL
> What about the science fiction
> fair?

> SAM
> Just ask Gordon to go. He likes
> science fiction.

Gordon walks over. Neal and Sam exit.

> GORDON
> I don't like science fiction. I
> love, love, love it. Do you want
> your mom to drive, or should mine?
> Maybe my mom should drive because
> she does all my make up in the
> parking lot before I go in.

Bill rolls his eyes.

> BILL
> Great.

CUT TO:

INT. NICK'S BASEMENT - LATER

Nick is laying back on his couch like a sloth. He eats chips
and stares off into space. Lindsay is sitting up straight,
sober and bored. A record is playing which has a lot of
drums.

(CONTINUED)

CONTINUED:

> LINDSAY
> I thought you said this was going
> to be fun.

> NICK
> It is fun.

> LINDSAY
> What's fun about this?

> NICK
> What's not fun about this? Listen
> to that drum fill. This guy's
> amazing. You know hard that is?
> (beat)
> You want to walk to the market and
> get some Drakes Cakes?

> LINDSAY
> No! Why do you do this? You're an
> amazing guy when you're not stoned.

> NICK
> Don't start with that. I've been
> waiting all week for this moment.

> LINDSAY
> I know you have and it's sad.
> You're wasting your life away.

> NICK
> You don't know what you're talking
> about. You take one hit, you don't
> inhale and then you criticize me
> and say I'm lame. What do you know?
> You've never been high. Who are you
> to judge me?

> LINDSAY
> Look at you, you're addicted.

> NICK
> Oh, please.

> LINDSAY
> You are. This is the highlight of
> your week? Sitting on the couch
> eating chips, dreaming of Drakes
> Cakes?

(CONTINUED)

CONTINUED: (2)

> NICK
> Is it better to sit there with a
> board up my butt like you? Not
> enjoying anything. Not feeling
> anything. You're exactly like your
> dad but you don't want to admit it.
> You're a drag.

He takes out the pot and throws the bag at her.

> NICK (CONT'D)
> Here. I'm really addicted. How will
> I live without it?

He starts to walk away.

> NICK (CONT'D)
> Grow up, Lindsay. You don't know
> everything. In fact, when it comes
> to pot, you know nothing.

He exits.

CUT TO:

INT. CAFETERIA - DAY

Alan sits at a table with a few friends including ERNIE
HAHUTH.

> ALAN
> Check out Mr. Peanut.

ANGLE ON: BILL eating his lunch alone.

> ERNIE
> He's probably eating a peanut
> butter and jelly sandwich, the
> liar.

Bill gets up and walks over to Gordon.

> ALAN
> Let's find out if he's lying.

Alan grabs a small paper cup filled with cafeteria peanuts
and walks over to where Bill was sitting.
ANGLE ON: BILL AND GORDON

> BILL
> Gordon, I don't think I can go to
> the convention.
> (MORE)

(CONTINUED)

CONTINUED:

                BILL (CONT'D)
I forgot my mom wants me to clean
our garage that day.

                GORDON
Oh, that's too bad. I was going to
lend you my Yoda mask.

ANGLE ON: ALAN putting a few peanuts in Bill's sandwich. Alan
walks back to his table.

                ALAN
Well, sit back and watch the
fireworks.

ANGLE ON: BILL walking back to the table. He sits down. Sam
and Neal walk over with their trays.

                BILL
Are you guys going to join me?

                SAM
Yeah. Why?

                BILL
I just thought maybe I was too
geeky to eat with.

                NEAL
You are, but we're too hungry to
care.

They sit down. Bill bites his sandwich. He looks troubled.

                BILL
This is crunchy.

                SAM
So?

                BILL
Crunchy, like peanuty crunch

                NEAL
Should we get Ms. Foote so you two
can discuss it?

                BILL
Did you guys put something in my
sandwich?

                NEAL
No.

(CONTINUED)

24.

CONTINUED: (2)

We see and hear Alan and his friends cracking up. Bill stares at him.

>   ALAN
>   Now what happens, Haverchuck?
>   Should we call an ambulance?

They all start laughing.

>   BILL
>   Yes.

Bill turns white. He starts having trouble breathing. This is very serious. His upper body falls onto the table.

>   SAM
>   Oh my God, Bill.

SMASH CUT TO:

INT. CAFETERIA - MOMENTS LATER

CLOSE UP: Bill is on a stretcher that is flying through the cafeteria being pushed by two paramedics. Ms. Foote and Mr. Kowchevski follow, looking concerned.

Sam and Neal watch it go, in a daze.

ANGLE ON: ALAN looking scared to death.

FADE OUT.

END OF ACT TWO

ACT THREE

FADE IN:

INT. HOSPITAL HALLWAY - DAY

GLORIA HAVERCHUCK, Bill's ex-stripper mom, is sitting in the hallway outside of Bill's hospital room. She's pretty but a little trashy looking, with big hair. She looks upset.

Sam, Neal and Jean come down the hall. Sam and Neal are running.

>   SAM
>   Mrs. Haverchuck! Mrs. Haverchuck!

They run up to her.

(CONTINUED)

CONTINUED:

> NEAL
> How's Bill? Is he still alive?

> GLORIA
> Yes. The doctor's in there with him
> right now.

> JEAN
> Oh, my God, Gloria. I'm so sorry.

> GLORIA
> This hasn't happened in years. Last
> time he ate a peanut, he was in a
> coma for two days. The doctor said
> he almost didn't make it.

Sam and Neal exchange freaked out looks.

> SAM
> He's not gonna die, is he?

> GLORIA
> Of course not.

She starts to get upset. Jean puts her arm around her.

> JEAN
> Come, sit down.

They walk away a bit, then sit down.

> NEAL
> Sam, could you not use the word
> "die" in a hospital?

> SAM
> You asked if he was still alive.

> NEAL
> Yes, but that's an optimistic
> question. Alive is good. Die is
> bad. Trust me on this stuff. My
> dad's a dentist.

Just then, a DOCTOR comes out of Bill's room.

> DOCTOR
> Mrs. Haverchuck, Bill's still
> unconscious.

Sam and Neal exchange looks.

(CONTINUED)

CONTINUED: (2)

> DOCTOR
> We've given him a shot of
> epinephrine, but his vital signs
> are still weak. We're just going to
> have to wait and see how his body
> reacts.

> GLORIA
> But he's going to be okay, right?

> DOCTOR
> (forcing a smile)
> We'll just have to wait and see.

He goes back inside the room. Gloria looks scared. She looks
at Jean, who also looks scared. They hug each other. Sam and
Neal look in shock.

> SAM
> Oh, man...

CUT TO:

INT. MR. ROSSO'S OFFICE- DAY

Ken and Daniel enter Mr. Rosso's office. He is speaking to
FRANK, a thirty year old burn out.

> MR. ROSSO
> Hey, guys. Could you give me a
> moment? I'm just finishing up with
> an old student.

> KEN
> Okay.

> MR. ROSSO
> Oh forgive me, Frank. This is
> Daniel Desario and Ken Miller.

> DANIEL
> How's it going?

> KEN
> Hey.

> FRANK
> What's up, guys?

He looks at Ken's 'Pink Floyd' shirt.

(CONTINUED)

CONTINUED:

> FRANK
> You into Floyd, man?

> KEN
> Yeah.

> FRANK
> I saw them at the pyramids.

> DANIEL
> In Egypt?

> FRANK
> You bet your ass.

> KEN
> I don't think they've played the
> pyramids.

> FRANK
> Yeah, you're right. I'm thinking of
> 'The Dead.' I just got confused
> because I went with the same guy to
> both shows. Tim. He went here.
> Class of '68. You know him?

Daniel and Ken shoot each other a glance.

> DANIEL
> What's his last name?

> FRANK
> Tim... Tim... Tim... something. He
> was a friend of a friend, actually.
> I saw Floyd at the laser dome. They
> weren't there, but it was their
> music. Have you been up there?

> KEN
> Uh-huh.

> FRANK
> That place is wild.
> (long pause)
> It makes you think.

> MR. ROSSO
> Well, thanks for lunch, Frank.
> We'll do it again soon.

(CONTINUED)

CONTINUED: (2)

> FRANK
> Definitely, Jeff.
> (to Ken and Daniel)
> See you, man. Shine on, you crazy
> diamonds.

He exits. Rosso waits until Frank is out of earshot.

> MR. ROSSO
> That was for your benefit. I want
> you to remember that man.

> DANIEL
> Why?

> MR. ROSSO
> 'Cause he's fried out of his mind.
> He's Mr. Wake and Bake.

> KEN
> So?

> MR. ROSSO
> He's your future. Keep burning the
> bong at both ends and you'll wind
> up just like him.

> DANIEL
> I'm telling you, I was getting rid
> of my pot.

> MR.,ROSSO
> How dumb do I look?

> KEN
> Do you really want to know?

> MR. ROSSO
> I can have you expelled for this,
> but I'm going to give you a break.
> Learn from Frank. Or you'll be
> Frank. It's your choice.

> DANIEL
> Fine.

> MR. ROSSO
> Do we understand each other?

> KEN
> As much as that's possible.

(CONTINUED)

CONTINUED: (3)

> MR. ROSSO
> Wait here a second. I've got some
> pamphlets I want to give to you.

Mr. Rosso exits.

> KEN
> He's gonna smoke our weed.

> DANIEL
> Or sell it to Frank.

CUT TO:

INT. LINDSAY'S ROOM - DAY

MUSIC UP: STEVE MILLER "FLY LIKE AN EAGLE"

Lindsay holds the bag of pot. She contemplates the pot for a
moment, then she opens a window. She pours the marijuana onto
a record album. She hesitates, then begins rolling a joint.

Quick shots of Lindsay attempting to roll the joint. The
paper ripping. Doing it wrong. Too small. Too big. Spilling
it.

CUT TO:

INT. HOSPITAL HALLWAY - DAY

Sam and Neal are standing in the hallway outside Bill's room.
Jean and Gloria are drinking coffee in the seats on the other
side of the door.

As they speak, Sam attempts to put a crinkled dollar bill in
a change machine which keeps rejecting it.

> SAM
> What if Bill dies?

> NEAL
> He won't die.

> SAM
> But what if he does? We were so
> mean to him today.

> NEAL
> What if he thinks we put the
> peanuts in his sandwich?

(CONTINUED)

CONTINUED:

>   SAM
>   (thinks, then...)
>   He's gotta get better. If he needs
>   an organ, I'll give him mine.

>   NEAL
>   What if he needs a liver? You've
>   only got one.

>   SAM
>   Maybe we can both give half.

He finally gets change. He uses the money to buy some candy
from an old handle pull candy machine.

>   NEAL
>   (hesitates)
>   Uh... okay. I guess.

>   SAM
>   If he... he might be mad at us
>   forever.

>   NEAL
>   What if Bill's ghost starts to
>   haunt us? He might start coming
>   into our rooms at night and
>   throwing things at us.

>   SAM
>   He wouldn't do that. He's our
>   friend. Right?

They both consider this for a second.

>   NEAL
>   That's true. We've all known each
>   other since kindergarten. That's
>   gotta count for something.

>   SAM
>   Yeah. I mean, maybe he'd be like
>   Casper the Friendly Ghost and he'd
>   hang out with us and nobody could
>   see him but us and then we'd keep
>   getting caught talking to him but
>   everybody would think we were crazy
>   like Wilbur on "Mr. Ed."

(CONTINUED)

CONTINUED: (2)

> NEAL
> Or maybe we'd start a detective
> agency and we could solve crimes
> because Bill's ghost could go
> undercover and nobody could see
> him.

> SAM
> Whoa, that'd be cool.

Just then, they hear Bill's mom burst into tears for the
first time. Jean hugs her.

> JEAN
> That's okay, Gloria. That's okay.

Sam and Neal look at each other.

> SAM
> It wouldn't be like that, would it?
> He'd just be dead and gone,
> wouldn't he?

Neal nods "yes." They go back to being freaked out.

> CUT TO:

INT. LINDSAY'S ROOM - DAY

Lindsay holds the burning embers of what is left of the
joint. She puts them out and chucks it out her window. She
sits on her bed and breathes deeply. Does she like it? Does
she dislike it? It is very scientific. Clearly, she is very
high.

There is a knock at the door. Lindsay jumps up in a panic.
She fans air out the window, fearing he'll smell the smoke.
Then she chucks the baggie of pot, and all the remnants off
the album cover out the window.

> LINDSAY
> (scared)
> Yeah.

Harold enters. Lindsay tries not to panic.

> HAROLD
> Lindsay, what are you doing?

> LINDSAY
> Dad, what are you doing home?

> (CONTINUED)

CONTINUED:

>   HAROLD
>   I forgot my wallet. What are <u>you</u>
>   doing home?
>
>   LINDSAY
>   What am I doing home? You mean why
>   am I home? Or what am I
>   doing...here?
>
>   HAROLD
>   I mean what are you doing here?!
>   You're supposed to be baby-sitting
>   for the Johnson's.
>
>   LINDSAY
>   I am?
>
>   HAROLD
>   Yeah. You better get over there or
>   they are going to be really mad.
>
>   LINDSAY
>   I've got to cancel. I
>   have...homework.
>
>   HAROLD
>   Lindsay, you are not canceling on
>   them. I'll have to hear about it
>   for months from Ted Johnson at my
>   Kiwanis meetings. That guy's just
>   looking for reasons to grouse. Do
>   your homework over there.

Lindsay stares, not knowing what to do.

>   HAROLD (CONT'D)
>   Are you all right?
>
>   LINDSAY
>   Yeah, I'm just...tired. You know,
>   woman problems.
>
>   HAROLD
>   I don't want to hear about it. Just
>   get going.

Harold exits. Lindsay looks panicked.

                                              CUT TO:

INT. HOSPITAL HALLWAY - DAY

Sam and Neal are sitting in silence outside Bill's door. Sam
is staring down. He hears footsteps. He looks down the hall
and his eyes go wide.

SAM'S POV: Alan White is standing at the end of the hallway,
looking tough.

> SAM
> (elbowing Neal)
> Uh, oh. What's he doing here?

> NEAL
> You don't think he's so mean he'd
> beat us up now, do you?

Just then, Alan's father, BEN, walks around the corner and
smacks Alan on the back of the head.

> BEN
> I told you to move it.

> ALAN
> Ow. Watch it.

> BEN
> Yeah, I'll watch it--right upside
> your head.

Ben grabs Alan by the arm and drags him down the hallway. Sam
and Neal exchange a look.

> BEN (CONT'D)
> (to Jean and Gloria)
> Which one of you is Bill's mother?

> GLORIA
> I am.

Ben pushes Alan toward her.

> BEN
> My son has something he'd like to
> say.

Alan stops in front of Gloria. He looks uncomfortable. He
throws a look back at his father, who gives him a "go ahead
or I'll kill you" look.

(CONTINUED)

CONTINUED:

>   ALAN
>   I...I was the one who put a peanut
>   in Bill's sandwich.
>   (quickly)
>   But I thought he was faking. He's
>   always lying about stuff. I didn't
>   know he was really allergic, I
>   swear.

>   JEAN
>   Oh, my goodness.

>   ALAN
>   Let me talk to him. I'll tell him
>   I'm sorry.

>   GLORIA
>   (stone-faced)
>   You can't talk to him because he's
>   unconscious and in critical
>   condition. And you'd better believe
>   he's not lying about that.

Gloria just gives Alan an icy stare and turns away. Sam and
Neal shake their heads. Alan looks freaked.

>   CUT TO:

INT. MILLIE'S KITCHEN - DAY

Lindsay has just entered.

>   LINDSAY
>   Millie, I need your help.

>   MILLIE
>   What is it? Did you forget your
>   social studies book again?

>   LINDSAY
>   No, I'm baby-sitting and I want you
>   to come with me.

>   MILLIE
>   (skeptical)
>   Really? Why?

>   LINDSAY
>   Because it will be fun.

>   MILLIE
>   You're lying to me. I can tell.

>   (CONTINUED)

CONTINUED: (2)

>   LINDSAY
> How can you tell?

>   MILLIE
> I <u>know</u> you.

>   LINDSAY
> Okay Millie, I'm going to tell you,
> but you have to swear--

>   MILLIE
> You're high.

>   LINDSAY
> What?

>   MILLIE
> You're on the pot.

>   LINDSAY
> How could you tell?

>   MILLIE
> I'm not dumb, Lindsay. I know what
> high people look like. I went to a
> Seals and Crofts concert last
> summer.

>   LINDSAY
> You can't tell anyone. I didn't
> want to. Nick talked me into it.
> I'm really stoned now and I don't
> know what's going to happen. I feel
> really weird.

>   MILLIE
> This is why you want me to baby-sit
> with you. So you won't freak out
> and boil the baby in a pot?

>   LINDSAY
> I'm not gonna boil the baby in a
> pot. I just need some help. Do you
> really think I would boil a baby in
> a pot?

>   MILLIE
> Fine, I'll go with you. But just
> for the safety of the child.

>   LINDSAY
> Thank you.

(CONTINUED)

CONTINUED: (3)

> MILLIE
> No, thank your dealer.

Lindsay rolls her eyes and they exit. Lindsay takes the pizza with her.

CUT TO:

INT. HOSPITAL HALLWAY - DAY

Alan walks toward the geeks. As soon as they see him coming they walk away.

Alan stares at Bill's crying mother. He looks scared. Alan looks at Bill's door, then slowly walks over to it. He looks to make sure that the geeks aren't watching and slips inside.

CUT TO:

INT. BILL'S HOSPITAL ROOM - CONTINUOUS

Bill is laying in a bed with machines and wires hooked all over him. It's a pretty scary scene. The BEEP BEEP BEEP of the heart monitor is the only sound. Bill is unconscious.

Alan looks at him and looks more freaked out than ever.

> ALAN
> (to himself)
> Whoa...

Alan slowly approaches the bed. KLANK! His foot hits a metal rolling stool, which rolls a few feet. Alan looks nervously back at the door, then at Bill.

> ALAN
> (quietly)
> Sorry, Haverchuck.
> (then)
> Hey, are you awake? Haverchuck?
> You're not faking, are you?

No. Bill lays there, unconscious.

> ALAN
> Oh, man, dork. Don't die. I'm
> warning you. If you die, I'll...

Alan stops. He has no idea what he's saying. This flips him out more. He really softens.

(CONTINUED)

CONTINUED:

> ALAN (CONT'D)
> I didn't think you were really
> allergic. You know, you're always
> saying stupid stuff. Remember that
> time in History when the teacher
> asked who was President during the
> Korean war and you said Alan Alda?
> And you really believed it.

Nothing from Bill. Alan walks right up to the bed and stares
at Bill.

> ALAN (CONT'D)
> Look, I'm sorry, okay? I didn't
> mean to put you in the hospital. I
> was just goofing on you.
> (beat)
> You know, it's not like you guys
> have ever been nice to me. I bet
> you don't even remember when we
> were in fourth grade. I actually
> used to think that you guys were
> really cool.

Alan really starts to get choked up. He takes a deep breath.

> ALAN (CONT'D)
> Remember when you brought that
> model of the Saturn 5 in for Show-
> and-Tell? I asked you guys if I
> could shoot rockets off with you
> but you said no. So, what, I'm
> supposed to be nice to you guys all
> the time? I liked comic books and
> science fiction and all that stuff
> too, but you guys never asked me to
> hang out.

Alan stares another beat, then starts to head out of the
room. He turns back.

> ALAN (CONT'D)
> Haverchuck, look. Please don't die.
> I promise I'll be nice to you,
> okay? Even if you do something
> really stupid. Just <u>don't die</u>,
> Haverchuck. Please don't die.

(CONTINUED)

CONTINUED: (2)

Alan now has a couple tears of fear and desperation running
down his face. He then composes himself and slips back out
the door. A moment later Bill groggily opens his eyes.

CUT TO:

INT. THE JOHNSONS' HOME - DAY

Lindsay and Millie listen to instructions from MR. and MRS.
JOHNSON. Sitting on the couch is six year old RONNIE JOHNSON.
Lindsay looks completely freaked out as she listens to the
instruction. She attempts to look normal by basically not
moving a muscle, but she winds up looking nervous and
intense.

                    MR. JOHNSON
          ...he's already eaten. If he says
          he's hungry that means he wants
          junk food. The junk food drawer is
          the bottom one next to the sink.
          You can give him one thing. He'll
          say he's allowed more, but he's
          not.

Lindsay can't take it anymore.

                    LINDSAY
          Will you excuse me? I have to use
          the bathroom.

Lindsay attempts to walk casually to the bathroom, but she is
stiff legged and self conscious as she moves. Millie
continues to listen to the instructions.

                    MRS. JOHNSON
          We'll be back at nine o'clock.
          We've left the number where we'll
          be in the kitchen.

CUT TO:

INT. THE JOHNSONS' BATHROOM - CONTINUOUS

Lindsay walks into the bathroom. She closes the door behind
her. She stands there looking like she is going to have a
panic attack. She breathes short, fast breaths.

Lindsay catches herself in the mirror. She looks at herself.
She stares into the reflection of her eyes. What is
happening? She looks scared.

(CONTINUED)

CONTINUED:

Finally, she breaks the gaze with herself and listens to the rest of the Johnson's instructions to Millie. She hears them exit, then walks out of the bathroom.

CUT TO:

INT. THE JOHNSONS' LIVING ROOM - CONTINUOUS

Lindsay walks out of the bathroom toward Millie and Ronnie. Ronnie senses her discomfort.

>   RONNIE
>   You look sick.

>   LINDSAY
>   I'm fine.

>   RONNIE
>   You look like you're going to throw
>   up.

>   LINDSAY
>   I'm not going to throw up. Don't
>   say that!

>   MILLIE
>   Lindsay, don't yell at him.

>   LINDSAY
>   I'm not yelling at him.

>   RONNIE
>   (almost crying)
>   You're yelling at me.

>   MILLIE
>   Don't get upset, Ronnie. Lindsay
>   just feels sick.

>   RONNIE
>   I know. That's what I said.

>   MILLIE
>   You know what would be fun? Let's
>   play hide and go seek.

>   RONNIE
>   Is she playing?

Millie answers Ronnie but is directing her comments to Lindsay with a slightly terse tone.

(CONTINUED)

CONTINUED:

> MILLIE
> No, she's going to lay down in the
> other room.

Lindsay gets the hint and walks toward the stairs.

> RONNIE
> Good. I don't like her.

CUT TO:

INT. HOSPITAL HALLWAY - CONTINUOUS

Sam and Neal are in the hallway.

> MAUREEN
> Sam!

They turn to see Vicki and Maureen running down the hallway.
They're both visibly upset as they run up to Sam and Neal.

> VICKI
> We just heard about Bill. Oh my
> God, is he all right?

> NEAL
> We don't know.

> MAUREEN
> How are you guys? This is so
> horrible.

And with this, Maureen throws her arms around Sam. Vicki
looks at Neal, then puts her arm around his shoulder.

> NEAL
> We're okay. We're just worried
> about Bill.

> MAUREEN
> (releasing her grip)
> Well, what's happening?

> NEAL
> He's in critical condition.

> MAUREEN
> Oh my God.

Maureen hugs Sam again, this time tighter than before. Sam
and Neal exchange looks. They weren't expecting this.

(CONTINUED)

CONTINUED:

Alan watches this from the other side of the hall. He looks sad.

ANGLE ON: Jean and Gloria are sitting drinking coffee.

                    GLORIA
          I feel so guilty.

                    JEAN
          Why?

                    GLORIA
          This is all my fault. If I took
          care of myself more when I was
          pregnant with Bill, maybe he
          wouldn't get allergies like this.

                    JEAN
          Don't blame yourself. We didn't
          know back then. When I was pregnant
          with Sam I never thought twice
          about nutrition.

                    GLORIA
          I was drinking a lot back then.

                    JEAN
             (speechless)
          Oh, well, you know...

                    GLORIA
          Getting high. Popping pills. This
          is all my fault. Bill has such a
          hard time in school, you know? Kids
          hassling him. His dad left us. I
          didn't want this kind of life for
          him.

                    JEAN
             (reaching for something)
          When Sam was four months old... I
          dropped him on a brick patio. He
          had a hairline fracture of his
          skull.

                    GLORIA
          Really?

                    JEAN
          Yeah.

                                        (CONTINUED)

CONTINUED: (2)

                    GLORIA
          Thanks, Jean.

                                        CUT TO:

INT. JOHNSONS' MASTER BEDROOM - DAY

MUSIC UP: BILLY JOEL'S "CAPTAIN JACK"

Lindsay is sitting down reading an Encyclopedia.

INSERT SHOT: The section on "Marijuana." We see the image of
a marijuana leaf. Several phrases are visible which describe
the effects.

Lindsay reads intensely. She needs information to get a
handle on this new feeling.

Suddenly, Ronnie bursts in the door.

                    RONNIE
             (tagging Lindsay)
          You're it! You're it! You're it!

                    LINDSAY
          I'm not it. I'm not even playing.

                    RONNIE
          You're it. You're it. I found you.

                    LINDSAY
          I wasn't even hiding.

                    RONNIE
          Stop cheating. It's my turn to hide
          now. You're cheating.

                    LINDSAY
          I'm not cheating. Just give me some
          space, man.

Lindsay runs into the hall in a panic.

                                        CUT TO:

INT. THE JOHNSONS' HALLWAY - CONTINUOUS

Lindsay runs out into the hall. Millie sees her and gets
alarmed.

                    MILLIE
          Oh my God, Lindsay, what happened?

                                        (CONTINUED)

CONTINUED:

>   LINDSAY
>   That kid's in there. He found me.
>
>   MILLIE
>   He's just a little boy.
>
>   LINDSAY
>   Well, I can't handle him right now.
>   (starts to cry)
>   What am I doing here? This house is
>   freaking me out. I don't like it.
>   Maybe I should lay down outside and
>   then just walk home when I feel
>   better.
>
>   MILLIE
>   No, just go in the living room.
>   I'll put Ronnie to bed, and then
>   I'll take care of you.
>
>   LINDSAY
>   Thanks, Millie.

Millie turns to walk away.

>   LINDSAY (CONT'D)
>   Millie.
>
>   MILLIE
>   Yeah.
>
>   LINDSAY
>   How long does this last?

FADE OUT.

<u>END OF ACT THREE</u>

<u>ACT FOUR</u>

FADE IN:

INT. JOHNSONS' LIVING ROOM - NIGHT

Lindsay and Millie are sitting in the living room. Lindsay is
laying on the couch under a blanket, Millie sits in an
armchair. The Johnsons' dog is sleeping across from them.

>   LINDSAY
>   Nick's stoned all the time. He
>   deals with his parents when he's
>   high, goes to class high. Why would
>   he do that?

(CONTINUED)

CONTINUED:

                    MILLIE
          Because he's unhappy.

Lindsay considers this. She nods her head, emphatically.

                    LINDSAY
          That's right. That's right, Millie.
          He's unhappy. And we're all
          unhappy. We're all unhappy. That's
          the thing about life. That's the
          horrible thing about life.

                    MILLIE
          I'm not unhappy.

                    LINDSAY
          Yes, you are. We all are.

                    MILLIE
          Well, not like you guys.

                    LINDSAY
          Why not?

                    MILLIE
          Because I know that God's taking
          care of me.

At first, Lindsay laughs, but then considers this very
seriously.

                    LINDSAY
          I don't believe in God.

                    MILLIE
          I know. That's why you're unhappy.
          That's why you're stoned.

                    LINDSAY
          But it's just - God doesn't make
          sense; it's not logical.

                    MILLIE
          Well, it may not be logical. But I
          have faith. I feel His presence and
          that's enough for me.

                    LINDSAY
          Once I dreamt I met Jesus. I was in
          the shower and He brought me some
          soap. Yellow soap.

                                        (CONTINUED)

CONTINUED: (2)

> MILLIE
> (excited)
> Maybe you had a vision. Maybe He
> came to you in your sleep.

Lindsay goes wide-eyed at the thought, but then shakes it
off.

> LINDSAY
> It was just a dream, Millie.

Lindsay has another profound thought.

> LINDSAY (CONT'D)
> Millie! Millie!

> MILLIE
> What?

> LINDSAY
> What if <u>this</u> is a dream? What if
> all of this is a dream?

Lindsay looks over at the Johnsons' dog sleeping.

> LINDSAY (CONT'D)
> (loud whisper)
> What if it's a dream and it isn't
> even our dream? What if it's that
> dog's dream? Maybe we're all just
> existing in his mind and all of a
> sudden he'll wake up to go drink
> out of the toilet and then we'll be
> gone. What would happen to us if
> that dog wakes up? It'll be over.

Millie stands up.

> MILLIE
> Life is not this dog's dream. We
> live in God's world.

Millie walks toward the dog.

> LINDSAY
> What are you doing?

> MILLIE
> I'm going to wake up that dog.

(CONTINUED)

CONTINUED: (3)

> LINDSAY
> Don't. Don't wake up the dog,
> Millie.

> MILLIE
> It'll be okay Lindsay.

> LINDSAY
> Don't do it. I'm serious. Please. I
> don't want you to do it.

> MILLIE
> Just have faith Lindsay. Have
> faith.

> LINDSAY
> No, no, no, no.

Millie picks up the dog by its paws and shakes it.

> MILLIE
> Arise doggy! Arise!

> LINDSAY
> Millie, no!

The dog wakes up.

ANGLE ON: Lindsay's eyes go wide with terror.

ANGLE ON: The dog starts licking Millie's face, happily.

> MILLIE
> Believe, Lindsay! Believe!

Lindsay starts to laugh.

> LINDSAY
> I hate you, Millie.

She walks over and pets the dog.

> MILLIE
> See, everything is all right.

The dog starts licking Lindsay's face. They both laugh
hysterically as the dog licks Lindsay and paws at her.

                                        CUT TO:

INT. BILL'S HOSPITAL ROOM - NIGHT

The DOCTOR leads Gloria and Jean into the hospital room. Sam and Neal trail behind.

> JEAN
> What's wrong? I--

Gloria looks over and her eyes go wide.

GLORIA'S POV: Bill is sitting up, drinking an orange juice. He looks groggy but okay.

> BILL
> Hi, Mom.

> GLORIA
> Billy!

She runs over and hugs Bill, causing him to spill orange juice on his lap.

> BILL
> Mom, you're making me spill.

She starts kissing his face. He squirms to get away. Jean looks happy. Sam and Neal look overjoyed. They run to the other side of the bed.

> SAM
> Bill, you're alive!

> NEAL
> I knew you'd make it!

> BILL
> Did I almost die?

> SAM
> Yeah.

> BILL
> Cool.

> DOCTOR
> Now, look, he's been through a lot
> and his body has a lot of
> recovering to do, so let's give him
> some quiet time to sleep and get
> stronger.

(CONTINUED)

CONTINUED:

                    JEAN
          That's a good idea. C'mon, Gloria.
          C'mon, boys.

                    GLORIA
          Yes, Billy, you rest up.

She gives him another big kiss. Bill squirms away.

                    BILL
          Mom, cut it out. I'm not going
          anywhere.

                    GLORIA
          Yes, you are. You're going straight
          to the White House.

She turns and heads out with Jean, excited. The doctor looks
at Sam and Neal.

                    NEAL
          Sir, could we just have one minute
          alone with our friend?

                    DOCTOR
          Okay, but make it quick.

The doctor and the nurse exit.

                    SAM
          Are you okay, Bill?

                    BILL
          Yeah. I can't get the smell of
          bacon out of my nose but that
          always happens after I pass out.

                    NEAL
          Bill, guess what? Vicki and Maureen
          showed up. And they were <u>crying</u>.

                    BILL
          Really? Because of me?

                    SAM
          Yeah. They were really worried
          about you.

                    BILL
          Oh, man. Send them in here.

                                        (CONTINUED)

CONTINUED: (2)

>   SAM
>   They're in the bathroom.
>
>   NEAL
>   But, Bill, I was thinking. Um... I
>   mean, ever since they thought you
>   were dying, well... they've kinda
>   been hanging all over us.
>
>   BILL
>   Wow...
>
>   NEAL
>   Yeah, and if they find out you're
>   okay, well, we won't have time to
>   close the deal. You know what I
>   mean?
>
>   BILL
>   No.
>
>   NEAL
>   I think that Sam and I could really
>   make some headway with them if you
>   could just, you know, keep dying
>   for a few more minutes.
>
>   BILL
>   Really?
>
>   NEAL
>   Yeah.

Bill thinks. Then...

>   BILL
>   Okay. But only if you promise to go
>   to the sci-fi fair with me.
>
>   SAM
>   Are you kidding? We were gonna do
>   that anyway.
>
>   BILL
>   Really?
>
>   NEAL
>   Of course.
>
>   BILL
>   Man, you guys are the best.

(CONTINUED)

CONTINUED: (3)

They all smile at each other. Sam and Neal pat Bill on the shoulders, happy to have him back.

CUT TO:

INT. NICK'S BASEMENT - NIGHT

Nick, Ken and Daniel are sitting on the couch.

> DANIEL
> (annoyed)
> I hate Mr. Rosso. I think I even
> hate him more than I hate
> Kowchevski. At least Kowchevski
> doesn't pretend he's not a jack-
> ass.

> KEN
> That guy Frank is probably some
> hippie actor friend of his.

> DANIEL
> No way. Nobody's that good an
> actor. That guy is fried out of his
> gourd.

> NICK
> What do people do when they're not
> stoned?

> KEN
> I don't know. Relate to one
> another.

> DANIEL
> I don't want to relate to anyone.

> NICK
> I want to relate to Lindsay. But
> she's so smart and straight. I
> don't know if it can ever work.

> DANIEL
> It certainly won't work if you're
> smoking weed.

> KEN
> She's too sweet and perfect for
> that.

CUT TO:

INT. JOHNSONS' HOUSE - NIGHT

Lindsay is sitting on the couch with the Johnsons' dog laying next to her, his head on her lap. Millie walks over with a large piece of Tupperware and a box of "Froot Loops."

> MILLIE
> Your Fruit of Loops, Madame.

She pours the cereal in the Tupperware and hands it to Lindsay.

> LINDSAY
> Thanks, Millie. You're the best.

She begins to eat.

> LINDSAY (CONT'D)
> (mouthful of Froot Loops)
> Oh, man, this is good. This is
> really hitting the spot. You know
> why this is so good? Because it was
> made by food scientists. You know
> what I hate, though? When you eat
> too many Loops and they tear up the
> roof of your mouth and then you
> drink some juice and it stings.
> That's the worst.

Lindsay sets down the bowl and picks up a potato chip sandwich. She bites into it. It CRUNCHES loudly. Millie gets up.

> LINDSAY (CONT'D)
> Barbecued potato chip sandwich.
> There's nothing better.

> MILLIE
> I'm gonna put on some music. Maybe
> that'll help get the monkey off
> your back.

> LINDSAY
> Millie. That's silly.

Millie gives her a look and opens the Johnson's console stereo. Lindsay starts to turn into a friendly drunk as Millie starts flipping through 8 track tapes.

(CONTINUED)

CONTINUED:

> LINDSAY (CONT'D)
> You're such a great friend. I don't
> know what I would have done without
> you. You really saved me.

Millie puts in a tape. A MAC DAVIS song comes on.

> LINDSAY
> This song is the best.

Millie sits next to Lindsay as Lindsay takes another loud
bite from her potato chip sandwich and listens to Mac Davis.

> LINDSAY
> God, we used to love Mac Davis.
> Remember when we used to watch his
> show?

> MILLIE
> Yeah. You used to wish you had a
> pillow stuffed with his hair.

> LINDSAY
> Just because it was so fluffy
> looking. God, I love Mac Davis.
>   (beat)
> You know who else I love, Millie?
> You. I love you. You're really my
> best friend. Why aren't we friends
> anymore?

> MILLIE
> I thought we were.

> LINDSAY
> We are, but...you know. We're not,
> really. And I don't know why. I
> mean, we're still the same people
> we were when we were five. But it's
> different now.

> MILLIE
> You're different now.

> LINDSAY
> You're right. But I'm not going to
> be different anymore. I'm going to
> be the same. And we'll be best
> friends.

(CONTINUED)

CONTINUED: (2)

> MILLIE
> You know Lindsay, I feel sorry for
> you.

> LINDSAY
> Why?

> MILLIE
> Because tomorrow, when you're not
> loaded, you're not gonna believe in
> God and you're not gonna want to be
> my friend.

> LINDSAY
> Millie, that is not true. I swear.

> MILLIE
> I hope not.

> LINDSAY
> I hope so, too.

CUT TO:

INT. HOSPITAL HALLWAY - DAY

Vicki and Maureen are sitting with Sam and Neal. Maureen has
her arm around Sam.

> VICKI
> You guys are so strong. If Maureen
> was sick I don't know what I'd do.

Vicki takes Neal's hand and holds it in hers. He almost
faints.

> MAUREEN
> What are the doctors saying now?

> SAM
> He's about the same.

> MAUREEN
> Oh, no.

> VICKI
> God, we should go yell at the
> doctors or something. You know,
> like they do on TV. It always makes
> them think to do something they
> hadn't thought of.

(CONTINUED)

CONTINUED:

Maureen sees two doctors walking down the hall.

                    VICKI
              (to the doctors; mean)
       Hey! You!

                    NEAL
       Uh, actually, Bill's doing a little
       better. The doctor told us things
       are looking up.

                    MAUREEN
              (relieved)
       I wish we could see him.

                    SAM
       Uh, no, he needs his rest. He's not
       out of the woods yet.

The girls stand and drink their pops. Sam and Neal exchange
looks. Sam makes a "do something" face at Neal.

                    NEAL
              (to both girls)
       So, when this is all over and
       Bill's back to normal, Sam and I
       were thinking maybe you two would
       like to go goofy golfing with us.

Sam and Neal stare at the girls nervously. The girls look at
each other.

                    MAUREEN
       Yeah, sure, that'd be fun.

                    SAM
       Really? Great.

                    VICKI
       Yeah. I'd love that.
              (to Maureen)
       Oh, and we should invite Sheila.
       She's always trying to get us to go
       goofy golfing with her.

                    NEAL
       Sure, bring her along. The more the
       merrier.

                    VICKI
       Yeah, and we should ask Jimmy and
       Rick.

                                  (CONTINUED)

CONTINUED: (2)

>   MAUREEN
> Oh, yeah, and Cindy and Todd, too.
> I bet we can get a whole bunch of
> people.
>> (to Sam and Neal)
> That's a great idea, you guys.
> We're gonna have so much fun.

Sam and Neal force smiles at them, then give each other a
"what were we expecting" look.

>   CUT TO:

INT. WEIR KITCHEN - NIGHT

Lindsay is now sober. She is doing homework on the kitchen
table. There is a knock at the back door.

>   LINDSAY
> Who is it?

>   NICK (O.S.)
>> (through the door)
> It's Nick.

Lindsay goes over to the door and opens it. Nick is standing
there.

>   NICK (CONT'D)
> Hey, I just wanted to tell you
> that, I've been thinking a lot
> about today.

>   LINDSAY
> Me, too.

>   NICK
> I think you're right. I gotta quit
> smoking.

>   LINDSAY
> Really?

>   NICK
> Yeah. I'm sorry I was such a jerk.
> I was just... high.

>   LINDSAY
> It's okay. I understand.

>   NICK
> Do ya?

>   (CONTINUED)

CONTINUED:

>   LINDSAY
>   Uh-huh. You're a great guy, Nick.
>   And when you're stoned that guy
>   disappears.

>   NICK
>   I know, I know. Where does he go?

>   LINDSAY
>   I don't know, but I miss him.

They share a nice moment. Then...

>   NICK
>   Hey, can I get that pot back from
>   you?

>   LINDSAY
>   What?

>   NICK
>   No, no, it's not what you think. I
>   want to take it back to Mark and
>   get my money back.

>   LINDSAY
>   I don't have it. I tossed it out
>   the window when my dad walked in my
>   room.

>   NICK
>   Oh.

>   LINDSAY
>   We can go look for it, but it
>   probably went all over the place.

>   NICK
>   That's all right. I probably
>   couldn't be trusted with it anyway.
>   Well, I better get going.

>   LINDSAY
>   Nick?

She takes his arm and pulls him in for a small but meaningful
kiss. He looks surprised, then very pleased.

>   NICK
>   I'll see you this weekend.

>   (CONTINUED)

CONTINUED: (2)

                    LINDSAY
          Yeah, I'll see you.

Nick takes off, looking happy. Lindsay closes the door,
looking happy too.

                                        CUT TO:

INT. HOSPITAL HALLWAY - DAY

Alan walks up to Gloria and Jean.

                    ALAN
          Mrs. Haverchuck? Is Bill okay?

                    GLORIA
          Yes he is, thank God.

Alan looks very relieved. Ben comes up to Gloria.

                    BEN
          I can't tell you how sorry I am
          about all this. If there's anything
          we can do to help, please let us
          know.

                    GLORIA
          I think your son could apologize to
          Bill now.

                    BEN
          Consider it done.

Ben grabs Alan by the arm and drags him over to Bill's room.

                    ALAN
          Ow, Dad, I was gonna do it anyway.

                    BEN
          Yeah, well, now you can. Get in
          there.

Ben pushes Alan through the door.

                                        CUT TO:

INT. BILL'S HOSPITAL ROOM - CONTINUOUS

Alan flies into the room, startling Bill.

                    ALAN
          Hey, Haverchuck.

                                    (CONTINUED)

CONTINUED:

> BILL
> Oh, hi, Alan.

> ALAN
> See, I knew you wouldn't die. I
> can't believe you'd be such a wuss
> that you'd die from one peanut.

> BILL
> Are you glad I didn't die?

> ALAN
> Yeah, I am for my sake. The last
> thing I want is to end up in juvie
> for killing you.

Bill just gives Alan a goofy smile.

> ALAN (CONT'D)
> What are you looking at, dork?

> BILL
> I heard you. You care about me. I
> heard everything you said.

> ALAN
> I don't care about you.

> BILL
> Yes, you do. You think I'm cool.

> ALAN
> How'd you like me to pound you?

> BILL
> How'd you like to go to the sci-fi
> fair with me, Sam, Neal and Gordon
> this weekend?

This stops Alan. He looks surprised, then quickly regroups.

> ALAN
> I'm not gonna hang out with you
> losers.

> BILL
> Why not? You know you want to.

> ALAN
> No, I don't.

(CONTINUED)

CONTINUED: (2)

> BILL
> Yes, you do.
> (sincere)
> C'mon, it's okay. We won't tell
> anybody. And it'll be fun. George
> Takei's gonna be there and
> everything.

Alan studies Bill, trying to see if he's goofing on him. Bill
looks very sincere.

> ALAN
> I don't know. It might be kind of
> weird.

> BILL
> No, it wouldn't. It'd be cool. And
> if you want, we can shoot off some
> rockets when we get back.

Alan just gives him a skeptical look. Bill shrugs.

> BILL (CONT'D)
> We're leaving Gordon's house at ten
> o'clock Saturday morning. If you
> want to come with us, just show up.

Alan stares a beat, then turns to go. He stops at the door.
Doesn't look back.

> ALAN
> Hey, Haverdork.

> BILL
> What?

> ALAN
> (staring at the door)
> ...I'm sorry.

> BILL
> It's okay, just don't do it again.
> I could die.

> ALAN
> I know.

And with that, Alan exits.

CUT TO:

EXT. WEIR HOUSE - NIGHT

We see a figure looking through the ground around the bushes outside of Lindsay's window.

We move closer and see that it is Nick, holding a flashlight, carefully picking up hunks of pot and putting them in a baggie.

                                                    CUT TO:

INT. BILL'S HOSPITAL ROOM - NIGHT

Bill is dozing. His eyes flutter and he wakes up. He looks around groggily, then looks down at his hand. Sees something. His eyes go wide.

BILL'S POV: Ms. Foote is sitting next to him, holding his hand and stroking it.

                    MS. FOOTE
          Are you okay, Bill?

                    BILL
          I am now.

Bill gives her a huge smile.

                                                    CUT TO:

EXT. GORDON CRISP'S HOUSE - DAY

Sam, Neal and Bill are gathered out on the driveway. Sam and Neal are dressed in 'Star Wars' costumes. Bill is dressed like 'Dr. Who.'

                    NEAL
          When'd you get a Dr. Who outfit?

                    BILL
          My mom bought it for me for not
          dying. I really cleaned up this
          time.

                    SAM
          Really? Man, I wish I had
          allergies. I really want a C3PO
          mask.

Just then, Gordon Crisp walks up.

                                                (CONTINUED)

CONTINUED:

>   GORDON
>   Hey, guys.

>   SAM
>   Gordon, where's your make-up?

>   GORDON
>   I told you, my mom does it in the
>   parking lot before I enter. It
>   stays fresher that way. She'll be
>   out in a minute.

ANGLE ON: ALAN, who is watching the geeks from a few houses away. He is sitting on his bike.

ALAN'S POV: The geeks dressed in their Star Wars clothes are laughing and goofing around.

Alan looks like he wants to go over. Then...

>   ALAN
>   Oh, man. I just can't do it.

Alan gives them a semi-sad, semi-relieved look and heads off on his bike.

>   FADE OUT.

<u>THE END</u>

FREAKS AND GEEKS

"DEAD DOGS AND GYM TEACHERS"

Episode #14

Written by Judd Apatow and Bob Nickman

Directed by Judd Apatow

The biggest event in my childhood was my parents' divorce. They separated when I was in seventh grade, got back together shortly afterward, then broke up for good when I was headed into ninth grade—right when puberty was hitting. I was a mess. They fought for years afterwards and didn't settle all of their legal issues till I was in college. It was ugly and unnecessarily so.

So I was determined to share this pain with you, the viewing audience. I had two ideas for how we could explore broken homes on the show. I wanted Bill's former stripper mom to begin dating his macho gym teacher, and I wanted Neal's parents to go through a very nasty, protracted divorce. This way, we could explore how weird it is when your parents begin dating, while also showing what it is like when you only see one of your parents on Sunday and that day is usually interrupted by a trip to a Broadway show.

Tom Wilson is one of my favorite actors. I am very proud of his work on this episode portraying Mr. Fredricks, the gym teacher. He is a very complex character who lives for me to this day. Martin Starr's work is perfect. He is funny and devastating as he attempts to face his mom's sexuality and a future with a new father figure.

My favorite scene is the one in which Bill comes home after school and makes a grilled cheese sandwich, then eats it with a piece of chocolate cake and milk while watching *The Dinah Shore Show*. He laughs at Garry Shandling performing stand up as The Who performs "I'm One."

That is how I spent most of my afternoons during junior high school and high school. It would be terribly sad if watching all of those hours of television didn't result in me being able to work as a writer as an adult. Jake Kasdan said it was the most truthful thing I had ever done, and he is correct. It is very sad, but it also shows how television and comedy can be your friend when you have nobody else to help you get through a difficult time. Sometimes I try to figure out why I was so drawn to comedy as a little boy. I think I appreciated the fact that there were people out there who said that life wasn't fair, that the system is bullshit. I needed to know I wasn't alone in my misery. Comedians, the Marx Brothers, the cast of

Saturday Night Live, they became my friends who would tell me that the world is crazy but it's alright, you can survive and you can have fun in spite of it. I hope my work has done that for other people.

—Judd Apatow

FREAKS AND GEEKS

"DEAD DOGS AND GYM TEACHERS"

CAST LIST

LINDSAY WEIR
SAM WEIR
HAROLD WEIR
JEAN WEIR
DANIEL DESARIO
NICK ANDOPOLIS
BILL HAVERCHUCK
NEAL SCHWEIBER
KEN MILLER
KIM KELLY
MILLIE KENTNER
ALAN WHITE
COACH FREDRICKS
MARK
GORDON CRISP
GLORIA HAVERCHUCK
MRS. KENTNER
MIKE
ERNIE

FREAKS AND GEEKS

"DEAD DOGS AND GYM TEACHERS"

SET LIST

INTERIORS:

MCKINLEY HIGH SCHOOL
    /HALLWAY
    /CAFETERIA
    /GYM
    /CLASSROOM
    /BAND ROOM
WEIR HOUSE
    /LIVING ROOM
    /KITCHEN
    /LINDSAY'S BEDROOM
NICK'S HOUSE
    /BASEMENT
BILL'S HOUSE
    /KITCHEN
    /LIVING ROOM
    /BILL'S BEDROOM
MR. FREDRICKS' CAR
KIM'S CAR
MAGIC BUS
GO-CART TRACK
    /BATHROOM

EXTERIORS:

DEAD END STREET
GO-CART TRACK
    /ENTRANCE
WOODED YARD

FADE IN:

INT. GYM - DAY

The geeks, BILL, NEAL and SAM are in gym class. Also in attendance are GORDON, ALAN, ERNIE and the jock, MIKE. Everyone is playing full court basketball except a small group of kids, including Sam and Gordon.

The students run down the court.

                    FREDRICKS
          Hustle it up, girls!

Ernie hits a jump shot. Everyone runs to the other side of the court, except Bill who looks exhausted. The ball is thrown to Neal who immediately passes it to Alan who puts in an effortless lay up.

Mike grabs the ball and sees that his teammate Bill is already on the other side of the court.

                    MIKE
          Bill!

Bill's eyes widen in panic. The ball is thrown all the way across the court to him. He catches it, then looks at the basket. He is twenty feet away. Everyone starts running toward him.

                    NEAL
          Bill, run! Put it in!

                    SAM
          Oh, no.

                    GORDON
          This won't be pretty.
              (to Bill)
          Pass it!

Bill runs to the basket. He is still wide open, but everyone is moments away from reaching him. He reaches the basket, and attempts a lay up while running full speed. He doesn't get the ball off fast enough so he winds up throwing it way too hard at the backboard as he passes below it. The ball just bounces off really hard, never coming close to the net.

                    MIKE
          Nice shot.

                                        (CONTINUED)

CONTINUED:

> ERNIE
> I told you you shouldn't have
> passed to him.

> FREDRICKS
> Hey, hey, hey!

Fredricks blows his whistle, then runs onto the court. The
geeks look scared.

> FREDRICKS (CONT'D)
> Shut your mouths! Haverchuck gave
> it his best shot. He just needs to
> practice.

> ALAN
> You've got that right.

> MIKE
> Okay, let's play already.

> FREDRICKS
> Hold up.

He walks to Bill, who looks scared - like he's about to be
hit.

> FREDRICKS (CONT'D)
> How is Bill going to improve if we
> don't take a moment and show him
> how to do it correctly?

Everyone moans.

> BILL
> Mr. Fredricks, you don't have to.

> FREDRICKS
> It's my job.
> (to a kid)
> Throw me the ball.
> (to Bill)
> Now Bill, when you shoot a lay-up
> it's important to remember that you
> dribble, then you get two free
> steps without dribbling, then you
> release with your right hand,
> aiming at the top right corner of
> the square on the backboard. Okay,
> try it.

(CONTINUED)

CONTINUED: (2)

                    BILL
        Now?

                    FREDRICKS
        Yes, now.

Bill sighs. Sam and Neal squirm. Bill dribbles the ball, then
basically does the same thing. Everyone laughs.

                    FREDRICKS (CONT'D)
        That was...better, I guess. Just
        make sure you jump up toward the
        hoop. Okay, try again.

                    ALAN
        Oh my God, we're going to be here
        all day.

                    FREDRICKS
        Hey, White, you're no Dr. J either.
        Go on, Bill.

Bill takes a deep breath, concentrates, then dribbles the
ball and puts it up and in the hoop. Bill looks more relieved
than happy.

                    SAM
        Thank God.

Fredricks walks up to him. He puts his hand on his shoulder.

                    FREDRICKS
            (gently)
        See, Bill. You can do it. You can
        do anything. You just need to learn
        how. So, whenever you have trouble
        with something in class, just give
        me a holler and I'll show you how
        to do it. All right, buddy?

                    BILL
        Uh... yeah.

Fredricks walks away. Sam and Neal walk over to Bill.

                    SAM
        What was that about?

                    BILL
            (nervous)
        I don't know.

(CONTINUED)

CONTINUED: (3)

                    NEAL
          I think Mr. Fredricks is in love
          with you.

                                        CUT TO:

          OPENING TITLE SEQUENCE

                ACT ONE

FADE IN:

INT. WEIR KITCHEN - DAY

The Weirs are having breakfast. Harold is dressed for work.
He is looking at the album cover for The Who's "Who Are You?"

                    HAROLD
          Sure, Lindsay, you can go to see
          The Who. And on the way, we can
          stop by the undertaker's and fit
          you for your coffin.

                    LINDSAY
          Dad, don't make a big deal out of
          this. It would be so much fun.

                    HAROLD
          Of course it would be fun. What's
          not fun about sitting in a cloud of
          marijuana smoke for three hours
          watching some maniac wag his bloody
          tongue?

                    LINDSAY
          Dad, that's not The Who, that's
          Kiss.

                    SAM
          Yeah, The Who smash their guitars.

                    LINDSAY
          They don't do that anymore. Mom,
          they wrote a rock OPERA.

                    JEAN
              (to Harold)
          I don't know what the big deal is.
          She's been to concerts before. We
          took her to see Rich Little last
          summer.

                                        (CONTINUED)

CONTINUED:

                    SAM
               (as Carson)
          May an overfed yak go poo-poo on
          your Buick.

Harold laughs.

                    LINDSAY
          Rich Little isn't a concert.

                    HAROLD
          Oh yeah? Tell that to the two
          thousand people who were laughing
          their butts off.

                    JEAN
          I hear they're very loud.

                    SAM
          They're in the Guinness Book of
          Records as the loudest band on
          Earth.

                    LINDSAY
          Sam.

                    SAM
          Hey, if I'm not allowed to see
          "Kentucky Fried Movie" ever, then
          why should you be able to see The
          Who?

                    LINDSAY
          Dad, how am I going to become an
          adult if you never treat me like
          one?

                    HAROLD
          Fine. I'll tell you what. Let me
          listen to one of their records. If
          there's nothing objectionable on
          it, I'll let you go.

                    LINDSAY
          Thanks, Dad. I'm sure it's fine.

                    HAROLD
          Don't get ahead of yourself. I'll
          be listening to it backwards, too.

                                        CUT TO:

INT. SCHOOL HALLWAY - DAY

Sam, Neal and Bill are talking as they walk to Sam's locker.

>   NEAL
> We have to go to this new go-cart
> track. Go-Cart City. I hear the
> cars go like fifty miles an hour.

>   BILL
> My mom won't let me go go-cart
> riding. She says those places are
> death traps.

>   NEAL
> I want to get a dirt bike. My
> neighbor, Gary Frank, has one.

>   SAM
> My dad always says you can get in
> as many car accidents as you want,
> but one motorcycle accident and
> you're dead.

>   NEAL
> It's a dirt bike. You can't get in
> an accident.

>   BILL
> Oh yeah? These kids used to ride
> dirt bikes on Slatzky's farm and
> Slatzky didn't like everyone riding
> there so he put up a wire and this
> one kid got his head cut off.

>   SAM
> I heard that story. His head was
> talking for a minute after it got
> separated from his body.

>   BILL
> Could you imagine that? Getting
> your head chopped off and watching
> your body still driving across a
> field.

>   NEAL
> What _don't_ you guys believe?

>   CUT TO:

INT. CAFETERIA - DAY

Nick, Ken and Daniel are having lunch. Nick is holding a
guitar and an instructional guitar book.

> NICK
> I'm telling you, man. I don't mean
> to degrade Led Zeppelin, but The
> Who are genius. I saw them two
> weeks ago in Indianapolis. I had a
> religious experience.

> KEN
> I can't wait till they hit Detroit.
> I hope my ears bleed.

> DANIEL
> You know what? My cousin Lloyd has
> that old school bus he got at the
> city auction. We should all drive
> together...on our "Magic Bus."

> KEN
> You mean our "Magic <u>School</u> Bus."

> DANIEL
> Shut up.

> NICK
> I hope Lindsay gets to go. I wanna
> write her a song and play it for
> her on my guitar.

> DANIEL
> Yeah, that's a good idea.

> KEN
> You don't even play guitar.

> NICK
> Yes, I do. I'm like Townshend, self-
> taught. I'm the master. Check out
> this riff.

Nick plays "Michael Row Your Boat Ashore" from his guitar
book. They all laugh as Mr. Kowchevski walks up.

> KEN
> Yeah, you rock.

(CONTINUED)

CONTINUED:

> MR. KOWCHEVSKI
> Hey Coco, this isn't the cafeteria
> from "Fame." Keep it down.

CUT TO:

INT. CAFETERIA - DAY

Lindsay and Kim are walking toward the lunch line.

> KIM
> He tape recorded them fooling
> around and then he played it to
> everyone in the lobby.

> VOICE (O.S.)
> Is that Lindsay Weir?!

Lindsay turns to see Mrs. Kentner, Millie's mom, a sweet, conservative woman, walking with Millie and carrying full lunch trays.

> LINDSAY
> Oh, hi Mrs. Kentner. Hi Millie.

> MRS. KENTNER
> I haven't seen you in ages. Did
> Millie take you for all your lunch
> money playing Uno again?

She laughs at her joke. Lindsay forces a chuckle, too.

> KIM
> (mocking)
> You should give it another go,
> Lindsay. God knows you've been
> practicing your Uno.

Millie gives Kim a look. She knows she's mocking her mother.

> MRS. KENTNER
> Hello, I'm Marianne Kentner.
> Millie's mother.

> KIM
> Hi. I'm Linda. Linda Lovelace.

> MRS. KENTNER
> Oh, what a pretty name. It's nice
> to meet you, Linda.

Lindsay quickly changes the subject.

(CONTINUED)

CONTINUED:

> LINDSAY
> So, what brings you to McKinley
> today?

> MILLIE
> We're having lunch.

> KIM
> Together? At school?

> MRS. KENTNER
> Our schedules are so busy now, it
> seems the only time we see each
> other is five minutes in the
> morning and Sunday at church. And
> you can't talk there.

> KIM
> (to Millie, quietly)
> God forbid.

> MILLIE
> Come on, Mom. Let's go. My macaroni
> and cheese is getting cold.

> MRS. KENTNER
> Okay. Nice meeting you, Grace. Bye,
> Lindser.

They exit. Kim calls after them.

> KIM
> Maybe Lindser and I'll stop by for
> some doubles at Uno.

> MRS. KENTNER
> (perky)
> We'll be ready for you.

> CUT TO:

INT. BILL'S HOUSE - DAY

Bill stands alone in the kitchen making a grilled cheese
sandwich. He puts it on a plate, grabs a cup of milk and a
box of Entemann's chocolate cake and heads over to the couch.

He turns the TV on and sits down. He watches "The Dinah Shore
Show." As Dinah interviews Garry Shandling, Bill eats his
grilled cheese. Between bites he takes bites of the chocolate
cake. Then he has a sip of milk.

(CONTINUED)

CONTINUED:

It is clearly a daily ritual. He watches the TV impassively.
He never smiles or reacts. Just zones out.

The door opens. It is Bill's mother GLORIA.

> GLORIA
> Hey, little man.

> BILL
> (not looking up)
> Hi, Mom. What's up?

She talks as she puts down some groceries and her jacket.

> GLORIA
> It was dead at lunch today. I made
> eighteen bucks in tips. How's
> anybody supposed to live on that?

> BILL
> (scared)
> Are you gonna start dancing again?

> GLORIA
> No way!

> BILL
> Good.

> GLORIA
> Besides, they don't want an old
> broad like me anymore.

She walks over to Bill.

> GLORIA (CONT'D)
> Oh, Billy, we have a guest coming
> over for dinner tonight.

> BILL
> Dad?

> GLORIA
> No. A new friend.

> BILL
> Another new friend?

> GLORIA
> Actually, it's someone special.

Bill looks grossed out.

(CONTINUED)

CONTINUED: (2)

>   BILL
> Who's so special?

>   GLORIA
> It's someone you know.

>   BILL
> Not Neal's dad.

>   GLORIA
> Vic Schweiber? Uch. You gotta be
> kidding. It's someone I met at your
> school. Remember when I had to come
> in for that parent teacher
> conference because you were having
> problems in gym.

>   BILL
> Yeah.

>   GLORIA
> Well, I've been seeing... Mr.
> Fredricks.

>   BILL
> My gym teacher?

>   GLORIA
> Physical Education teacher.

>   BILL
> Oh, no. You can't.

>   GLORIA
> He's a very nice man.

>   BILL
> No, he's not. He's a jerk. He's a
> dumb jock.

>   GLORIA
> He is not. You just don't know him
> that well.

>   BILL
> I know him better than you.

>   GLORIA
> I doubt that. We've been seeing
> each other for a little while.

(CONTINUED)

CONTINUED: (3)

                        BILL
          What? Why didn't you tell me
          before?

                        GLORIA
          I didn't want to upset you. I
          wanted to make sure it was serious
          first.

                        BILL
          It's serious?

                        GLORIA
              (smile)
          I think so.

                        BILL
          Oh, no.

                        GLORIA
          Are you upset?

                        BILL
          Yes! You can't do this. The other
          kids will kill me. You'll make my
          life worse than it already is.

                        GLORIA
          Bill, don't say that.

                        BILL
          You have to stop seeing him.

SFX: THE DOORBELL

                        BILL (CONT'D)
          Who's that?

                        GLORIA
          It's him. I invited him over for
          dinner.

                        BILL
          Well un-invite him.

                        GLORIA
          It won't be so bad. You'll see.

She walks to the door.

                        GLORIA (CONT'D)
          Be nice.

(CONTINUED)

CONTINUED: (4)

She opens the door. It is Mr. Fredricks.

>   GLORIA (CONT'D)
>   Hi, Ben.

She hugs and kisses him on the cheek. Bill's eyes widen in
shock.

>   MR. FREDRICKS
>   Hi, Gloria. You look great.

>   GLORIA
>   Thanks. I think you know my son,
>   Bill.

He looks over and sees Bill.

>   MR. FREDRICKS
>   You mean the lay-up machine. Sure
>   do. How's it going big guy?

Bill's mouth opens but no sound comes out.

>   CUT TO:

INT. KIM'S CAR - NIGHT

Kim and Lindsay are in Kim's car getting ready to back out of
Lindsay's driveway. Kim is behind the wheel. Lindsay is in
the passenger seat. The STEREO is cranking.

>   KIM
>   Howie's only gonna be at the store
>   till five.

>   LINDSAY
>   How much did the tickets cost?

>   KIM
>   Forty apiece. But The Who never
>   tour. I heard this might be their
>   last tour ever.

>   LINDSAY
>   I hear Fleetwood Mac is great in
>   concert.

>   KIM
>   I heard Stevie Nicks is a witch.

>   LINDSAY
>   What do you mean?

>   (CONTINUED)

CONTINUED:

>   KIM
>   She does witch stuff. She casts
>   spells on people. She cast a love
>   spell on Lindsay Buckingham.
>
>   LINDSAY
>   I like all her shawls.
>
>   KIM
>   Maybe I should be a witch. Cut off
>   a lock of Daniel's hair and stick
>   it to a voodoo doll. Every time he
>   got out of line, I'd jam him with a
>   pin.
>
>   LINDSAY
>   I don't know. Voodoo is pretty
>   serious.
>
>   KIM
>   Well, I'm serious. I think it's
>   about time I had some supernatural
>   powers...

Suddenly, there is a LOUD THUD. Kim and Lindsay both are
jostled as the car drives over something.

>   KIM (CONT'D)
>   What the hell?!
>
>   LINDSAY
>   What was that?
>
>   KIM
>   Aw, crap. My car's falling apart
>   again.
>
>   LINDSAY
>   I think you hit something.
>
>   KIM
>   Nah, must be my shocks are out of
>   line or something.
>
>   LINDSAY
>   Maybe it was a squirrel. We should
>   go back and see.
>
>   KIM
>   (after a beat)
>   Nah, we can't be late.
>   (MORE)

(CONTINUED)

CONTINUED: (2)

                KIM (CONT'D)
          The world will survive with one
          less squirrel.

Kim's eyes are peeled to the road. Lindsay looks concerned.

                                CUT TO:

INT. BILL'S KITCHEN - NIGHT

Bill, Gloria and Mr. Fredricks sit around the table eating
dinner. Bill looks miserable. Mr. Fredricks is filled with
hopeful, positive energy.

                MR. FREDRICKS
          The soup was cold. I'd be mad, too.

                GLORIA
            (laughing)
          Hey, I serve it, I don't cook it.

They notice Bill, not taking part in their conversation.

                MR. FREDRICKS
          Bill, did you see "Rocky Two?" I
          thought it was even better than the
          first one. That Carl Weathers is
          ripped.

                BILL
          No.

                GLORIA
          Bill just saw a movie. What movie
          was it?

                BILL
          "Stripes."

                MR. FREDRICKS
          Oh, I saw that.

                GLORIA
          Did you like it?

                MR. FREDRICKS
          Nah. That Bill Murray's a wise ass.

Bill can't believe what he's hearing.

                MR. FREDRICKS (CONT'D)
          Someone needs to slap some respect
          into that guy.

(CONTINUED)

CONTINUED:

Bill puts down his fork.

> BILL
> Bill Murray is the funniest man in
> the world.

Mr. Fredricks realizes he has made a mistake. He attempts to
recover.

> MR. FREDRICKS
> Well, I guess comedians are
> supposed to be wise asses.
> (getting nervous)
> Gloria, you should have seen Bill
> in gym class today. I'm telling
> you, Bill, if you applied yourself,
> you could be playing for the school
> basketball team next year. You've
> definitely got the height for it.

Bill is silent.

> GLORIA
> Maybe Ben could give you some
> private lessons.

> BILL
> Who's Ben?

> MR. FREDRICKS
> (laughs)
> I am.

Bill doesn't laugh.

> BILL
> Oh.

CUT TO:

INT. SCHOOL HALLWAY - DAY

Kim and Lindsay walk down the hall together.

> KIM
> I told her - if she's not gonna
> give me any money for lunch, at
> least put a Ding Dong in the pantry
> so I don't starve to death.

They pass by Millie, who is at her locker. She has obviously
been crying. Lindsay stops.

(CONTINUED)

CONTINUED:

> LINDSAY
> Millie? What's wrong?

> MILLIE
> (in tears)
> Goliath's dead.

> LINDSAY
> Oh my god. Millie.

> KIM
> Who's Goliath?

> LINDSAY
> Goliath's her dog. What happened?

> MILLIE
> Some maniac hit him with their car
> last night.

Millie can't finish her sentence - she's too distraught.

> LINDSAY
> A car hit him?
> (Millie nods)
> That's horrible. I'm so sorry,
> Millie.

> MILLIE
> He must have gotten out.

REACTION - On Kim, her mouth drops open. She is reeling - she knows that she is the culprit.

> MILLIE (CONT'D)
> The worst part is - they didn't
> even stop. He must have been in the
> street for hours. Who would do
> that?

Millie wipes her tears. The bell rings.

> MILLIE (CONT'D)
> I'm gonna be late for class. See ya
> later.

> LINDSAY
> Yeah, see ya' later, Millie.

Millie nods, sniffling. She walks away. Kim and Lindsay lock eyes, full of guilt.

(CONTINUED)

CONTINUED: (2)

> KIM
> Oh, my god, we killed Millie's dog.

And off their mortified looks, we...

> FADE OUT.

<u>END OF ACT ONE</u>

<u>ACT TWO</u>

FADE IN:

INT. SCHOOL HALLWAY - DAY

Bill, Neal and Sam are walking down the hallway.

> SAM
> "MASH" is not funny.

> NEAL
> What? Klinger isn't funny?

> SAM
> You <u>would</u> like Klinger.

Mr. Fredricks comes walking toward them.

> MR. FREDRICKS
> Hey, Billy. I'm still stuffed from
> your mom's pot roast. I couldn't
> even eat breakfast this morning.
> But it was goo-ood.

Bill stares at him. Shocked and embarrassed.

> MR. FREDRICKS (CONT'D)
> Well, I'll see ya' in gym class big
> guy.

He pats Bill on the shoulder, then heads off.

> SAM
> What the hell was that?

> BILL
> What?

> NEAL
> He ate your mom's pot roast?

(CONTINUED)

CONTINUED:

> BILL
> I don't want to talk about it.

> SAM
> You have to talk about it.

> BILL
> Okay, I'll tell you, but you can't
> say a word.

> NEAL
> What? Tell us.

> BILL
> My mom is dating Mr. Fredricks.

Sam and Neal are too shocked to speak.

> BILL (CONT'D)
> Well, say something.

> NEAL
> I heard Radar O'Reilly has almost
> no fingers.

> SAM
> Yeah, that's why he's always
> carrying a clipboard.

> CUT TO:

INT. CAFETERIA - DAY

Kim and Lindsay cross and join Daniel and Ken at a table.

> KIM
> You guys, I killed Millie's dog.

> KEN
> With your bare hands?

> KIM
> No, I ran over it.

> DANIEL
> (disturbed)
> You are really sick.

> KIM
> I didn't do it on purpose, doofus.

> (CONTINUED)

CONTINUED:

                    LINDSAY
Yeah, it was an accident.

                    DANIEL
Your first roadkill. I'm proud of
you, babe.

                    KEN
I always say - girl plus car equals
dead animal.

                    LINDSAY
We have to tell Millie.

                    KIM
Why? It's not gonna bring her dog
back. It'll just upset her.

                    KEN
It's not like you ran over a human
being. It's just a dog.

                    KIM
That's even worse. I love dogs.

                    KEN
Why? Dogs suck. They're lazy and
dumb. They don't even really like
people. They're just kissing our
asses so we'll feed them.

Kim spots...

At another table, Millie sits alone, eating and looking glum.

Kim nudges Lindsay - pointing out Millie.

                    KIM
Lindsay. Look.

                    LINDSAY
Oh, god. Poor Millie.

                    KIM
She's just sitting there by
herself. We should invite her to
sit with us.

                    LINDSAY
Really?

(CONTINUED)

CONTINUED: (2)

> KIM
> I'm gonna bring her over here. But
> she doesn't know it was me who
> killed her dog. So don't say
> anything. I mean it.

> KEN
> She's killed once. She'll do it
> again.

The Freaks watch, surprised as Kim gets up and walks over to
Millie's table. Kim taps Millie on her shoulder.

> KIM
> Hey.

> MILLIE
> What?

> KIM
> You wanna come over and sit with
> us?

> MILLIE
> That's okay. I'm not feeling very
> social.

> KIM
> (sweet)
> Come on. You shouldn't be by
> yourself right now. Seriously.

Kim picks up Millie's tray. Millie has no choice but to
follow. Kim and Millie sit at the Freaks table. Millie looks
uncomfortable. The Freaks acknowledge her.

> LINDSAY
> Hey, Millie. How you holding up?

> MILLIE
> Terrible.

Ken breaks the awkward silence.

> KEN
> I'm hungry. I could go for a corn
> dog about now. Or maybe a chili
> dog. Oooh, devil dog.

Kim glares at Ken.

(CONTINUED)

CONTINUED: (3)

>   DANIEL
>   So some jerk drove over your dog,
>   huh?
>
>   MILLIE
>   Yeah.
>
>   DANIEL
>   That sucks. If someone did that to
>   my pet, I'd kill the guy.
>   (with a glance toward Kim)
>   Or girl.
>
>   MILLIE
>   I don't want to hold hatred in my
>   heart. The Bible says "Blessed are
>   the peacemakers."
>
>   DANIEL
>   But doesn't the Bible also say "an
>   eye for an eye?" I'd like to find
>   that guy and smoosh him, like he
>   smooshed your dog.
>
>   KIM
>   The guy probably doesn't know he
>   hit your dog. If he did, I'm sure
>   he'd feel really bad.
>
>   MILLIE
>   (nods)
>   It's just sad. Goliath was too
>   young to die.
>
>   DANIEL
>   You know, Millie, sometimes it's
>   good to get out your anger.

Daniel points to the BAKED POTATO on her tray.

>   DANIEL (CONT'D)
>   There's the guy that drove over
>   your dog.

Millie stares at the potato.

>   DANIEL (CONT'D)
>   Now hit him. Give him what he
>   deserves.

Millie lightly slaps the potato.

(CONTINUED)

CONTINUED: (4)

> DANIEL (CONT'D)
> Harder.

> LINDSAY
> Daniel...

> DANIEL
> He's a dog-killer, Millie. You're
> gonna let him get away with that?

Millie stabs the potato with her fork. The Freaks are
stunned, even Daniel. Millie breaks into a grin, then
giggles.

> KEN
> I think somebody feels better.

> CUT TO:

INT. GYM - DAY

Sam, Neal and Bill are the first ones in gym class. As they
speak, their classmates arrive.

> SAM
> How come you didn't tell us?

> BILL
> I just found out yesterday. He had
> dinner with us. It was really
> weird.

> NEAL
> At your <u>house</u>?

> BILL
> Yeah.

> SAM
> Well, what are you gonna do?

> BILL
> What can I do? My dad hasn't even
> called in three months. My mom's...
> lonely.

That's a little heavy for Neal and Sam.

> NEAL
> Tell your mom to dump him. He's a
> gym teacher.
> (MORE)

(CONTINUED)

CONTINUED:

                    NEAL (CONT'D)
          Even if he wasn't the biggest jerk
          on Earth, he has a terrible job.
          There's no upward mobility. It's
          not like he can become a CEO of the
          school.

                    BILL
          But she really likes him. And he
          doesn't act the same with her as he
          does with us. He's all sweet and
          phony.

                    SAM
          Does anyone else know?

                    BILL
          No. And you better not tell anyone.

                    NEAL
          You think they're gonna get
          married?

                    BILL
          No. She usually only dates guys
          for a few weeks.

                    SAM
          I'm sure this will be over before
          you know it.

                    BILL
          I hope so.

                                        CUT TO:

INT. CLASSROOM - DAY

Millie is sitting in class. Kim takes a seat next to her as
other students file in. Millie looks at Kim, unsure.

                    KIM
          How's it going?

                    MILLIE
          Okay. You?

                    KIM
          I don't know. Mr. Perlick is gonna
          kill me. I didn't do any of the
          assignment.

                    MILLIE
          Me, either.

                                        (CONTINUED)

CONTINUED:

                    KIM
        You're kidding me?

                    MILLIE
        I was up all night crying.

Kim stares at her a beat.

                    KIM
        I know how you feel. I had a dog
        and it got sick so my mother
        MURDERED it.

                    MILLIE
        That's cruel.

                    KIM
        I hate my mother.

                    MILLIE
        What was your dog's name?

                    KIM
        Bobo. He was like a member of the
        family. He was so smart. He would
        sit and watch TV with me. He loved
        TV.

                    MILLIE
        So, how'd he die?

                    KIM
        Well, he was epileptic. All of a
        sudden he would froth at the mouth
        and his little legs would freeze up
        and he'd start shaking and then
        he'd poop and he'd get his little
        paws in the poop and he'd smear it
        all around...it wasn't his fault.

                    MILLIE
              (sympathetic)
        Aw.

                    KIM
        I didn't mind, but my parents
        couldn't take it. They didn't even
        tell me they were gonna put him to
        sleep. One day he was just gone.

Millie looks at Kim sympathetically.

                                        (CONTINUED)

CONTINUED: (2)

> MILLIE
> I'm putting Goliath to rest under
> his favorite tree. You wanna come?

Kim nods. They share a moment.

CUT TO:

INT. GYM - DAY

The class is gathered. Sam and Neal stand next to each other.
Strangely, Bill stands off to the side, alone. Mr. Fredricks
walks to the group.

> NEAL
> (quietly to Sam)
> Here comes Bill's future dad.

> SAM
> Neal, we said we wouldn't make
> jokes.

> NEAL
> We can make jokes to each other.
> Just not to Bill.
> (beat)
> I can kinda see why Mr. Fredricks
> is going out with her. Bill's mom's
> pretty hot. For a mom.

> SAM
> It's your friend's mother, you
> weirdo. I hope Mr. Fredricks
> doesn't start dating your mom.

> NEAL
> Hey, that's not funny.

Mr. Fredricks speaks to the group.

> MR. FREDRICKS
> All right, everyone. We have some
> potential basketball superstars in
> this class, so we're going to spend
> today working on our fundamentals.
> Who knows, maybe one of you will
> make the school team next year.

He looks at Bill.

(CONTINUED)

CONTINUED:

> MR. FREDRICKS (CONT'D)
> First we're gonna warm up with ten
> laps around the gym.

Everyone moans.

> BILL
> Mr. Fredricks?

> MR. FREDRICKS
> Yes, Bill.

> BILL
> I can't run.

> MR. FREDRICKS
> Why?

> BILL
> 'Cause I have better things to do.

Sam and Neal look at each other. This is bad.

> MR. FREDRICKS
> Excuse me.

> BILL
> I have better things to do than run
> around a gym a bunch of times then
> try to throw a stupid ball in a
> hoop.

Mr. Fredricks doesn't know what to do. He is being challenged
on his home turf. He tries to remain calm.

> MR. FREDRICKS
> Oh really, Bill? What better things
> do you have to do?

> BILL
> Anything. Read the comics. Go to
> the bathroom. Pick my nose. Eat it.
> They're all more important than gym
> class.

Alan starts cracking up.

> ALAN
> Oh, he's so dead. Kill 'em, Mr.
> Fredricks.

(CONTINUED)

CONTINUED: (2)

> MR. FREDRICKS
> Shut up, Alan! For once in your
> life shut your big, stinking trap!
> Okay?

> ALAN
> He's the one who-

> MR. FREDRICKS
> Well, I'm talking to you. Just shut
> up. I am trying to run a class
> here. I do not need your constant
> comments and incessant cackling.
> You got me?

> ALAN
> Okay.

Mr. Fredricks looks at Bill. He's not sure what to do.

> MR. FREDRICKS
> You're gonna run those laps. And
> you're gonna do the drills because
> in this gym I am the teacher and
> you are the student.

Bill starts walking away.

> BILL
> You can't tell me what to do.

> MR. FREDRICKS
> Keep walking and you're in big
> trouble Mr. Haverchuck.

> BILL
> What are you gonna do, call my mom?

> MR. FREDRICKS
> Bill!

> BILL
> Leave me alone!

Bill walks away defiantly. Mr. Fredricks just stares. Alan
turns to Ernie.

> ALAN
> (quietly)
> I never thought I'd say this, but
> Haverchuck is the king.

(CONTINUED)

CONTINUED: (3)

He holds back a laugh.

FADE OUT.

<u>END OF ACT TWO</u>

<u>ACT THREE</u>

FADE IN:

EXT. WOODED YARD - DAY

A tearful Millie sticks a make-shift cross into the freshly spread dirt, covering her dead dog's grave. The cross reads - "GOLIATH - 1965 - 1981. REST IN PEACE." Kim and Lindsay look very sad and guilty.

> MILLIE
> We should kneel.

The three girls kneel down before the gravesite.

> MILLIE (CONT'D)
> We are here today to say good-bye to Goliath. My dog. Goliath, you were more than a pet. You were my friend. You were always there for me. My entire life.

Millie gets choked up.

> MILLIE (CONT'D)
> But I know you're with Jesus now. And you're happy in Heaven with all the other dogs and you can run and play and you'll never have to be on a leash again. 'Cause there are no leashes in heaven. You'll always be my favorite puppy. I love you, Goliath.

Kim is moved. She smiles at Millie.

> MILLIE (CONT'D)
> Lindsay, do you want to say something?

> LINDSAY
> No. That's okay.

Millie looks disappointed.

(CONTINUED)

CONTINUED:

> KIM
> Say something, Lindsay.

> LINDSAY
> Goliath, you were a sweet dog. You
> had nice fur. I always had fun
> playing with you. And even though
> you're gone, we are not sad because
> you lived a long, long, happy life.

> KIM
> That's right. A long, happy life.

> LINDSAY
> We'll miss you.

Millie smiles, appreciative. She takes out a single flower
and lays it underneath the cross. The girls stare at the
cross in silence for an extended moment.

> CUT TO:

INT. LINDSAY'S ROOM - DAY

Lindsay, Kim and Millie are in Lindsay's room. Millie is
about to leave.

> MILLIE
> Thanks, guys.

> LINDSAY
> Where are you going?

> MILLIE
> I'm gonna go pack all Goliath's
> things in a box and take it to the
> animal shelter.

> KIM
> You know what you need? You need to
> go out and let off some steam.

> LINDSAY
> Yeah.

> KIM
> Hey, why don't you come with us to
> The Who concert?

Lindsay looks concerned.

> (CONTINUED)

CONTINUED:

> MILLIE
> Really?

> LINDSAY
> Kim. She doesn't have a ticket.

> KIM
> So, we get her a ticket.

> MILLIE
> (intrigued)
> I've never been to a rock concert
> before.

> KIM
> You're fifteen years old and you've
> never been to a concert?

> MILLIE
> I saw <u>Godspell</u>. Does that count?

> KIM
> Millie, you've gotta go. You're
> gonna love it. Just think,
> thousands of people, rockin' out.

> LINDSAY
> Millie, your mom would never let
> you go.

> KIM
> Why not?

> MILLIE
> (to Kim)
> My mom thinks rock is the music
> Satan plays on the elevator to
> Hell.

> KIM
> It's not Black Sabbath, it's the
> Who. You're this straight A goody
> two shoes. It's not like you're
> gonna drop acid and have sex in the
> parking lot.

> MILLIE
> Speak for yourself.

Kim and Millie crack up. Lindsay looks nervous.

>   CUT TO:

INT. BILL'S KITCHEN - MORNING

MUSIC UP: THE WHO

Bill is eating cereal at the breakfast table. He is wearing
a white T-shirt and pajama bottoms. Mr. Fredricks walks into
the kitchen wearing boxer shorts and a white T-shirt.

                MR. FREDRICKS
        Good morning, Bill.

Bill is too shocked to speak. Mr. Fredricks walks to the
refrigerator and drinks some orange juice straight from the
carton.

Bill glares at him, so he grabs a mug from the cupboard and
pours the O.J. in it. He turns and we see the mug says "BILL"
on it (or the mug is Bill's Darth Vader Burger King mug).

             MR. FREDRICKS (CONT'D)
         (holds out the carton)
      You want some? It's good.

                BILL
      No, thank you.

Bill's mom enters wearing a bathrobe. Bill can't believe his
eyes. He gets up and walks away.

                        CUT TO:

INT. SCHOOL HALLWAY - DAY

Lindsay is walking down the hall. She spots Kim and Millie
hanging together.

                  KIM
        Hey, Lindsay. Did your old man make
        up his mind about the Who concert
        yet?

                LINDSAY
        Nah, but count me in. He's just
        making me sweat it.

                MILLIE
        Hey, after school, Kim and I are
        going to the record store. You
        wanna come?

                LINDSAY
      Umm...what?

                         (CONTINUED)

CONTINUED:

> MILLIE
> I'm gonna buy some Who albums so I
> can sing along at the concert.

> LINDSAY
> Millie, you're gonna go to the Who
> concert? What about your parents?

> MILLIE
> They said I could go.

> LINDSAY
> You're kidding.

> MILLIE
> No. They're letting me do anything
> I want since my dog died. I had
> Fresca for breakfast.

> LINDSAY
> I think I'm gonna...go home. We
> have all that trig homework. Right,
> Millie? Trig?

> MILLIE
> Oh, that's right. I forgot about
> that.

> KIM
> Blow it off. You're in mourning.
> You can't be expected to do
> homework.

> MILLIE
> Good point. I guess I'm gonna blow
> it off. Oh my god, I'm so bad.

> KIM
> Millie, I'll meet you out front
> after school. You're gonna wear
> your big coat to the store, right?

> MILLIE
> Yeah.

Kim walks away.

> MILLIE (CONT'D)
> She loves my big coat. She's been
> talking about it all day.

(CONTINUED)

CONTINUED: (2)

> LINDSAY
> Millie, please don't wear your big
> coat.

> MILLIE
> I can't believe I used to be so
> scared of her. She's really cool.

Lindsay looks a little shocked.

> MILLIE (CONT'D)
> You know, Lindsay, when you started
> hanging out with them, I felt bad
> for you because I thought you were
> turning into a dirtbag. But now I
> realize you were just...exploring.

> LINDSAY
> What do you mean?

> MILLIE
> Well, when Goliath got run over, I
> started questioning things. And I
> realized that's how you felt when
> your Grandma died. Right?

> LINDSAY
> Well, yeah, but I think it's
> different, you know? A dog and a
> person. A person's a much bigger
> deal.

> MILLIE
> Maybe, but your Grandma didn't lie
> in the street for three hours.
> > (a beat)
> Anyway, I've been kinda judging you
> and I'm sorry. See ya'.

Millie exits.

CUT TO:

INT. WEIR LIVING ROOM - DAY

Harold and Jean are sitting on the couch listening to a Who
album.

MUSIC UP: SQUEEZEBOX

Harold listens to the banjo driven intro.

(CONTINUED)

CONTINUED:

                    HAROLD
          This isn't so bad. Kinda catchy.

They listen to the words.

                    THE WHO
                 (on the record)
          Mama's got a squeezebox she wears
          on her chest and when daddy gets
          home he never gets no rest, because
          they're playing all night.

                    HAROLD
          Is it just me or is this squeezebox
          filthy?

                    JEAN
          I think it's about an accordion.

                    HAROLD
          Are you sure?

                    JEAN
          Sounds like it.

They listen some more.

                    THE WHO
          "They go, in and out and in and out
          and in and out. You know they're
          playing all night. And the music's
          alright. Mama's got a squeezebox,
          daddy never sleeps at night."

                    HAROLD
          That is not about an accordion!

                                        CUT TO:

INT. SCHOOL HALLWAY - DAY

Lindsay sees Kim.

                    LINDSAY
          Hey, Kim.

                    KIM
          Hey, Lindsay.

                    LINDSAY
          I'm thinking maybe we should tell
          Millie the truth.

                                        (CONTINUED)

CONTINUED:

> KIM
> We can't do that.

> LINDSAY
> We have to.

> KIM
> Why?

> LINDSAY
> 'Cause she's gonna wind up getting
> in trouble.

> KIM
> Why, 'cause she's hanging out with
> us?

> LINDSAY
> What's the difference, you're just
> hanging out with her because you
> feel guilty.

> KIM
> No, I'm not. She's kind of funny.

> LINDSAY
> You don't even know Millie. She's
> smart, she's into her church. She
> gets along great with her family.

> KIM
> And what? We're scum?

> LINDSAY
> That's not what I'm saying.

> KIM
> Well, what are you saying?

> LINDSAY
> I just don't think we should
> interfere with her life.

> KIM
> You're the one who's interfering.
> I'm just hanging out with her. And
> she's way more fun than you. You're
> a control freak.

> LINDSAY
> Don't be a jerk, Kim.

(CONTINUED)

CONTINUED: (2)

>   KIM
> What are you worried about? If
> Millie hangs out with us you'll
> have nobody to run to when you get
> scared of your bad friends?

Kim walks away.

>   LINDSAY
> Kim.

>   KIM
>   (turns back)
> And if you tell her, I'll kick your
> ass.

Kim exits. Lindsay is stunned and frustrated.

>   CUT TO:

INT. BILL'S LIVING ROOM - AFTERNOON

Gloria is speaking with Mr. Fredricks on the couch.

>   MR. FREDRICKS
> I don't know what else I can do. If
> he hates me, he hates me.

>   GLORIA
> He doesn't hate you.

>   MR. FREDRICKS
> It's true. I've tried to be a nice
> guy. It's not my fault his father
> didn't play catch with him so he's
> bad at sports.

>   GLORIA
> Oh, Ben. Don't start with that.

>   MR. FREDRICKS
> He's undermining my authority,
> Glor. They see Bill get away with
> it one day, the next day they're
> all mouthing off.

>   GLORIA
> He's just...having a hard time with
> this.

>   MR. FREDRICKS
> Well, so am I.

(CONTINUED)

CONTINUED:

>   GLORIA
>   Ben, you just need to hang out with
>   him more. You need to get to know
>   each other better.
>
>   MR. FREDRICKS
>   He doesn't want to know me. He
>   doesn't care.
>
>   GLORIA
>   Don't be such a baby.
>   (sweetly)
>   You should take him somewhere
>   special. Show him you like him.
>
>   MR. FREDRICKS
>   Like where, to the movies? I'm not
>   seeing that "Stripes" crap again.
>
>   GLORIA
>   He's been bugging me to go to this
>   Go-Cart City. I always say no, but
>   maybe you could--
>
>   MR. FREDRICKS
>   Really? I love Go-Cart City. Great.
>   I'll take him there.
>
>   GLORIA
>   So, that place is not a deathtrap?
>
>   MR. FREDRICKS
>   They lose two or three kids a year,
>   tops.

                                        CUT TO:

INT. WEIR KITCHEN - DAY

Lindsay is speaking to Harold and Jean.

>   LINDSAY
>   You're not going to let me go?
>
>   HAROLD
>   We heard about the squeezebox.
>
>   LINDSAY
>   I can't believe you. I'm like the
>   only kid in the entire school who's
>   not allowed to go to a rock
>   concert.

                                        (CONTINUED)

CONTINUED:

> HAROLD
> Maybe their parents don't care if
> their kids hang out in a cloud of
> reefer smoke hoping an M-80 doesn't
> blow up in their face, but we do.

> JEAN
> Maybe we could chaperone you. We
> could just sit behind you. You
> wouldn't even know we were there.

> LINDSAY
> Mom, I am not going with you.

> JEAN
> Lindsay.

> LINDSAY
> (changing tactics)
> Dad, I understand your concerns. I
> have them myself, but I think I can
> handle it. And I wouldn't bother to
> fight you... but Millie's going.

> JEAN
> Millie is?

> LINDSAY
> Yeah, her parents said she could
> go. So, I kind of wanted to go with
> her to make sure she was okay.

Jean looks at Harold. Harold looks annoyed.

> JEAN
> Aw, Lindsay, you're a good girl
> aren't you?

> LINDSAY
> Yes. And I think I can handle
> myself.

> JEAN
> Maybe she is old enough to go.

> HAROLD
> Fine, just don't get involved in
> any of that squeezebox business.

> CUT TO:

INT. BILL'S ROOM - DAY

Bill is hanging out with Neal and Sam. They are playing a
board game. Maybe one plays an old electronic hand-held
football game.

> BILL
> He's fat. He's a gym teacher and
> he's not even in good shape. You
> ever notice how you never see him
> run, or take part in any of the
> games?

> NEAL
> That's because he can't. It's like
> I always say, those who can, do.
> Those who can't, teach. Those who
> can't teach, teach gym.

> SAM
> You stole that from "Annie Hall."

Neal glares at Sam.

> SAM (CONT'D)
> Maybe he's not such a bad guy.

Bill's eyes widen.

> BILL
> What?

> SAM
> I'm just saying it's possible. We
> don't know him that well. And he
> did let you be a Captain in gym
> class.

> BILL
> (sarcastic)
> Oh, then I guess I should start
> calling him daddy.

> SAM
> Well...he was nice to me in sex ed.

> NEAL
> Yeah, but he laughed when I got hit
> in the pistachios in dodge ball.

(CONTINUED)

CONTINUED:

>   BILL
> Yeah. What kind of guy laughs at
> that?

>   SAM
> You laughed, too.

>   BILL
> That's because Neal's my friend.
> I'm allowed to.

Mr. Fredricks appears at the doorway.

>   MR. FREDRICKS
> Hey guys.

>   SAM/BILL/NEAL
> Hey.

>   MR. FREDRICKS
> Bill, I was just wondering,
> tomorrow maybe you might want to go
> to Go-Cart City with me.

>   BILL
> Um--

>   NEAL
> We'd love to go.

Bill turns to Neal.

>   MR. FREDRICKS
> We? Oh? Oh, well.., okay. We'll all
> go. You want to go, Sam?

>   SAM
> Uh, sure.

>   MR. FREDRICKS
> Great. Okay, Bill?

>   BILL
> I guess so.

>   MR. FREDRICKS
> All right. The four men are going
> to have some fun.

Mr. Fredricks exits.

(CONTINUED)

CONTINUED: (2)

> BILL
> (to Neal)
> Thanks a lot, Neal.

> NEAL
> Hey, no one else is gonna take us
> there. It's all the way out in the
> boonies.

> BILL
> So? I don't want to go with him.

> NEAL
> Why not? You know he's going to pay
> for everything. We'll ditch him
> then drive go-carts all day. It'll
> be fun.

> SAM
> It won't be so bad, Bill.

CUT TO:

INT. LINDSAY'S ROOM - DAY

Lindsay stands at her closet, trying to pick an outfit for
the concert. There's a KNOCK at her door.

> MILLIE (O.S.)
> Hey, Lindsay.

Lindsay turns to see Millie, wearing a brand-new black T-
shirt with a picture of the Who.

> LINDSAY
> Hey, Millie. What you been up to?

> MILLIE
> Kim and I went to the mall. It was
> soooo fun.

> LINDSAY
> Really? What did you do?

> MILLIE
> Kim bought me this shirt. And we
> bought a bunch of Who albums so I
> could educate myself. And then we
> just hung out and talked.

(CONTINUED)

CONTINUED:

> LINDSAY
> Sounds like fun. I'm glad you guys
> are hitting it off.

> MILLIE
> You know, I used to think she was a
> dirtbag, but she's really sweet. I
> just think she doesn't like
> everyone to know that.

> LINDSAY
> Yeah, you're probably right.

> MILLIE
> Who would have thought that me and
> Kim Kelly would become such fast
> friends?

> LINDSAY
> Not me.

> MILLIE
> Now I know what you see in those
> guys. They're fun.

> LINDSAY
> So, you're excited about going to
> the concert?

> MILLIE
> I really am getting excited. But
> I'm also kind of nervous. All those
> stories about concerts aren't true,
> are they, Lindsay? Nobody's gonna
> put LSD in my pop or throw a
> firecracker at me, are they? 'Cause
> if they are, I'm not gonna go.

> LINDSAY
> (long beat)
> No, Millie. There's nothing to
> worry about. Just stick by me, and
> we'll have a good time.

> MILLIE
> All right. Well, then let's put on
> one of these records and rock out!

(CONTINUED)

CONTINUED: (2)

> LINDSAY
> All right, Millie, let's rock...
> out.

CUT TO:

INT. MR. FREDRICKS' CAR - DAY

MUSIC UP: GARY NUMAN'S "CARS"

Mr. Fredricks is driving. The geeks all sit in the back seat.

> MR. FREDRICKS
> Hey, you guys want some gum?

> NEAL
> Sure.

Mr. Fredricks hands them sticks of gum which they all put in their mouth.

> MR. FREDRICKS
> This is supposed to be one of the
> best tracks in Michigan.

> SAM
> Now I'm beginning to get really
> excited.

Bill looks annoyed at Sam.

> NEAL
> Bill, what's the matter with your
> mouth?

Bill opens his mouth. It is black.

> BILL
> What?

> SAM
> Your spit is black.

> BILL
> Yours is, too.

Sam puts his finger on his tongue, then looks at it.

> NEAL
> Wait a minute. I know what this is.

(CONTINUED)

CONTINUED:

> BILL
> Is it bad?

> SAM
> Is it a disease?

> NEAL
> No, it's gag gum.

Mr. Fredricks starts laughing.

> MR. FREDRICKS
> I got it at the joke shop. I didn't
> think it would work. You should
> have seen the looks on your faces.

> BILL
> (quietly sarcastic)
> Heh-heh.

Mr. Fredricks reaches into a bag and pulls out a few items
from the joke shop.

> MR. FREDRICKS
> I heard that you guys were into
> comedy so I got you guys some
> presents from there.

He hands them all gifts.

> SAM
> Oh, cool.

Bill looks at his.

> BILL
> Fake dog doody.

> MR. FREDRICKS
> Yeah, isn't that crazy?

> SAM
> An ice cube with a fly in it...
> (or something better)
> ...Wow, it looks pretty real.

> MR. FREDRICKS
> I tried that on your mom, Bill. It
> totally works.

> BILL
> Sorry I missed it.

(CONTINUED)

CONTINUED: (2)

> NEAL
> Fake vomit.
> (to Sam and Bill)
> Oh, this is the one I don't have.
> Peas and carrots. Thanks, Mr.
> Fredricks.

> MR. FREDRICKS
> You're welcome.

CUT TO:

INT. NICK'S BASEMENT - DAY

Nick is playing his guitar as Ken listens. The song is basically three chords.

> NICK
> (singing)
> "You made me believe in dreams...
> In a land of jagged rocks...You're
> my moonstone, my gypsy queen...You
> freed my spirit from its locks."

ANGLE ON: Ken is trying desperately not to laugh.

> NICK (CONT'D)
> (singing)
> Specters of your love haunt my
> heart...The key to yours you never
> gave...Lady L, we were worlds
> apart....You lived in a castle, I
> lived in a cave."

Nick ends the song with a long, pretentious flourish. He looks at Ken expectantly.

> KEN
> Seriously man, don't sing this to
> her.

> NICK
> What?

> KEN
> Don't do it. I'm not even close to
> kidding. Don't make the same
> mistake twice. As your friend, I
> beg you.

> NICK
> What's the matter with it?

(CONTINUED)

CONTINUED:

> KEN
> "Lady L"?

> NICK
> Well, I didn't want to use her
> actual name.

> KEN
> You couldn't think of anything
> less... queer?

> NICK
> Hey, as long as I'm honest about my
> emotions, there's nothing to be
> ashamed of.

> KEN
> That's where you're wrong.

CUT TO:

EXT. GO-CART TRACK - DAY

The gang runs up to the go-cart track.

> MR. FREDRICKS
> Okay, here we are. GO-CART CITY!

> SAM
> Check it out.

Neal and Sam run to the track's fence. Bill slowly walks
over. Mr. Fredricks watches him with concern.

> MR. FREDRICKS
> What do you think, Bill? Pretty
> cool, huh?

> BILL
> Yeah, pretty cool.

Bill heads toward his friends. Mr. Fredricks watches him go.

> MR. FREDRICKS
> All right, let's race.

FADE OUT.

<u>END OF ACT THREE</u>

ACT FOUR

FADE IN:

EXT. GO-CART TRACK - DAY

Neal, Sam, Bill and Mr. Fredricks are sitting in their go-carts at the starting line.

>   NEAL
>   This is so great. Thanks, Mr.
>   Fredricks.

>   SAM
>   Yeah, thanks.
>   (to Bill)
>   My dad would never take me here.

>   MR. FREDRICKS
>   It's my pleasure. Now, get ready
>   for a race because I'm not going
>   easy on you guys.

>   NEAL
>   You're gonna be the loser.

>   MR. FREDRICKS
>   Oh, you think so. I bet a triple
>   ice cream cone I kick your butts.

>   SAM
>   You're on.

>   MR. FREDRICKS
>   You in, Bill?

>   BILL
>   (warming up)
>   Yeah. Get ready to buy me that ice
>   cream.

Fredricks smiles. They are given the flag to begin racing. They take off.

Their cars fly around the track. Bill has some trouble in the beginning. He has no rhythm with his car. Neal is in the quick lead. Mr. Fredricks is in third, probably because his car can't go as fast with someone his size in it. Bill is in last.

As they go around their second lap Bill starts getting into it. He passes Mr. Fredricks.

(CONTINUED)

CONTINUED:

                    MR. FREDRICKS
        No way!

                      BILL
        Eat my dust, Fredricks!

Bill attempts to pass Sam on the right. He can't get through
so he quickly turns to the inside of the track and buzzes by
him.
ANGLE ON BILL: A GIGANTIC SMILE ON HIS FACE

Neal looks back and sees Bill right on his butt. Bill gets
even with him.

                    BILL (CONT'D)
        That ice cream cone is mine!

                      NEAL
        Never!

They jockey for position for a few moments, then Bill passes
him on the right.

Bill sees the finish line up ahead. He will win. But then
Fredricks, gaining speed, flies past Neal and Sam.

Bill sees Fredricks, he is shocked.

Fredricks attempts to pass on the inside, Bill blocks him.
Fredricks attempts to pass on the outside. His wheel clips
Bill's wheel.

Bill spins out and hits a stack of hay.

Mr. Fredricks crosses the finish line in first place.

Sam, Neal and Mr. Fredricks jump out of their cars and run to
Bill. Neal and Sam are laughing and screaming, having a great
time. Mr. Fredricks looks very happy as well.

                    NEAL (CONT'D)
        Bill, that was incredible.

                      SAM
        You should have seen yourself spin
        out. It was so cool.

Bill jumps out of his car and throws his helmet down. Mr.
Fredricks is confused.

                    MR. FREDRICKS
        What is it, Bill?

                                          (CONTINUED)

CONTINUED: (2)

> BILL
> I hate you!

> MR. FREDRICKS
> What?

> BILL
> You always have to win! Everything
> is about winning to you. You never
> think about how other people feel.

> MR. FREDRICKS
> I'm sorry, Bill, I--

> BILL
> Just leave me alone!

Bill storms off. Mr. Fredricks looks sad. Sam and Neal are
stunned.

> CUT TO:

EXT. DEAD END STREET - DAY

Lindsay walks across the school parking lot. Her eyes go wide
as she sees a wildly painted small school bus. RANDOM FREAKS
are gathered around in admiration.

Daniel, Ken, and Kim exit the bus proudly as Lindsay
approaches.

> DANIEL
> How do you like the Magic Bus?

> LINDSAY
> It's amazing.

> KIM
> Wait 'til you see the inside.

> DANIEL
> (to Kim)
> Once Lloyd gets some money, he's
> gonna take out the last three rows
> of seats and put in a water bed.

> KIM
> Excellent.

> DANIEL
> I'm gonna go do a sound check on
> the speakers.

> (CONTINUED)

CONTINUED:

Daniel heads back into the bus. Seconds later, groovy Who music pounds across the parking lot.

> LINDSAY
> Have you seen Millie?

> KIM
> She's over there talking to Stroker
> and them.

We see Millie, in her freaky outfit, talking to a long-haired guy and his friends. She's dancing a little and the guys are digging it.

Lindsay watches, totally disturbed. MARK approaches.

> MARK
> I never thought I'd say this, but
> that Millie chick is kinda hot.

Lindsay is dumbstruck.

> MARK (CONT'D)
> I like it when good girls cross
> over. They're always trying to make
> up for lost time.

> LINDSAY
> Shut-up. And stay away from her.

> MARK
> What are you, her mother?

Lindsay calls out to Millie.

> LINDSAY
> Millie!

Millie looks over and gives Lindsay a blithe wave, then turns her attention back to the Freak Guys.

> LINDSAY (CONT'D)
> Millie!

> WOMAN'S VOICE
> Millie!

Everyone turns. A very angry Mrs. Kentner is in her idling car.

(CONTINUED)

CONTINUED: (2)

Millie's face drops. As Mrs. Kentner parks, Millie and
Lindsay exchange looks of doom.

                                        CUT TO:

INT. GO-CART PARK BATHROOM - LATER THAT DAY

Sam is looking around for someone. He finds Mr. Fredricks
sitting by himself, smoking a cigarette. He looks miserable.

                    SAM
          You're not supposed to smoke those.
          You taught us that in health class.

                    MR. FREDRICKS
          You're right.
               (putting it out)
          It's the first one I've had in six
          years.

                    SAM
          Mr. Fredricks, are you all right?

                    MR. FREDRICKS
          I'm fine.

                    SAM
          Bill didn't mean it.

                    MR. FREDRICKS
          Yeah, he did. I wasn't trying to
          win, I was just having fun.

                    SAM
          We were, too.

                    MR. FREDRICKS
          He hates me. Do all the kids in
          class hate me?

                    SAM
          No. Maybe a couple.

                    MR. FREDRICKS
          Bill's never gonna like me, is he?

                    SAM
          He will. It's just gonna take a
          really long time.

                                        (CONTINUED)

CONTINUED:

                    MR. FREDRICKS
    Oh, boy.

                                CUT TO:

EXT. DEAD END STREET - DAY

Mrs. Kentner has shown up and walks directly to Millie. All
the freaks are watching.

                    MRS. KENTNER
    Millie, I thought we agreed you
    weren't going to this concert.

                    MILLIE
    I didn't agree. You did.

                    MRS. KENTNER
    Well, you're not going.

                    MILLIE
    Yes, I am.

                    MRS. KENTNER
    What? Don't talk back to me.

                    MILLIE
    Mom, this is important to me. I
    mean, I'm a straight A student.
    I've never done anything wrong in
    my life.

                    MRS. KENTNER
    Millie, you're still a kid.

                    MILLIE
    Mom, I'm fifteen!

                    MRS. KENTNER
    You don't know the type of things
    that could happen.

                    MILLIE
    I can't believe you don't trust me.
    It's not like I'm gonna drop acid
    and have sex in the parking lot.

Mrs. Kentner can't believe what she's hearing.

                    MRS. KENTNER
    Millie, you get in the car. I'm
    taking you home. Right now.

                            (CONTINUED)

CONTINUED:

> MILLIE
> No. Just leave me alone.

Mrs. Kentner is stung.

> MRS. KENTNER
> Fine. Do what you want to do. You
> obviously don't care what I think.

She turns and walks away. Millie can't believe what she just
did.

> MARK
> Nice.

CUT TO:

EXT. ENTRANCE TO THE GO-CART PARK - DAY

Bill sits on or in the car. Mr. Fredricks sees him. He
tentatively walks over and sits down next to him. Bill stares
ahead silently.

> MR. FREDRICKS
> I'm sorry, Bill. I don't think I've
> bothered to understand just how
> hard this is on you. We've known
> each other a little in class this
> year. I thought we knew each other.
> I guess we don't know each other at
> all. And I know you think I'm this
> stupid, jock gym teacher. And
> you're probably right. But I'm also
> a man who...loves your mother very
> much. She's a very special woman.
> She's had a hard time these last
> few years...

> BILL
> What do you know about it?

> MR. FREDRICKS
> Only what she tells me. But, I
> think she deserves to be happy. And
> I can make her happy. I've never
> cared about someone as much as I
> care about your mother. And
> nothing in this world is more
> important to her than you, Bill. I
> know you don't want anyone to
> replace your father. I would never
> try to do that.
> (MORE)

(CONTINUED)

CONTINUED:

> MR. FREDRICKS (CONT'D)
> But maybe we can try to be friends.
> I'd like that. And, I know your
> mother would. I might not turn out
> to be as bad a guy as you think I
> am.

Mr. Fredricks gets up and walks away. A moment later Bill
puts his face in his hands and starts to cry.

> CUT TO:

INT. MAGIC BUS - DAY

Everyone is partying before the concert. Daniel yells to
everyone.

> DANIEL
> Okay, people, listen up. Rules of
> the road. There are no rules!

Everyone cheers and whoops.

> DANIEL (CONT'D)
> But I do need five bucks from
> everyone for gas.

The crowd groans a little and they start collecting money.
Nick approaches Lindsay, holding his guitar. Ken is sitting
nearby.

> NICK
> I'm really glad you're going.

> LINDSAY
> Me, too. The Who are the best.

> NICK
> Yeah. Townshend's been a huge
> influence on my songwriting.

> LINDSAY
> Yeah?

> NICK
> Actually, I wrote a song for you.

> LINDSAY
> You did?

> NICK
> (sheepishly)
> Hey.
> (MORE)

> (CONTINUED)

CONTINUED:
                    NICK (CONT'D)
          (beat)
     Can I play it for you?

                    LINDSAY
     Sure.

Nick positions himself to play the guitar. Ken leaps up,
grabs Nick's guitar and shouts to everyone.

                    KEN
     Hey, look at me! I'm Pete
     Townshend!

Ken starts smashing the guitar. It breaks into pieces as the
onlooking concertgoers cheer him on.

                    MARK
     This is gonna be the craziest party
     ever!

                    DANIEL
     Break out the cold ones!

People start opening their coolers of beer. Nick looks at
Lindsay, pretending this is the cool joke he and Ken had
planned.

                    NICK
     Pretty wild, huh?

                    LINDSAY
     Yeah, sure was.

Nick goes over to Ken, who hands him the smashed guitar.

                    NICK
     What the hell?

                    KEN
     Trust me, man. This is the biggest
     favor I ever did for you.

                    NICK
     You're buying me a new guitar.

                    KEN
     No, I'm not.

                    NICK
     Yes, you are.

                    KEN
     No.

                                        (CONTINUED)

CONTINUED: (2)

ANGLE ON: Millie, who sits next to Kim and Lindsay in the
seat behind the driver's seat occupied by Daniel. Millie
looks distraught.

>   LINDSAY
> You okay?

>   MILLIE
> My mom was really upset.

>   KIM
> Hey, it'll be cool. You gotta start
> training 'em sometime.

>   MILLIE
> I've never seen her like that. I
> feel kinda sick.

She sees Daniel passing beers around.

>   MILLIE (CONT'D)
> Can I have one of those?

>   DANIEL
> Abso-freakin'-lutely.

Millie takes the beer and pops it open. Lindsay looks at Kim
desperately.

>   LINDSAY
> Millie, you don't drink.

>   MILLIE
> I am so ready for this.

Kim looks at her, concerned.

>   MILLIE (CONT'D)
> Bottom's up!

Millie raises the beer to her mouth.

>   KIM
> I killed your dog.

>   MILLIE
> What?

>   KIM
> I was the one who ran him over. I'm
> so sorry.
>   (MORE)

(CONTINUED)

CONTINUED: (3)

> KIM (CONT'D)
> I didn't even know I did it until
> you said something at school.

Millie thinks Kim must be kidding.

> MILLIE
> That's not very funny you know.

> KIM
> It's true, Millie.

Millie realizes it is true.

> MILLIE
> Why didn't you say anything? Why
> didn't you tell me?

> KIM
> I don't know. We didn't know how.

> MILLIE
> Lindsay?

Lindsay hangs her head.

> LINDSAY
> I'm sorry, Millie.

Millie stands.

> MILLIE
> Go to hell. All of you!

Millie exits the bus, furious. There is a long stunned
silence.

> KEN
> Way to kick off a party, Kim.

> KIM
> Shut-up.
> (to Lindsay)
> God, she's really mad.

> LINDSAY
> Good.
> (beat)
> I'd better go talk to her.

> KIM
> What about the concert?

(CONTINUED)

CONTINUED: (4)

>   LINDSAY
>   Go without me.

Lindsay starts to leave and turns back to Kim

>   LINDSAY (CONT'D)
>   (sincerely)
>   Thanks, Kim.

Lindsay exits. Kim sighs and slumps in her seat.

>   NICK
>   Come on, Daniel, let's get mobile.
>   The Who waits for no one.

Daniel starts the bus and turns on the stereo to the
appropriate song of the Who. We see them drive out of the
parking lot. Lindsay walks in the opposite direction.

>   CUT TO:

INT. LINDSAY'S ROOM - DAY

Lindsay and Millie are playing Uno. There is some Who music
on the stereo. Millie throws down a card.

>   MILLIE
>   Uno!

>   LINDSAY
>   Go again?

>   MILLIE
>   Sure.

Millie starts to shuffle the deck and deal.

>   LINDSAY
>   I'm glad we didn't go. Those
>   concerts are so loud.

>   MILLIE
>   Yeah, and I hear the bathrooms
>   smell really bad and it's not safe
>   to sit.

>   LINDSAY
>   Can you imagine trying to hold it
>   in for four hours?

They laugh. Lindsay goes to her desk and takes something out
of a drawer. It is a photograph.

>   (CONTINUED)

CONTINUED:

>   LINDSAY (CONT'D)
>   I found this picture the other day.
>   I thought you might like it.

INSERT: A picture of a six year old Lindsay and Millie
standing on either side of a giant Great Dane. They are
dwarfed by his size.

>   MILLIE
>   Wow, I remember that. That was the
>   day Goliath ate those steaks right
>   off the barbecue.

>   LINDSAY
>   Your dad was pretty upset.

>   MILLIE
>   Yeah.
>   (beat)
>   He was a good dog, huh, Lindsay?

>   LINDSAY
>   Yeah, he was a good dog.

Lindsay nods. They share a moment.

>   LINDSAY (CONT'D)
>   So, you wanna finish the game?

>   MILLIE
>   I'd better get home.
>   (beat)
>   I don't know what I'm gonna say to
>   my mom.

>   LINDSAY
>   You want me to go with you?

>   MILLIE
>   No. I've got to do this myself. See
>   ya'.

>   LINDSAY
>   Yeah.

Millie starts to exit and turns back.

>   MILLIE
>   You better come with me.

(CONTINUED)

CONTINUED: (2)

Lindsay stands up and they exit.

                                    CUT TO:

INT. BILL'S LIVING ROOM - NIGHT

Mr. Fredricks sits on the couch watching a hockey game on
television. Bill walks in the room

                    MR. FREDRICKS
          I'm sorry, Bill. Did you want to
          watch something?

He stands up and hands Bill the remote control to the T.V.
Bill takes it then sits down on the floor about five feet in
front of Mr. Fredricks.

He turns the channel until he finds "Dallas." He watches for
a few moments. Mr. Fredricks watches, feeling awkward from
the silence. Finally Bill speaks.

                    BILL
          That's Bobby and Pamela.

Mr. Fredricks is taken aback by Bill speaking to him.

                    MR. FREDRICKS
          Oh.

                    BILL
          Pamela's brother Cliff Barnes is
          JR's nemesis so JR hates Pamela,
          too.

                    MR. FREDRICKS
          Yeah?

                    BILL
          JR is evil so Bobby has to always
          protect her.

                    MR. FREDRICKS
          So Bobby's a good guy?

                    BILL
          Yeah, but now he's caught in a
          Ewing land battle.

                    MR. FREDRICKS
          What land?

                                    (CONTINUED)

62.

CONTINUED:

                    BILL
          Would you be quiet? I'm trying to
          watch the show?

                    MR. FREDRICKS
          Sorry.

                    BILL
          I'll explain it to you during the
          commercial.

Mr. Fredericks smiles as he waits for the commercial.

                                        FADE OUT.

                    THE END

FREAKS AND GEEKS

"NOSHING AND MOSHING"

Episode #15

Written by J. Elvis Weinstein

Directed by Jake Kasdan

I was chomping at the bit to write this script. The downside of writing episode one was that I had to wait months until it was my turn to write a first draft again. Sure I had contributed along the way, but now I could really put my stink on something...something that never aired on NBC. I'd like to think they were *afraid* to air it, I mean who wants a show you canceled to win an Emmy, let alone a rare Pulitzer for "dramedy"? Yep, I'd like to think that.

I think the "Daniel goes punk" index card was on the storyboard since week one, now I had to run with it. I decided since punks hate posers, and Daniel was doing just that to impress a girl, he should pay—really get the Fonzie kicked out of him. I think James Franco really brilliantly portrayed both the appeal of punk to someone who is already angry, as well as how exhausting that total dedication to anger can be. One concern was portraying the 1980 "scene" as non-cartoony as possible, but as always on the show, the casting, wardrobe, and art departments kicked ass.

The other side of the show was a continuation of "The Garage Door" episode following Neal coping with the knowledge of his father's marital infidelity. Since I first met him, I wanted to make Samm Levine cry—now was my chance.

The first draft I handed in had the dramatic arc playing out at a family Bar Mitzvah. I was then informed we couldn't afford to stage both a Bar Mitzvah and a punk club...the Bar Mitzvah was canceled. Mazel Tov.

Once I brought my weeping down to a manageable sob, we decided to make it a party at the Schweibers' for Dr. S's patients. That's also when the ventriloquism came into the picture. I would have to do something that so many actual ventriloquists had failed at...make ventriloquism funny. Making it emotionally poignant seemed easy by comparison.

The production of this episode was really fun. Jake K. is a great director and a terrific collaborator. Also, every member of the McKinley faculty in this episode was played by a dear friend of mine. Plus, I got to write a drunk scene for Joe Flaherty, one of the few actors for whom I've ever felt truly safe doing so. I even got some of my music choices in.

If you enjoy reading this script half as much as I enjoyed writing it, I'm sorry. Writing isn't really that much fun. If you enjoy it as much as I enjoyed turning it in when I was done, you're in for a treat. I won't spoil the ending for those of you who don't have cable or a DVD player.

—J. Elvis Weinstein

FREAKS AND GEEKS

"NOSHING AND MOSHING"

<u>**CAST LIST**</u>

LINDSAY WEIR
SAM WEIR
HAROLD WEIR
JEAN WEIR
DANIEL DESARIO
NICK ANDOPOLIS
BILL HAVERCHUCK
NEAL SCHWEIBER
KEN MILLER
KIM KELLY
MR. ROSSO
MR. KOWCHEVSKI
DR. SCHWEIBER
MRS. SCHWEIBER
BARRY SCHWEIBER
MR. LACOVARA
SEIDELMAN
JENNA ZANK
KATEY DESARIO
MR. BOTWINICK
CHEERLEADER
PIERCING GIRL
MOHAWK GUY
BALD MAN (MR. LANTZ)
KID
FRESHLY PIERCED GUY
BIG PUNK

FREAKS AND GEEKS

"NOSHING AND MOSHING"

SET LIST

INTERIORS:

MCKINLEY HIGH SCHOOL
    /HALLWAY
    /BIOLOGY CLASSROOM
    /ROSSO'S OFFICE
    /DETENTION ROOM
    /CAFETERIA
WEIR HOUSE
    /DINING ROOM
    /LIVING ROOM
    /KITCHEN
SCHWEIBER HOUSE
    /LIVING ROOM
    /DINING ROOM
    /NEAL'S ROOM
DANIEL'S HOUSE
    /DANIEL'S BEDROOM
MINI MART
THE ARMPIT PUNK CLUB
    /MEN'S ROOM

EXTERIORS:

MCKINLEY HIGH SCHOOL
    /SMOKING PATIO
    /PARKING LOT
DANIEL'S HOUSE
    /FRONT PORCH
MINI-MART
NICK'S HOUSE
    /FRONT YARD
SCHWEIBER HOUSE
KIM'S HOUSE

<u>TEASER</u>

FADE IN:

INT. NEAL'S BEDROOM - DAY

Close up of a hand pushing the play button on a tape
recorder.

MUSIC UP: PAUL FEIG'S "SPACE FUNK"

CLOSE UP: Bill's Face. He is dancing. We widen out till we
reveal his entire body doing the Re-run dance from "What's
Happening."

ANGLE ON: SAM AND NEAL WATCHING IN HORROR.

                         SAM
               That's not sexy.

                         BILL
               Yes, it is.

                         NEAL
               You look like you're having a
               seizure.

                         BILL
               Women love good dancers. Girls
               don't even care that Re-run is fat
               because he's a good dancer.

                         SAM
               Bill, please stop. You're making me
               sick.

                         BILL
               All right, now you guys get up and
               try it. Come on, shake it Sam, you
               won't break it.

Neal turns off the tape.

                         BILL (CONT'D)
               Hey, you cut me off in mid-funk.
               You always say you wanna impress
               the ladies, Neal. Well, this is the
               way.

                         NEAL
               It's never worked for you.

                                        (CONTINUED)

CONTINUED:

> BILL
> Because I've never done it for any
> ladies. If I did, I'd be fighting
> them off with a stick.

> NEAL
> Guys, let's get serious. That is
> not going to impress the ladies.
> Trust me.

> BILL
> Oh, and you know what is.

> NEAL
> I do, as a matter of fact. Because
> I've found the thing that's gonna
> change our lives. It's gonna make
> us money, bring us respect and
> power.

Neal pulls a suitcase out from under his bed.

> NEAL (CONT'D)
> And it's all right here in this
> suitcase.

> SAM
> What is it?

> NEAL
> Think you can handle it?

> BILL
> Yes! Open it.

> NEAL
> Are you sure?

> SAM
> Just open it already!

Neal opens the suitcase with his back to the guys. Sam and
Bill's eyes go wide in expectation. Neal turns around,
holding a ventriloquist's dummy.

> NEAL
> Fellows, say hello to Morty.
>   (as the dummy)
> Hi there, dummies!

As Sam and Bill exchange looks, we...

CUT TO:

ALTERNATE OPENING

FADE IN:

INT. NEAL'S BEDROOM - DAY

          DR. SCHWEIBER
Hey kiddo, how was school?

          NEAL
   (a little coldly)
Fine.

          DR. SCHWEIBER
How's the schtick coming along?
Should I call Edgar Bergen and tell
him to retire?

          NEAL
Not until I have a tight ten.

          DR. SCHWEIBER
A what?

          NEAL
Ten minutes of killer material.

          DR. SCHWEIBER
Wow, that sounds serious. Do I get
to see a little?

          NEAL
Not yet. Pretty soon.

          DR. SCHWEIBER
All right, but I want a front row
seat at your world premiere.

          NEAL
You got it.

Neal chuckles. The door shuts. His expression immediately
goes hostile. The Dummy's head turns toward him.

          DUMMY
What a jerk.

          NEAL
Morty, be nice. That's my father
you're talking about.

          (CONTINUED)

CONTINUED:

The dummy just turns its head and stares at Neal. Neal
stares back.

CUT TO:

OPENING TITLE SEQUENCE

ACT ONE

FADE IN:

INT. MINI MART - AFTERNOON

DANIEL, NICK, and KEN are browsing the snack-cake aisle after
school. Daniel looks very out of it. Ken stands holding a
packet of mini-donuts.

> NICK
> I'm gonna get a drink; I've got
> serious cotton-mouth. You guys want
> anything?

> KEN
> Orange.

> NICK
> Daniel?

> DANIEL
> (snapping out of a daze)
> What? Oh, yeah, anything with
> caffeine -- except Yellow Blast. I
> hear that stuff shrinks your nards.

Nick goes off to the cooler.

> KEN
> Man, you've been a waste case all
> day.

> DANIEL
> Yeah, I didn't get any sleep last
> night.

The two move down the aisle to the cigarette carton case.

> KEN
> (nudge, nudge)
> Kim keep you up?

> DANIEL
> No, my Mom.

(CONTINUED)

CONTINUED:

Ken looks confused and a bit disgusted. Daniel looks up
towards the check-out counter and sees that the clerk is busy
ringing out a customer.

> DANIEL (CONT'D)
> She was up all night praying and
> freaking out because my Dad's
> workman's comp is gonna run out.
> Throw me a screen.

Ken moves and stands in front of Daniel, obscuring the
clerk's view of him.

> KEN
> That sucks.

Daniel pulls a carton of cigarettes off the rack and sticks
it in his jacket. It creates a slight bulge.

> DANIEL
> Yeah, and there's no way in hell he
> can go back to work. He can barely
> make it to the can.

They casually move away from the case.

> KEN
> Can't you sue the company or
> something?

> DANIEL
> No, man. The system sucks. We're
> totally getting screwed over.

Daniel casually sticks a can of cheesefood in his jacket.
Nick rejoins the guys with the drinks.

> NICK
> (indicating girl behind
> the counter)
> Hey, isn't that Jenna Zank?

The guys turn to look at JENNA ZANK, 17, a very pretty, very
PUNK girl in a Gas N' Gulp uniform shirt. Part of her hair is
shaved, the other part dyed electric blue. She is reading a
copy of "SLASH" magazine.

> DANIEL
> (studying her)
> Is it? Didn't she drop out?

(CONTINUED)

6.

CONTINUED: (2)

> KEN
> Why would you drop out and then
> stay in Chippewa? That's crazy.

> NICK
> Man, she used to be so hot.

> DANIEL
> She still is.

> KEN
> If you like clowns.

> DANIEL
> I hang out with you, don't I?

Daniel slips a pack of cookies into his pocket. He looks up
and sees Jenna staring right at him. He turns around.

> DANIEL (CONT'D)
> (sotto)
> I'll meet you guys outside.

Daniel walks towards the door. Out of the corner of his eye
he looks at Jenna. She is still looking at him, watching him
walk.

ANGLE ON; Two POLICEMEN coming in the door, holding empty
coffee travel mugs.

Daniel's face tenses for a second, then he slaps on a smile
and steps aside for the nice officers giving them an "After
you" gesture. He looks over at Jenna. She is staring right at
him. Their eyes meet. The police barely notice Daniel as they
walk by. He slips out the door.

CUT TO:

INT. LIVING ROOM/KITCHEN - NIGHT

Harold sits in his chair reading the newspaper. Jean is in
the kitchen making dinner. They yell to each other from the
opposing rooms. Lindsay sits on the couch doing homework.

> JEAN
> Harold, we have to go or the
> Schweibers will be offended. We
> missed it last year.

> HAROLD
> We didn't miss anything. It's the
> same party every year. It's smarmy.
> (MORE)

(CONTINUED)

CONTINUED:

> HAROLD (CONT'D)
> You don't see me having a soiree
> for everyone that buys a tennis
> racquet at my store.

> JEAN
> Harold, we have to go.

> LINDSAY
> Mom, I don't have to go, do I?

> HAROLD
> Yes.

> JEAN
> No.

Harold looks at Jean.

> HAROLD
> Why not? She's a part of this
> family? Sam's going.

> LINDSAY
> He's friends with Neal. Who am I
> supposed to talk to?

> HAROLD
> He's your dentist, too.

> LINDSAY
> Fine, I'll switch dentists.

> HAROLD
> (to Jean)
> Say, there's an idea.

> JEAN
> Harold, you're acting like a child.
> (settling it)
> We're going. Lindsay, you don't
> have to.

Harold grumbles. Lindsay smiles.

> CUT TO:

EXT. DANIEL'S FRONT PORCH - MORNING

Daniel comes out his front door, looking annoyed. Close
behind him comes his mother, KATEY DESARIO, 40, and not a
young 40. She is wearing a housedress and a large cross
around her neck. She comes out the door after him.

> (CONTINUED)

CONTINUED:

                    KATEY
               (aggravated)
          Daniel, come back here. I need you
          to run to the drug store and pick
          up your father's prescriptions.

He stops and turns around.

                    DANIEL
          Mom, I gotta go, I'm gonna be late
          for music.

                    KATEY
          You know I can't leave him alone.
          He might fall.

                    DANIEL
          Call Joey. He's not working.

                    KATEY
          Tell me about it. I'm supposed to
          trust your brother with those
          painkillers? Never again.

                    DANIEL
          Fine, I'll pick them up after
          school. But I gotta go. I can't get
          anymore tardies.

                    KATEY
          It can't wait. Your father's in
          pain. You have to do it now. C'mon,
          Daniel, I need your help here.

                    DANIEL
          What do you want me to do? I'm in
          high school!

                    KATEY
          When it's convenient for you, you
          are. You're eighteen. What, are you
          trying to be the world's oldest
          junior?

                    DANIEL
          You want me to drop out so I can
          bring home $2.50 an hour?

                    KATEY
          You think I'd turn that down?
          C'mon, Danny, what am I supposed to
          do here?

                                    (CONTINUED)

CONTINUED: (2)

> DANIEL
> What do you mean, what are you
> supposed to do? You're supposed to
> take care of Dad, and I'm supposed
> to go to school. It's called
> Wednesday.

She gives him a look. He turns and walks away.

> KATEY
> Where are you going?

> DANIEL
> I'm going to get the stupid
> painkillers.

CUT TO:

INT. MCKINLEY HIGH - HALLWAY - DAY

SAM, BILL, and NEAL are standing at Neal's locker. Neal works
the padlock.

> SAM
> Can I dump my history book in there
> until after next period?

> NEAL
> I don't have a lot of extra room.

Neal undoes the lock and opens his locker.

> BILL
> (scared)
> Ahh!

ANGLE ON: Neal's DUMMY staring out from the locker.

> SAM
> You're bringing the dummy to school
> now?

> NEAL
> It's called a "figure," not a
> "dummy". A dummy is someone who
> calls it a dummy.

> SAM
> (indignant)
> Oh, is it?

Neal takes it out of the locker.

(CONTINUED)

CONTINUED:

> BILL
> No, don't take it out.

Bill looks around to see if anyone is looking.

> NEAL
> It's just Morty, Bill.

> DUMMY
> Yeah, what's your problem?

> BILL
> Tell it not to talk to me.

> DUMMY
> You got a problem? Want a piece of
> me, stringbean?

> BILL
> Shut up, already.

> NEAL
> Sorry. I need to squeeze in
> rehearsal time whenever I can. My
> brother's coming home this weekend
> so I'm not going to have much time.

> SAM
> What are you rehearsing for? Is
> there some talent show or
> something?

> NEAL
> For life. I'm taking control. I
> can't rely on my crazy parents
> anymore. I can make big bucks with
> this.

> BILL
> I doubt it. Ventriloquism isn't
> funny.

> NEAL
> I guess you've never seen a little
> show called "Soap." That guy's
> hilarious. And now he's rich,
> thanks to ventriloquism.

Sam and Bill look at each other and give up. Neal closes the
dummy in his locker and the geeks head down the hallway. Neal
thinks, then looks at them.

(CONTINUED)

CONTINUED: (2)

                         NEAL (CONT'D)
              When Barry gets home this weekend,
              I'm going to tell him about our
              Dad.

                         SAM
              What? About that woman?

                         NEAL
              Uh-huh.

                         SAM
              You think that's a good idea?

                         NEAL
              I have to do it. Barry should
              know.

As the geeks head off, Kim comes storming down the hall. We
go with her as she spots Daniel down the hall.

                         KIM
                    (yelling)
              Hey, Desario!

                         DANIEL
                    (yelling back)
              What?

                         KIM
              Where the hell were you this
              morning? You have my notes!

                         DANIEL
              I got hung up.

                         KIM
              Thanks a lot. I failed a test
              because of you!

                         DANIEL
              What are you talking about?

A passing Lindsay sees the commotion and walks over.

                         KIM
              It was an open notes test. I left
              my bag in your car last night.

                         DANIEL
              That's my fault you're too stupid
              to take your bag out of my car?

                                        (CONTINUED)

CONTINUED: (3)

> KIM
> Don't call me stupid, man.

> DANIEL
> You know what? I was tardy in music
> this morning, so I got bigger
> things to worry about than your
> stupid test.

Lindsay rolls her eyes, not in the mood for another Kim and Daniel fight. She walks away. We FOLLOW her around the corner, where she finds the enormous SEIDELMAN picking up a cheerleader.

> CHEERLEADER
> Put me down!

> SEIDELMAN
> (laughing)
> C'mon, you know you love me.

> CHEERLEADER
> You're crushing my ribs!

Seidelman laughs, thinking the girl is joking. Lindsay sees she's clearly not. Lindsay storms over to Seidelman.

> LINDSAY
> Put her down!

> SEIDELMAN
> What, we're just having fun.

> CHEERLEADER
> No, I'm not! Put me down!

Seidelman LAUGHS. Lindsay gets an angry look. She winds her foot back and kicks him hard in the leg.

> LINDSAY
> I said put her DOWN!

Seidelman releases the cheerleader.

> SEIDELMAN
> Ow! That hurt, you burn-out.

MR. BOTWINICK, a middle-aged, snotty teacher comes out of a classroom and sees the commotion.

INT. BIOLOGY CLASS

Mr. Lacovara holds a stack of reports written by his
students.

>   MR. LACOVARA
>   Neal, I don't see your report here.

>   NEAL
>   Oh, I did it.

>   MR. LACOVARA
>   Where is it?

Neal points to his head.

>   NEAL
>   In my mind.

The class laughs. He looks around at the class, pleased at
response.

>   NEAL (CONT'D)
>   I didn't write it down because I
>   didn't want to kill a tree.
>   Did you know our forests are
>   disappearing at a rate...

>   MR. LACOVARA
>   Neal!

>   NEAL
>   Hector.

The class laughs again. Neal winks at them.

>   MR. LACOVARA
>   Okay, that's it. You just bought
>   yourself a ticket to the
>   principal's office.

Neal gets up.

>   NEAL
>   (as he exits)
>   To see Jerry. I love that guy. He
>   owes me money.

>   MR. LACOVARA
>   (firmly)
>   Neal, that's over the line. It's
>   not funny.

(CONTINUED)

CONTINUED:

Neal is stung.

> NEAL
> (softly, without moving
> his lips)
> Funnier than your stupid jokes.

Sam gives Bill a "what is he doing?" look. Bill shrugs back.

> MR. LACOVARA
> Okay, Mr. Schweiber, gather up your
> stuff. You just bought yourself a
> trip to the office.

> NEAL
> What? I didn't say anything. I
> didn't even move my mouth!

> MR. LACOVARA
> Please, I'm a man of science.
> (without moving his lips)
> Get out.

The class chuckles. Neal gives a deep angry sigh.

                                                    CUT TO:

INT. ROSSO'S OFFICE - DAY

Neal sits in front of Rosso with a hanky on his nose. HOOONK!
Rosso blows his nose loudly. He clearly has a cold.

> ROSSO
> Sorry, friend. Picked up a little
> bug the other night. Long story.

> NEAL
> Look, Mr. Rosso, I'm sorry I
> mouthed off in class. I'll
> apologize to Mr. Lacovara. I
> promise it won't happen again.

Neal starts to get up to leave. Rosso stops him.

> ROSSO
> Neal, have a seat. Here's what I
> see - a kid whose grades have taken
> a sudden tumble and for the first
> time, starting to get into trouble.
> Now in my business, we call those
> warning signs.
> (MORE)

                                                    (CONTINUED)

CONTINUED:

                    ROSSO (CONT'D)
          I'm here to help you but I can't
          help you if you won't talk to me.

And with this, Rosso breaks into a barrage of HACKING COUGHS.

                    ROSSO (CONT'D)
               (finally stopping)
          Sorry.

                    NEAL
          Really, Mr. Rosso. Everything's
          fine.

                    ROSSO
          Neal, sometimes we like to say that
          everything's fine. Because really
          things aren't fine.

                    NEAL
          Everything's fine.

                    ROSSO
          I've had kids lying to me since
          before you were born. You're new to
          it and you're not good at it.
          C'mon, you're gonna feel a whole
          lot better if you talk.

Neal looks at him silently for a moment. Rosso settles in,
showing Neal he can wait.

                    NEAL
               (intense)
          Okay. You want me to talk? You
          think it will help? Great. My
          father is having an affair, my
          mother doesn't have a clue, and now
          I have to decide whether or not to
          tell her. There, I talked about it,
          and you're wrong, I don't feel
          better. Now can I go?

Rosso is frozen.

                                        CUT TO :

INT. MINI MART - AFTERNOON

Jenna is behind the counter, reading a *People* magazine. She
hears the BELL on the door as it opens, she quickly puts the
People back on the rack. She looks to see Daniel entering. He
walks to the counter.

                                        (CONTINUED)

CONTINUED:

> DANIEL
> Hey.

She just stares at him.

> DANIEL (CONT'D)
> How's it goin'?

Still nothing.

> DANIEL (CONT'D)
> I don't know if you remember me...
> from McKinley... Daniel?

> JENNA
> I don't know. Maybe.

> DANIEL
> Yeah... Out on the patio? I used to
> see you sometimes... So, how's the
> dropping out going?

> JENNA
> Better than the staying in was. A
> lot fewer idiots hassling me all
> the time.

> DANIEL
> That's cool.

> JENNA
> Do you want something or are you
> just waiting for me to turn my back
> so you can steal more stuff? You
> know, I could have had you thrown
> in jail.

> DANIEL
> So, why didn't you?

She shrugs. Then looks away--

> JENNA
> Didn't you have that psycho
> girlfriend?

> DANIEL
> Uh... Yeah, but...she and I don't
> share the same interests anymore.

> JENNA
> That's too bad.

(CONTINUED)

CONTINUED: (2)

> DANIEL
> Yeah. You know, like she's not into
> current affairs. I am. She's not a
> punker. I am.

> JENNA
> Really? You know what punkers don't
> do? Call themselves "punkers." Who
> do you listen to?

> DANIEL
> I didn't bring the list.

> JENNA
> No, c'mon, I'm just curious.

> DANIEL
> The Clash, Iggy, The Ramones, The
> Pistols...

> JENNA
> All the obvious guys.

> DANIEL
> I like some more obscure stuff,
> too. Who are you into?

> JENNA
> Black Flag, X, Agent Orange, The
> Buzzcocks.

> DANIEL
> (faking it)
> Yeah, they're cool.

> JENNA
> Well, you look a lot more like
> Black Sabbath than Black Flag.

> DANIEL
> You know, I was going to dye my
> hair,
> (re: her hair)
> but someone bought the last bottle
> of bleach.

Daniel smiles. Jenna sneers back, but it quickly dissolves
into a smile. After a beat, she grabs a Sharpie off the
counter, grabs Daniel's arm, and pushes up his sleeve. She
scribbles "775 Elm" on his arm with the Sharpie.

(CONTINUED)

CONTINUED: (3)

> JENNA
> That's where I'll be tomorrow
> night. It's called The Armpit. It's
> downtown. Puss is playing.

She takes her fingernail and scratches a line under the
address. Daniel winces slightly.

> JENNA (CONT'D)
> Maybe I'll see you there.

Daniel smiles at her, containing his wince.

> DANIEL
> Definitely.

Another customer walks up to the counter.

> JENNA
> Watch out, I gotta ring this guy
> up. Wait over there. I'll be done
> in a second.

Daniel steps over to the side and watches her ring up the
customer with great interest.

> FADE OUT.

END OF ACT ONE

ACT TWO

FADE IN:

EXT. MCKINLEY PARKING LOT - DAY

CLOSE-UP on Daniel's forearm. The address is still there and
the scratch under it is red and inflamed.

> KEN (V.O.)
> It's a good thing the club isn't on
> East Renaissance Boulevard. You'd
> need stitches.

PULL BACK to reveal Daniel, Nick, and Ken leaning against the
back of Daniel's car while he shows them his arm.

> DANIEL
> So, what do you say? You guys wanna
> go with me?

(CONTINUED)

CONTINUED:

>   KEN
> Sure, what the hell. I like a good
> freak show.

>   NICK
> I don't know man, I don't like punk
> very much. They aren't very good
> musicians, they just play loud to
> cover.

>   DANIEL
> So what!? It's what they're saying
> that's important.

>   NICK
> What are they saying?

>   DANIEL
> They're saying "Screw the system,
> make up your own rules..."

>   KEN
>   (interrupting)
> Get a stupid haircut.

Nick laughs.

>   DANIEL
> Yeah, you're right. It doesn't have
> the power of an important work like
> "Lady L."

>   NICK
> Hey, I'd like to hear the song you
> write.

>   CUT TO:

INT. DETENTION ROOM - DAY

Lindsay sits in a room populated by the bottom end of the
McKinley Bell curve. Mr. Botwinick patrols the room. Lindsay
is the only one in the room doing homework. Seidelman is
sitting at a nearby desk, giving Lindsay a dirty look.

>   MR. BOTWINICK
> Ms. Weir, what are you doing?

He is standing over her.

>   LINDSAY
> What? I'm just doing my homework.

>   (CONTINUED)

CONTINUED:

>   MR. BOTWINICK
> That's not allowed in here.

>   LINDSAY
> What?

>   MR. BOTWINICK
> This is detention, not a study
> hall. The point is to spend time
> thinking about what you've done.

>   LINDSAY
> What? Why would you want to keep
> people in detention from studying
> for once in their lives? Isn't that
> the point?

The whole of the room gives Lindsay a dirty look.

>   MR. BOTWINICK
> Maybe you'll find out the answer
> when you come in after school
> tomorrow.

>   LINDSAY
> That's insane.

>   MR. BOTWINICK
> All right, and Friday.

Lindsay sighs with a "This is bullshit" look on her face.

>   CUT TO:

INT. SCHOOL HALLWAY - DAY

The hall is empty except for a janitor who is mopping the
floor.

Lindsay and Kim come crashing through the double doors at the
end of the hall.

>   LINDSAY
> I hate Mr. Botwinick. I hate that
> cow Seidelman. Is every man in this
> school an idiot? It's this school
> that does it. I hate this school.

>   KIM
> I broke up with Daniel.

>   (CONTINUED)

CONTINUED:

> LINDSAY
> Really?

> KIM
> Yeah.

> LINDSAY
> That's good, right?

> KIM
> Yeah. I think so.

> LINDSAY
> Well, then... congratulations.

> KIM
> Thank you.

CUT TO:

INT. SCHWEIBER DINING ROOM - EVENING

Neal, Dr. Schweiber, and MRS. SCHWEIBER are eating dinner.
Morty the Dummy is seated in a chair next to Neal. Neal seems
lost in his own world. He hasn't eaten much.

> DR. SCHWEIBER
> Oh, by the way, I just got a late
> riz-vip from Jim Narotsky. A "D"?
> Geez, did you spell your name right
> at least? What happened?

> NEAL
> I don't know, I guess I studied
> wrong.

> MRS. SCHWEIBER
> This is a few grades like this now,
> honey. Do you think maybe Morty is
> distracting you a little bit from
> your studies?

> NEAL
> No.

> MRS. SCHWEIBER
> Well, maybe you shouldn't take him
> to school anymore.

> NEAL
> It's not the ventriloquism!

(CONTINUED)

CONTINUED:

> DR. SCHWEIBER
> Hey, calm down, buddy, we're just
> talking.

> MRS. SCHWEIBER
> We just want to make sure you're
> all right.

> NEAL
> (over-reacting)
> Yes! I'm fine. Why is everyone on
> my case today!?

> MRS. SCHWEIBER
> I'm not trying to get on your case,
> I just want to know if something's
> wrong.

> NEAL
> I had a couple of bad tests. I'll
> do better, I promise!

> DR. SCHWEIBER
> All we ask is that you try your
> hardest.

> NEAL
> I will. Can I be excused? Willie
> Tyler and Lester are on the
> Hollywood Squares this week. I
> gotta watch.

He starts to get up.

> MRS. SCHWEIBER
> Sure.

> DR. SCHWEIBER
> But tomorrow, why don't you leave
> Morty at home.

CUT TO:

INT. CAFETERIA - DAY

Neal sits with the Geeks with Morty on his lap. Sam and Bill
are horrified and trying to look like they're not with him.
People are walking by and snickering. Morty flirts with
girls at the next table.

(CONTINUED)

CONTINUED:

> MORTY
> Hey, how about I lose the chump and
> you and me get out of here?

A couple of girls at the next table laugh and look away.

> BILL
> Sam, do you see another table open?

> SAM
> Neal, people are looking at us.

> BILL
> Yeah, and not in a good way.

> NEAL
> What are you talking about? I'm
> killing.

> SAM
> Would you please put that thing
> back in your locker?

> MORTY
> Who are you calling a thing?

Seidelman walks up to the table.

> SEIDELMAN
> Nice doll, Schweiber. Did it come
> with a dress?

Sam and Bill look up, startled.

> MORTY
> Nice head, Seidelman, did it come
> with a neck?

Seidelman's face turns angry. Sam and Bill's turn scared.

> NEAL
> Morty, be quiet!
>   (to Seidelman)
> I just can't control him sometimes.

> SEIDELMAN
> Yeah, well you better.

Sam and Bill are getting plenty nervous.

(CONTINUED)

CONTINUED: (2)

> DUMMY
> Don't worry, I won't use any big
> words.

> SEIDELMAN
> I'm gonna kick your butt,
> Schweiber.

> NEAL
> What? It's not me, it's him!

Seidelman starts toward Neal menacingly. Sam and Bill jump
to their feet.

> SEIDELMAN
> Oh, yeah? Well, I'll kick your butt
> and he can talk about it.

KOWCHEVSKI rushes in just in time.

> KOWCHEVSKI
> Hey!

He pulls Seidelman off.

> KOWCHEVSKI (CONT'D)
> Seidelman, knock it off! Why don't
> you pick on someone your own size.
> There's a bus in the parking lot.

He shoves Seidelman off on his way. Sam and Bill finally
exhale. Neal hasn't moved.

> NEAL
> Thanks, Mr. Kowchevski. Some people
> just don't appreciate art.

> MORTY
> Yeah, you're my hero.

> KOWCHEVSKI
> You're a glutton for punishment,
> aren't you, Schweiber?

He walks away. Sam and Bill look annoyed.

                                              CUT TO:

INT. DETENTION ROOM - DAY

Lindsay is sitting in detention, bored. She looks over and
sees a guy drop a pencil on the ground so he can look up a
girl's skirt. Lindsay rolls her eyes in disgust.

CUT TO:

INT. WEIR KITCHEN - AFTERNOON

Sam and Bill come in the back door with their backpacks and
stuff.

> SAM
> All I know is, it's gotta stop. I
> don't even like being around him
> anymore.

> BILL
> That dummy almost got us killed.

> SAM
> (mimicking Neal)
> It's not a dummy, it's a figure!

Bill laughs. They plop their stuff down on the table. Sam
opens the refrigerator and takes out a pitcher of orange
juice.

> BILL
> He shouldn't even be messing with
> that stuff.

> SAM
> What do you mean?

> BILL
> I mean did you ever see that movie
> "Magic"?

> SAM
> Yeah, I saw it with you. Remember
> we were supposed to be seeing
> "Grease?"

Sam takes out two glasses and fills them with juice.

> BILL
> Yeah. Well, what if he has the kind
> of dummy that was in "Magic"? One
> minute it's fun and games, the next
> minute it's...
> (MORE)

(CONTINUED)

CONTINUED:

> BILL (CONT'D)
> (a la "Fats" from Magic)
> "Hey, Schmucko, why don't you kill
> Bill."

> SAM
> That was a movie, Bill. The dummy's
> not talking. It's Neal and he's
> driving me crazy. I know he's going
> through a hard time but I kinda
> don't care.

> BILL
> (after a beat)
> Do you get to be a jerk just
> because your dad's having an
> affair?

As they ponder this, we...

CUT TO:

INT. DANIEL'S BEDROOM - NIGHT

Daniel's room is small and sloppy. On the walls are a few
posters (The Ramones, Zeppelin, Alice Cooper, some muscle
cars), a DEAD END road sign, and a few drawings (maybe his).
A few mismatched stereo components are stacked on a little
kid desk. Daniel opens the door and enters carrying a paper
bag.

> DANIEL
> (to someone down the hall,
> in a hushed voice)
> I know, I'll be quiet.

He shuts the door.

> DANIEL
> (to himself)
> He's always trying to sleep.

Daniel takes off his jacket and tosses it on the floor. He
opens the bag, taking out a few new LPs: X - "Los Angeles,"
BLACK FLAG - "Damaged," and AGENT ORANGE - "Living in
Darkness." He opens up the Black Flag Album, takes out the
record and puts it on his turntable.

MUSIC UP: BLACK FLAG'S "Rise Above"

We hear the music trickling out of a set of earphones. Daniel
turns the volume up so you can clearly hear it coming out of
the phones. It must be really loud with them on. He puts them
on.

(CONTINUED)

CONTINUED:

At first he almost winces from the volume, then a look of
intense concentration comes over his face as he tries to soak
it in completely.

FADE OUT.

END OF ACT TWO

ACT THREE

FADE IN:

INT. MCKINLEY HIGH - HALLWAY - DAY

End of the day. The Geeks are walking together. Neal holds
his dummy under his arm.

>   NEAL
>   Where were you guys at lunch? You
>   missed a good show. Morty and I had
>   the lunch ladies cracking up. I
>   pretended there was a guy drowning
>   in the beans.
>   (does a voice)
>   Help me. Gurgle gurgle.

>   SAM
>   Sorry we missed it.

The guys turn the corner. Neal's face lights up.

ANGLE ON: NEAL'S P.O.V.

Down the hall, we see BARRY SCHWEIBER, 20, standing at Neal's
locker, looking around. He is basically a bigger, preppier
version of Neal.

Neal rushes ahead of the Geeks towards Barry.

>   NEAL
>   Barry!

Barry sees Neal coming towards him.

>   BARRY
>   Groucho!

Neal laughs. Sam and Bill arrive.

>   NEAL
>   (to Barry)
>   What are you doing here!?

(CONTINUED)

CONTINUED:

> BARRY
> I made good time driving in, so I
> thought I'd come by and see the old
> prison.
>> (re: dummy)
> What's this? You studying CPR?

> SAM
> Hi, Barry.

> BARRY
> Hey, Sam! You look good.

> SAM
> Really?

> BARRY
> Yeah. You're looking like a stud.
> Won't be long till you blow off
> these guys and get some real
> friends.

> BILL
> Hey!

> BARRY
> Sorry, Bill. Wow, you're getting
> huge.

> BILL
> Thanks.

> BARRY
> Wasn't that you fighting the Six
> Million Dollar Man? On no, that was
> Bigfoot.

> BILL
> Ha-ha.

Barry and Neal laugh, followed by Sam.

> BARRY
> I'm just messing with you 'cause I
> like you so much.

Bill gives a perfunctory laugh.

> LINDSAY (O.C.)
> Sam.

Lindsay walks up to Sam.

(CONTINUED)

CONTINUED: (2)

>   LINDSAY (CONT'D)
> I've got detention. If Mom asks
> where I am, don't tell her.

>   NEAL
> Detention? Not my Lindsay.

>   LINDSAY
>   (turning around)
> I'm not your Lindsay.
>   (noticing Barry)
> Oh, hi... Barry. How are you?

>   BARRY
> Lindsay.
>   (he soaks her in)
> Damn.

>   LINDSAY
> What?

>   BARRY
>   (flirty)
> What's going on with the Weirs?
> They all look so hot lately. Neal,
> you've got to spend some more time
> over there.

>   NEAL
> Believe me, I've been trying.

>   LINDSAY
> So, how's college?

>   BARRY
> I can't tell you, it would make you
> feel bad.

>   LINDSAY
> Really?

>   BARRY
> It's unbelievable. There's no
> detention, there's no--

Mr. Kowchevski walks over.

>   BARRY (CONT'D)
> Mr. Kowchevski.

>   MR. KOWCHEVSKI
> Hey, stragglers, get to class.

(CONTINUED)

CONTINUED: (3)

> BARRY
> Hey, fat ass, why don't you shove
> it?

> MR. KOWCHEVSKI
> Okay, you're going to the
> principal's office.

> BARRY
> I'm not going anywhere. I graduated
> two years ago.

> MR. KOWCHEVSKI
> Then get the hell out of here.

Barry walks away.

> BARRY
> Hey, Lindsay, come to the party.
> I'll tell you all about college.

> LINDSAY
> Okay.

> BARRY
> See ya, Neal.

> MR. KOWCHEVSKI
> Only thing I hate more than a high
> school kid is a college kid.

CUT TO:

INT. SCHWEIBER DINING ROOM - EVENING

The Schweiber family is having a nice "Welcome home, Barry"
dinner. Mr. and Mrs. Schweiber and Neal are laughing as Barry
tells them a story.

> BARRY
> Fraternities are lame, Dad.

> DR. SCHWEIBER
> They are not.

> BARRY
> Do you know what they make you do
> to get into a fraternity? You have
> to pick up a meatball with your
> rear end and if you can't run with
> it to the other side of the room
> they make you eat it.
> (MORE)

(CONTINUED)

CONTINUED:

> BARRY (CONT'D)
> Is that what you want me doing? You
> actually want to pay to have me
> take part in that activity?

> DR. SCHWEIBER
> If it will help you get a job when
> you graduate, then I'm all for it.

> MRS. SCHWEIBER
> Is that what you did at your
> fraternity?

> DR. SCHWEIBER
> No, it was much harder. We did it
> with an ice cube.

> MRS. SCHWEIBER
> Neal, showbiz is looking better and
> better.
>   (to Barry)
> Have you narrowed in on a major
> yet?

> BARRY
> Well, I'm leaning towards
> undeclared.

> NEAL
> With a minor in sitting on your
> ass.

> MRS. SCHWEIBER
> That's a dollar.

> BARRY
> Yeah, well it's either that or pre-
> law.

> DR. SCHWEIBER
> Now we're talking!

> BARRY
>   (mock whispering to Neal)
> Not really, but look how excited
> they get when I say it.

They all laugh.

> DR. SCHWEIBER
> So, how are the ladies treating
> you?

(CONTINUED)

CONTINUED: (2)

> BARRY
> (smiling)
> I do all right. Right now, I'm just
> playing the field a little bit.

> DR. SCHWEIBER
> Good idea. Don't get tied down too
> young. You're a Schweiber man,
> irresistible to the ladies!

Barry chuckles. A wave of contempt sweeps over Neal.

> DR. SCHWEIBER (CONT'D)
> Isn't that right, honey?

> MRS. SCHWEIBER
> That's right. And I'm the lucky gal
> who gets three Schweiber men all to
> myself.

She leans over and lovingly grabs Neal's face. Neal musters a smile for her.

> CUT TO:

INT. DANIEL'S BEDROOM - DAY

MUSIC UP: "YOUR PHONE'S OFF THE HOOK BUT YOU'RE NOT" BY X

The music is playing loud in Daniel's room. He is bending over his leather jacket with a bottle of Liquid Paper using the little brush to finish painting a white "Anarchy" symbol on the back of his jacket. He leaves it to dry and goes to the mirror to look at himself. He is wearing a sleeveless, sliced up, white T-shirt, holey jeans, and combat boots. He takes a pen knife and slices another rip into the leg of his jeans. He's still not satisfied. He grabs a towel and puts it over his shoulders. He grabs a bottle off the dresser and reads off it for a second, then removes the cap and starts dumping the liquid into his hair.

> CUT TO:

INT. NEAL'S BEDROOM - DAY

Neal is sitting on his bed with a cigar box and his hand made up like Senor Wences' puppet. He pulls the string and opens the box.

> NEAL
> (high voice)
> Kiss for you.
> (MORE)

(CONTINUED)

CONTINUED:

>   NEAL (CONT'D)
>   (deep voice-opens box)
>   No, not for me.
>   (Neal's voice)
>   Close the door.
>   (deep voice-open box)
>   Close the door.
>   (Neal's voice)
>   Okay?
>   (deep voice-open box)
>   Alright.
>   (high voice to Barry)
>   Kiss for you?

>   BARRY
>   Okay, now you're creeping me out.

>   NEAL
>   It's good, huh?

>   BARRY
>   I didn't like that stuff when Senor
>   Wences did it. But you kind of pull
>   it off.

>   NEAL
>   I'm putting together a whole big
>   act. It's going to be so great.
>   (beat)
>   There's something I've been wanting
>   to tell you... it's about Dad.

>   BARRY
>   What about him?

>   NEAL
>   I don't know how to say it, you're
>   gonna be upset.

>   BARRY
>   Just say it.

>   NEAL
>   (takes a big breath)
>   I think Dad is cheating on Mom.

Barry is silent for a moment. Neal anxiously waits for a
response.

>   BARRY
>   How did you find out?

(CONTINUED)

CONTINUED: (2)

> NEAL
> It's a long story, but I'm pretty
> sure I'm right.

> BARRY
> Oh, you're right.

> NEAL
> What?

> BARRY
> Dad cheats on Mom. I've known for
> years.

> NEAL
> Really?

> BARRY
> Yeah. I spotted him once at a
> movie. He was with some redhead.

> NEAL
> Did he see you?

> BARRY
> I don't know, but that year he
> bought me a car for my birthday.

> NEAL
> Why didn't you tell me?

> BARRY
> Why would I tell you?

> NEAL
> Because I live here. Did you tell
> Mom?

> BARRY
> No!

> NEAL
> But he's making a fool of her!

> BARRY
> So, you want to tell her so they
> can get divorced?
> Then they'll sell the house. You'll
> only get to see Dad on the
> weekends. Stay at his new
> apartment. Is that what you want?

(CONTINUED)

CONTINUED: (3)

>   NEAL
> Well, I'm gonna tell her.

>   BARRY
> Neal, don't do it. Nothing good
> will come of it. Just ride this
> out. You'll be in college before
> you know it.

>   NEAL
> That's easy for you to say. You're
> already gone.

                                        CUT TO:

INT. WEIR LIVING ROOM - EVENING

Harold, Jean, and Sam are dressed for the party, ready to
walk out the door.

>   JEAN
>   (calling out)
> Bye, Lindsay, we won't be back too
> late.

>   LINDSAY (O.C.)
> Wait a minute!

>   HAROLD
> Here it comes, "Dad, can I borrow
> some money?"

ANGLE ON: Lindsay, coming out of her room in a dress, looking
beautiful.

>   LINDSAY
> I decided to come with you.

>   JEAN
> Honey, you look great. What made
> you change your mind?

>   LINDSAY
> Umm, Dad was right. I'm a part of
> this family, so I should go.

Sam rolls his eyes. They start to exit.

>   HAROLD
> Did you hear that, Jean? I was
> right about something.
>   (MORE)

                                        (CONTINUED)

CONTINUED:
                    HAROLD (CONT'D)
          We should take a picture of this
          moment or something.

The door shuts.

CUT TO:

EXT. NICK'S FRONT YARD - NIGHT

Nick and Ken are standing at the curb, waiting for Daniel.
They are wearing their normal Freakwear®.

                    NICK
          If this really sucks, you'll help
          me get him out of there, right?

                    KEN
          No, I like things that suck.

                    NICK
          He'd better not ditch us to go off
          with Jenna Zank.

                    KEN
          If he does, I'll clock him in the
          head and take his keys.

Daniel's car pulls up in front of them. They open the
passenger door and start to get in.

MUSIC: "THE PASSENGER" BY IGGY POP coming from the car
speakers.

Nick and Ken look at Daniel. He sits there grinning at them,
his hair now bleached WHITE BLONDE, and spiked. Ken and Nick
bust out laughing. Daniel's grin turns into a sneer.

                    DANIEL
          Just shut up and get in.

                    KEN
               (getting into the back
                seat, laughing)
          Hey, Edgar Winter called. He needs
          his hair back for a gig tonight.

Nick climbs into the front passenger seat.

                    NICK
               (trying to stifle his
                laugh)
          I think you look good, man...

                                        (CONTINUED)

CONTINUED:

Daniel gives him an "I'm waiting" look.

>   NICK (CONT'D)
>   Can I use you to clean out my ear
>   later?

He breaks into big laughter.

>   DANIEL
>   We'll see who looks out of place
>   when we get downtown.

Nick shuts his door. Daniel peels out.

>   CUT TO:

INT. SCHWEIBER LIVING ROOM - NIGHT

MUSIC UP: "Sweet Caroline" by Neil Diamond.

The party is on. Several people mingle about, many gathered
by the buffet table. The Weirs have just arrived. Dr.
Schweiber moves to greet them. Harold pastes on a smile.

>   DR. SCHWEIBER
>   The Weirs are here! Glad you could
>   make it this year.

They exchange handshakes and hugs.

>   DR. SCHWEIBER (CONT'D)
>   Jean, you look terrific. You too,
>   Lindsay. You're a real knockout.
>   Let me get you guys a drink. Sammy,
>   I know Neal and Bill are around
>   here somewhere.

Sam heads off to find them. Harold and Jean walk into the
party. Harold, subtly holds out his keys to Jean.

>   HAROLD
>   I'm giving these to you now. There
>   is no way I'm gonna spend all night
>   listening to the same old set of
>   dentist jokes without plenty of
>   anesthesia.

Jean takes the keys with an annoyed eye roll.

(CONTINUED)

CONTINUED:

ANGLE ON: Lindsay standing alone. She casually looks around until she spots Barry across the room, talking to an older couple. He eventually sees her, and signals to her with his eyebrows and a smile. She smiles back at him.

                                                    CUT TO:

INT. THE ARMPIT - NIGHT

Daniel, Nick, and Ken enter the loud, dingy punk club. The place is full of people in various stages of punkdom. The dance floor is a sea of strange haircuts bouncing up and down and slamming into each other as the band onstage plays a loud, cheap and easy-to-clear punk song. Daniel is happy, he doesn't look out of place. Nick is wincing from the noise.

                    DANIEL
          Isn't this great?

                    KEN
          No one carded us. I like it.

                    DANIEL
          That's right, man, no rules! You
          can do what you want here.

                    NICK
          I'm not sure what that is.

                    KEN
          I am. I'll be at the bar.

                    NICK
          I'll go with you.

The three head towards the bar. Their path is impeded by a BIG PUNK with a mohawk, wearing pants and suspenders, no shirt. They stop in their tracks. The guy takes a swig of his drink and sprays it up into the air from his mouth. Nick and Ken dodge the shower. Daniel takes the brunt.

                    BIG PUNK
               (screaming)
          YEAH!

Daniel shakes some liquid off his head like a dog then gets right up in the Big Punk's face, smiling.

                    DANIEL
               (screaming)
          YEAH!

                                              (CONTINUED)

CONTINUED:

The big punk gives a strange nod of approval. Nick and Ken shoot each other an "Uh-oh" look.

FADE OUT.

<u>END OF ACT THREE</u>

<u>ACT FOUR</u>

FADE IN:

INT. SCHWEIBER HOUSE - NIGHT

MUSIC UP: "I AM, I SAID" - by Neil Diamond

Lindsay and Barry are standing off in the corner of the party, engrossed in conversation.

>   BARRY
>   If one more person asks me what my
>   major is going to be I'm going to
>   snap.

Lindsay doesn't say anything. She just smiles.

>   BARRY (CONT'D)
>   You want to ask me now, don't you?

>   LINDSAY
>   No, I don't.

>   BARRY
>   Oh, you want to ask so bad.

>   LINDSAY
>   Not if you're going to snap.

>   BARRY
>   I honestly have no idea. Do you
>   know what you're going to major in?

>   LINDSAY
>   Not a clue. Probably in just being
>   glad I'm out of high school.

>   BARRY
>   You'll love college. You're perfect
>   for it.

>   LINDSAY
>   (liking the sound of that)
>   Really?

(CONTINUED)

CONTINUED:

> BARRY
> Absolutely. After high school all
> the dumb, slutty popular girls wind
> up in Junior College, or community
> college. You actually never see
> them again for the rest of your
> life. It's like they've fallen off
> the planet. But the smart, pretty
> girls who nobody payed attention to
> in high school, in college, they
> rule. And you're gonna be their
> queen.

> LINDSAY
> (loves that)
> Yeah? Thanks.

A middle-aged BALD MAN taps Barry on the shoulder.

> BALD MAN
> Barry.

Barry turns around to see the man.

> BARRY
> (not recognizing him)
> Hi.

> BALD MAN
> Dr. Melvin Latz, one of your
> father's partners.

> BARRY
> Oh, hi! How are you?

> BALD MAN
> Fine, good to see you. How's
> school? Have you chosen a major?

Barry shoots Lindsay a glance. She tries to hold back a
laugh.

> BARRY
> (solemnly)
> I'm thinking about African tribal
> poetry.

                                                    CUT TO:

INT. THE ARMPIT - NIGHT

Daniel and Nick are standing together. Nick still has a
pained look on his face. Daniel is scanning the room.

>   DANIEL
>   I don't see her.

>   NICK
>   Damn. Let's go.

>   DANIEL
>   Shut up, man. It's still early, she
>   didn't write what time on my arm.

Ken returns to the trio, looking pissed.

>   NICK
>   Where are the drinks!?

>   KEN
>   The bartender is a bastard! He
>   keeps ignoring me. He's only
>   serving people with stupid
>   haircuts... Daniel, you go.

>   DANIEL
>   Bite me. Hey! There she is.

We see Jenna and her blue head disappear into the crowd.

>   DANIEL (CONT'D)
>   See you later.

Daniel dashes off after her. She seems to slither through the
crowd easily while Daniel is having a harder time. A guys
shoulder slams into him, knocking him off balance.

>   DANIEL (CONT'D)
>   (over his shoulder)
>   Excuse me.

He trods on for a few steps and gets slammed into again.

>   DANIEL (CONT'D)
>   (turning around)
>   Hey!

The punk who slammed him ignores him and keeps walking.
Daniel collects himself.

(CONTINUED)

CONTINUED:

> DANIEL (CONT'D)
> (resolute, to himself)
> All right, let's go!

He takes a few steps, then winds up, and slams his shoulder into a PUNK passing him. The guy whips around.

> PUNK
> (wild)
> What's your problem!?

> DANIEL
> Nothing, man! Someone pushed me.
> Sorry.

The Punk gives him a dirty look but decides to move on. Daniel sees Jenna within earshot.

> DANIEL (CONT'D)
> (calling out)
> Jenna.

Jenna turns around. Daniel walks to her.

> DANIEL
> Hey.

> JENNA
> (with an attitude)
> What?

> DANIEL
> Whaddya mean "what"? You invited me here.

He holds up his arm to show her the address.

> JENNA
> (dropping the attitude)
> Oh, it's you. You look different.

> DANIEL
> This is the real me.

> JENNA
> Yeah?

> DANIEL
> Yeah.

(CONTINUED)

CONTINUED: (2)

>   JENNA
> Well, does the real you want to
> dance? Because I do.

>   DANIEL
> Let's do it.

Daniel follows Jenna out on the dance floor. They begin to
pogo along with the crowd. Slamming into people and each
other.

>   JENNA
>   (shouting over the music)
> How do you like the band?

>   DANIEL
>   (also shouting)
> They're great! Puss Rules!

>   JENNA
> Puss is on next.

>   DANIEL
>   (covering)
> Yeah... I know... they rule.

He smiles at her. Someone slams Daniel hard and knocks him
out of frame. Jenna rolls her eyes, but smiles as if she's
somewhat charmed.

                                                    CUT TO:

INT. SCHWEIBER LIVING ROOM - NIGHT

MUSIC UP: "HOT AUGUST NIGHT" by Neil Diamond.

Harold and Jean are standing with The Schweibers and others
as listening to Dr. S. telling a joke.

>   DR. SCHWEIBER
> So, the dentist shoots back "Make
> up your mind, I gotta adjust the
> chair."

The group laughs. Harold laughs harder than anyone, too hard.
Jean looks at him strangely,

>   DR. SCHWEIBER (CONT'D)
> Another drink, Harold?

                                              (CONTINUED)

CONTINUED:

> HAROLD
> (jovial)
> Don't mind if I do.

He hands Dr. S. his glass.

> JEAN
> (a little embarrassed by
> Harold)
> I better not, I'm driving.

ANGLE ON: Lindsay and Barry are sitting on a couple of
folding chairs in the corner of the room, talking intensely.

> BARRY
> I mean, come on, he's a former
> actor. Bush is the former head of
> the C.I.A. Who do you think is
> really running the show?

> LINDSAY
> I never thought of it that way. But
> do you really think John Hinckley
> was working for him?

> BARRY
> Not directly, but yes. At least I
> find it easier to believe than that
> fakakte Jodie Foster story.

> LINDSAY
> Fakakte?

> BARRY
> Fakakte. It's Yiddish for... lame.

> LINDSAY
> I see.

> BARRY
> You want to go for a stroll? All
> these weird people in my house are
> making me nervous.

> LINDSAY
> Yeah, great.

The two get up to leave.

(CONTINUED)

CONTINUED: (2)

>   BARRY
> Look, that guy's not even using a
> coaster.

                                    CUT TO:

INT. THE ARMPIT - NIGHT

The punk band wails at the same fevered tempo. Daniel and
Jenna are moshing big time. Both are having a good time.
Nearby, a couple of guys are surfing prone on top of the
crowd.

>   DANIEL
>   (fist pumping in the air)
> Wooooo!

One of the crowd surfers gets close to Daniel then all of a
sudden his heavy combat boot flies into the back of Daniel's
head with a loud thud. Daniel goes down. As he hits the floor
the crowd swallows him up and he starts to get trampled.

>   DANIEL (CONT'D)
>   (disoriented, panicked)
> Hey! Get off! Ah!

He struggles to get up. Jenna helps him up and quickly off
the dance floor.

>   JENNA
>   (not overly concerned)
> Are you okay?

>   DANIEL
>   (breathing heavily)
> Yeah, I'm fine.

He feels the back of his head where he took the boot then
looks at his hand. It's got blood on it.

>   DANIEL (CONT'D)
> Where's the bathroom?

>   JENNA
>   (pointing)
> Over there.

>   DANIEL
> I'll be right back.

                                    CUT TO:

EXT. SCHWEIBER HOUSE - NIGHT

Lindsay and Barry are walking outside the party.

                LINDSAY
    ...and he was into me, but he was
    stoned all the time. You smoke?

                BARRY
    No. You crazy? I get paranoid.

                LINDSAY
    Me, too. That stuff, it's fakakte.

                BARRY
      (laughs)
    That's very good.

                LINDSAY
    What were we talking about?

                BARRY
    Your friends.

                LINDSAY
    Yeah. They're funny and fun and all
    that, but it's not like they
    challenge me or inspire me. Is that
    terrible to say?

                BARRY
    Yes, it's very bad. No. Relax. You
    think too much.

                LINDSAY
    It's hard not to.

                BARRY
    The funny part is you get to
    college and all that high school
    stuff disappears. It's like a do-
    over.

                LINDSAY
    You're way too into college.

                BARRY
    I get a commission on everyone I
    bring in. No, I mean you get there
    and nobody knows you were a
    mathlete or a burn-out so you can
    start fresh. Be who you want to be.
      (MORE)

(CONTINUED)

CONTINUED:

                    BARRY (CONT'D)
          Take me for instance. When I was in
          high school, I got beat up more
          than Neal. But when I got to
          college, I didn't say I'm the kid
          who gets his butt kicked every day.
          I said, I'm the handsome, dashing
          Jew. And they believed it.

                    LINDSAY
          I believe it.

                    BARRY
          See.

                    LINDSAY
          But, who do I want to be?

                    BARRY
          Give me the weekend and I'll come
          up with something good. But I'm
          thinking... fisherman? Matador?

They laugh.

                    LINDSAY
          Stablemaster.

Barry kisses her.

                                        CUT TO:

INT. THE ARMPIT - MEN'S ROOM - NIGHT

Daniel is standing at the sink holding a wad of bloodsoaked
paper towels to the back of his head. Several punk guys mill
in and out behind him. Daniel takes the wad away from his
head to see if the bleeding stopped. A GUY with a mohawk
behind him inspects the wound.

                    MOHAWK GUY
          Nice battle scar, man.

                    DANIEL
          Thanks.

                    MOHAWK GUY
          Quite a night, huh?

                    DANIEL
          Yeah.

                                        (CONTINUED)

CONTINUED:

                    MOHAWK GUY
          Can you believe how many posers
          there are out there?

                    DANIEL
          Yeah... I know, it sucks.

                    MOHAWK GUY
                (re: Daniel's head)
          Oh, it's still oozing a little.

Daniel puts the towel back against his head.

                    DANIEL
          Thanks.

The guy exits. Daniel takes a good look at himself in the
mirror.

                                        CUT TO:

INT. SCHWEIBER'S HOUSE - NIGHT

Sam, Neal, and Bill are sitting on the couch watching the
party. Sam is still eating.

                    BILL
          You know, "Fantasy Island" is on,
          we could go watch that.

Neal doesn't answer. He is staring across the room with an
angry look on his face.

ANGLE ON: Neal's POV - His parents across the room laughing
and talking to a group of people. His Dad has his arm around
his Mom.

                    NEAL
                (sotto mocking)
          Yeah, look at me, I'm such a good
          husband, blah, blah, blah.

ANGLE ON: Dr. Schweiber picking up a spoon and tapping it
against his glass. The room quiets down and focuses on him.
He raises his glass.

                    DR. SCHWEIBER
          I'd like to propose a toast: To my
          wife, without whom we'd all be
          hungry and without whom my life
          wouldn't be complete.

                                        (CONTINUED)

CONTINUED:

The crowd lets out a collective "Awwww."

Dr. Schweiber squeezes his wife and plants a big kiss on her cheek.

>   NEAL
>   This sucks, I gotta get out of
>   here.

Neal rushes out of the room. Bill and Sam watch him go.

>   CUT TO:

EXT. SCHWEIBER HOUSE - NIGHT

MUSIC UP: "LOVE ON THE ROCKS" by Neil Diamond.

Neal is walking alone outside in a dark mood, almost on the verge of tears. He walks along for a little bit then turns the corner to discover Lindsay and Barry making out, hot and heavy.

>   NEAL
>   (bottoming out)
>   No.

Lindsay and Barry are startled. They pull apart quickly.

>   BARRY
>   Hey, buddy.

>   LINDSAY
>   (flustered)
>   Uh, hi, Neal.

>   NEAL
>   Don't let me interrupt, I was
>   just...

He feels his voice start to quiver.

>   NEAL (CONT'D)
>   Uh... out for... a...

Rather than have them see him break down, he turns around and bolts. Lindsay and Barry look at each other, concerned.

INT. SCHWEIBER LIVING ROOM - NIGHT

Neal rushes in the door, head down, and heads towards his room. He is intercepted by his dad.

>   (CONTINUED)

CONTINUED:

> DR. SCHWEIBER
> (cheerful)
> I've been looking all over for you.

> NEAL
> (breathing heavy)
> What.

> DR. SCHWEIBER
> Everyone wants to see your
> ventriloquism!

> NEAL
> (out of the question)
> No. Not now.

> DR. SCHWEIBER
> Come on, what friendlier audience
> are you ever going to find?
> (turning to the room)
> Hey everyone? Who wants to see
> Neal's ventriloquism act?

The whole room applauds and cheers. Neal is mortified.

> DR. SCHWEIBER
> Come on, go get your dummy.

Neal gets an angry, resolved look on his face.

> NEAL
> It's called a figure.

He turns and marches off towards his room.

INT. THE ARMPIT - NIGHT

Daniel wanders back out into the club. He finds Jenna who has
gathered with the rest of a small group gathered around
something going on.

> JENNA
> How's your head?

> DANIEL
> No problem, just another battle
> scar.

The small group cheers. Daniel looks and sees they're
cheering for a guy who just had his nose pierced with a
safety pin by a girl sitting in a chair.

(CONTINUED)

CONTINUED:

> FRESHLY PIERCED GUY
> (soaking up the applause)
> Thank you, thank you very much.

He struts around showing off his new orifice.

Just then a big, good looking Punk comes up behind Jenna and throws his arms around her. She turns around to see who it is.

> JENNA
> Billy!

She throws her arms around him and gives him a big hug. Daniel is bothered.

> PIERCING GIRL
> (holding up a fresh safety
> pin)
> Who's next?

Daniel looks at Jenna, still hugging the guy, then at the piercer.

> DANIEL
> I am.

He kneels down in front of the girl and tilts his head back. She puts a piece of ice on his nostril.

> PIERCING GIRL
> I just have to numb it for a
> minute.

Nick walks up to the group, curious why they're gathered. He looks down on the floor and sees Daniel.

> NICK
> What are you doing, man?!

> DANIEL
> Don't worry about it.

> PIERCING GIRL
> Are you ready?

> DANIEL
> Yeah. Do it.

She puts the open safety pin up to Daniel's nostril.

(CONTINUED)

CONTINUED: (2)

                    PIERCING GIRL
          Okay, on "three" I'll push it
          through. One...

                    NICK
          Daniel, this is stupid.

                    PIERCING GIRL
     Two...

ANGLE ON: DANIEL'S P.O.V. - We see the hand up to his nose,
and beyond that we see Jenna making out with Billy.

                    PIERCING GIRL (CONT'D)
     Three.

                    DANIEL
     Wait!

He leaps to his feet.

                    DANIEL (CONT'D)
               (in pain)
     Ahhh!

                    NICK
               (cringing and looking
                away)
     Jeez.

The pin has not gone through Daniel's nose, but it has gone
into it and is now sticking out of it.

                    PIERCING GIRL
          You wimp. You ruined it.

Daniel takes out the pin, throws it on the floor and walks
away. Nick follows.

                    NICK
          Can we get out of here now? This
          place is making me sick.

                    DANIEL
          Hell, yes. Where's Ken?

ANGLE ON: Ken on the dance floor. He's dancing alone,
sweating profusely, wildly slamming anyone within five feet
of him, hard. He has a maniacal grin on his face.

                                        CUT TO:

INT. SCHWEIBER LIVING ROOM - NIGHT

Neal is sitting on a dining room chair with his dummy on his lap. He has a confident look about him. Bill and Sam are smiling, waiting for him to suck.

                    NEAL
          Good evening, everyone. Morty, say
          hello to the nice people.

                    MORTY
          Hello, nice people!

                    ALL
             (mixed with laughter)
          Hi, Morty!

                    MORTY
          Why are these people so funny
          looking?

                    NEAL
          What do you mean?

                    MORTY
          Their teeth. They're terrible.

Everyone laughs, Dr. Schweiber included.

                    MORTY (CONT'D)
          Have they ever heard of a
          toothbrush?

The audience chuckles.

                    NEAL
          Behave! These people are my Dad's
          patients.

                    MORTY
          Your dad's a doctor?

                    NEAL
          Not a real doctor, he's a dentist.

Dr. Schweiber forces a laugh.

                    MORTY
          Oh. So, these people pay him to fix
          their teeth.

(CONTINUED)

CONTINUED:

>   NEAL
>   That's right.
>
>   MORTY
>   Well, I'd get my money back. That
>   woman over there, her teeth are so
>   bad she could play professional
>   hockey.
>
>   NEAL
>   You really seem to hate dentists.
>
>   MORTY
>   Yeah, me and everyone else on the
>   planet. Executioners are more
>   beloved than dentists. At least
>   executioners don't lie and say this
>   won't hurt.
>
>   NEAL
>   Do you ever go to the dentist?
>
>   MORTY
>   No.
>
>   NEAL
>   Why not?
>
>   MORTY
>   I already have a hand in one end of
>   me, I don't need one in the other.
>   Ooh, I hate dentists.
>
>   NEAL
>   Could we get to the act already?
>
>   MORTY
>   Sure thing, friend. What's the
>   difference between a dentist and a
>   proctologist?
>
>   NEAL
>   What?
>
>   MORTY
>   One's a doctor of the ass, and
>   one's an ass who's a doctor.

The room gasps except for Harold who can't control his
laughter. Jean elbows him.

                                        (CONTINUED)

CONTINUED: (2)

> NEAL
> That's not very nice.

> MORT
> What's the difference between a
> dentist and a brand new pair of
> leather shoes?

> NEAL
> What?

> MORTY
> A brand new pair of leather shoes
> doesn't give you an unnecessary
> root canal so he can build an
> addition onto his house.

Dr. Schweiber looks very annoyed. He is getting ready to make
a move.

> NEAL
> That's not funny, Morty.

> MORTY
> Why did Dr. Schweiber become a
> dentist?

> NEAL
> Why?

> MORTY
> He failed medical school.

People are getting uncomfortable.

> NEAL
> That's not even a joke. Dr.
> Schweiber is a great dentist.

> MORTY
> Suck up. Sounds like someone's
> bucking for a new bicycle.

> NEAL
> I'm not sucking up, I'm telling the
> truth.

> MORTY
> Well, he ain't working on me. I
> wouldn't let this guy put me under.
> (MORE)

(CONTINUED)

CONTINUED: (3)

> MORTY (CONT'D)
> You'll wake up with your wisdom
> teeth gone along with your
> virginity.

ANGLE ON: Barry and Lindsay walking in the back of the room
surprised to see what's going on.

> DR. SCHWEIBER
> (jumping in)
> Okay, that's enough, Neal.

> MORTY
> (mimics)
> That's enough, Neal. Get a load of
> this moron, he thinks Neal's
> talking.

> NEAL
> Please, Morty. Think about the nice
> people. You're ruining the party.

> MORTY
> This party sucks every year. Why
> should tonight be any different?

Dr. Schweiber rushes towards Neal.

> DR. SCHWEIBER
> Okay, show's over.

He pulls Neal off the stage.

> DR. SCHWEIBER (CONT'D)
> Thank you, Neal and Morty.

> MORTY
> You're out of order. You're out of
> order.

Dr. Schweiber covers the dummy's mouth.

> MORTY (CONT'D)
> You're all out of order. This whole
> dentist practice is out of order.

> NEAL
> (in a rage to dad)
> Get your hands off me!

He pulls the dummy away from his dad and runs off into his
room.

Mrs. Schweiber goes after him. Barry catches her.

(CONTINUED)

CONTINUED: (4)

                    BARRY
          Do you want me to talk to him?

                    MRS. SCHWEIBER
          No honey, I have to.

She heads off.

                    DR. SCHWEIBER
               (to the room, forcing a
                smile)
          Sorry about that. There's plenty
          more to eat and drink everyone.
          Enjoy!

ANGLE ON: Bill and Sam

                    BILL
               (whispering to Sam)
          I told you the dummy would take him over.

                                        CUT TO:

INT. NEAL'S BEDROOM - NIGHT

Mrs. Schweiber enters to see Neal laying face down on the bed
crying. She rushes to him, sits down and strokes his back.

                    MRS. SCHWEIBER
          Shhh. It's okay, it's okay.

                    NEAL
               (crying)
          I told him I didn't want to do it!

                    MRS. SCHWEIBER
          I know. It's all right. Shhhh. Now
          will you tell me what's wrong?

                    NEAL
          No. I don't want to talk about it.
          I'll be fine! I just want to be alone.

Neal continues to cry. She gives him a hug and a kiss on the
forehead.

                    MRS. SCHWEIBER
               (worried)
          Okay, but I'll just be in the other
          room if you need me.

She gets up and turns around to leave.

                                        (CONTINUED)

CONTINUED:

>   NEAL
>   (blurting it out)
>   Dad's cheating on you.

Mrs. Schweiber turns around, shocked by what she's just heard. Neal begins sobbing uncontrollably. Mrs. S. sits down on the bed with him and holds him while he sobs.

>   MRS. SCHWEIBER
>   It's okay, honey, calm down, it's
>   okay.

>   NEAL
>   I'm sorry, I had to tell you.

>   MRS. SCHWEIBER
>   No, no, don't be sorry, you should
>   never have had to deal with this.
>   I should've... I didn't think you'd
>   find out.

>   NEAL
>   (confused)
>   What... you know?

She looks in his eyes and nods slowly.

>   MRS. SCHWEIBER
>   I've known for a while. And I'm
>   okay, Neal, I'll be fine.

>   NEAL
>   So are you two going to get... you
>   know...

>   MRS. SCHWEIBER
>   Everything will be fine, Honey, try
>   not to worry about it. I want you
>   to know, nothing is more important
>   to me than you and your brother.
>   I'm so proud of you both.

She starts to well up. Neal starts to sob some more. Mom holds him tight.

>   NEAL
>   I'm sorry about doing that act.

>   MRS. SCHWEIBER
>   What sorry? You were hilarious.

Neal smiles.

(CONTINUED)

CONTINUED: (2)

>   NEAL
>   Yeah? Did you like the thing about
>   the hand in one end?

>   MRS. SCHWEIBER
>   It was great.

>   NEAL
>   Yeah, it killed. I made that up
>   right there.

>   MRS. SCHWEIBER
>   Wow!

She hugs him tighter.

>   CUT TO:

INT. SCHWEIBER LIVING ROOM - NIGHT

The House is emptying out. Several people are leaving. A
drunken Harold and tipsy Jean along with Sam and Bill, come
up to Lindsay and Barry.

>   HAROLD
>   Where's that kid? He was hilarious.

>   JEAN
>   Come on, Lindsay, honey, we'd
>   better get going.

>   HAROLD
>   Where are we going?

He wanders off, Sam and Bill follow.

>   LINDSAY
>   (laughing)
>   You guys are hammered!

>   JEAN
>   No, not hammered dear, tipsy maybe.
>   Your father, he's hammered.

She holds out the keys.

>   JEAN (CONT'D)
>   You're driving.

>   LINDSAY
>   I'll be right there.

>   (CONTINUED)

CONTINUED:

                    JEAN
          Okay.

She notices Barry standing there and realizes there's
something going on. A big grin comes over her face.

                    JEAN (CONT'D)
          Take your time.

She walks off.

                    LINDSAY
          I guess I gotta go.

                    BARRY
          I wish I could. This could be a
          long night for the Schweibers.

He takes a pen out of his pocket, grabs a napkin off a table
and writes on it. He hands it to Lindsay.

                    BARRY (CONT'D)
          Here's my number at school. Call me
          sometime.

                    LINDSAY
          Thanks.

                    BARRY
          And try to stay out of detention.

He kisses Lindsay on the cheek. She smiles.

                    BARRY (CONT'D)
          Bye.

                    LINDSAY
          Bye.

Barry walks off. Lindsay collects herself from her
sophisticated evening then heads off.

                                                  CUT TO:

EXT. SCHWEIBER HOUSE - NIGHT

UNDER MUSIC...

Track with -- the Weirs, as they leave the party. Harold is
clearly a little tipsy. Jean hands the keys to Lindsay, who
is distracted, happy. PUSH ON-- Lindsay, as she drops just
behind the family, in her own world.

INT. NEAL'S BEDROOM - NIGHT

Neal sits on his bed, reflecting on the night he's had. He
glances over to Morty, propped against the wall in the
corner. After a beat, he starts LAUGHING.

INT. SCHWEIBER HOUSE/LIVING ROOM - NIGHT

Mrs. Schweiber cleans up plastic cups, from the buffet. Dr.
Schweiber escorts the last of his guests to the door. As he
passes, she throws him a look -- deep in thought.

EXT. KIM'S HOUSE - NIGHT

Daniel, beaten, bloodied and blonde, stands in front of the
door, debating whether or not to knock. After a beat, it
seems as though he's decided not to. He begins to walk away,
when suddenly, the door OPENS -- it's Kim. He turns to her
and they take each other in for a moment. She starts to
laugh. Not a mean laugh, an understanding one. Then she hugs
him, and he holds her tight.

                                                FADE OUT.

                        THE END

FREAKS AND GEEKS

"SMOOCHING AND MOOCHING"

Episode #16

Written by Steve Bannos

Directed by Jake Kasdan

I remember it like yesterday. It was a balmy day in January of 2000 and I was enjoying the success of a "Sleeper Hit TV Show" and living high on the Apatow Hog (and a damn succulent Hog it is). *Freaks and Geeks* had hit its stride, and the episodes were locked until the end of the season. I had kept busy for months writing and revising more outlines and drafts of "The Missing Bus" than I could keep track of (nine outlines and three drafts), and I was ready to coast until it shot in a few weeks.

I was enjoying a leisurely afternoon drive southbound to the Commerce Casino, where I would have ultimately been financially ass-paddled by the locals in a game of seven card stud, when my cell phone rang. It was Judd. Now, what in the hell would Judd Apatow be doing calling me on my cell phone? Doesn't he have a hit show to helm? I immediately perked up, figuring he wanted to pick my brain about some super narrow geek trivia about *Mad Magazine* or monsters, and I was ready to oblige. But his tone was serious and almost apologetic. He got right to the point. "The Missing Bus" script was getting shelved—as in the shelf in the trash can. The news was appropriately devastating, but I continued to drive. Judd's tone of seriousness now addressed a more grave problem at hand. A new script needed to be written in one week. No time to waste, I turned the shitbox around and headed back north to Raleigh Studios and started all over again.

At this point in the season, Judd and Paul pretty much knew we were being canceled, so it was time to quickly tie up the big picture stories—specifically Sam and Cindy becoming a real couple and then ultimately their breakup. They also wanted to finally feature Joe Flaherty in an episode.

The "Smooching" story, specifically a creepy party where kids were making out, came from a real life story. Sadly, the only element in the episode that I wasn't satisfied with was the makeout party. I envisioned the house to be scarier, the kids older, and all the girls much more experienced and sluttier. It all seemed a tad bit too friendly and lacked the filthy peepshow sexuality fear that I envisioned.

I couldn't wait to tell Martin Starr (my favorite cast member) that not only did I write him smooching with a red-hot girl, but I wrote him into a black turtleneck to make him look like James Bond while he was doing it. He drooled in anticipation (as opposed to his usual drooling). Martin's performance in the "Seven Minutes in Heaven" scene was absolutely inspired!

The "Mooching" story gave Joe Flaherty (also my favorite cast member) a real chance to shine. Shine on, you crazy Canadian Diamond! The last scene with Lindsay in the bedroom is possibly the most heart tugging and sincere moment in the entire run of the show. Joe was incredible!

In fact, the whole cast was incredible! Paul and Judd were incredible! The show was incredible! And the whole trip was incredible!

Please enjoy the script.

—Steve Bannos

FREAKS AND GEEKS

"SMOOCHING AND MOOCHING"

<u>CAST LIST</u>

LINDSAY WEIR
SAM WEIR
HAROLD WEIR
JEAN WEIR
DANIEL DESARIO
NICK ANDOPOLIS
BILL HAVERCHUCK
NEAL SCHWEIBER
KEN MILLER
KIM KELLY
MR. LACOVARA
CINDY SANDERS
HARRIS
GORDON CRISP
VICKY APPLEBY
MR. ANDOPOLIS
SEAN
MAUREEN
MONA
GUY

FREAKS AND GEEKS

"SMOOCHING AND MOOCHING"

SET LIST

INTERIORS:

MCKINLEY HIGH SCHOOL
        /HALLWAY
        /BIOLOGY CLASSROOM
        /CAFETERIA
        /UNDER THE STAIRS
WEIR HOUSE
        /DINING ROOM
        /LIVING ROOM
        /KITCHEN
        /LINDSAY'S BEDROOM
        /SAM'S ROOM
        /HALLWAY
NICK'S HOUSE
        /BASEMENT
        /LIVING ROOM
SCHWEIBER HOUSE
        /NEAL'S ROOM
BILL'S HOUSE
        /BILL'S BEDROOM
MONA'S HOUSE
        /LIVING ROOM
        /HALLWAY
        /BEDROOM
        /LAUNDRY ROOM

EXTERIORS:

MCKINLEY HIGH SCHOOL
        /UNDER THE BLEACHERS
GARAGE SALE
MONA'S HOUSE

<u>TEASER</u>

FADE IN:

EXT. GARAGE SALE - DAY

NICK and KEN are walking around a neighborhood garage sale, looking at all the junk.

> KEN
> Man, people have a lot of crap. How does anyone get more than one toaster?

Ken points to a table with several toasters. Nick bends down to a box filled with old books.

> NICK
> (thinking)
> I don't know, man. I can never figure out why they have all these old books. Do you think they read them all and didn't like them?

> KEN
> I don't know. My mom always reads these stupid romance books and leaves them on the back of the toilet and then someone always ends up knocking them into the bowl.

> NICK
> How does that happen?

> KEN
> I don't know. It's the bathroom. Weird things happen in there.

Nick gets up and his eyes go wide.

> NICK
> Ken, check it out!

They walk over to a table that has a beat-up set of bongos sitting on it.

> NICK (CONT'D)
> Bongos, man. Now we can play "Evil Ways." And you know what? This'll bring the Andopolis kit up to an even thirty pieces.

(CONTINUED)

CONTINUED:

> KEN
> Wouldn't this make it thirty-one?

> NICK
> (thinking)
> I don't know, man. Technically,
> even though the bongos are two
> drums, they're considered to be a
> single instrument.

> KEN
> Then I shall henceforth refer to
> them as "The Bongo."

Nick smiles and happily grabs the bongos as he digs a few
bucks out of his pocket.

                                                    CUT TO:

INT. NICK'S BASEMENT - MOMENTS LATER

Dim basement. Nick and Ken bump around upstairs.

> NICK (O.S.)
> Hey, Ken, get out of the fridge.

> KEN (O.S.)
> I need some fuel.

> NICK (O.S.)
> No, put that beer back, man. My dad
> knows how many are in there. He's
> already pissed at me.

Nick and Ken descend the stairs, Nick carrying the bongos.

> KEN
> Why? He see your report card?

> NICK
> Yeah. And I was practicing
> "American Band" while he was trying
> to watch "Sixty Minutes."

They hit the bottom of the stairs, take the turn toward the
play area, and stop dead in their tracks.

NICK'S POV: Where Nick's drums used to be, there is now
nothing except a few scraps of drum hardware. THE DRUMSET IS
GONE. Only the stool remains.

Nick and Ken stare. Nick looks beyond shocked.

                                              (CONTINUED)

CONTINUED:

>   KEN
> Uh... Nick. Where's your drums?

Nick just stares in shock.

>   CUT TO:

OPENING TITLE SEQUENCE

ACT 1

FADE IN:

INT. NICK'S LIVING ROOM - DAY

MR. ANDOPOLIS, uniform still on, tie loosened, drink in hand, sits in his chair. Nick stands before him, looking very upset.

>   MR. ANDOPOLIS
> I think you'd better lower your
> voice, son.

>   NICK
> You had no right to give my drums
> away!

>   MR. ANDOPOLIS
> I think those drums were making you
> go deaf. Otherwise, you would have
> heard all the times I told you to
> clean up your act.

>   NICK
> You know I've been trying.

>   MR. ANDOPOLIS
> Yeah. With a little more effort,
> you might just end up living in a
> cardboard box.

>   NICK
> You have no right to give away my
> personal property.

>   MR. ANDOPOLIS
> The only personal property you
> should be worried about is your
> future.

>   NICK
> But--

>   (CONTINUED)

CONTINUED:

> MR. ANDOPOLIS
> We're done talking.

And with this, Mr. Andopolis opens his newspaper and starts reading. Nick looks like he wants to say more but just turns and heads out the door.

He stops in the doorway. Turns back. Flat faced.

> NICK
> You owe me money.

Mr. Andopolis lowers his paper and gives Nick an "are you talking to me?" look. Nick just stares, challenging nervously.

> MR. ANDOPOLIS
> Are you talking to me?

> NICK
> I paid for those drums. You gave them away. You owe me for them.

> MR. ANDOPOLIS
> That's fine, Nick. You can deduct it from the last sixteen years of rent that you owe me.

> NICK
> I don't owe you anything. But you owe me for those drums. I want my money. Right <u>now</u>.

> MR. ANDOPOLIS
> Go get it from your drug dealer.

> NICK
> (yelling)
> Give me my MONEY!

Mr. Andopolis gets up. You don't yell at this guy. He holds a hard stare on Nick, who stares at him, nervously defiant.

> MR. ANDOPOLIS
> We're finished talking.

> NICK
> (after a beat)
> I'm outta here. Enjoy all the peace and quiet.

(CONTINUED)

CONTINUED: (2)

Nick stares down his dad, then turns and exits the front
door, SLAMMING it behind him. Mr. Andopolis watches him go.
He looks tired and fed up.

                                              CUT TO:

INT. SCHOOL HALLWAY - MORNING

SAM, NEAL, and BILL are walking down the hall.

                    NEAL
          I want to get a dirt bike. My
          neighbor, Gary Frank, has a KX 80.
          It's so cool.

                    SAM
          They're dangerous.

                    NEAL
          No, they're not.

                    BILL
          Really? These kids used to ride
          dirt bikes on Slatzky's farm and
          Slatzky didn't like it so he put up
          a wire and this one kid got his
          head cut off.

                    SAM
          I heard that story. His head was
          talking for a minute after it got
          separated from his body.

                    NEAL
          What don't you guys believe?

Sam and Bill look at Neal like he's nuts. Then they see CINDY
SANDERS and TODD SCHELLINGER pass in the hallway without
acknowledging each other.

                    NEAL (CONT'D)
          What was that?

                    SAM
          What?

                    NEAL
          Cindy and Todd didn't say hi to
          each other.

                    BILL
          So?

                                         (CONTINUED)

CONTINUED:

>   NEAL
> Maybe they broke up.

>   BILL
> Maybe they just had a lover's spat.

>   NEAL
> It looked like more than a lover's
> spat.

>   SAM
> What if they broke up for good?

>   BILL
> I don't know. My mom had a spat
> with Mr. Fredricks the other night
> and she told him he was ten pounds
> of crap in a five pound bag. He got
> mad but then he ended up spending
> the night.

Sam stares at Cindy in the distance wondering "what if?"

                                        CUT TO:

INT. CAFETERIA - DAY

The freaks are sitting around their table in the cafeteria.
Nick looks depressed. He moves his neck around, in pain.

>   NICK
> Anybody want to give me a neckrub?

>   KEN
> Think I'll pass. Maybe one of those
> hippies'll do it for you.

Ken points over to the Deadhead table. LAURIE and VICTOR are
sitting there eating.

>   KIM
> They kinda look like that couple
> from "The Joy of Sex."

>   DANIEL
> How'd a high school guy grow a
> beard like that?

>   KEN
>   (a la Calgon commercial)
> Ancient Deadhead secret.

                                        (CONTINUED)

CONTINUED:

>   KIM
> God, Nick, I can't believe you
> slept on Daniel's floor. That
> carpet's infested.

>   NICK
> Well, it's better than sleeping in
> my Maverick... kinda.

>   LINDSAY
> Are you going home tonight?

>   NICK
> No. No way. I'm never going home.
> Not if that fascist is living
> there.
>   (to Ken)
> Can I crash at your place tonight?

>   KEN
> No. My dad would have a conniption
> fit. He won't even let my grandma
> stay over. He's got issues.

>   DANIEL
> You can stay at my house again as
> long as you remember to flush the
> toilet. You almost gave my mom a
> heart attack this morning.

>   NICK
> No offense, man, but your house is
> kinda depressing and...
>   (scratching his scalp)
> ...I think I got chiggers from your
> floor.

>   DANIEL
> Gee, I'm sorry. I didn't realize I
> had royalty sleeping in my room
> last night.

Nick makes a face, then looks at Lindsay. She knows what's
coming.

>   NICK
> Hey, Lindsay, any chance I could
> stay at your place?

(CONTINUED)

CONTINUED: (2)

> LINDSAY
> Oh... God, Nick. If it was up to me
> you could, but there's just no way
> my dad'd let you. He's worse than
> Ken's dad when it comes to stuff
> like that.

> KEN
> Yeah, but nice try, Nick.

> NICK
> Shut up, man.

> KEN
> You should have cried. You would
> have been in.

Nick gives Ken a dirty look, then goes back to his food.
Lindsay sighs, looking like she feels guilty. Behind them,
Neal walks by with his lunch tray. He goes over to...

THE GEEK TABLE

Neal comes over and sits with Sam and Bill, who are mid-
conversation.

> SAM
> "There's something wrong with these
> cans. He hates these cans." "The
> Jerk" is a perfect movie. There
> isn't one scene in it that isn't
> hilarious.

> NEAL
> (matter of fact)
> "Caddyshack" is better.

> BILL
> Way better. Ted Knight's the
> funniest. "Spaulding. You'll get
> nothing and like it."

> SAM
> That movie is so uneven. Half of it
> rules, but half of it sucks.
> "Stripes" is like that, too. You
> couldn't even tell me what happened
> in the second half of that movie.

(CONTINUED)

CONTINUED: (3)

> NEAL
> They were reassaigned to Europe to
> work on a top secret mission
> concerning an urban assault
> vehicle...

Just then, Cindy walks up to the table. They all look
embarrassed about their conversation.

> CINDY
> Sam, can I talk to you for a
> second?

> SAM
> Oh, uh... sure.

> CINDY
> (looking at Bill and Neal)
> Over here.

Sam exchanges a look with Neal and Bill. Neal nods "go on" to
Sam. Sam gets up and heads over to Cindy. They are about
eight feet away from Neal and Bill.

> CINDY
> (quietly)
> Sam... I broke up with Todd.

> SAM
> (trying to hide excitement)
> Really? Wow. Uh, I'm sorry.

> CINDY
> Don't be. Todd's a jerk. He's only
> interested in one thing. All these
> jocks are.

> SAM
> Huh.

> CINDY
> I was wondering. Are you gonna be
> home tonight?

> SAM
> Uh, yeah... Sure.

> CINDY
> Good. I'm gonna call you. I really
> need someone to talk to.

(CONTINUED)

CONTINUED: (4)

> SAM
> Uh, yeah. Anytime. I'm around.

Cindy gives Sam a big, grateful smile, then leans in and kisses him on the cheek. Sam looks shocked. He tries to recover as Cindy gives him another smile, a smile that's more than a "you're just like my sister" smile and heads back off.

Sam watches her go, stunned. He's in love.

ANGLE ON: NEAL AND BILL. They've heard the whole thing. They look surprised. Then Neal smiles.

> NEAL
> Oh my God. It's happening.

Off Bill's nervous look, we...

                                                        CUT TO:

INT. WEIR DINING ROOM - NIGHT

Sam is sitting at the dinner table. He's touching his cheek where Cindy kissed him, a million miles away. Jean looks up from her food and sees him.

> JEAN
> Sam, are you okay? Is there
> something wrong with your cheek?
> Are you getting a pimple?

> SAM
> No. I... just had an itch.

> JEAN
> Well, if you want me to swab it
> with a little alcohol, let me know.

Sam looks embarrassed. Lindsay goes back to some discussion she's been having with Harold.

> LINDSAY
> Give me one good reason why there
> can't be a woman president.

> HAROLD
> It's called three irrational days
> per month. I would have no issue
> with it the other twenty-seven
> days, but we're talking about the
> bomb here.

                                                    (CONTINUED)

CONTINUED:

> JEAN
> Oh, Harold.

> LINDSAY
> That's stupid, Dad. You know, guys
> get periods, too. It all has to do
> with body tides.

> HAROLD
> My body does not have a tide.

Lindsay's about to argue when, DING DONG.

> JEAN
> Oh, no. Don't those religious
> people have anything better to do?

INT. WEIR LIVING ROOM/FRONT DOOR - CONTINUOUS

Harold goes to the front door. He opens it, revealing Nick
standing there.

> NICK
> Hey, Mr. Weir. Is Lindsay here?

> HAROLD
> She's eating dinner.

> NICK
> Ooo, I can tell. It smells great in
> there.
> (closes his eyes)
> Wait a minute. Let me guess. Pot
> roast.

> HAROLD
> Congratulations.

Lindsay comes around the corner. Looks confused.

> LINDSAY
> Hey, Nick. What's up?

> NICK
> Oh, hey, I was just dropping by to
> say hey. But I didn't know you'd be
> eating. You guys eat late, don't
> you?

(CONTINUED)

CONTINUED:

> HAROLD
> Yes, because I work all day and
> like to have a nice quiet meal with
> my family after I close the store.

> NICK
> Oh. That's cool. I admire that.

They all stand there for a beat. Nick's not getting the hint.
Finally, Jean comes around the corner.

> JEAN
> Oh, hello, Nick.

> NICK
> Hey, Mrs. Weir. I was just saying
> that pot roast smells great.

He gives her a big smile. It's obvious he's fishing for an
invitation.

> JEAN
> Oh. Well, you want to join us for
> dinner? We've got plenty of food.

Both Lindsay and Harold give Jean a look.

> NICK
> Oh, man, that would rock. I haven't
> eaten dinner yet. Is it okay with
> you, Mr. Weir?

> HAROLD
> (what's he going to say?)
> Yeah... it would rock.

Nick smiles happily. Lindsay doesn't.

CUT TO:

INT. WEIR DINING ROOM - NIGHT

Nick is wolfing down a plate of pot roast like he hasn't
eaten in days. Harold and Lindsay both look uncomfortable
having him there.

> NICK
> Mmm, man, this pot roast rocks,
> Mrs. Weir. You're a way better cook
> than my mom.

(CONTINUED)

CONTINUED:

> JEAN
> Oh, well, Nick. I'm sure your
> mother does fine. You don't get to
> be as tall as you are without
> somebody doing something right.

> NICK
> Hey, Mr. Weir, you sell sleeping
> bags, right? What's a good cheap
> one?

> HAROLD
> Are you going camping?

> NICK
> No, I'm just spending a lot of time
> sleeping on people's floors and I
> could use a good bag.

Lindsay looks at Nick. She can see right through him.

> JEAN
> Why on earth are you sleeping on
> people's floors?

> NICK
> I left home. My dad and I got in a
> fight and he kicked me out.

> LINDSAY
> Nick, he didn't kick you out.

> NICK
> He gave away my drums. It wasn't an
> invitation to stay.

> HAROLD
> Wait a minute. He wouldn't just
> give them away. The man must have
> had a reason.

> NICK
> Yeah, a stupid one. He thinks they
> were "interfering" with my
> schoolwork. I think my schoolwork
> is "interfering" with my drums.

> HAROLD
> (stares a beat)
> How are you doing in school?

(CONTINUED)

CONTINUED: (2)

>   NICK
>   Terrible.

Nick goes back to his food. Harold stares at him. The family waits for Harold to go into lecture mode. Instead...

>   HAROLD
>   Why don't you spend the night over
>   here? You can sleep on the couch.

>   LINDSAY
>   What?

Lindsay looks at her dad, completely surprised. Sam looks shocked, too. Even Jean seems a little thrown.

>   NICK
>   Really? You mean it, Mr. Weir?

>   HAROLD
>   Yeah.

And with this, Harold goes back to his food. Lindsay looks at Nick. He gives her a big smile and nod that says "we did it." Lindsay forces a weak smile. Nick is now going to be living in her house.

>   FADE OUT.

END OF ACT ONE

ACT 2

FADE IN:

INT. WEIR LIVING ROOM - NIGHT

Harold is in the dining room, doing paperwork for his store at the cleared off table. Jean is putting away the dishes. Sam and Lindsay are sprawled out in the living room doing their homework. Nick looks at them strangely.

>   NICK
>   I can't believe you guys actually
>   have an official homework time.
>   This is wild.

(CONTINUED)

CONTINUED:

                    LINDSAY
               (whispering)
        Yeah, my dad started the "quiet
        homework time" a few years ago
        'cause Sam was always running
        around like a crazy man after
        dinner.

                    SAM
        I was ten. I couldn't help it. I
        had a sugar rush.
               (beat)
        Hey, Nick, do you sleepwalk?

                    NICK
        I don't think so. Why?

                    SAM
        Bill sleepwalks. Once, when I slept
        over at Bill's, he got up, walked
        over to his toy chest, opened it up
        and peed in it.

They laugh.

                    HAROLD
          (from the other room)
        Hey, I hear voices.

Lindsay and Sam make a face at each other, give Nick a look
and go back to their homework. Nick watches them a beat, then
grabs his notebook and his science book.

Nick handles his books like he was handling nuclear waste.
It's clear he hasn't encountered study materials much. He
opens his binder, then opens his textbook, then looks around.

                    NICK
          (quietly, to Lindsay)
        Um, can I borrow a pen?

Lindsay nods and hands him a pen. He gives her a thank you
smile but she's engrossed in her reading. Nick looks at Sam,
who's scribbling notes as he reads from a textbook.

Nick reads for a second, gets bored, flips the pages, then
looks at some pictures in the book. Nudges Sam.

                    NICK
        Hey, check it out. That's some
        guy's real brain. That brain once
        made some guy talk.

                                   (CONTINUED)

CONTINUED: (2)

Sam forces a smile and shrugs, then goes back to his
homework. Nick looks at the book again. Tries to read. After
a few seconds, he taps Sam on the arm.

> NICK
> (pointing at something in book)
> Hey, what's DNA?

> SAM
> Well, Mr. Lacovara says it's like a
> blueprint that tells all the
> chemicals in your body what to do.

> NICK
> Lacovara. He caught me stealing a
> vat of chocolate pudding out of the
> kitchen once. He was cool about it.

Lindsay and Sam shush him. Nick makes a "sorry" face and goes
back to his books.

DISSOLVE TO:

INT. WEIR LIVING ROOM - A LITTLE LATER

Lindsay and Sam are gathering up their books. Nick closes his
science book.

> NICK
> Man, that was the longest hour of
> my life.

RING RING. The kitchen telephone rings. Sam looks up,
expectant.

> JEAN
> Sam, telephone. It's Cindy.

Sam runs into the kitchen.

> NICK
> Cindy, huh? Sam's got a girlfriend?

> LINDSAY
> No, just a girl who wants to be
> friends with him.

> NICK
> I know what that's like.

(CONTINUED)

CONTINUED:

Lindsay gives Nick a look. She wasn't expecting a shot like this. Nick looks like he knows he just overstepped his bounds.

> NICK (CONT'D)
> I was... just joking.

Nick goes back to his reading as Lindsay gives him a suspicious look. This comment has really bugged her.

CUT TO:

INT. WEIR KITCHEN - CONTINUOUS

Sam runs in as Jean holds the phone out to him. He grabs the phone, goes to speak, then puts his hand over the mouthpiece.

> SAM
> Mom, can I have some privacy?

> JEAN
> What? Oh, of course, Sammy.

Jean giggles and walks out of the kitchen. Sam closes the door behind her. He's about to talk when he sees...

SAM'S POV: Harold is sitting at the dining room table, staring at him through the kitchen window.

Sam walks over and shuts the door to the dining room, then pulls the sliding kitchen window shutters closed, too. Once he's convinced he's shut himself off, he speaks into the phone.

> SAM
> Hello? Oh, hi, Cindy. No, I'm glad
> you called... Really? No, that's
> okay. I finished my homework. Yeah,
> I can talk all night.

And with this, an extremely happy Sam sits down at the kitchen table and starts having a real conversation with Cindy Sanders.

MUSIC UP: ELO'S "TELEPHONE LINE"

A short montage of Sam talking on the phone. In a series of TIME DISSOLVES, we see Sam sitting in different places in the kitchen, talking, laughing, having a great time on the phone.

(CONTINUED)

CONTINUED:

> SAM (CONT'D)
> (a different line in each
> dissolve)
> I'd have to say Paul McCartney./No,
> he really stuck a whole Zotz up his
> nose! Serious./If he doesn't
> appreciate you, what are you gonna
> do? I mean, maybe Todd isn't the
> right guy for you./I think
> Lakeside's a way better mall than
> Macomb./I heard he got killed in
> Vietnam./ Purple. Or orange,
> Sometimes./ Yeah, I'd like to live
> in the forest, too.

By the end, Sam hangs up and looks completely happy and in love.

> CUT TO:

INT. LINDSAY'S ROOM/HALLWAY - NIGHT

Lindsay is laying in bed, eyes open, thinking. It's late. TAP TAP TAP. Someone's at the door. Her eyes go wide.

> LINDSAY
> (loud whisper)
> Who is it?

> NICK (O.C.)
> (whispering through door)
> It's me. Nick.

> LINDSAY (O.C.)
> What do you want?

> NICK (O.C.)
> I need to tell you something.

Lindsay looks around, panicked. She gets up and goes to the door. Continues to whisper through it.

> LINDSAY
> Nick, I can't open the door. If my
> dad wakes up, he's gonna kill you.

> NICK
> No, don't open the door.

IN THE HALLWAY

> (CONTINUED)

CONTINUED:

We reveal that Nick is standing at Lindsay's door wearing nothing but a pair of brightly-striped bikini underwear with his face close to the door, whispering into it. INTERCUT WITH LINDSAY.

> NICK (CONT'D)
> I just wanted to say thank you. I think it's really cool of you and your folks for letting me stay here.

> LINDSAY
> It's okay. Go back to sleep.

> NICK
> No, yeah. I really appreciate it. You know that, right?

Lindsay looks desperate to end this moment.

> LINDSAY
> I know, Nick, I know. Just please don't wake up my dad.

> NICK
> I won't. Good night.

> LINDSAY
> Good night.

Lindsay goes back to her bed. She's not enjoying this. CRACK! There's a noise in the living room.

> CUT TO:

INT. WEIR LIVING ROOM - CONTINUOUS

Nick has just stubbed his toe on the counter and is jumping around holding his foot trying not to make a noise.

> NICK
> (quietly to himself)
> ...ow, ow, ow, ow...

Lindsay comes out of her room and GASPS LOUDLY when she sees Nick hopping around in his bikini underwear. Nick turns and sees her.

> NICK (CONT'D)
> (loud whisper)
> Lindsay, don't look!

> (CONTINUED)

CONTINUED:

Before Lindsay can move, Sam comes out of his room in his
Star Wars pajamas and takes in the scene. Lindsay turns and
sees him.

                    SAM
          Uh... hey.

                    LINDSAY
          Sam, go back to bed.

Lindsay looks back at Nick, gets embarrassed and runs back
into her room, leaving Sam staring at Nick.

                    NICK
          Cool pajamas.

                    SAM
          Thanks.

                                        CUT TO:

INT. SCHOOL HALLWAY/BIOLOGY CLASSROOM - MORNING

Bill is walking. Cindy calls to him.

                    CINDY
          Bill.

Bill looks like she's talking to another Bill. She walks
right up to him and takes him by the arm. He is very
uncomfortable.

                    CINDY (CONT'D)
          Bill, I need to talk to you.

She walks him into their empty biology class. As they speak,
kids begin to enter.

                    CINDY (CONT'D)
          About yesterday.

                    BILL
          That wasn't me. It was Neal. He
          just blamed it on me.

                    CINDY
          What?

                    BILL
          Oh. What?

                                        (CONTINUED)

CONTINUED:

> CINDY
> Yesterday Sam and I had the best
> conversation. It lasted like hours.
> It was like we were instant best
> friends.

> BILL
> Yeah.

> CINDY
> Bill, I know I can trust you with
> this because we were lab partners.
>   (beat)
> I like Sam.

> BILL
> Me, too.

> CINDY
> No, I really like Sam.

> BILL
> Oh.

> CINDY
> Do you think he likes me?

> BILL
> Um... it's hard to tell.

> CINDY
> I just thought that maybe you could
> find out if he likes me.

> BILL
> O-Okay.

> CINDY
> But don't tell him I like him.

> BILL
> Oh. Okay.

> CINDY
> But if he does like me you can tell
> him. And tell him to ask me to
> Mona's party.

Sam and Neal enter. Cindy looks instantly nervous.

(CONTINUED)

CONTINUED: (2)

>   CINDY (CONT'D)
>   (quickly)
>   Thanks, Bill. You're the best.

She runs to her seat. Sam and Neal see this, and look
intrigued.

>   MR. LACOVARA
>   Everyone take your seats. We've got
>   a busy class ahead of us.

Bill sits across the way from Sam and Neal.

>   SAM
>   (mouths the words)
>   What just happened?

>   BILL
>   Cindy wanted me to find out--

>   MR. LACOVARA
>   Gentleman, can we save the
>   intellectual debate for the
>   cafeteria? Anyway... today we will
>   be having a pop quiz.

Everyone moans.

>   MR. LACOVARA (CONT'D)
>   Funny, the people who did their
>   homework didn't moan.

Sam looks like this will be the longest fifty minutes of his
life. Bill looks freaked.

>   CUT TO:

EXT. UNDER THE BLEACHERS - DAY

Lindsay and Kim are hanging out under the bleachers. At the
opposite end are Nick, Daniel and Ken.

>   KIM
>   So, what'd he do? Knock on your
>   door in the middle of the night?

>   LINDSAY
>   Yeah, how'd you know?

>   (CONTINUED)

CONTINUED:

>   KIM
> It's a total guy thing. It's like
> they all read the same book. I bet
> he told you he just wanted to talk.

>   LINDSAY
> No, he said he wanted to thank me.

>   KIM
> That's even worse. Did he try to
> give you a back rub?

>   LINDSAY
> No.

>   KIM
> He will. If he offers to give you a
> foot massage, run.

>   LINDSAY
> What am I gonna do, Kim? It's just
> too weird having him there.

>   KIM
> Kick him out. Tell him you know
> what he's doing and it's not going
> to work.

>   LINDSAY
> I can't do that.

>   KIM
> Well, then you're in for a long
> night.

Lindsay SIGHS, frustrated.

NICK, DANIEL and KEN are hanging out on the other side.
Daniel throws a look over at Kim and Lindsay.

>   KEN
> So, Nick, sleeping at Lindsay's
> house. That's a pretty good scam.

>   NICK
> Shut up, man.

>   DANIEL
> Here's what you've gotta do. Get
> her to stay up watching TV with
> you.
>   (MORE)

(CONTINUED)

CONTINUED: (2)

                    DANIEL (CONT'D)
          Then, once her parents go to bed,
          offer to give her a back rub. If
          you do it right, you're in.

                    NICK
          That's sick, man. You really think
          I'd do that?

                    KEN
          I'd do it.

                    NICK
                (offended)
          Hey, Lindsay and I are just
          friends. I think it's cool her
          parents are letting me stay there.

                    DANIEL
          Fine. Sorry for bringing it up.

They sit in silence for a beat. Then...

                    NICK
          I mean, if she came out in the
          middle of the night and told me she
          was in love with me, I wouldn't
          turn her away or anything.

Daniel and Ken laugh as Nick gets an embarrassed smile.

                                        CUT TO:

INT. SCHOOL HALLWAY - DAY

Sam, Neal and Bill are talking.

                    SAM
          I don't believe you.

                    BILL
          It's true.

                    SAM
          If this is a joke and you are
          setting me up I will stop being
          your friend. I'm not kidding.

                    BILL
          It's true.

                    NEAL
          You've got to ask her to that
          party.

                                        (CONTINUED)

CONTINUED:

> SAM
> I don't even know Mona.

> NEAL
> What's the difference? That's what
> Cindy wants.

> BILL
> I think she wants to be your
> girlfriend.

> SAM
> Oh, man.

> NEAL
> This is what you've been dreaming
> about. You've got to be a man and
> go get her.

> SAM
> I know, but...

> NEAL
> But what?

> SAM
> I'm scared.

> BILL
> Me, too.

> NEAL
> Well, they're not.

They see Cindy turn the corner with several jocks by her
side. Sam looks panicked.

> NEAL (CONT'D)
> I can hear what they're saying
> right now. "Excuse me, Cindy? Would
> you like to go to Mona's with me?"
> "Well, I was hoping Sam would ask
> me but since he doesn't seem to be
> interested, well, okay, Thor."

> SAM
> All right, shut up. I'll go ask her
> out.

(CONTINUED)

CONTINUED: (2)

Sam thinks a beat, takes a deep breath, gets up and starts the long walk over to Cindy's locker. Neal and Bill watch him go.

                                                    FADE OUT.

                        END OF ACT 2

                            ACT 3

FADE IN:

INT. SCHOOL HALLWAY - DAY

MUSIC UP: ELO'S "SHOWDOWN"

Sam walks slowly and nervously toward Cindy. He seems to be having a hard time taking a deep breath.

SAM'S POV: Cindy is talking to all the popular kids (mainly guys), including Vicki and Maureen, almost holding court with them. It's going to be a big deal to wade into this group.

Sam looks more nervous than before. But he steels himself and walks up to the table.

ANGLE ON: NEAL AND BILL. They watch, holding their breath. Neal looks nervous, too. Bill looks worried.

Sam walks through the popular kids and up to Cindy.

                        SAM
            Uh, Cindy. Can I talk to you for a
            second?

                        CINDY
            Sure.
                (to everyone)
            I'll see you guys at practice.

They exit.

                        CINDY (CONT'D)
            What's up?

Sam's face goes blank. He's completely thrown.

                        SAM
            I was wondering... if you might
            want to come to Mona's party with
            me?

                                                (CONTINUED)

CONTINUED:

> CINDY
> I'd love to.

> SAM
> Really?

> CINDY
> Really.

ANGLE ON: BILL AND NEAL

> NEAL
> It just happened. Look, they're
> smiling. It's on.

> BILL
> What if Sam starts going out with
> Cindy and stops hanging out with
> us?

> NEAL
> He won't. He'll help us get in with
> Cindy's friends. Like Vicki. I love
> her.

> BILL
> I thought you said they were like
> pod people. A cult.

> NEAL
> They are. But that's one cult I
> wouldn't mind joining. Bring on the
> pods.

ANGLE ON: SAM AND CINDY

> SAM
> Okay, well I'll meet you there.

> CINDY
> This is gonna be so much fun. Call
> me later.

> SAM
> I will.

There is an awkward moment, then Cindy gives Sam a quick peck
on the mouth. Sam goes white.

(CONTINUED)

CONTINUED: (2)

> CINDY
> See ya'.

Cindy walks away. Neal and Bill walk over.

> NEAL
> I'm so happy I could cry.

Bill looks concerned. Sam looks overwhelmed.

CUT TO:

INT. WEIR LIVING ROOM - NIGHT

The quiet hour. Lindsay and Sam are doing their homework. Harold is working in the dining room. Jean is reading the newspaper. Nick is flipping through his textbook, bored. He seems very comfortable hanging in the Weir house. After a beat, Nick gets up and wanders off down the hallway.

A few moments pass in silence. Then, we hear the beginning of RUSH'S "TOM SAWYER" faintly in the distance. Lindsay and Sam exchange looks.

Rush starts to get louder and louder. Harold and Jean look up. Harold shakes his head, trying to ignore it. The song gets louder and starts THUMPING through the wall from Lindsay's room. Harold gets up angrily and heads to the bedroom. Lindsay watches him go, then gets up and sneaks after him to eavesdrop.

CUT TO:

INT. LINDSAY'S BEDROOM/HALLWAY - CONTINUOUS

Nick is laying on the floor next to Lindsay's stereo. The music is very loud. Harold comes in and turns down the stereo. INTERCUT WITH LINDSAY LISTENING IN THE HALLWAY.

> HAROLD
> Nick, this is quiet hour.

> NICK
> Oh, yeah, I know. Was I being too
> loud?
> (off Harold's look)
> Man, I'm sorry.

> HAROLD
> Aren't you supposed to be doing
> your homework?

(CONTINUED)

CONTINUED:

> NICK
> Um... me? Uh, I don't know. I mean,
> I was.

> HAROLD
> You were? Then maybe you oughta
> finish it.

> NICK
> (trying to joke)
> Mr. Weir, you're starting to sound
> like my dad.

> HAROLD
> Yeah? Well, then your dad's a smart
> man.

This gets Nick. He suddenly looks upset.

> NICK
> Hey, you know what?
> (pointing at the stereo)
> I'm a drummer. This _is_ my homework.

> HAROLD
> (giving Nick a look)
> Oh, c'mon, Nick. This isn't
> homework. It's screwing around. If
> you're really a drummer, your
> homework would be practicing your
> drums.

> NICK
> Don't you think I want to? My dad
> gave my drums away!

This stops Harold.

> HAROLD
> So, then get two sticks and go
> pound on a rock. That's what a guy
> who really wanted to be a drummer
> would do if someone gave his drums
> away.

Nick gives Harold a strange look. Harold gets very fatherly.
Lindsay listens to all this in the hallway. She looks
confused, a little jealous at Harold's cool tone with Nick.

(CONTINUED)

CONTINUED: (2)

> HAROLD (CONT'D)
> When I was in high school, I was
> working in a department store
> learning all about retail and I
> still got straight A's. Don't tell
> me you can't find time to do both
> things. You can't be that easy on
> yourself, Nick. Push yourself.
> You're a smart kid.

Nick just looks at Harold. Is this sinking in or not? In the
hall, Lindsay leans in, waiting to hear what Nick will say.
Finally...

> NICK
> Thanks, Mr. Weir. That's really
> cool of you to say.

Harold gives him a nod. Starts to leave, then turns back.

> HAROLD
> And by the way, that drummer you're
> listening to is terrible.

> NICK
> What? That's Neal Peart. He's the
> greatest alive.

> HAROLD
> Ah, he couldn't drum his way out of
> a cardboard box. You want to hear
> drumming? I'll play you some
> drumming.

                                                    CUT TO:

INT. WEIR LIVING ROOM - NIGHT

Harold and Nick are standing around the stereo. Jean is
sitting on the couch. Harold takes out a Gene Krupa album,
"Drummer Man" and ceremoniously takes it out of its sleeve,
puts it on the turntable and puts the needle on it.

MUSIC UP: GENE KRUPA'S "DRUMMER MAN"

The wild drums of Gene Krupa blast out of the stereo. It's
immediately amazing. Nick's in awe.

> JEAN
> Oh, Harold, it's our song.

                                              (CONTINUED)

CONTINUED:

> NICK
> This guy's amazing. Where'd you
> hear about him?

> HAROLD
> You kidding? I grew up listening to
> Gene Krupa.

> NICK
> How'd he learn to play like that?

> HAROLD
> (joking)
> I don't know. Maybe he took a
> lesson.

Nick listens intently, tries to follow along air-drumming.

> NICK
> Wow, that's insane. Nobody can do
> that. Maybe I should take a lesson.

Nick goes back to listening to the record, studying it.
Harold watches Nick and sees how into it he is.

                                                    CUT TO:

INT. LINDSAY'S BEDROOM - NIGHT

Lindsay is in her room doing her homework. Sam taps on the
door and comes in.

> SAM
> Hey, can I ask you something?

> LINDSAY
> Sure.

> SAM
> Well, uh... Cindy and I are going
> to a party together and... I think
> it's kind of a date.

> LINDSAY
> Really? Are you nervous?

> SAM
> Yes. Cindy kissed me goodbye in
> school today and I didn't know what
> to do. I just stood there.

                                              (CONTINUED)

CONTINUED:

>   LINDSAY
> She kissed you?

>   SAM
> Yeah. And what if she wants to kiss
> me at the party for real?

>   LINDSAY
> Don't worry about it. You can't
> kiss wrong. When it happens, you'll
> know what to do.

>   SAM
>   (not convinced)
> I guess. It's just... I mean, I've
> never had a girlfriend before. I
> don't know what to do with any of
> it.

>   LINDSAY
> Just be yourself, Sam. 'Cause
> that's why she likes you. Be a
> gentleman, don't get weird, don't
> smother her. Let her come to you.

>   SAM
> Did Nick smother you?

>   LINDSAY
> Nick was so into me it just made me
> want to move to another country. I
> mean, he's still completely in love
> with me. That's why it's so weird
> having him in the house.

Just then, they hear Jean and Harold LAUGH. They exchange a
look and head out the door to see what's up.

                                              CUT TO:

INT. WEIR LIVING ROOM - CONTINUOUS

Lindsay and Sam walk out of the hallway and stop. They look
surprised.

SAM AND LINDSAY'S POV: Jean and Nick are dancing around the
room doing the jitterbug. Harold is clapping along. They're
having a great time.

Sam looks at Lindsay.

                                         (CONTINUED)

CONTINUED:

> SAM
> Uh, I don't think Nick's in love
> with you. I think he's in love with
> Mom and Dad.

Off Lindsay's completely confused look, we...

CUT TO:

INT. CAFETERIA - DAY

Sam, Bill and Neal, Harris and Gordon are sitting together.

> HARRIS
> I heard about your good fortune.
> Congratulations, Sam.

> SAM
> Thanks.

> GORDON
> She's the one who should be
> thankful. You're a catch.

> NEAL
> So, Sam, do you think you can get
> me and Bill into Mona's party?

> SAM
> Oh... I don't know. I never thought
> about it.

> NEAL
> Well, think about it.

> BILL
> I don't want to go.

> HARRIS
> Why not? Everyone wants to go to a
> make out party.

> SAM
> It's a make out party?

> GORDON
> Cool.

> BILL
> You're not going to French kiss
> Cindy, are you, Sam?

(CONTINUED)

CONTINUED:

> NEAL
> Of course he's going to. What do
> you think he's going to do? Kiss
> her on the cheek?

> SAM
> (still freaked)
> Nobody told me it was a make out
> party.

> HARRIS
> Well, you better get ready to make
> out or she's gonna think you don't
> like her.

> BILL
> French kissing's gross. I would
> never French kiss in a million
> years.

> NEAL
> Why the heck not?

> BILL
> Hello? Germs? Spit? Mucus? Old
> bits of food? Do the math on <u>that</u>.
> I mean, why do you even have to use
> your tongue? Aren't you supposed to
> kiss with your lips?

> NEAL
> Yeah, but using your tongue makes
> it a real kiss.

> BILL
> But why? What's the point? Are you
> supposed to lick the inside of her
> mouth? Do you lick her teeth? Do
> you make your tongue hard or soft?

> SAM
> God, Bill, enough.

> BILL
> Well, I want to know, since
> everybody seems to think this
> French kissing stuff is so great.

> NEAL
> You're supposed to put your tongue
> against her tongue.

(CONTINUED)

CONTINUED: (2)

                    BILL
          What if she puts her tongue too far
          into my mouth and I have a gag
          reflex?
                (then; horrified)
          What if I throw up? What if I
          throw up all over her? What if I
          throw up in her mou--

                    SAM
          Bill! Shut up! You're making me
          sick.

                    BILL
          Well, I'm telling you both right
          now, I'm never doing it.

                    NEAL
          Well, I am. So, what do you say,
          can we go?

                    SAM
          I don't know. If I take you, I have
          to take Gordon and Harris...

                    GORDON
          I don't want to go. I'm saving my
          virginity for my wife.

                    HARRIS
          I have a date with Judith. Every
          night is a make out party for us.

Neal stares at Sam.

                    SAM
                (to Neal)
          Fine. I'll get you in.

                    NEAL
          Yes!

As Neal celebrates, Bill looks sick to his stomach.

                    BILL
                (flatly)
          Whoopee.

                                        CUT TO:

INT. UNDER THE STAIRS - DAY

Lindsay, Kim and Ken are hanging out. Lindsay yawns.

                    LINDSAY
          Man, I'm so tired. Nick and my dad
          were up playing those stupid jazz
          records all night. I think he's in
          love with my parents.

                    KEN
          Huh, boy. That's the oldest trick
          in the book.

                    KIM
          Yeah, really. I didn't think Nick
          was desperate enough to pull that
          one out.

                    LINDSAY
          I don't know. He seems like he's
          really into them. I mean, he made
          my mom and dad breakfast this
          morning.

                    KEN
          Did he wear an apron?

                    KIM
          Maybe he thinks that this is like
          one of those countries where
          parents arrange marriages.

                    KEN
          Yeah, maybe your dad'll trade you
          to him for a herd of cattle.

Kim laughs. Lindsay just shakes her head.

                    LINDSAY
          I don't know. My dad's being all
          understanding and stuff. I don't
          get it. If I ever ran away from
          home, he'd kill me.

                    KIM
          It's just some weird male bonding
          thing. Guys are all the same, no
          matter how old they are.

                    KEN
          I agree.

                                        (CONTINUED)

CONTINUED:

> LINDSAY
> Well, I think I'm gonna tell my
> parents to tell Nick that tonight's
> the last night. I want my house
> back.

                                                    CUT TO:

INT. NEAL'S BEDROOM - DAY

Bill and Neal are sitting around in Neal's bedroom. Neal
pulls an empty wine bottle out from under his bed.

> NEAL
> These make-out parties all start
> the same way -- Spin the Bottle.
>   (holding up bottle)
> The bottle is the key to our make-
> out future. And the ability to
> control the spin of the bottle is
> going to make the difference
> between a good evening and a bad
> one.

> BILL
> You can't control a bottle.

> NEAL
> Oh, can't I? Just watch. I've been
> working on this for days. Sit
> anywhere and I'll make it point at
> you.

Bill scoots over. Neal puts down the bottle, makes a few
visual calculations and spins the bottle. It lands on Bill.

> BILL
> Wow, how'd you do that?

> NEAL
> It's all about finger control. Move
> somewhere else. I'll show you.

Bill moves to the opposite side. Neal puts his hand on the
bottle and starts lining things up.

> NEAL
> You have to train yourself to
> always make the bottle spin two
> full rotations.
>   (MORE)

                                              (CONTINUED)

CONTINUED:

                    NEAL (CONT'D)
          Once you get the feel for that, you
          add or subtract a small percentage
          of thrust based on the position of
          your target.

Neal spins again. It once again lands on Bill.

                    BILL
          That's amazing.

                    NEAL
          All I can say is "hello, ladies."

                    BILL
          What if nobody wants to kiss... us?

                    NEAL
          That's the genius part of this
          game. They'll have to.

                    BILL
          I just don't want to see that
          disappointed look on their faces
          when it lands on me.

                    NEAL
          Bill, who cares if they look
          disappointed? All I care about is
          if they look disappointed after the
          kiss. And they won't with me
          because I plan on delivering the
          goods.

                    BILL
          What goods?

                    NEAL
          Super lip action. A great kiss can
          make a girl fall in love with you.
          Even one that doesn't like you at
          all. And that's going to happen
          with me tonight. Hopefully with
          Vicki.

                    BILL
          Do people French kiss when they
          play spin the bottle?

                    NEAL
          Most don't. I do.

                                        (CONTINUED)

452

CONTINUED: (2)

                          BILL
                 My stomach hurts.

                                                    CUT TO:

MONTAGE - INTERCUT THE THREE GEEK BEDROOMS

MUSIC UP: ELO'S "DO YA"

INT. BILL'S BEDROOM - DAY

Bill is looking in the mirror at himself, eating Oreos. He
puckers his lips and looks at himself. Tries to look sexy.
Then he sticks out his tongue and inspects it. He makes a
face that shows the thought of French kissing makes him want
to barf. Then he smiles broadly, revealing that his teeth are
completely stained with Oreos. He looks worried.

INT. SAM'S BEDROOM - DAY

Sam is going through his closet looking for clothes. He pulls
out what looks like his church clothes and holds them up.
Decides against it and puts them back. Pulls out the Parisian
Nightsuit. Looks at it and tosses it back in. He sighs, no
idea what to wear.

INT. NEAL'S BEDROOM - DAY

Neal is in full playboy mode. He is acting sexy to something
out of frame. He has a robe on as a smoking jacket. He
suavely makes his way over to the bed, to reveal that his
ventriloquist dummy is laying on the bed. Neal comes up to it
and slowly moves in for a kiss. He makes the mouth open and
gives the dummy a deep soul kiss.

END OF MONTAGE - MUSIC OUT

                                                    FADE OUT:

                        END OF ACT 3

                           ACT 4

FADE IN:

EXT. MONA'S HOUSE - THAT NIGHT

A few kids are visible inside. The geeks walk up. Neal and
Bill are wearing turtlenecks.

                                              (CONTINUED)

CONTINUED:

> NEAL
> Bill, take off your turtleneck.
> That's my look.

> BILL
> I can't. I'm not wearing anything
> underneath. Besides, I happen to
> look cool in a turtleneck.

> NEAL
> So do I. Everyone looks cool in
> them -- that's the point. But we
> can't both wear them.

> BILL
> Well, I can't go in without a
> shirt.

> NEAL
> All right, fine. I'll take mine
> off. Thanks a lot.

Neal pulls it off -- it's a DICKY. Stuffs it in his pocket.

> BILL
> (chuckling)
> Nice dicky.

> SAM
> Guys, be cool.

> NEAL
> You be cool.

> SAM
> Just don't embarrass me.

> NEAL
> What are you, ashamed of us? Don't
> embarrass me.

> SAM
> Fine, be that way.

Sam walks up to the door. He takes a deep, nervous breath. He
opens the door.

CUT TO:

INT. MONA'S BASEMENT - CONTINUOUS

MUSIC UP: THE ROMANTICS' "GIMME ONE MORE CHANCE"

(CONTINUED)

CONTINUED:

The Geeks slowly walk in. They look around, trying to look like they belong there. It's a normal looking house, a bit on the pre-fab, depressing side with white walls and stark looking furniture. Not exactly romantic. Cindy walks up. She looks adorable in a fuzzy pink sweater. Sam melts.

                    CINDY
          Hi, Sam. Hi, guys. You look great.

                    SAM
          So do you, Cindy. You look
          beautiful.

                    CINDY
          Oh, Sam. You're so sweet. I'm so
          happy you're here.
               (takes Sam by the arm)
          Come on.

Sam gets an excited, yet nervous look. He smiles at her and they head into the party. Neal and Bill look around. Many popular kids walk by them. They feel stared at. Neal looks nervous. He doesn't move.

                    BILL
          Are we going in or what?

                    NEAL
          Don't rush me.

                    BILL
          Are you okay?

                    NEAL
          Remember that scene in the
          beginning of "Animal House" when
          Flounder went to the fraternity,
          and they didn't think he was cool
          so they put him in the room with
          the blind guy and the Indian guy? I
          feel like we're about to be sent to
          that room.

                    BILL
          So? Blind guys are cool. They have
          supersonic hearing.

                    NEAL
          You're right. Let's mingle.

                                        CUT TO:

INT. WEIR DINING ROOM - EVENING

Nick is setting the table with Jean as Lindsay stands watching.

> JEAN
> You kids have a good day today?

> LINDSAY
> I don't know. It was okay.

> NICK
> I had a fantastic day today, Mrs.
> Weir. I took my first drum lesson
> ever.

> LINDSAY
> Drum lesson?

Harold walks into the dining room, ready for dinner.

> HAROLD
> Hey, yeah, how'd that go, Nick?

> NICK
> Really cool. The teacher, Terry
> Breese, taught me how to hold the
> sticks jazz style.
> > (demonstrates with knife
> > and fork)
> Like this.

Nick plays a paradiddle on a hot pad.

> LINDSAY
> Where'd you get the money to take
> lessons?

> NICK
> Your dad.

Lindsay looks at her dad, shocked.

> HAROLD
> Nick's going to work part time as a
> stockboy at my store to pay for his
> lessons.

> JEAN
> Lessons? Good for you. All right,
> just let me get the ham and we'll
> eat.

(CONTINUED)

CONTINUED:

Jean heads to the kitchen. Nick runs after.

                    NICK
          Wait, let me, Mrs. Weir. Hams can
          be heavy.

Nick exits. Lindsay turns to Harold. Stunned. Perplexed.

                    LINDSAY
          Dad... that was really nice of you.

                    HAROLD
          What do you mean?

                    LINDSAY
          You're playing records for Nick,
          you're getting him drum lessons,
          letting him stay at the house.
          What's the deal?

                    HAROLD
          I'm helping the kid out. What, you
          don't want me to?

                    LINDSAY
          I'm just trying to figure out why
          you're so nice and logical when
          Nick has a problem but when I do,
          you just yell at me.

                    HAROLD
          Because I expect more out of you.
          Nick's father is a hard man. My old
          man was the same way.

                    LINDSAY
          Yeah, I know the feeling.

                    HAROLD
          Lindsay, trust me. You don't.

Harold gives her a sobering look. Lindsay looks a little
surprised.

                    HAROLD
          By the way, any time you wanna
          dance with me to Gene Krupa, I'm
          around.

Just then, Nick comes back in carrying a ham on a platter.

                                              (CONTINUED)

44.

CONTINUED: (2)

> NICK
> Who wants ham?

CUT TO:

INT. MONA'S BASEMENT - LATER

About eight kids sit on the floor in a circle playing Spin the Bottle. Cindy and Sam are playing, along with Maureen and Vicki. Neal and Bill sit and watch. The bottle is pointing at Cindy. One of the guys gives Cindy a kiss. Sam looks bothered by this. Cindy looks very embarrassed. MONA, a slutty popular girl, laughs.

> MONA
> God, look at you, Cindy. You're
> beet red.

> CINDY
> Why's the bottle keep landing on
> me?

> MONA
> I guess you're just lucky. Okay,
> whose spin?

> GUY
> Mine.

The GUY spins a Boone's Farm Strawberry Wine bottle. Sam holds his breath. Fortunately, it lands on another girl.

> MONA
> Ooooh, yeah! That's three times
> for you guys. Now it's Seven
> Minutes in Heaven!

Everyone "ooohhs." Bill whispers to Neal.

> BILL
> What's that?

> NEAL
> That means they have to go into a
> closet together for seven minutes.

> BILL
> And do what?

Neal gives Bill a "figure it out" look. Bill looks disturbed as the couple heads off to a closet. Everyone giggles.

(CONTINUED)

CONTINUED:

A couple of kids who aren't in the game run over and put
their ears against the door of the closet.

> MONA
> All right, Cindy. Your spin.

Cindy makes a face at Sam and spins. Sam is clearly
frustrated. The bottle stops on Sean. Cindy blushes.

> CINDY
> God, what's wrong with that bottle?
> I'm sorry, Sam.

> SEAN
> I'm not.

Sam tries to make a cool face. Cindy walks to Sean on her
knees and gives him a quick peck on the lips. Sam glances
back at Neal and Bill. They shrug.

> SEAN (CONT'D)
> What was that?

> MONA
> Nice kiss, Cindy. When do you start
> wearing your nun's clothes?

> CINDY
> (laughing)
> Shut up, Mona.

Meanwhile, another guy spins. It lands on Cindy again. She
looks very embarrassed. They kiss. Sam's jealousy rises --
he's had it.

> SAM
> Hey, Cindy, do you want to walk
> around or something?

> CINDY
> Yes, <u>please</u>. We'll see you guys
> later.

> THE GROUP
> Wooooooo.

> CINDY
> Shut up. God.
> (to Neal)
> Two spots are open, Nate.

Neal's eyes light up. Neal pulls Bill over and they fill in
the spots. Neal sits next to Vicki. Gives her a big smile.

(CONTINUED)

CONTINUED: (2)

                    NEAL
          Hello there.

                    SEAN
          Great. Two more guys.

The players look at them like they're aliens. Bill looks
sick. Neal rubs his hands together, ready for action.

                                        CUT TO:

INT. WEIR LIVING ROOM - NIGHT

The Weirs are in their quiet hour positions -- Harold at the
table working, Lindsay doing homework, Jean reading the
paper. Nick is reading a beginning drum book, writing notes
on the exercise musical staff in its pages. DING DONG.

                    JEAN
          My goodness, who could that be at
          this hour?

Harold gets up, goes to the door and opens it. It's Mr.
Andopolis.

                    MR. ANDOPOLIS
          Mr. Weir? I'm looking for Nick.

Nick looks up, completely surprised, as does Lindsay and
Jean.

                                        CUT TO:

INT. MONA'S BASEMENT - LATER

SPIN THE BOTTLE MONTAGE.

MUSIC UP: QUEEN'S "TIE YOUR MOTHER DOWN"

- Neal excitedly spins the bottle. It lands on Bill. Neal's
bummed.

- Another boy spins. It lands on a girl. They kiss deeply.

- Bill spins. It lands on Vicki. She cringes, then holds out
her hand. Bill reluctantly kisses it.

- Neal spins the bottle. It lands on Bill.

- Bill spins the bottle. It lands on Vicki. She offers her
cheek. Bill gives her a peck.

                                        (CONTINUED)

CONTINUED:

- Neal spins the bottle. It lands on Bill.

- Another boy spins. It lands on a girl. They make out.

- Mona spins the bottle. It lands on a boy. She gives him a huge, deep kiss. It's obviously someone she likes. Bill stares at them, horrified.

- Neal spins the bottle. It lands on Bill.

- Another couple kiss. And another. And another.

- Neal spins the bottle. It lands on Bill. Everyone laughs.

END MONTAGE

> NEAL
> Hold it! This isn't fair! There's obviously something wrong with the bottle. Bill, switch places with someone. This is ridiculous.

Bill switches places with a hesitant PRETTY GIRL.

> NEAL (CONT'D)
> I'm spinning again.

Neal warms up, really goes through his bottle-spinning calculations, aiming to hit the pretty girl, and spins. The bottle spins and spins and begins to slow down.

Neal stares at the pretty girl, barely able to contain himself. The bottle stops on Bill. Neal rolls back.

> NEAL (CONT'D)
> NOOOOOO!

> SEAN
> Just kiss him and get it over with!

Everybody LAUGHS. Neal stews. Bill looks embarrassed.

                                        CUT TO:

INT. WEIR LIVING ROM - NIGHT

Harold opens the door. Mr. Andopolis steps in.

> HAROLD
> Yes.

                                        (CONTINUED)

CONTINUED:

                    MR. ANDOPOLIS
          Hello, I'm Nick's father.

                    HAROLD
          Oh. Harold Weir. It's a pleasure to
          meet you, sir.

Mr. Andopolis gives Harold a terse smile. He's not
comfortable with any of this. He sees Nick.

                    MR. ANDOPOLIS
          C'mon, Nick. It's time to go home.

Nick looks around at the Weirs. Nobody really knows what to
do. Nick gets up.

                    NICK
               (intimidated)
          Yeah. Okay.

                    HAROLD
               (to Mr. Andopolis)
          Hey, could I talk to you in the
          kitchen for a minute?

                    MR. ANDOPOLIS
               (not into it)
          Sure.

They head into the kitchen. Nick watches them go. He doesn't
look happy.

                                                    CUT TO:

INT. WEIR KITCHEN - CONTINUOUS

Harold and Mr. Andopolis come in. Harold gestures for Mr.
Andopolis to have a seat at the table. Mr. Andopolis just
stops and stands, declining the offer. Harold stays standing.

                    MR. ANDOPOLIS
               (desperate to leave)
          Thanks for letting Nick stay here.

                    HAROLD
          Well, it was our pleasure. That's
          quite a kid you've got there.

                    MR. ANDOPOLIS
               (not smiling)
          Yeah.

                                              (CONTINUED)

CONTINUED:

                    HAROLD
          So, you gave his drums away, huh? I
          guess they must be pretty
          distracting.

                    MR. ANDOPOLIS
          You have no idea.

                    HAROLD
          Well, the things kids get into.
          When I was a kid, I was always
          bringing dogs home.

Mr. Andopolis nods.

                    HAROLD (CONT'D)
          He's having some trouble in school,
          huh?

                    MR. ANDOPOLIS
          Yes, sir.

                    HAROLD
               (after a beat)
          I guess teenagers need to try all
          sorts of things. I guess sometimes
          we just have to let them be kids--

                    MR. ANDOPOLIS
          Harold, how old is your boy?

                    HAROLD
          Fourteen.

                    MR. ANDOPOLIS
          Call me when he turns sixteen.

And with this, Mr. Andopolis turns and heads out of the
kitchen.

                                        CUT TO:

INT. MONA'S BASEMENT - LATER

Vicki spins the bottle. It slows down and stops on Bill.
Vicki looks horrified.

                    MAUREEN
          Oooo, that's three! Vicki and Bill
          are going for Seven Minutes in
          Heaven.

                                        (CONTINUED)

CONTINUED:

                    THE GROUP
          "Vicki and Bill, sittin' in a
          tree..."

                    VICKI
          Shut up, you guys.

Vicki looks at Bill with utter disdain. He forces a nervous
smile at her that says he's not into this either.

                    VICKI (CONT'D)
          Come on, let's get this over with.

She grabs Bill by the shirt and leads him to the laundry
room. SLAM! The door shuts behind them. Neal watches this,
very upset that it's not him.

                    NEAL
          All right. It's my spin.

Several girls get up and head off to the kitchen, leaving
mostly guys sitting around.

                    NEAL (CONT'D)
          Good idea. Why don't we take a
          break.

                                                CUT TO:

INT. MONA'S HOUSE/HALLWAY - NIGHT

Sam has Cindy by the hand and is walking her through the
house toward the back.

                    CINDY
          I'm so glad you could make it
          tonight, Sam. I was hoping we could
          spend some time together.

                    SAM
          Yeah, so was I.

Sam and Cindy exchange innocent smiles as they stroll. A
couple snuggles and kisses in the darkness. Sam looks over at
them. Seems to get confidence from them. He looks at Cindy,
then sees an open doorway. He peeks inside.

                    CINDY
          What are you doing, Sam?

                                           (CONTINUED)

CONTINUED:

> SAM
> Cindy, would you come in here with
> me? I just want to talk to you in
> private. Don't worry.

> CINDY
> (nervous, coquettish)
> Okay, Sam.

Sam takes her hand and leads her inside.

CUT TO:

INT. WEIR LIVING ROOM - NIGHT

The Weirs are seeing Nick off. Mr. Andopolis stands in the
doorway. He seems tired and worn out.

> MR. ANDOPOLIS
> Thanks again. I hope he wasn't too
> much trouble.

> JEAN
> No trouble at all.

Mr. Andopolis gives them a nod and heads off. Nick watches
him go. Turns back to the Weirs.

> NICK
> You sure you don't want to adopt
> me?

They force smiles at him but we see they all feel bad.

> LINDSAY
> You gonna be okay, Nick?

> NICK
> Yeah, I'm fine. Hey, at least he
> came looking for me. I never
> expected that.

Harold and Jean force smiles at him. Jean gives him a kiss on
the cheek.

> JEAN
> You stop by any time you want.

> NICK
> Thanks. I will.
> (to Harold)
> I'll see you at the store tomorrow?

(CONTINUED)

CONTINUED:

> HAROLD
> You'd better.

> NICK
> Thanks. I'll see you at school,
> Lindsay.

> LINDSAY
> Yeah. See you.

Nick gives them a weak smile and heads out. The Weirs watch
him go, then exchange looks.

> JEAN
> I never should have broken up with
> him... for you.

> CUT TO:

INT. MONA'S LAUNDRY ROOM - NIGHT

It's dark. A little light seeps in from under the door. We
can just barely see Bill and Vicki. Vicki heaves an impatient
SIGH.

> VICKI
> (after a long beat)
> Don't even think about it.

> BILL
> I wasn't thinking about anything.

> VICKI
> Good.

Bill sighs. A few beats pass.

> BILL
> The fabric softener smells good.

> VICKI
> Just stay away from me, okay?
> You're not going to touch me and
> you are <u>not</u> going to kiss me. Got
> it?

Bill stares at her, then gets an angry look.

> BILL
> You know what? You're a jerk.

> (CONTINUED)

CONTINUED:

>   VICKI
>   Excuse me?

>   BILL
>   You're a jerk. I couldn't be less
>   happy to be in here with you, so
>   don't keep acting like you think
>   I'm hoping I can kiss you. It's
>   actually the last thing in the
>   world I'd like to do right now.

Vicki looks surprised at Bill's outburst. Bill just sits
there stewing.

>   CUT TO:

INT. BEDROOM - NIGHT

Sam leads Cindy into a guest bedroom. It is lit only by a
small night light in the wall, making it a moody, romantic
place. She is acting very coy and innocent.

>   SAM
>   Well... here we are.

>   CINDY
>   (very nervous)
>   Yeah. Here we are.

Sam looks around and sees a clock radio. He gets an idea and
walks over to it.

>   CINDY (CONT'D)
>   What are you doing, Sam?

>   SAM
>   I thought we should have a little
>   music.

Sam clicks on the radio. He spins the dial, looking for a
song.

>   CUT TO:

INT. MONA'S LAUNDRY ROOM - NIGHT

Bill and Vicki are standing there. A long beat. Then...

>   VICKI
>   I'm sorry, Bill. That wasn't nice
>   of me.

>   (CONTINUED)

CONTINUED:

                    BILL
          Don't worry about it. You only
          have...

Bill hits the button on his digital watch. His face is lit up
by a red glow of the L.E.D.

                    BILL (CONT'D)
          ...three minutes and twenty six
          seconds 'til your seven minutes in
          heaven are over.

                    VICKI
          Where'd you get that watch?

                    BILL
          I won it in a raffle. It costs
          three hundred and fifty dollars in
          stores.

                    VICKI
          Wow. That's pretty cool.

There's a long beat.

                    BILL
          Can I ask you a question?

                    VICKI
          What?

                    BILL
          What's it like being pretty?

                    VICKI
          You think I'm pretty?

                    BILL
          Well, you were voted prettiest girl
          in school last year.

                    VICKI
             (laughs)
          I don't know. This is the only way
          I've ever looked.

                    BILL
          I think people are nicer to you
          when you're pretty.

                    VICKI
          Why would you say that?

                                        (CONTINUED)

CONTINUED: (2)

> BILL
> 'Cause they're not nice to <u>me</u>.

They laugh.

> VICKI
> Bill, that's not true. I see you.
> You're always laughing.

> BILL
> Really?

> VICKI
> Yeah, you always look like you're
> having a good time. What are you
> laughing about?

> BILL
> I watch movies in my head.

Vicki stares at him a beat, then smiles. Bill smiles back.

> CUT TO:

INT. LINDSAY'S BEDROOM - NIGHT

MUSIC UP:

Lindsay's on her bed, listening to music. She looks out her door and sees Harold walking by. She sits up.

> LINDSAY
> Hey, Dad.

He stops in the doorway.

> LINDSAY (CONT'D)
> It was really nice what you did for
> Nick.

Harold just gives her a smile. Lindsay smiles back.

> HAROLD
> I'm sorry if you think I don't
> treat you right sometimes.

> LINDSAY
> (with a smile)
> I didn't say that, Dad. I just wish
> you'd talk to me the way you talk
> to Nick.

(CONTINUED)

CONTINUED:

> HAROLD
> Do you know what the difference is
> between you and Nick? You're my
> daughter, and every second that
> you're out of this house, every
> second that I can't see you and
> know what you're doing, is absolute
> torture for me.

> LINDSAY
> I can't just stay home all the
> time.

> HAROLD
> I know.
>   (beat)
> Why not?

They laugh, possibly hug.

CUT TO:

INT. BEDROOM - NIGHT

Sam is still searching for a good radio station as Cindy
watches him, looking around nervously. Finally...

MUSIC UP: STYX "COME SAIL AWAY"

Sam turns and gives Cindy a look.

> CINDY
> Oh, my gosh, Sam. Remember this
> song? This was our first dance.

> SAM
> Yeah, I remember.

They share a very nice moment. Sam looks completely confident
and in love. Cindy is glowing.

CUT TO:

INT. MONA'S LAUNDRY ROOM - NIGHT

Bill is talking animatedly to Vicki.

(CONTINUED)

CONTINUED:

> BILL
> And then the cans behind Steve
> Martin all start springing holes
> and Steve Martin goes, "Hey,
> there's something wrong with these
> cans." And then he sees the guy
> shooting and goes "That guy hates
> these cans."

Bill cracks up. Vicki laughs. There's a long beat.

> VICKI
> Ah, what the hell.

> BILL
> What the hell what?

> VICKI
> Don't ever tell anyone this
> happened.

And with this, Vicki grabs Bill and gives him the hugest
French kiss ever. Bill's eyes go wide, then we see that as
he's kissing Vicki he has a gigantic smile on his face.

> CUT TO:

INT. BEDROOM - NIGHT

MUSIC UP: STYX "COME SAIL AWAY"

Sam walks up to Cindy. He's ready to give his first real
kiss. Cindy looks at him, blushing. They lock eyes. Sam takes
a deep breath and moves closer. It's a very sweet, very
romantic moment.

> SAM
> Cindy... can I kiss you?

> CINDY
> Oh, Sam.
> (then)
> You can do more than that.

And with this, Cindy pushes Sam back on the bed and clicks
off the light. Darkness.

> SAM (O.S.)
> What are you doing?

> (CONTINUED)

CONTINUED:

> CINDY (O.S.)
> What do you think? It's called
> second base.

> SAM (O.S.)
> But... I thought you didn't like
> guys like Todd who were only
> interested in one thing.

> CINDY (O.S.)
> Yeah, I don't. All those guys care
> about is football. But you're
> different, Sam.

And with this, we HEAR Cindy jump on Sam. Sam GASPS.

CUT TO:

INT. MONA'S BASEMENT - NIGHT

Neal stands at the door to the closet that Bill is in. He knocks on the door.

> NEAL
> Hey Bill, your seven minutes were
> up seven minutes ago. Hello! Can
> you hear me in there?!

CUT TO:

INT. MONA'S BASEMENT - NIGHT

Neal sits on a couch holding the bottle from the game. He examines it to see if it's weighted properly. Bill sits down, looking very happy.

> NEAL
> Bill, I'm sorry. You were right. We
> shouldn't have come here. This
> party sucks. Let's get out of here.
> (as they walk off)
> That Vicki is one cold fish, huh?

They get up and exit.

FADE OUT:

<u>THE END</u>

FREAKS AND GEEKS

"THE LITTLE THINGS"

Episode #17

Story by Jon Kasdan and Judd Apatow and Mike White

Written by Jon Kasdan

Directed by Jake Kasdan

"The Little Things" was the first piece of writing I ever had produced, and thus, a seminal work in my life. Perhaps I would be a far more popular and mysterious literary figure today if it had also been the last piece of writing I ever had produced. It wasn't. There are several, at least four, episodes of another coming-of-age series that bear my name. And while that one yielded more short-term benefits, i.e. girlfriend, money, my own crappy hotel suite in beautiful Wilmington, North Carolina, I sometimes wonder if perhaps I squandered the "hip, young comedy writer" status which came from having worked on "Fs&Gs." Perhaps. Who knows.

I do know this—if I could go back in a time machine to the day before we started shooting this episode, there are several things I would have done differently. For example, I probably wouldn't have boycotted the set because Paul and Judd had completely rewritten me the previous evening. So what if I'd spent upwards of six months working on those forty pages of script. Who cares? Rewriting is a necessary part of the process and I should have been less precious about the arbitrary words that I agonized over for, well, quite some time. I should have swallowed my dignity and enjoyed watching my older brother direct what had been quietly dubbed, "The Episode Formerly Written by Jon Kasdan." I also probably wouldn't have gotten all misty-eyed in the presence of Natasha Melnick, for she is oh-so-cute and I really wanted her to think of me as a confident, attractive suitor rather than, ya know...pathetic, whiner guy. And finally, I almost certainly would not have gone on to write for "The Teen Show that Shall Not Be Named," but rather faded into obscurity and poverty with my untarnished record and my one awesome credit. Oh the benefits of hindsight.

If I could take credit for "The Little Things" I would. And, come to think of it, I have in several strip clubs around Los Angeles. But the reality is that this episode, like so many others, represents what Paul and Judd did best. It is at once outrageously funny and incredibly tender. As irreverent as it is honest. And if you need proof look no further than their truly graceful handling of "ambiguous genitalia," which manages to be hilarious without ever being mean spirited. And that, I've always believed, is the secret to this whole, wacky, wonderful series. I am proud of whatever contribution I was able to make and I am proud to have my name in the credits.

—Jon Kasdan

FREAKS AND GEEKS

"THE LITTLE THINGS"

<u>**CAST LIST**</u>

LINDSAY WEIR
SAM WEIR
HAROLD WEIR
JEAN WEIR
DANIEL DESARIO
NICK ANDOPOLIS
BILL HAVERCHUCK
NEAL SCHWEIBER
KEN MILLER
KIM KELLY
MILLIE KENTNER
CINDY SANDERS
MR. ROSSO
MR. KOWCHEVSKI
HARRIS
GORDON
SEAN
VICKI APPLEBY
TODD SCHELLINGER
MR. MAINZER
MR. LACOVARA
AMY ANDREWS
AGENT MEARA
MIKE

FREAKS AND GEEKS

"THE LITTLE THINGS"

SET LIST

INTERIORS:

MCKINLEY HIGH SCHOOL
    /HALLWAY
    /CAFETERIA
    /MR. ROSSO'S OFFICE
    /TEACHER'S OFFICE
    /UNDER THE STAIRS
    /REC ROOM WITH COMPUTER
    /BOYS BATHROOM
    /STAIRS
    /KOWCHEVSKI'S CLASSROOM
    /BIOLOGY CLASSROOM
    /ADMINISTRATION OFFICE
WEIR HOUSE
    /DINING ROOM
    /LIVING ROOM
    /HALLWAY
    /SAM'S BEDROOM
AMY'S HOUSE
    /BEDROOM
NICK'S HOUSE
    /BEDROOM
KEN'S HOUSE
    /KEN'S BEDROOM
MOVIE THEATER

EXTERIORS:

MCKINLEY HIGH SCHOOL
    /BLEACHERS
    /FOOTBALL FIELD
    /PARKING LOT
FREAK HANG-OUT
AMY'S HOUSE
NEIGHBORHOOD STREET

FADE IN:

INT. WEIR DINING ROOM - NIGHT

The Weirs are having dinner. CINDY SANDERS is there, sitting
at the table next to SAM, her new boyfriend.

HAROLD and JEAN are completely charmed by her outward
charisma, while LINDSAY remains slightly wary.

                HAROLD
      So, if this new sporting goods mega-
      store opens at the mall, we're in
      for a real fight.

                CINDY
      If I was them, I would be the
      nervous ones. People in this town
      are very loyal. I wouldn't shop at
      that mega-store if you paid me.

                HAROLD
      I like this girl.
         (to Lindsay)
      Isn't she great, Lindsay?

                LINDSAY
      Yeah, she's... great.

                JEAN
      So, I hear that something exciting
      is happening this week at school.

                CINDY
      That's right. Vice President George
      Herbert Walker Bush is coming to
      speak at an assembly in the
      cafeteria.

                JEAN
      Why in the cafeteria?

                CINDY
      Because Mr. Bush wants it to be
      very informal. So, he's going to
      come at lunch and eat with us.

                                (CONTINUED)

CONTINUED:

>   HAROLD
> I wish there was some way I could
> get the Vice President to stop by
> my store. You can't pay for that
> kind of publicity. But these
> politicians, they only visit
> diners. God knows why.

>   SAM
> The most exciting part is that
> Cindy, because she's head of the
> Young Republican Club, gets to
> introduce him.

>   JEAN
> That's a big honor. Lindsay?
> Isn't it, Lindsay?

>   LINDSAY
> Yeah, if you're a Republican.

>   HAROLD
> And you're not?

>   LINDSAY
> No, I'm a Democrat.

>   HAROLD
> Oooh, what a rebel. Everyone's a
> Democrat until they have some
> money. Then they come to their
> senses.

                                        CUT TO:

INT. WEIR HALLWAY - NIGHT

After dinner, Cindy and Sam are walking back toward his
bedroom.

>   CINDY
> Sam, let's play in your room.

>   SAM
>   (confused)
> Okay... we can play in my room.

They enter his room.

INT.   SAM'S BEDROOM - CONTINUOUS

Cindy enters the bedroom followed by Sam. She seems unusually comfortable given how little time she's spent here. She closes the door behind Sam and proceeds to the window where she begins closing the blinds. Sam is perplexed.

                    SAMMY
          Cindy...

                    CINDY
          Yes, Sammy?

                    SAM
          What are you doing?

                    CINDY
          I'm creating our secret love nest.
               (he still doesn't get it)
          So we can make out, silly.

Cindy walks back across the room.

                    SAM
          We can't. My parents are in the
          next room.

                    CINDY
          Remember when you wanted to slow
          dance with me, but the music sped
          up? Well, now's your chance to slow
          dance.

                    SAM
          Now?

                    CINDY
          Yes, now.

She puts her arms around him.

                    CINDY (CONT'D)
               (singing)
          I'm sailing away. Set an open
          course, for the virgin seas.
               (to Sam)
          Now you sing.

                    SAM
          Uh... I've got to be free. Free to
          face the life that's ahead of me.
               (MORE)

(CONTINUED)

CONTINUED:

                    SAM (CONT'D)
          On board I'm the Captain... so
          climb aboard.

                    CINDY
          You're such a good singer. You
          should sing the national anthem at
          one of our games. Keep going.

                    SAM
          And we'll try, the best that we can
          To ca-rry on.

                    CINDY
          Now dance for me, Sam.

She starts humming the song.

                    SAM
          No. I can't.

                    CINDY
          Come on. You're so cute when you
          dance. That's why I hate dancing
          with you cause I can't watch you
          dance. Come on.

Sam starts dancing uncomfortably as she hums.

                    CINDY (CONT'D)
          That's so great. Todd would never
          do this.

                                        CUT TO:

                            ACT ONE

FADE IN:

INT. SCHOOL HALLWAY - DAY

NICK, DANIEL and KEN are under the stairs. They watch as
Cindy Sanders walks by with several girls. They are holding
American flags for hanging and red, white and blue pennants,
banners, etc. Four SECRET SERVICE MEN walk by from the other
direction.

                    KEN
          What, are the Blues Brothers doing
          a show in town tonight?

                    DANIEL
          No, George Bush is coming to speak
          at the school.

                                        (CONTINUED)

CONTINUED:

>   NICK
>   The porn star?
>
>   KEN
>   He's the Vice President of the
>   United States of America.
>
>   NICK
>   So, how am I supposed to know? I
>   didn't vote for him.
>
>   DANIEL
>   You're not old enough to vote,
>   doofus.
>
>   KEN
>   You are.
>
>   DANIEL
>   Shut up.
>
>   NICK
>   Good one, Ken.

Just as he says this, AMY walks over with LINDSAY. They've
been talking and joking as old friends do. Amy is wearing her
marching band uniform and it looks cute.

>   AMY
>   The band is gonna play "Hail to the
>   Chief" when Bush arrives for the
>   assembly. There's a lot of tuba in
>   it. I'm really nervous.

She walks over to Ken and puts her arms around his waist. He
puts his arm around her shoulder. They look very happy.

>   LINDSAY
>   I wouldn't worry about it too much,
>   Amy. I don't think George Bush is
>   gonna be judging the band.
>
>   DANIEL
>   Don't kid yourself. One wrong note
>   and we'll never hear from you
>   again.

Just then, MR. KOWCHEVSKI walks up. The freaks look surprised
to have him invading their freak space.

>   (CONTINUED)

CONTINUED: (2)

>   MR. KOWCHEVSKI
> All right, you guys. Beat it.
> There's no hanging under the
> stairs.

>   DANIEL
> Since when?

>   MR. KOWCHEVSKI
> Since the Vice President is coming.
> Secret Service wants all these
> areas cleared.

>   DANIEL
> But where will we plan our coup?

>   MR. KOWCHEVSKI
> Don't even joke, Desario. I could
> have you thrown in jail just for
> saying that.

The freaks GROAN and slowly start to move. Amy moves away
from Ken.

>   AMY
>   (to Ken)
> I've gotta get to practice anyway.
> If I screw up "Hail to the Chief"
> it's gonna be on your head.

>   KEN
> Do you want to hang out tonight?

>   AMY
> On a school night?

>   KEN
> Oh, you're right, what was I
> thinking?

Amy laughs and punches him playfully. They look very happy.

>   CUT TO:

INT. SCHOOL HALLWAY - DAY

SAM, NEAL and BILL are walking down the hall.

>   SAM
> Would you rather be like the guy in
> "The Dead Zone" or the kid in
> "Firestarter"?

>   (CONTINUED)

CONTINUED:

>   NEAL
>   Definitely "Firestarter". It's way
>   cooler to light things on fire with
>   your mind than see the future.

>   BILL
>   I don't want to light anything on
>   fire or see the future. Those
>   people are always grabbing their
>   heads...
>   (acts it out)
>   Ouch! This damned power.

They all start cracking up. Cindy walks up.

>   CINDY
>   What's wrong, Bill?
>   Did you eat a peanut?

>   SAM
>   No, we're just goofing around.

Sam kisses her hello. Neal and Bill react appropriately.

>   CINDY
>   Sam, can I talk to you for a
>   minute?

>   SAM
>   Oh. Okay. Uh... I'll see you guys
>   later.

Cindy hands Sam her books. She then takes his other hand and
leads him--

INTO THE ALCOVE.

>   SAM (CONT'D)
>   What did you want to talk about?

>   CINDY
>   I was hoping you could help me with
>   my French.

Cindy grabs Sam and starts mauling him. Sam is taken by
surprise.

ANGLE ON: Neal and Bill peer around the corner and see what's
going on.

                                              (CONTINUED)

CONTINUED: (2)

>   BILL
>   Is Sam better looking than us? Is
>   that why this is happening?

Neal shoots Bill a look.

>   NEAL
>   He's not better looking than me.

>   BILL
>   Maybe he's cooler than us. I mean,
>   look at who he's with and look who
>   we're with.

>   NEAL
>   Hey, you're with me. And I'm cool.

>   BILL
>   If you say so.

Neal looks annoyed.

                                              CUT TO:

INT. MR. ROSSO'S OFFICE - DAY

Lindsay is sitting across from MR. ROSSO. He has a very
pleased-with-himself look on his face.

>   MR. ROSSO
>   Lindsay, old Jeff Rosso's about to
>   make your day. You've heard of a
>   guy named Vice President George
>   Bush, haven't you?

>   LINDSAY
>   Yeah.

He shows her a head shot of George Bush.

>   MR. ROSSO
>   Well, I've arranged for you to ask
>   him the first question during his
>   informal Q and A with the student
>   body.

>   LINDSAY
>   I don't want to do that.

>   MR. ROSSO
>   Why?

                                         (CONTINUED)

CONTINUED:

>   LINDSAY
> Because I'm a Democrat.

>   MR. ROSSO
> So?

>   LINDSAY
> I wouldn't have voted for Reagan if
> I was old enough. Why would I want
> to talk to his lackey?

Mr. Rosso stares at her. His smile fades. He suddenly starts
to look upset. Something has snapped inside him.

>   MR. ROSSO
> Gee, I don't know. Maybe because
> he's the second most powerful man
> on Earth? Maybe because we live in
> a country where we're actually
> allowed to question our leaders
> without fear of being hacked to
> death by a machete?

>   LINDSAY
> Mr. Rosso, I didn't mean...

>   MR. ROSSO
> You know what? Forget it. I don't
> want you to talk to the Vice
> President. There's plenty of other
> students here who actually care
> about their country. I guess me and
> all my hippie friends were just
> wasting our time at Berkeley
> demonstrating and stopping an
> unjust war. We probably shouldn't
> have bothered.

>   LINDSAY
> Mr. Rosso, please stop.

Rosso's demeanor changes immediately. He starts pleading.

>   MR. ROSSO
> Oh, c'mon, Lindsay. I was so
> excited for you to do it. You're a
> special person and it's your
> destiny, whether you like it or
> not, to be interacting with world
> leaders.

(CONTINUED)

CONTINUED: (2)

>   LINDSAY
>   Do you really believe that?

Rosso smiles.

>   LINDSAY (CONT'D)
>   Okay, Mr. Rosso. I'll do it.

>   MR. ROSSO
>   (smiling big)
>   I got the best job in the world.
>   Twelve grand a year and I'm
>   overpaid.

Just then, the door to Rosso's office opens. A Secret
Serviceman, AGENT MEARA, enters.

>   AGENT MEARA
>   Sir, we need you and the young lady
>   to leave this office.

>   MR. ROSSO
>   Uh... is there anything wrong?

>   AGENT MEARA
>   No, sir. We're securing the area.
>   We need to inspect and then cordon
>   off all of these offices until
>   after the Vice President's visit.

>   MR. ROSSO
>   But where am I supposed to work?

>   AGENT MEARA
>   Sir, that's not my problem.

>   MR. ROSSO
>   (to Lindsay)
>   Isn't this exciting?

INT. CAFETERIA - DAY

Bill and Neal are eating alone. They see Sam sitting with
the popular kids, including Vicki. They look very bored
without him.

>   BILL
>   (looking at Vicki)
>   Remember when I made out with
>   Vicki?

She looks at Bill, then turns away.

>   (CONTINUED)

CONTINUED:

> NEAL
> I am so sick of that lie.

> BILL
> (matter of fact)
> You know, I like you when Sam's
> around. But when he's not around,
> I don't.

> NEAL
> (with little emotion)
> Are you serious?

> BILL
> Kind of.

> NEAL
> (with little emotion)
> Do you want to fight?

> BILL
> (flatly)
> Bring it on.

They go back to eating their food. Gordon and Harris come
over and sit down with them.

> GORDON
> Hi guys, what's happening?

> BILL
> We wouldn't know. It's all going
> on over there.

Bill indicates Sam at the table with the girls.

> HARRIS
> "Once you start down the dark path
> forever will it dominate your
> destiny." At least that's what Yoda
> always says.

AT SAM AND CINDY'S TABLE

Sam is surrounded by Cindy and her friends which include
VICKI, MIKE, TODD, and RICK. Sam sits between Cindy and her
ex-boyfriend Todd.

> CINDY
> It's not like cheerleaders have to
> be pretty but their cheerleaders
> aren't at all. They're dirty.

(CONTINUED)

CONTINUED: (2)

>   SAM
> Um... I saw some of the Lincoln
> cheerleaders at the mall and they
> were eating a lot of pizza.

>   VICKI
> You know, it's disrespectful to
> their team and to their school. If
> I was their student body, I
> wouldn't allow it.

>   TODD
> Hey, not all our cheerleaders are
> pretty.

>   CINDY
> Shut up.

>   TODD
> I wasn't talking about you. Get
> over yourself.

Sam is silent.

>   CINDY
> Aren't you going to defend me, Sam?

>   SAM
> He said he wasn't talking about
> you.

>   CINDY
> So, you're just gonna let it go?

Sam is speechless.

>   TODD
> Why are you starting? I like Sam.
> What do you want, to see us fight?

Todd chuckles.

>   MIKE
>   (jokes)
> I'd like to see that.

ANGLE ON: NICK EXITING THE FOOD LINE

Nick is staring at Sam sitting next to Cindy.

(CONTINUED)

CONTINUED: (3)

> NICK
> I'm now officially the only guy in
> the world without a girlfriend.

CUT TO:

SAM'S BEDROOM - DAY

MOUSETRAP, the goofy game by Milton Bradley. Sam, Neal, and
Bill are sitting on the carpet finishing up their game. Bill
rolls the dice and celebrates.

> BILL
> Yes! I get to set the mouse trap in
> motion.

Bill turns the crank and sets the mouse trap in motion. The
geeks watch impassively as it runs through its machinations.
It ends with the cage coming down on Sam and Neal's mice.

> BILL (CONT'D)
> Mousetrap! I win!

> NEAL
> Congratulations. Maybe you can get
> the school to start a team.

Neal and Sam shrug and begin breaking the game down and
putting it in the box. Sam's mind is clearly somewhere else,
it had been the whole game.

> BILL
> Sam, don't worry. It's just a game.
> You're really good at "Kerplunk."

> SAM
> No, it's just, this thing with
> Cindy. It's kinda not what I
> thought it would be. Cindy's...
> sorta boring.

> BILL
> Really?

> SAM
> I mean, I don't know. It's just
> weird hanging out with her friends,
> and all she ever wants to do is
> make-out and stuff.

(CONTINUED)

CONTINUED:

                    NEAL
          Oh yeah, that's boring. I'd kill
          to be that bored.

                    BILL
          Well, maybe you're not doing this
          right. I mean, aren't you supposed
          to go out on dates and stuff?

                    SAM
          Well, we went to the mall twice.
          And once we went to a football
          game, and after the game we went
          to... a different mall.

                    BILL
          Why don't you take her on a date
          where you do something you like to
          do?

                    SAM
          I don't know. I guess I could. I
          don't know if she'd be into it.

                    BILL
          Then why are you going out with
          her?

                    NEAL
          Why? Because she's a Goddess! Am I
          the last sane man left on this
          godforsaken planet? Good lord, pass
          her over here. I'd move to the mall
          if she wanted me to.

                    SAM
          Okay, I'll do it. Just shut up
          already.

                                        CUT TO:

INT. AMY'S ROOM - NIGHT

Amy's bedroom is a very feminine place, with horse posters,
ballet dancer figurines and music boxes. There's also a lot
of band stuff, like trophies. The room is pink and very
girly. Amy and Ken are sitting on the floor across from each
other.

                    AMY
          How come we never hang out at your
          house?

                                        (CONTINUED)

CONTINUED:

                       KEN
Because I hate it there.

                       AMY
Are you serious?

                       KEN
Yes, I'm serious. How come everyone
always thinks I'm joking? I think
it has something to do with my
voice.

                       AMY
But why? Your parents seem so nice.

                       KEN
They're... they're not bad people.
They're good at what they do. I
guess raising me wasn't one of the
things they learned to do at
college.

                       AMY
Then why are you such a great guy?

                       KEN
Because I was raised by a nanny.

                       AMY
Really?

                       KEN
Yeah. Catherine. She was nice. But
she moved back to Virginia and now
me and my parents are forced to
talk to each other again. It's
pretty weird. They're just like,
"Go to school. Oh, you got in
trouble. Well... try harder." Then
they go on their way. But I turned
out okay, I guess.

Amy stares at him.

                       AMY
I'm glad you told me.

                       KEN
                  (uncomfortable)
Yeah... well.

(CONTINUED)

CONTINUED: (2)

                    AMY
          It's really important that we tell
          each other everything. Don't you
          think?

                    KEN
          Yeah, sure.

                    AMY
          I want to tell you something about
          myself. It's really important, but
          you have to promise me you won't
          freak out.

                    KEN
          I'm very hard to freak out.

                    AMY
          I'm serious. You promise?

                    KEN
          Okay, but if you killed someone or
          something...

                    AMY
          No, I didn't kill anyone. Well,
          when I was born...

                    KEN
          Wow, this is an old story.
              (off her look)
          I'm sorry. Please tell me.

                    AMY
          When I was born, now this is not
          that uncommon, when I was born I
          had the potential to be either male
          or female.

                    KEN
          Yeah. Me, too.

                    AMY
          No, I mean I was born with both
          male and female parts.

                    KEN
          You mean, like a snail?

                                        (CONTINUED)

CONTINUED: (3)

> AMY
> Kind of. So, my parents and the
> doctors made the decision that I
> should be a girl. Thank God,
> because that's what I really am.

> KEN
> Uh-huh.

> AMY
> It's just a big part of my life and
> I thought you should know.

> KEN
> I'm glad you told me.

> AMY
> Is this too weird for you?

> KEN
> No. You're all girl now?

> AMY
> Yeah.

> KEN
> Then it's okay. If I was dating
> you when you were just born it
> might be different, but now you're
> a girl, so... it's okay.

> AMY
> I'm so glad.

She hugs him.

> KEN
> Hey, I had my appendix out. What's
> the big deal?

> AMY
> I knew I could tell you.

FADE OUT.

<u>END OF ACT ONE</u>

(CONTINUED)

<u>ACT TWO</u>

FADE IN:

INT. BIOLOGY CLASS - MORNING

All the students are walking out of class. Sam walks over to
Cindy. They speak in the now empty class.

                    SAM
          So... how's it going?

                    CINDY
          I think I'm gonna get a B in math.
          I am so relieved.

                    SAM
          Hey, Cindy, I was thinking that
          maybe.., you might wanna go out
          with me, on a date. Like a real
          date, ya know?

          Oh, Sam, you are the sweetest. Of
          course I'll go out with you on a date.

                    SAM
               (relieved)
          It's gonna be really fun.

                    CINDY
          Oh, I know it will be. I always have
          fun with you. You know what we could
          do? The football team is going to
          go to this batting cage, goofy
          golfing-type place. Then afterwards
          they want to go swim in this lake.

                    SAM
          Uh, Cindy? I was kinda hoping... I
          mean, I'm thinking that I should
          plan the date. Like a surprise, ya
          know? I'll take you out. It'll be
          my treat.

                    CINDY
          Oh, I get it. You wanna take out
          your girlfriend like a real
          gentleman.

                    SAM
          Yeah.

                                        (CONTINUED)

CONTINUED:

> CINDY
> That is so romantic. And you know
> what else?

> SAM
> What?

> CINDY
> I even think it's a little...
> (whispering)
> ...sexy.

Cindy hugs Sam. MR. MAINZER walks over.

> MR. MAINZER
> Hey, Valentino. You can paw on Ms.
> Sanders after school.

CUT TO:

INT. SCHOOL HALLWAY - DAY

Ken and Amy are walking down the hall. Things are decidedly
awkward between them.

> KEN
> Wow, sixth period already.

> AMY
> Yeah.

> KEN
> Did you have a good lunch?

> AMY
> The cafeteria food looked gross, so
> I had an apple.

> KEN
> It was actually pretty good. If
> you like salisbury steak.

> AMY
> Well, I've got to get to math.

> KEN
> I've got to get to chemistry.

They stop, then Amy looks at Ken, waiting for a kiss. Ken
looks uncomfortable.

(CONTINUED)

CONTINUED:

He gives her a hug but pats her on the back as he does it, like guys do when they hug. They separate and Amy gives him a disappointed look.

> KEN (CONT'D)
> I'll call you later.

Amy forces a smile and takes off. Ken watches after her, in complete turmoil. Just then, Mr. Rosso walks by.

> MR. ROSSO
> Hey, Ken. How's it hangin'?

> KEN
> What? Oh... it's hangin'.

Lindsay rounds the corner and sees Mr. Rosso. She comes over and catches him.

> LINDSAY
> Mr. Rosso, here's my questions for
> Bush.

> MR. ROSSO
> (not stopping)
> Cool. I'm on my way to talk to his
> people right now. I'll pass these
> by them. Good work, sister.

He smiles and heads off, leaving Lindsay standing with Ken.

> LINDSAY
> Hey, what's up?

> KEN
> Nothing.

> LINDSAY
> Have you seen Amy? I need to ask
> her something.

> KEN
> She went that way.

> LINDSAY
> Thanks.
> (starts; turns back)
> Hey, Ken, I'm glad you and Amy hit
> it off. You really surprised me.
> You're a sweet guy.

(CONTINUED)

CONTINUED: (2)

                    KEN
          Yeah, that's me. Sweet guy.

Lindsay gives Ken a big smile. Ken forces one back as Lindsay
takes off. Ken looks more confused than ever.

                                              CUT TO:

INT. ADMINISTRATION OFFICE - DAY

Lindsay and Kim are hanging out. Lindsay is writing in her
notebook.

                    LINDSAY
          What should I ask him?

                    KIM
          Ask him something really tough. Put
          him on the spot. I mean, what would
          he not want to talk about?

                    LINDSAY
          Well, they say that Reagan had Iran
          delay the release of the hostages
          until after he was elected.

                    KIM
          Oooo, you should ask him about
          that. Write that down. I bet he
          flips.

                    LINDSAY
          Cool.

Lindsay writes it down as Kim thinks, getting into it.

                    KIM
          We need another one like that.
          What other dirt do you have on him?

                    LINDSAY
          He was the head of the CIA.

                    KIM
          That's it! Ask him if he ever
          killed a guy. I bet he did. Those
          guys are all like spies and stuff.

                    LINDSAY
               (as she writes)
          I think I want to ask him about
          trickle-down economics.

                                         (CONTINUED)

CONTINUED:

> KIM
> That's boring. Nobody wants to hear
> about that. Gimme that notebook. I
> want to ask him who killed Kennedy.

Kim grabs the notebook from Lindsay.

> LINDSAY
> Or about the aliens at Roswell.
> Area 51!

Lindsay and Kim laugh. Then Lindsay takes the notebook back.

> LINDSAY (CONT'D)
> C'mon, Kim, I've gotta write some
> real questions.

CUT TO:

INT. REC ROOM WITH COMPUTER - DAY

Sam, Neal, Bill, Gordon and Harris are hanging out while
Harris noodles around on a very primitive looking computer.

> GORDON
> If it was me, I'd take her to a
> Broadway show.

> SAM
> Broadway? We're in Michigan.

> GORDON
> Dinner theater. They're doing "The
> Odd Couple" at Larry's. Two of the
> guys who quit M*A*S*H are in it.

> NEAL
> Oh, the guys who quit were the best
> ones.

> SAM
> It just has to be perfect. Maybe I
> should take her to a great movie.

> BILL
> "The Jerk" is playing at the
> discount theater.

(CONTINUED)

CONTINUED:

                    NEAL
          That's not exactly romantic.

                    HARRIS
          Laughter is the ultimate
          aphrodisiac. Get a woman laughing
          and you're getting a woman loving.

                    BILL
          Uch.

                    NEAL
          You have to get her a really good
          present.

                    SAM
          How good?

                    HARRIS
          She will judge your level of
          interest based on how much money
          you spend.

                    SAM
          How much should I spend?

                    NEAL
          How much do you have?

                    SAM
          Two hundred dollars, but it's in
          bonds. I can't get to it for three
          years.

                    BILL
          Why don't you make something for
          her? Like out of paper mache.

                    GORDON
          That's a good idea. It's from the
          heart.

                    NEAL
          I'll lend you money.

                    SAM
          How much?

                    NEAL
          As much as you need. Just don't
          screw this up. You're our ticket to
          electric ladyland.

                                    (CONTINUED)

CONTINUED: (2)

> SAM
> (to Harris)
> What kinds of presents do you buy
> Judith?

> HARRIS
> Judith has very particular tastes.
> All she really ever wants are
> scented oils and plenty of time
> with her man.

> BILL
> You should buy Cindy shampoo.

> SAM
> What?

> BILL
> Well, she has long hair. Buy her
> really good shampoo. The kind with
> the conditioner already in it.

> NEAL
> No! She'll think you're telling
> her her hair is dirty. You might as
> well buy her deodorant.

> GORDON
> I'd write her a poem. Maybe a
> haiku.

> BILL
> What's a haiku?

> GORDON
> It's a poem with five syllables,
> seven syllables, then five. It's
> like...
> (counts syllables)
> "Cindy is my girl. She is pretty
> to me...
> (beat)
> ...yes. I like her a lot."

> NEAL
> That's great. Here's a poem she
> might like: Cindy has B.O. Her hair
> is stinky, also. Here is some
> shampoo."
> (beat)
> I'll have the money for you by
> morning.

EXT. BLEACHERS/FOOTBALL FIELD - DAY

It's early afternoon and the field is not in use. Rotating
sprinklers water the grass, clicking loudly as they move. Ken
and Amy are watching from the top row of the bleachers.
There's a space between them as they sit. The silence is a
little awkward. Amy finally turns to Ken.

                AMY
     I can't take this any more. Why are
     you acting like this?

                KEN
     Acting like what?

                AMY
     You can't even look at me.

Ken looks at her.

                KEN
     I'm looking.

                AMY
     What are you thinking about what I
     told you?

                KEN
     Nothing. You told me. I'm fine
     with it.

                AMY
     You're not fine with it. You're
     acting all weird.

                KEN
     How's a guy supposed to act when
     his girlfriend tells him...
     something like that.

                AMY
     I don't know... but you're not
     reacting at all.

                KEN
     I don't know what to say. You took
     care of it, right?

                AMY
     Yeah.

                         (CONTINUED)

CONTINUED:

               KEN
Everything's kosher. I mean,
there's nothing I can do. I can't
change it.

               AMY
You are such a jerk.

               KEN
Amy, tell me what to say, 'cause
clearly you have something in mind.

               AMY
You can't be this dumb.

               KEN
Apparently I can be this dumb, so
do you want to help me out?

               AMY
Do you still like me?

               KEN
Yes.

               AMY
And you can live with this?

               KEN
Live with what? You took care of
it. You're not going back, are ya'?
It's over. Move on.

               AMY
I can't just move on. I think about
this all the time.

               KEN
Yeah, and now you're making me
think about it all the time.

               AMY
Ken, you don't understand. It's not
that easy. No matter what the
doctors did there's always going to
be a part of me that's...

               KEN
A guy?

               AMY
Forget it.

               (CONTINUED)

CONTINUED: (2)

> KEN
> I think I'm beginning to
> understand.

CUT TO:

INT. SAM'S BEDROOM - DAY

Sam is sitting on his bed, thinking. Jean walks in with some
of Sam's freshly folded clothes.

> JEAN
> Hey, honey. Whatcha doing?

> SAM
> Mom, I want to give Cindy a gift. I
> was thinking about buying her a
> charm for her charm bracelet. I
> guess you're supposed to get her
> half a heart and I keep the other
> half. But I don't know.

Jean takes a moment to think about, finally, an idea occurs
to her, a great idea. She gives Sam a smile.

> JEAN
> I've got the perfect gift.

INT. WEIR LIVING ROOM - MOMENTS LATER

CLOSE UP on a thick copper necklace. It's old and a little
tarnished.

> SAM (O.C.)
> What is it?

REVEAL that Jean and Sam are standing in the living room.
She's showing Sam the necklace.

> JEAN
> Your grandmother gave me this
> necklace when I was about Cindy's
> age. It's an heirloom. Oh, I
> thought it was the most elegant
> thing I had ever seen. And I'm sure
> if your grandmother knew how
> important this was to you.., she'd
> want you to have it. After all,
> this is your first love.

(CONTINUED)

CONTINUED:

                    SAM
                (warmly)
            Thanks, Mom.

                                        CUT TO:

INT. NICK'S BASEMENT - NIGHT

Daniel and Ken are sleeping over at Nick's. Ken lays on the
couch. Daniel and Nick are on the floor.

                    KEN
            I think I'm gonna break up with
            Amy.

This stops Daniel and Nick in what they're doing.

                    NICK
            Why?

                    KEN
            I can't tell you.

                    DANIEL
            Oh, man. Has she been cheating on
            you with some band geek? I'll bet
            it's that trumpet guy.

                    KEN
            No, I just don't think we're
            really... right for each other.

                    NICK
            Are you kidding, man? You two are
            like a perfect couple.

                    KEN
                (dead serious)
            Alright. Look, I'm going to tell
            you guys something but you have to
            promise not to tell anyone and not
            to be jerks about it. Okay?

                    DANIEL
            Yeah, sure, man. That's cool.

                    KEN
            I'm serious, Daniel. If you guys
            crack one joke, you're dead. And if
            you tell Kim, I will personally
            make it so you never have kids. You
            got it?

                                        (CONTINUED)

CONTINUED:

The guys nod, sincere. Now they've got to know. Ken takes a deep breath.

> KEN (CONT'D)
> Amy's... not really a girl.

A long silence. Nick and Daniel just stare. Finally...

> NICK
> What?

> KEN
> I mean, she is but she's kinda part guy, too. She came out unique.

> DANIEL
> What's that mean?

> KEN
> (after a beat)
> It means she was born packing both a gun and the holster.

Nick and Daniel take this in. Nobody knows what to say. He stares at them, waiting.

> NICK
> Does she... still have the "gun?"

> KEN
> No, the doctors took it off when she was a baby.

> NICK
> Then she's a girl.

> DANIEL
> I don't think so. It doesn't work that way. I think you gotta get rid of her, man.

> NICK
> (to Daniel)
> That's not cool. It's not her fault. I mean, if a girl got her leg cut off in a farming accident, you wouldn't dump her, would you?

> DANIEL
> I would if she was a guy.

(CONTINUED)

CONTINUED: (2)

> KEN
> She's not a guy, Daniel. Man, I
> knew I shouldn't have told you
> this.

> NICK
> No, I'm glad you did. You had to.
> How are you supposed to hold that
> in?

Daniel's about to say something but Nick cuts him off with a
"don't" look. Daniel just nods. Ken thinks.

> KEN
> I don't want to break up with her.
> I really like her. I think I may
> even... love her.

> NICK
> Really?

> KEN
> Yeah.

> DANIEL
> (after a beat)
> Does that make you gay?

> KEN
> I'm not sure. Does it?

> DANIEL
> I was kidding.

> KEN
> ... oh...

FADE OUT.

END OF ACT TWO

ACT THREE

FADE IN:

INT. KEN'S BEDROOM - DAY

Ken sits on the floor leaning against his bed in his very
sparse bedroom. A few rock posters (Ted Nugent) and pictures
of hot rods are up. His stereo is on a cart in front of him.

(CONTINUED)

CONTINUED:

He has a pile of 8-track tapes in front of him. He picks up one and puts it in the stereo.

MUSIC UP: TED NUGENT'S "GREAT WHITE BUFFALO"

Ken listens for a second, then pulls it out. He picks up another tape. Puts it in.

MUSIC UP: DAVID BOWIE'S "FASHION"

Ken makes a face and pulls it out. Grabs another tape. Puts it in.

MUSIC UP: OZZY OSBOURNE'S "CRAZY TRAIN"

Ken looks unsure and pulls it out. Puts in another tape.

MUSIC UP: THE ROCKY HORROR PICTURE SHOW'S "SWEET TRANSVESTITE"

He listens for a few beats, then pulls a paper bag out from under his bed. Looks around and pulls two magazines out of the paper bag. One of them is Playboy. The other is Playgirl, with a studly guy on the cover.

Ken stares at both the magazines for a long moment, as if trying to decide. He looks pained. Then he tosses both magazines in the garbage.

MUSIC OUT.

                                                    CUT TO:

INT. TEACHER'S OFFICE - DAY

Ken and Mr. Rosso are crammed into a tiny teacher's office, the kind that Mr. Kowchevski has.

                    MR. ROSSO
          Sorry about the cramped conditions.
          The Secret Service kicked me out of
          my office. Oh, well, the price we
          pay for democracy, huh?

                    KEN
          If you say so.

                    MR. ROSSO
          So, what can I do for you?

                                              (CONTINUED)

CONTINUED:

> KEN
> I kind of wanted to ask some
> advice.

> MR. ROSSO
> That's what they pay me for.

> KEN
> Well... there's a slight chance
> that... I might be gay.

> MR. ROSSO
> I see.

> KEN
> And I thought you'd be a good
> person to talk to about it since
> you're gay.

> MR. ROSSO
> Ken, I'm not gay.

Ken stares at him for a beat.

> KEN
> You aren't?

> MR. ROSSO
> No.

> KEN
> I just always thought...

> MR. ROSSO
> Why did you think that?

> KEN
> Well, I don't know, you just have
> this way about you, and I've never
> seen you with a woman.

> MR. ROSSO
> I don't bring dates to school, Ken.
> (regrouping)
> Look, there's nothing wrong with
> being gay. It's just not my
> personal preference.

Ken just nods. Mr. Rosso studies him.

> MR. ROSSO (CONT'D)
> Why did you ask me this?

(CONTINUED)

CONTINUED: (2)

> KEN
> Um... I was just curious.
> (beat)
> I'd better get going.

> ROSSO
> Ken, you can stay and talk about
> this.

> KEN
> No, I can't.

Ken gets up and gets out of the room quickly. Mr. Rosso
stares after him, unsure what to think.

CUT TO:

EXT. MCKINLEY PARKING LOT - DAY

School is over for the day and all the students and faculty
are getting into their cars and heading home. Mr. Rosso's
keys are locked in his car. He's attempting to open it with a
slim-jim.

> MR. ROSSO
> Damnit!

Lindsay walks up to him. She seems anxious.

> LINDSAY
> Mr. Rosso?

> MR. ROSSO
> Oh, Lindsay...

> LINDSAY
> What's the matter?

> MR. ROSSO
> I locked my keys in my car.

> LINDSAY
> Do you need any help?

> MR. ROSSO
> (annoyed)
> I think I can handle it.

He struggles unsuccessfully to open the door. He's in a
terrible mood.

(CONTINUED)

CONTINUED:

>   MR. ROSSO (CONT'D)
>   Bush's people rejected your
>   questions. So, they've written one
>   for you. Here.

Rosso pulls a card out of his pocket and hands it to Lindsay.

>   LINDSAY
>   (reading)
>   "What is your favorite place to eat
>   in the state of Michigan?"

Her face falls. There's a long silence.

>   LINDSAY (CONT'D)
>   What happened?

>   MR. ROSSO
>   The Bush people found the ones you
>   wrote too sophisticated.

>   LINDSAY
>   "Sophisticated?" What does that
>   mean?

>   MR. ROSSO
>   That's code for "nice try but this
>   is a glorified photo opportunity."
>   (beat)
>   Look, I'm disappointed, too. But
>   let's try to keep a positive
>   perspective on all this. You're
>   still getting a chance to interact
>   with the Vice President of the
>   United States. That's historic.

>   LINDSAY
>   Yeah. And maybe, if we're lucky,
>   he'll tell us which steak house has
>   the best prime rib.

This stops Rosso. He looks at Lindsay. Lowers his voice.

>   MR. ROSSO
>   Look, don't you think I'm PO'd too?
>   I thought we were gonna get to have
>   an actual political conversation.
>   You can't win with these people.
>   You know what all my protesting
>   accomplished during the 60's at
>   Berkeley? I've got sixteen scars on
>   my head from a tear gas cannister.
>   (MORE)

>   (CONTINUED)

CONTINUED: (2)

> MR. ROSSO (CONT'D)
> We tried to get them to stop the
> war. They stopped when they felt
> like it. And now all my compatriots
> are getting rich working Wall Street
> and I can't get my keys out of my
> mother's car!

> LINDSAY
> So, that's it? We're gonna give up?
> There's nothing we can do?

> MR. ROSSO
> No, there is something we can do.
> You can go get Brooksie the janitor
> to come out here and help me.

Lindsay looks disappointed and heads off to get Brooksie.

CUT TO:

INT. MOVIE THEATER - NIGHT

The theater is only half occupied, still some time before the
movie begins. Sam and Cindy are sitting in their seats, at
the back of the theater. Sam feels the uncomfortable silence.

> CINDY
> ...And I told Todd that Republicans
> aren't selfish. They just don't
> believe that poor people should get
> hand-outs. They should get jobs.
> I mean, I think hand-outs make
> people lazy, don't you, Sam?

> SAM
> Uh... I guess so. I don't know.

> CINDY
> Well, they do. Todd never
> understood. He's a Democrat.

Sam nods, uncomfortable. Then he gets an idea.

> SAM
> Speaking of hand-outs...
> (he laughs weakly)
> ...I got you something.

> CINDY
> Really? Sam, you're the best
> boyfriend. What'd you get me?

(CONTINUED)

CONTINUED:

Sam digs in his pocket and pulls out the heirloom necklace. Holds it up to her.

> CINDY (CONT'D)
> What is it, Sam?

> SAM
> It's an heirloom necklace. It's been in our family for generations.

> CINDY
> How much did it cost?

> SAM
> I don't know. It's an heirloom.

> CINDY
> Oh, well, thank you, Sam. That's very sweet.

Cindy gives him a kiss.

> SAM
> Do you want me to put it on you?

> CINDY
> Well, no, because it's metal and it'll be really cold. I'll just put it in my purse.

She grabs her purse off the floor and drops it in. Sam forces a smile at her, not happy about her reaction to the necklace.

                                                  CUT TO:

INT. WEIR DINING ROOM - EVENING

Harold, Jean and Lindsay are sitting around the table, eating dinner. Lindsay is mid-rant.

> LINDSAY
> Isn't that stupid? They're afraid of real questions.

> HAROLD
> Lindsay, the man isn't coming to your school to be attacked by a bunch of pimply faced teenagers. You have to be polite to the man.

                                              (CONTINUED)

CONTINUED:

>   LINDSAY
>   Oh, so if you have a zit you're not
>   entitled to an opinion. Is that it?
>
>   JEAN
>   I just think it's nice that he's
>   coming. I'm sure he's a very busy
>   man.
>
>   LINDSAY
>   Busy doing what? Waiting for the
>   President to die so he can take
>   over?
>
>   JEAN
>   Take that back. And knock on wood.
>   Both hands.
>
>   HAROLD
>   There's a more important
>   opportunity to be had, Lindsay. I
>   was thinking that when you ask your
>   question you could mention my
>   store.
>
>   LINDSAY
>   What? That's sick.
>
>   HAROLD
>   Yeah, it'll be sick when I go out
>   of business and you're living on
>   the street. Your only party
>   affiliation is to the Weir party.
>   And we need help.
>
>   LINDSAY
>   Mom, stop him, please.
>
>   JEAN
>   Honey, this is serious. The mega-
>   store offers discounts your dad
>   can't.
>
>   HAROLD
>   It's all about volume. It's not a
>   big deal. All you have to do is
>   say, "Hi, I'm Lindsay Weir. My
>   father owns A-1 sporting goods out
>   on sixteen mile. What is your
>   favorite place to eat in Michigan?"

(CONTINUED)

38.

CONTINUED: (2)

> LINDSAY
> I can't believe you're asking me to
> do this.

> JEAN
> And could you wear one of your
> father's t-shirts?

Lindsay looks over at Harold. He holds up a t-shirt that reads "A-1 SPORTING GOODS" with the phone number and address written underneath. Lindsay just looks at both her parents like they're nuts.

CUT TO:

INT. MOVIE THEATER - NIGHT

Sam and Cindy are sitting in the dark theater as "The Jerk" plays on the screen. Cindy looks bored.

ANGLE ON SCREEN: "The Jerk" is playing. The guy-shooting-the-cans scene is on.

Sam mouths every word. Cindy doesn't get it at all. It doesn't take long for Sam to catch on because Cindy SIGHS loudly, impatient.

> SAM
> Are you okay?

> CINDY
> I guess so.

> SAM
> You want some popcorn or something?

> CINDY
> I don't know. Will popcorn make
> this movie funnier?

Sam takes it like a slug to the chest.

> SAM
> You don't think it's funny?

> CINDY
> No, it's really stupid. I mean, how
> old is that guy? He's got gray hair
> and he's acting like a five year
> old.

(CONTINUED)

CONTINUED:

Sam looks completely bummed and offended. They sit and watch
for a few beats.

> CINDY (CONT'D)
> Sam?

> SAM
> Yeah?

She starts mauling Sam in the dark. He suddenly rears back.

> SAM (CONT'D)
> Ow. What are you doing?

> CINDY
> Giving you something.

> SAM
> What are you giving me?

> CINDY
> You goof, I'm giving you a hickey.

Sam's eyes go wide in horror. He's being eaten by Cindy
Sanders in the middle of the best scene of "The Jerk."

CUT TO:

EXT. FREAK HANG-OUT - NIGHT

Daniel, Nick, Kim and Lindsay are hanging out.

> LINDSAY
> I'm telling you. Rosso's cool. It's
> weird. He's kinda like one of us.

> NICK
> Please don't say that. It scares
> me.

> LINDSAY
> Did you ever really look at him?
> He's actually sort of good looking.

> KIM
> Yeah, if you're into guys who look
> like Jesus.

> LINDSAY
>   (laughing)
> Shut up.

(CONTINUED)

CONTINUED:

They all laugh. Just then, Ken and Amy walk up. Ken is on
edge.

>   AMY
> Hi, everyone.

>   NICK/KIM/LINDSAY
> Hey, what's up?

Ken's face goes blank.

>   KEN
> "Hey guys?" What's that supposed to
> mean, Daniel?

>   DANIEL
> Uh... it means "Hello, you guys."

Ken gives him an icy look. Daniel panics.

>   DANIEL (CONT'D)
> Oh, no, man. I didn't mean it that
> way. I just meant--

Ken leaps forward and punches Daniel in the face. Kim screams
and everyone jumps back, completely surprised.

>   KIM
> What the hell, Ken?!

Amy takes in the situation. Her face drops. She gives Ken
an incredulous look.

>   AMY
> Oh my God, Ken...

And with this, she runs away. Everyone is completely
confused. Ken stares at them, then runs off after Amy.

>   LINDSAY
> Daniel, are you all right?

>   KIM
> Anybody want to tell me what that
> was all about?

>   DANIEL
> Nothing, Kim. Everything's fine.

>   KIM
> He just punched you. Why--

(CONTINUED)

CONTINUED: (2)

>   DANIEL
>   Kim! Leave it alone.

Nick helps Daniel up as Kim and Lindsay exchange looks.

CUT TO:

INT. WEIR LIVING ROOM - NIGHT

Sam is sitting on the couch in the living room, not watching TV. Just sitting there. Lindsay enters, shaken up from her night.

>   LINDSAY
>   You okay?

>   SAM
>   Yeah.

>   LINDSAY
>   Something go wrong on your date?

>   SAM
>   We went to see "The Jerk" tonight.
>   She didn't laugh once.

>   LINDSAY
>   Uh oh.

>   SAM
>   What's wrong with me? I mean,
>   Cindy's so pretty. How come I don't
>   like her?

>   LINDSAY
>   Sam, just because she's pretty
>   doesn't mean she's right for you.
>   All good looking people aren't
>   cool.

>   SAM
>   Yeah. I guess. Why's it got to be
>   so hard?

Lindsay studies Sam's face. She sees he's uncertain. Thinks a beat.

>   LINDSAY
>   I don't know. It always is. It was
>   like that with Nick and I. It just
>   never really felt quite right.

(CONTINUED)

CONTINUED:

> SAM
> What'd you do about it?

> LINDSAY
> I broke up with him.

> SAM
> I can't break up with Cindy.

> LINDSAY
> Why not?

> SAM
> (after a beat)
> Because... everybody'll think I'm
> crazy.

> LINDSAY
> (gently)
> Sam, you're only a freshman.
> Nobody's gonna give you a hard time
> if you don't have a girlfriend.
> None of your friends have one.

> SAM
> I know. They're the ones who'll
> think I'm crazy.

> LINDSAY
> They'll think you're more crazy if
> you stay with somebody you don't
> really like.

> SAM
> You don't know my friends.

> LINDSAY
> Yes, I do. And trust me, they don't
> know anything when it comes to this
> stuff. You've just gotta do
> whatever makes you happy. And you
> don't seem very happy right now.

Sam just looks at her. His face shows he knows she's right.

> LINDSAY (CONT'D)
> What's that on your neck?

> SAM
> A hickey.

(CONTINUED)

CONTINUED: (2)

> LINDSAY
> (trying not to laugh)
> Oh, man, Sam.

Sam gives her a hangdog look. She smiles apologetically.

CUT TO:

EXT. AMY'S HOUSE - NIGHT

Ken is banging on Amy's door. He has clearly been there a while. Amy does not respond and she does not appear.

> KEN
> Amy, come on. I want to talk to you.

Still no response. After a beat, Ken turns and walks away.

CUT TO:

EXT. NEIGHBORHOOD STREET - LATER

Ken is walking home. Daniel's Trans Am pulls up next to him.

> DANIEL
> Get in. I'll drive you home.

Ken looks over at Daniel. In that instant, they've forgiven each other in that silent private way that friends do. Ken gets into the car and rides off with his friend.

FADE OUT:

END OF ACT THREE

ACT FOUR

FADE IN:

INT. FRONT HALLWAY - DAY

Lindsay walks into the school. Mr. Rosso, wearing a nice suit and tie, comes out of the office and stops her. He's been waiting for her to arrive. He has his hair back in a pony tail and looks very neat.

> LINDSAY
> Mr. Rosso, you look great.

> MR. ROSSO
> I clean up nice. So, are you ready?

(CONTINUED)

CONTINUED:

                      LINDSAY
        Yeah. I guess.

                      MR. ROSSO
        We shouldn't get so worked up about
        it. Let's just have fun. The Vice
        President is here! This is
        exciting, isn't it?

Lindsay gives him a smile as he heads off, happy. Kim walks up.

                      KIM
        So, you're really gonna do it?

                      LINDSAY
        I have to.

Lindsay opens her shirt to reveal that she's wearing the A-1 Sporting Goods T-shirt.

                      KIM
        I can't believe you're doing it.

                      LINDSAY
        Well, believe it. I'm a member of
        the Weir party.

                                    CUT TO:

INT. HALLWAY- DAY

At Sam's locker, the geeks are gathered. Sam looks sick.

                      SAM
        My stomach hurts.

                      BILL
        My stomach would hurt too if I was
        breaking up with the prettiest girl
        in school.

                      NEAL
        I'm glad your stomach hurts. You
        know what that is? It's your body
        telling you you're making a big
        mistake.

                      SAM
        I'm not making a mistake. Just
        because a girl's pretty doesn't
        mean she's cool.

                              (CONTINUED)

CONTINUED:

> NEAL
> Sam, first of all, of course it
> does. Secondly, you're just scared.
> One day you're gonna be hanging out
> with your unattractive kids and
> your unattractive wife asking
> yourself, "why did I dump that
> goddess Cindy Sanders?"

> BILL
> Shut up, Neal. You just want him to
> go out with her so you get your
> kicks living vicariously.

> SAM
> I can't listen to this anymore.

Sam quickly walks away.

> BILL
> Have I ever told you about the time
> I made-out with Vicki Appleby?

> NEAL
> Shut up.

CUT TO:

INT. CLASSROOM/HALLWAY - DAY

Mr. Kowchevski is at his desk grading papers when he looks
out the door and sees Ken coming down the hall. Mr.
Kowchevski gets up and goes to the door.

> MR. KOWCHEVSKI
> Mr. Miller, would you mind stepping
> inside here? I want to talk to you.

> KEN
> (stopping)
> Am I in trouble?

> MR. KOWCHEVSKI
> (warmly)
> No, you're not.

Ken nods, unsure, and comes into the classroom. Kowchevski
motions for Ken to sit at a desk. Ken does. Kowchevski then
shuts the door and sits on the front of his desk, facing Ken.
Takes a deep breath. Uncomfortable.

(CONTINUED)

CONTINUED:

> MR. KOWCHEVSKI (CONT'D)
> Mr. Rosso told me, in confidence,
> that you've been having some
> problems. And I just want you to
> know... I understand.

Ken gives him a look.

> KEN
> Understand what?

> MR KOWCHEVSKI
> What you're going through. I'm gay
> myself.

> KEN
> You're gay?

> MR. KOWCHEVSKI
> Yes.

> KEN
> Really? Like all this time...
> you've been gay?

> MR KOWCHEVSKI
> We're here to talk about you.

> KEN
> You don't seem gay at all. You're
> not very... attractive.

> MR KOWCHEVSKI
> Hey, I do fine.

> KEN
> Is that why you're always yelling
> at us all the time? 'Cause you're
> secretly gay?

> MR KOWCHEVSKI
> No, I yell because you kids drive
> me crazy. You try teaching in this
> dungeon for twenty years. We'll see
> how great your mood gets.
> (tries to calm down)
> Anyway... I'm just saying... I
> understand.

> KEN
> Mr. Kowchevski, I'm not gay. I have
> a girlfriend.

(CONTINUED)

CONTINUED: (2)

> MR. KOWCHEVSKI
> Oh my God, I'm gonna kill Rosso. He
> did this to me last year. Ken, get
> out of here. And keep your mouth
> shut about this.

Ken stands up, and heads to the door, then stops.

> KEN
> I did talk to Mr. Rosso. I've just
> been... confused lately.

> MR. KOWCHEVSKI
> Well, hey, I was confused for a
> long time, too. In a small town
> it's pretty scary to admit who you
> are. But there's no shame in being
> gay.

> KEN
> It's just... I don't know if I am.
> I mean, how do you know?

> MR. KOWCHEVSKI
> Well .. let's see...
> (thinks, then quickly)
> Do you like guys.?

> KEN
> No.

> MR. KOWCHEVSKI
> Then you're not gay.

> KEN
> Are you sure?

> MR. KOWCHEVSKI
> That's kinda the key part of
> equation.

> KEN
> I guess that's true. Thanks Mr. K.

> MR. KOWCHEVSKI
> I'm always here.

> KEN
> Are you still going to give me a D
> in math?

(CONTINUED)

CONTINUED: (3)

                    MR. KOWCHEVSKI
          If you're lucky.

CUT TO:

INT. SCHOOL STAIRS - DAY

Lindsay is heading up the stairs in her A-1 Sporting Goods shirt. Amy is coming down in her band outfit. Amy sees Lindsay and turns to head back up the stairs. Lindsay runs after her.

                    LINDSAY
          Amy, Amy, wait!

Amy stops and turns to Lindsay, expecting the worst.

                    LINDSAY (CONT'D)
          Is everything ok?

                    AMY
          No!

                    LINDSAY
          What's going on?

                    AMY
          Like you don't know.

                    LINDSAY
          I don't.

                    AMY
          Yeah, right Lindsay.

                    LINDSAY
          I swear to God. Nobody will tell
          me anything.

Amy looks surprised at this.

                    LINDSAY (CONT'D)
          Do you want to tell me? Maybe I
          can help.

                    AMY
          I don't think you can. Just don't
          worry about it. I'll see you
          later, Lindsay.

                    LINDSAY
          I'll see ya. Good luck with "Hail
          to the Chief."

                                      (CONTINUED)

49.

CONTINUED:

Amy heads down the stairs, looking slightly relieved and deep
in thought. Lindsay watches her go, confused. Then
continues up the stairs. We see the back of her t-shirt
reads "WELCOME, GEORGE BUSH."

                                                    CUT TO:

INT. BOYS' BATHROOM - DAY

FLUSH! A stall door and Sam comes out. He doesn't look
well. He walks over to the sink and leans on it. Looks at
himself in the mirror. He looks very nervous. He turns on
the faucet and rubs some water on his face. Ken enters and
sees him.

                    KEN
              Hey, are you sick?

                    SAM
                 (embarrassed)
              I'm nervous.

                    KEN
              Because of George Bush?

                    SAM
                 (after a beat)
              I'm gonna break up with Cindy
              Sanders.

                    KEN
              Wow. Why?

                    SAM
              Well... she's just really different
              than I am.

                    KEN
              I know how that goes. I've been
              thinking about breaking up with my
              girlfriend, too.

                    SAM
              How come?

                    KEN
              It's complicated.

                    SAM
              Oh.
                 (then)
                      (MORE)

                                              (CONTINUED)

CONTINUED:

                    SAM (CONT'D)
          Me and Cindy just don't have
          anything in common. We never have
          anything to talk about. She doesn't
          like any of the stuff I like. She
          thought "The Jerk" was stupid.

                    KEN
          Are you serious? My girlfriend
          loves "The Jerk."

Sam's making himself nervous again. He sighs as Ken is
thinking about what Sam has said. Sam shrugs, sad.

                    SAM
          We just never really have any fun
          together.

                    KEN
          That's too bad. My girlfriend's
          pretty cool when it comes to that
          stuff.

                    SAM
          Then what's the problem?

                    KEN
             (after a beat)
          I don't know. Maybe there is no
          problem.

They both stand there for a second, lost in their own worlds.

                    SAM
          Well, I'm gonna go break up with
          Cindy Sanders.

                    KEN
          Good luck, buddy.

                    SAM
          Thanks.

Sam takes a deep breath and heads out. Ken watches him,
thinking.

                                             CUT TO:

INT. SCHOOL HALLWAY - DAY

MUSIC UP: ELO'S "SHOWDOWN"

Sam comes out of the bathroom, looking very nervous but
determined.

                                        (CONTINUED)

CONTINUED:

A few seconds later, Ken comes out, looking uncertain. He walks behind Sam for a few beats, then Sam turns and heads down a different hallway.

Ken continues onward.

                                                        CUT TO:

INT. SCHOOL HALLWAY - DAY

The school is buzzing with activity. Genuine excitement fills the air as anticipation of the Vice President's visit mounts.

Students are hauling tables out of the cafeteria, clearing more space for the assembly. Cindy is running all over the place, energized by the jitters.

Sam sees her from the end of the hall. After a moment of indecision, he slowly walks toward her.

                    CINDY
          Sam, oh my god, I've been looking
          all over for...
                    (noticing the turtleneck)
          What the hell is that?

                    SAM
          What?

                    CINDY
          You're wearing a turtleneck. Are
          you covering my hickey?

                    SAM
          Well, it's just... it's
          embarrassing. Don't get all mad.

                    CINDY
          Oh, thanks, Sam. I guess if you
          gave me a diamond ring, you
          wouldn't get mad if I was too
          embarrassed to wear it.

                    SAM
          I gave you a necklace and you've
          never worn it.

                    CINDY
          It was ugly.

                    SAM
          It was an heirloom.

                                              (CONTINUED)

CONTINUED:

> CINDY
> Don't start a fight, Sam. This is
> a big day for me.

> SAM
> I know. It's just...

Sam suddenly looks tired and frustrated. He looks Cindy in
the eye.

> SAM (CONT'D)
> Cindy... I don't wanna be your
> boyfriend anymore.

A moment of silence. They're both a little shocked by the
clarity of his words. It just came out. Cindy is flustered.

> SAM (CONT'D)
> I wanna go back to just being
> friends.

> CINDY
> Friends? You wanna be my friend?

> SAM
> Yeah. I really wanna just be your
> friend.

> CINDY
> No.

> SAM
> No?

> CINDY
> You can't break up with me. Sam,
> you're supposed to be nice. That's
> the only reason I'm going out with
> you.

> SAM
> I am nice. I'm just not having any
> fun. Are you?

Cindy is flustered. She doesn't have any idea how to react to
this development. She reaches into her purse.

> CINDY
> No, I'm not. And you can have your
> stupid, ugly heirloom back.

(CONTINUED)

CONTINUED: (2)

Cindy takes out the copper necklace and tosses it on the
ground at Sam's feet, then she storms off. Sam watches her,
pained but relieved. Neal and Bill walk up next to him. All
three watch her disappear around the corner.

> NEAL
> You did the right thing. You're
> too good for her.

> BILL
> Are you gonna sit with us at lunch
> again?

> SAM
> Yeah.

> BILL
> (looking at Neal)
> Thank God.

CUT TO:

INT. SCHOOL HALLWAY - DAY

MUSIC UP: PETE TOWNSHEND'S LIFEHOUSE VERSION OF "BABA
O'RILEY"

Ken is heading down the hallway, looking very determined. He
looks up ahead.

KEN'S POV: The band is gathered in the hall outside the
cafeteria, waiting to go in and play. There are three tubas
sticking up out of the middle of them.

Ken takes a deep breath, then heads toward the band. He gets
there and wades in, trying to get to the tubas.

He comes to the first one and taps on the tuba. The tuba
turns around. It's a guy. Ken makes an apologetic face and
squeezes through the band and comes up to the next tuba.

It looks like Amy from behind. Ken spins her around. It's a
different girl. She looks surprised. Ken nods and turns her
back around.

Then he looks over and sees the final tuba on the far edge of
the group. It's Amy. She's warming up, doesn't see him. We
see Ken call out her name. She looks over and gets an
uncertain look on her face.

(CONTINUED)

CONTINUED:

Ken pushes through the band and comes up to her. They stand face to face, Amy holding her tuba. Each trying to read each other's expressions.

>   KEN
>   I don't care.

>   AMY
>   You don't care?

>   KEN
>   No, I don't care. I just don't want
>   to talk about it anymore.

>   AMY
>   But you don't care?

>   KEN
>   I don't care.

Then, Ken gets a big smile. Amy smiles too and they attempt to embrace. However, the tuba makes this impossible.

And so, Ken leans in and he and Amy share a very sweet and tender kiss. All is well.

>   CUT TO:

INT. CAFETERIA - DAY

Students are filling in the lunch tables quickly, while many of their parents and siblings enter, taking their places along the walls. There's an excitement in the air.

A podium is set up at the front of the cafeteria. Cheesy red, white and blue bunting decorates the cafeteria.

Cindy Sanders is waiting by the podium for the event to begin. She wears a pretty dress and fancy braids. Her eyes are red. She tries to smile through her teary eyes.

Sam, Neal, and Bill are sitting at the geek table. All of a sudden, Millie runs up to Sam, very excited.

>   MILLIE
>   Sam. Oh my god. Everyone is talking
>   about you. They said you broke up
>   with Cindy Sanders because you
>   didn't wanna be tied down to one
>   girl. Is it true?

>   (CONTINUED)

CONTINUED:

> SAM
> Well, sorta...

SEAN walks by.

> SEAN
> Sam Weir. You are the man!

Neal and Bill look at Sam. He's becoming a god.

CUT TO:

INT.HALLWAY OUTSIDE CAFETERIA - SAME TIME

Students are filing into the cafeteria. We see the MASCOT enter. Mr. Mainzer walks in.

> MR. LACOVARA
> All right, everyone. Just eat like
> you'd normally eat.

Mr. Rosso straightens his tie and briskly walks to the door. Agent Meara is standing near the door debriefing his team. Another agent is checking names at the door, much like a bouncer. Rosso approaches him.

> MR. ROSSO
> Hello. My name's Rosso. It'll be on
> your list.

The Agent scans over his clipboard. Finally, he finds the name. He turns and whispers in the ear of Agent Meara, who quickly seems to get the picture. Agent Meara steps up to Mr. Rosso, who seems confused.

> AGENT MEARA
> Jeffery Theodore Rosso?

> MR. ROSSO
> Yes?

Agent Meara grabs Rosso by the arm and escorts him away from the door. Confused, Rosso is pulled down the hall.

> AGENT MEARA
> Mr. Rosso, are you now or have you
> ever been a member of the Taft
> Student's Alliance for a New
> America?

(CONTINUED)

CONTINUED:

> MR. ROSSO
> What? No. I mean, I might be on
> their mailing list somewhere from
> way back but I'm certainly not...

> AGENT MEARA
> I'm afraid your name has been red
> flagged as a security risk so I
> can't allow you to attend this
> assembly.

> MR. ROSSO
> There must be a mistake. I work
> here.

> AGENT MEARA
> Yes, I know. Now, if you'd allow me
> to guide you to a little holding
> area we have set up.

Rosso's face falls as they drag him away. Lindsay is heading
down the hall with an excited Harold and Jean in tow.

> JEAN
> Oh, there he is. Mr. Rosso, thanks
> so much for letting Lindsay do
> this.

> LINDSAY
> Mr. Rosso, what's going on? Where
> are you going?

> MR. ROSSO
> Well, it seems I'm a bit of a
> persona non grata here.

> LINDSAY
> What?

> MR. ROSSO
> Don't worry about it. It's cool,
> Lindsay. I guess I rocked the boat
> one too many times in my youth.
> It's no big deal. You just go in
> there and make the school proud.

He and Lindsay lock eyes for a moment. She can see in him
that distant flame of the radical that once was. He gives her
a smile.

> HAROLD
> I told you that guy was a kook.

(CONTINUED)

57.

CONTINUED: (2)

From inside the cafeteria, "Hail to the Chief" begins as Harold grabs Lindsay and Jean and hustles them inside.

ANGLE ON: ROSSO AND AGENT MEARA

> AGENT MEARA
> So, what do you teach here?

> MR. ROSSO
> Actually, I'm a guidance counselor.

CUT TO:

INT. CAFETERIA - DAY

MUSIC UP: "HAIL TO THE CHIEF"

The Marching Band is behind the podium, playing. Students are sitting at their lunch tables. All around the sides of the cafeteria are people watching, a couple of local news crews and photographers. Amy is playing with the band.

From the back, Ken watches Amy. At this moment, his heart is soaring. He smiles and begins to clap and cheer for her. She smiles at him as she plays. Daniel and Nick look up at Ken and smile.

ANGLE ON: CINDY CRYING

ANGLE ON: SAM FEELING GUILTY

ANGLE ON: BILL AND NEAL - HAPPY TO HAVE SAM BACK

ANGLE ON: THE WEIRS LOOKING PROUD

ANGLE ON: KIM EXCITED TO SEE LINDSAY ASK HER QUESTION

ANGLE ON: LINDSAY WAITING FOR HER MOMENT

Finally Ken can no longer contain his enthusiasm. He jumps to his feet and screams--

> KEN
> THIS SONG ROCKS!

The song ends.

ANGLE ON: THE STAGE

(CONTINUED)

58.

CONTINUED:

Cindy walks up to the podium and prepares to speak into the microphone. There is a long pause as she pulls herself together.

> CINDY
> Ladies and Gentleman. As the Republican National Committee's student liaison for McKinley High School, I am honored to present the Vice President Elect of the United States of America, George Bush.

The audience applauds loudly. Maybe more excited than anyone is Harold Weir, who stands with Jean on the sidelines.

CUT TO:

INT. MR. ROSSO'S OFFICE - DAY

Agent Meara is pouring out his guts to Mr. Rosso. In the background we hear the assembly over a radio (or school's public address system).

> AGENT MEARA
> It's not really what I thought it would be. Sometimes I have to guard an empty hallway for like twelve hours. Just stand there. You could go insane.

> MR. ROSSO
> Well, it's an important job.

> AGENT MEARA
> No, it's not. When's the last time you heard of a Vice President getting assassinated? It's never happened. And it never will, because, who cares? You know what I mean?

> MR. ROSSO
> So, there's no possibility for advancement?

> AGENT MEARA
> Yeah, I can guard a hallway for the President, whoopee. Before this you know who I covered? Mondale. And I thought nobody could be more boring than him. Boy, was I wrong.

(CONTINUED)

CONTINUED:

> MR. ROSSO
> So, it's never been fun.

> AGENT MEARA
> I was assigned to LBJ at the ranch
> for a while. He was fun. Told good
> stories, but then he died.
> (joking)
> Not my fault.

They laugh.

> MR. ROSSO
> Well, is this what you always
> wanted to do?

> AGENT MEARA
> I wanted to be CIA or FBI, but I
> had a friend at Service. Next thing
> you know, I've got ten years under
> my belt. Good pension. It's tough
> to switch gears.

> MR. ROSSO
> You've got to follow your dreams.
> If you're unhappy...

> AGENT MEARA
> I know, I know. You are so right.
> But what would I do? Quit?

> MR. ROSSO
> I've got a test here which reveals
> what type of job you are best
> suited for. Do you want to take it?

> AGENT MEARA
> Sure. Thanks, Jeff.

                                    CUT TO:

INT. CAFETERIA - CONTINUOUS

Mr. Lacovara steps up in front of the band.

> MR. LACOVARA
> Now we're going to open up the
> floor so the Vice President can
> take some questions from members of
> our student body. Our first
> question comes from Ms. Lindsay
> Weir.

                              (CONTINUED)

CONTINUED:

Lindsay stands. Looks back over at her parents. Harold and Jean give her supportive, expectant smiles.

> MR. LACOVARA (CONT'D)
> Miss Weir, go right ahead...

> LINDSAY
> Mr. Vice President, my name is Lindsay Weir. My father owns A-1 Sporting Goods on 16 mile road. My question is: as the former head of the CIA, would you finally tell us who killed President Kennedy?

We see reaction shots from all of our players, including:

ANGLE ON: NICK. At this moment, Lindsay is the goddess.

ANGLE ON: KIM. She busts out laughing.

ANGLE ON: HAROLD WEIR. His jaw drops in absolute horror.

ANGLE ON: JEAN. She shakes her head.

                                                    CUT TO:

INT. MR. ROSSO'S OFFICE - DAY

ON MR. ROSSO. He grins with delight and pride. AGENT MEARA smiles.

> AGENT MEARA
> Funny kid.

> MR. ROSSO
> One of McKinley's finest.

Mr. Rosso looks pleased as we...

                                              FADE TO BLACK.

                        <u>THE END</u>

FREAKS AND GEEKS

"DISCOS AND DRAGONS"

Episode #18

Written by Paul Feig

Directed by Paul Feig

With the end of the season and what we were pretty sure would be the end of our series fast approaching, Judd and I decided that the final episode should really work as our series finale, just in case the inevitable happened (which it did). And since this looked like it might be the last chance to write for these characters, I wanted to make sure that there weren't any favorite plot ideas that went to waste. There were three stories floating around that both Judd and I had been wanting to do. I had been trying to do a disco-themed episode based on something that had happened to me in high school. Then, I'd been dying to get the geeks involved in Dungeons and Dragons, since I'd never seen it portrayed in a positive light on TV and in movies. And, finally, Judd had come up with an idea when we first started writing the show that Lindsay should become a Deadhead.

So, when he and I huddled in his office to figure out the final episode, we listed out these three stories and basically said to each other, "Can we cram them all into one show?" And I, ever in search of a challenge (*why* I'll never know), said, "Sure!"

Of course, I was dumb enough to say this right before we broke for Christmas vacation. But since Judd had promised me that I would finally be allowed to direct an episode, I was more than happy to spend my much-needed vacation time toiling with what would turn out to be "Discos and Dragons."

First of all, let me say that part of this episode was written in Las Vegas. My wife and I had decided to go there for a short escape and ended up running into Judd and his "posse," which on that trip consisted of Adam Sandler, writer/director Steve Brill, *Rocky* star Carl Weathers, and the infamous Quentin Tarantino!

I was there with my posse, which consisted of my wife and my laptop computer.

I had written up my first pass of the story, which included the surprise ending with Lindsay and the Academic Summit. But some of my story was a bit too complicated (I had a whole subplot about Lindsay befriending the owners of a record store who would turn her on to the Grateful Dead), and I wasn't happy with it. So, Judd and I sat in a coffee shop next to the Sports Book in the Mirage and trimmed the story down, while his posse bet on the horses and my posse went shopping (well, my wife did, not my laptop—I think my laptop went to a strip club). I wasn't a huge expert on the Grateful Dead and so spent most of the next day sitting in the bathtub in my hotel room reading various Dead books so that I wouldn't make a fool out of myself in front of any Grateful Dead fans who happened to watch the show. And once my wife and I came home from Vegas, I spent the rest of the vacation finishing the script.

One of the things I'm most proud of in this episode is the fact that I got to show what really happened to me when I entered a dance contest at the teen disco at our local bowling alley. In the show, Nick is talked into entering by his current girlfriend, but I, alas, was talked into entering the disco contest by no one other than myself. I fancied myself a good dancer and figured that I could impress everyone if I got out there and did my thing. I did indeed do my thing (to the song "Disco Inferno"), which consisted of me simply dancing and spinning like an insane person you see living at a bus stop. I was sure at the time that the stunned faces on the women watching me were expressions of awe until, after I lost, I realized that they were actually looks of absolute disbelief at my incredible lack of talent. And then, to make things worse, the guy who danced after me started doing magic tricks, making a cane appear and pulling silk scarves out of his fist. He won, and I slinked out of the disco faster than you can say, "Play that funky music, white boy."

Anyway, this is the last script for *Freaks and Geeks*, and as proud as I am of it, it also makes me a bit sad, since it *is* the last script for *Freaks and Geeks*. Ever. But, hey, at least they let us make 18 episodes, right?

Thanks, enjoy, and if you haven't picked up a copy of the Grateful Dead's *American Beauty* and the latest *Dungeon Master's Guide*, then you'd better get crackin', friend. There's a lot of freakin' and geekin' to do.

—Paul Feig

FREAKS AND GEEKS

"DISCOS AND DRAGONS"

CAST LIST

LINDSAY WEIR
SAM WEIR
HAROLD WEIR
JEAN WEIR
DANIEL DESARIO
NICK ANDOPOLIS
BILL HAVERCHUCK
NEAL SCHWEIBER
KEN MILLER
KIM KELLY
HARRIS
MR. ROSSO
MR. KOWCHEVSKI
GORDON
SARA
MR. CASPER
MR. LACOVARA
MR. FLECK
VICTOR
LAURIE
JOCK(S)
FREAK STUDENT
DEEJAY
BOUNCER
BUS DRIVER
EUGENE

FREAKS AND GEEKS

"DISCOS AND DRAGONS"

<u>SET LIST</u>

INTERIORS:

MCKINLEY HIGH SCHOOL
 /HALLWAY
 /KOWCHEVSKI'S CLASSROOM
 /CAFETERIA
 /AUDIO VISUAL ROOM
 /EQUIPMENT ROOM
 /MR. ROSSO'S OFFICE
 /UNDER THE STAIRS
 /CAFETERIA
 /SOCIAL STUDIES CLASS
 /MR. ROSSO'S OFFICE
WEIR HOUSE
 /DINING ROOM
 /KITCHEN
 /LINDSAY'S BEDROOM
NICK'S HOUSE
 /BASEMENT
BOWLING ALLEY
DISCOTHEQUE
BUS

EXTERIORS:

BUS STATION
ANOTHER BUS STATION

FADE IN:

INT. BOWLING ALLEY - NIGHT

LINDSAY, KEN and KIM are sitting around at the bowling alley.
DANIEL is bowling. Lindsay is at the score table. The rest
are lounging on the bench, all wearing bowling shoes. In the
background, we hear the muffled sound of DISCO MUSIC. Daniel
throws a gutter ball.

              DANIEL
There's something wrong with these
lanes. I think they put down too
much oil.

              LINDSAY
        (looking up at clock)
Oh, man, it's nine. I've gotta go.
I've got two tests to study for.

              KEN
I hate the last week of school.
It's all tests. How am I supposed
to look forward to summer vacation
if I've got all these tests to
worry about?

              KIM
You could study.

              KEN
I could what?

Daniel and Ken laugh. Kim just rolls her eyes.

              KIM
        (to Daniel)
Don't you have some big test in
Kowchevski's tomorrow?

              DANIEL
Yeah. I'm ready for it. I'm paying
Dave Fleury twenty bucks to let me
cheat off his test.

              LINDSAY
Kowchevski's gonna nail you. He
knows you cheat.

(CONTINUED)

CONTINUED:

>   DANIEL
>   Yeah, but he moved me next to Dave
>   because he thinks he's the only kid
>   in class who won't let me cheat off
>   him. But everybody's got a price.

>   KIM
>   That's great, Daniel. You've
>   corrupted the last honest kid in
>   class. You must be very proud.

>   DANIEL
>   Prouder than if I was going to
>   summer school.

Just then, a couple of girls in disco dresses walk by,
LAUGHING. Ken looks at them, then at Daniel.

>   KEN
>   Is it time?

>   DANIEL
>   It's time.

The guys laugh and get up. They walk after the disco girls.
Kim just gives Lindsay a look.

>   KIM
>   Is it just me or are those guys
>   getting boring?

Lindsay gives Kim a smile and they get up and walk after
them.

>   CUT TO:

INT. DISCOTHEQUE - NIGHT

MUSIC UP: FOXY'S "HOT NUMBER"

A bowling alley "under age" disco, it's a converted cocktail
lounge that has a small dance floor in the middle and disco
lighting. A mirror ball hangs over the dance floor. The place
is not terribly crowded, about 30 people in their teens and
twenties.

The dance floor is half full. People dancing. In the middle
of them, a couple is doing the hustle. We see the girl is
SARA, the Abba girl from McKinley. We can't see who she's
dancing with.

>   (CONTINUED)

CONTINUED:

Daniel and Ken walk into the entrance of the disco. Lindsay
and Kim walk up behind them.

> KIM
> You guys, this is so stupid.

> KEN
> No, this is not stupid. This is a
> tradition.

Ken and Daniel exchange a look, nod to each other, then yell
inside at the top of their lungs...

> KEN & DANIEL
> DISCO SUUUUUUUUUUUUCKS!!!

Everybody inside turns and looks as Ken and Daniel wave.
People on the dance floor stop dancing. As they turn, they
part, revealing the dancers in the middle of the floor.

Suddenly, all the freaks' eyes go wide.

FREAKS' POV: In the middle of the dance floor is NICK. He
still has his arm around Sara from hustling. He sees the
freaks. He looks busted.

> KEN
> (in shock)
> Oh. My. God.

Off Lindsay and the freaks' surprised looks, we:

CUT TO:

OPENING CREDIT SEQUENCE

ACT ONE

FADE IN:

INT. WEIR KITCHEN - MORNING

HAROLD, Lindsay and Sam are at the kitchen table, doing their
morning breakfast routine. JEAN is cooking. Lindsay looks preoccupied.

> HAROLD
> Well, you two, I want you to figure
> out what days you're going to work
> at the store this summer.

(CONTINUED)

CONTINUED:

> SAM
> I want Fridays off. That's gonna be
> our Dungeons and Dragons day.

> JEAN
> Sam, you shouldn't play that game.
> I heard it's dangerous.

> SAM
> Mom, it's Bill, Neal, Gordon
> Harris and me sitting around a
> table. It's as dangerous as
> breakfast.

> LINDSAY
> Dad, can't I just get a job
> somewhere else? I can't spend
> another summer in your store. You
> don't even pay us minimum wage.

> HAROLD
> This isn't about pay. It's about
> family. Look around you. This
> kitchen, your clothes, the food on
> your plate. That's your pay.

> SAM
> We're working for bacon?

> HAROLD
> You're darn right you are. There's
> plenty of kids in the ghetto who'd
> give their eye teeth for bacon.

> LINDSAY
> Then let them work at the store.

> HAROLD
> You know what? It's time for you to
> start taking life a little more
> seriously, Lindsay. Are you ready
> for your finals?

> LINDSAY
> (impatiently)
> Yes, I've been studying.

> HAROLD
> I hope so. I read in the paper that
> it's become much harder to get
> accepted into good colleges.
> (MORE)

(CONTINUED)

CONTINUED: (2)

> HAROLD (CONT'D)
> There's a lot of very serious
> students out there.

> LINDSAY
> Dad, I'm studying.

> HAROLD
> (not even listening to
> her)
> You know, it's not too early to be
> thinking about your SATs and your
> ACTs. High school's gonna fly by
> and soon you'll be face to face
> with the rest of your life.

> SAM
> (joking)
> Gee, Dad. No pressure.

> HAROLD
> Laugh it up. You're next.

Sam makes a face at Lindsay. However, Harold's words seem to
have landed on Lindsay. She looks a little beaten down.

> CUT TO:

INT. SCHOOL HALLWAY - DAY

Daniel, Ken, Nick and Sara are walking down the hallway.
There are end-of-the-school-year banners up for yearbooks and
finals. Nick has his arm around Sara, who's wearing a disco
fedora hat. The freaks look very uncomfortable with Sara.
Daniel is studying Nick.

> SARA
> (energetic)
> I can't believe Nick hasn't told
> you he's been going to the disco.
> He's such an amazing dancer.

> KEN
> That's what I've always said.

> SARA
> No, it's true. It's probably
> because he's a drummer. You know
> what they say...

> DANIEL
> What do they say?

> (CONTINUED)

CONTINUED:

> SARA
> "Drummers do it with rhythm."

Sara giggles, squeezes Nick's waist. Ken and Daniel exchange a "this chick is weird" look.

> SARA
> You guys are coming to the disco on
> Friday, right?

> KEN
> Why would we do that?

> SARA
> Nick's gonna be in a dance contest
> and everything.

Daniel and Ken take this in, stunned, as they stop at Daniel's locker.

> DANIEL
> Wow, really, Nick?

> NICK
> (embarrassed)
> Yeah. I guess. I don't know.
> (trying to change the
> subject)
> Hey, Sara, we should probably get
> to class. They're gonna review
> stuff for finals.

> SARA
> Oh, yeah. Finals. Like, who cares,
> right?

The freaks all force smiles as Sara giggles. She's trying to fit in with them and it's not working. Daniel pulls out a twenty dollar bill.

> DANIEL
> Test time. Dave Fleury, I hope
> you've studied hard.

> SARA
> Oh, wow. Are you paying Dave Fleury
> to help you cheat or something?

Daniel looks at Sara, annoyed. Nick quickly jumps in.

(CONTINUED)

CONTINUED: (2)

> NICK
> (to Sara)
> Yeah, but don't say anything, okay?

> SARA
> Oh, no, of course not. I would
> never do that.

Nick starts to lead Sara away.

> NICK
> We'll see you guys later, okay?

> SARA
> Bye!

Nick and Sara take off. Daniel and Ken watch them go.

> KEN
> What in the name of God is going
> on? Is this the seventh sign of the
> Apocalypse?

> DANIEL
> I don't know, but I get the feeling
> that John Bonham's rolling in his
> grave.

ANGLE ON: LINDSAY AND KIM

Lindsay and Kim are standing by the lockers. They watch as
Nick and Sara walk by, arm in arm.

> KIM
> That's so sad.

> LINDSAY
> (shrugging)
> I don't know. Sara's cool.

> KIM
> Lindsay. Nick doesn't really like
> her. He's just using her to get
> over you. I bet he's hoping you'll
> get jealous.

> LINDSAY
> If that's true, it's kind of...
> awful.

(CONTINUED)

CONTINUED: (3)

>   KIM
>   I know. Guys do it all the time.
>   They don't know how to deal with
>   getting dumped, so they just pick
>   the easiest girl and jump right
>   into another relationship.

>   LINDSAY
>   (after a beat)
>   Man, I'm glad I'm not a guy.

As Kim and Lindsay ponder this...

>   CUT TO:

INT. ANOTHER PART OF THE HALLWAY - DAY

SAM, BILL and NEAL are walking down the hall after Sam has
taken some books out of his locker.

>   BILL
>   I can't wait to get my yearbook.
>   I'm only going to let girls sign it
>   so when I have kids, they'll think
>   I was a big stud.

>   SAM
>   I bet we find out some girls have
>   crushes on us. "Dear Sam, I've been
>   in love with you since September.
>   True love always."

>   NEAL
>   It never happens. Every girl always
>   writes the same thing in mine.
>   "Neal, you're a wild and crazy
>   guy." Nobody ever says wild and
>   sexy guy.

Just then, a couple of JOCKS run up behind the geeks.

>   JOCKS
>   Geek clean out!!!

And with that, they knock the geeks' books out of their hands
from the back and onto the floor. The jocks continue running
past, laughing and celebrating.

>   NEAL
>   (calling after them)
>   Thanks, guys. Real mature.

>   (CONTINUED)

CONTINUED:

Some other students laugh at the clean-outs. The geeks look humiliated. They pick up their books.

> SAM
> I hate this. Why do jocks think it's funny?

> BILL
> They think towel snapping's funny. They think clean-outs are funny. They think swirlies are funny. They think wedgies are funny. When do they have time to play sports?

> NEAL
> I don't know but I wish they would.

> SAM
> I'm so tired of being called a geek. I mean, what's so geeky about us? We're just guys.

HARRIS walks around the corner and up to the guys, holding a book. He speaks loud and proud. Passing students hear him and look over.

> HARRIS
> Gentlemen, good news.
> (shows them D&D book)
> New Dungeons and Dragons handbook at the gaming store. The "Deities and Demigods" cyclopedia. We're gonna have fun Friday night.

The geeks all exchange a look, then look around at passing students as they stand up.

> SAM
> Um, could we not talk about this right now?

> HARRIS
> What's the matter with you?

> SAM
> I don't know if I'm gonna be able to play that night.

> HARRIS
> Oh. Well, your loss.

(CONTINUED)

10.

CONTINUED: (2)

The geeks go into the A/V room as Sam looks depressed.

CUT TO:

INT. AUDIO VISUAL ROOM - CONTINUOUS

The geeks enter the A/V room. It has a desk and lots of
shelves filled with A/V catalogues and movie containers.
There are a few projectors and film strips on the counters.

MR. FLECK, the A/V teacher, is finishing a cigarette. He
butts it out.

                    MR. FLECK
          Oh, hey, guys. Sorry about the
          smoke. These things are gonna kill
          me. I know I might look cool with
          a cigarette in my hand but it's a
          crutch. Never forget that. Got it?

                    THE GEEKS
               (by rote)
          Yes, Mr. Fleck.

                    MR. FLECK
          So, how's tricks?

                    BILL
          They're okay. We got cleaned out.

                    MR. FLECK
          Jocks?

                    SAM
          Who else?

                    MR. FLECK
          Let me tell you about the jocks.
          Watch my hand.

Mr. Fleck illustrates his words by making a graph in the air.

                    MR. FLECK (CONT'D)
          This is a graph of their lives.
          "Ooh, I'm in Pee Wee football. I'm
          pretty good. What? I can be first
          string on the high school football
          team and wear a jacket with leather
          sleeves? Hooray."
               (stops his hand)
          That's where they are right now.
                    (MORE)

(CONTINUED)

CONTINUED:

> MR. FLECK (CONT'D)
> And when they gave you that clean-
> out, that was the pinnacle.
> (his hand starts going
> down)
> "I wanna play college ball. Excuse
> me? My GPA's not high enough to get
> a sports scholarship? All right, I
> guess I'll go to this crappy
> backwoods college. Ow, I just blew
> out my knee in practice. Oops, now
> I'm out of school and selling used
> cars. What? I'm fired? Hand me that
> bottle, man."

The geeks nod, taking this in.

> MR. FLECK (CONT'D)
> Now let's look at you guys.
> (hand going down)
> You get clean-outs, you get beaten
> up, you get called geeks, girls
> don't notice you, you're--

> BILL
> I thought this was supposed to make
> us feel better.

> MR. FLECK
> Hold on, Cool Breeze. Now, things
> start to get good.
> (hand going up)
> Hey, I got into an Ivy League
> school. Wow, chicks dig smart guys.
> Who knew? Look at me, I'm the head
> of a Fortune 500 company. Why, yes,
> Mr. Jock-Who-Cleaned-Me-Out, I <u>will</u>
> have fries with that."

Neal, Bill and Harris laugh. Sam looks unconvinced.

> SAM
> Yeah, but that's way in the future.
> We're gonna have to put up with
> this for three more years.

> MR. FLECK
> That's why you have to enjoy the
> small pleasures in life.

He pulls out a large film can. The geeks lean in and read it.
Neal, Bill and Harris get excited.

(CONTINUED)

CONTINUED: (2)

> HARRIS
> A sixteen millimeter print of
> "Monty Python and the Holy Grail?"

> MR. FLECK
> The A/V department over at Lincoln
> got it on loan from the Air Force
> base, so I traded them a copy of
> "Hemo the Magnificent" for it. It's
> ours for a week.

> NEAL
> Our own copy of "Grail." A/V is a
> paradise on Earth.

> BILL
> I'm so happy I think I'm going to
> cry.

The geeks celebrate as Mr. Fleck watches them, as happy as
they are. Sam, however, looks unconvinced. The BELL RINGS.

                                              CUT TO:

INT. KOWCHEVSKI'S CLASSROOM - DAY

Students are taking their seats in Mr. Kowchevski's class.
Mr. K is up front preparing to hand out tests. Daniel's
sitting at his desk, looking around. There's an empty desk
next to him.

> MR. KOWCHEVSKI
> All right, troops, let's find our
> seats. It's test time.

Daniel leans forward to another FREAK STUDENT.

> DANIEL
> Hey, man. Where's Dave Fleury? He's
> never late.

> FREAK
> Didn't you hear? He broke his arm
> in gym this morning. Fell off the
> ropes and missed the mat. It was
> hilarious.

> DANIEL
> Oh, no...
>   (then)
> You gotta let me copy off your
> test.

                                         (CONTINUED)

CONTINUED:

                    FREAK
          Sure, man, copy away. I ain't gonna
          get anything right but be my guest.

Daniel looks around, panicked. Then he gets up and sneaks
quickly out the door.

                                        CUT TO:

INT. SCHOOL HALLWAY - CONTINUOUS

Daniel heads around the corner into an empty hallway. Walks
over to a fire alarm. Looks around. The coast is clear. He
quickly breaks the glass to get to the alarm.

Right as he does, Mr. Rosso comes through the double doors at
the end of the hallway. Right as Daniel has his hand on the
alarm to pull it, Rosso calls out.

                    ROSSO
              (yelling over the alarm)
          There better be a fire, bro.

Daniel's completely busted.

                                        CUT TO:

INT. ROSSO'S OFFICE - DAY

Daniel is sitting before a stern looking Mr. Rosso.

                    ROSSO
          Think you're pretty cool, don't
          you, Mr. Desario?

                    DANIEL
          I don't think I'm cool.

                    ROSSO
          Yeah? You don't think you're the
          Fonz or something? If a jukebox was
          broken, you think you could hit it
          and it'd start playing?

                    DANIEL
              (insulted)
          I don't think I'm the Fonz.

                    ROSSO
          Yeah? Well, you act like somebody
          who thinks he's too cool to play by
          the rules.
                    (MORE)

                                      (CONTINUED)

CONTINUED:

                    ROSSO (CONT'D)
          Do you know how dangerous it is to
          pull a fire alarm? Do you know that
          if the fire department came out for
          a false alarm, they might miss a
          real fire? Maybe even at your
          house?

                    DANIEL
          Look, I'm really sorry, okay? I
          don't know what I was thinking.
          I'll never do it again.

                    ROSSO
          You forgot to say your dog ate your
          homework.

Daniel just rolls his eyes. Rosso stares at him a beat.

                    ROSSO
          I feel like we've been here before,
          Daniel. I'm a nice guy. But you
          know when I stop being nice? When
          people take advantage of my
          niceness. And that's what you've
          been doing. So, guess what? I'm not
          gonna be nice right now. How you
          like them apples?

                    DANIEL
          I like them fine, sir.

                    ROSSO
          Okay, cool guy. I've got a real
          cool way for you to spend the rest
          of the school year. You're now in
          A/V. Congratulations.

Daniel's face drops.

                                        CUT TO:

INT. SCHOOL HALLWAY - DAY

Lindsay is walking down the hallway when she looks and sees
Nick and Sara kissing each other good-bye. Nick gives Sara a
goodbye kiss, then turns to leave. He spots Lindsay. After an
awkward beat, he gives her a friendly nod and exits.

Lindsay continues walking, unnerved. Sara hurries to catch up
to her.

                    SARA
          Hey, Lindsay. Wait up.

                                        (CONTINUED)

CONTINUED: (2)

As Sara runs up, she slips and almost falls.

                SARA
          (nervous energy)
Whoa, man, I'm such a klutz. I can
barely walk around in real life but
somehow when I'm dancing, I'm super
coordinated. Weird, huh?

                LINDSAY
          (forced)
Yeah, that's wild.

                SARA
Do you ever go dancing, Lindsay?

                LINDSAY
Not really.

                SARA
Yeah, I got the feeling Nick was
kinda new to the whole dance scene.

Sara pulls a LIP GLOSS out of her pocket and puts some on.
Then she offers it to Lindsay.

                SARA (CONT'D)
You want some?

                LINDSAY
Oh, no thanks.

                SARA
          (chatty)
God, my lips are so chapped. I have
to keep putting more gloss on
because Nick keeps kissing it off.
He's such a good kisser, isn't he?

                LINDSAY
What?

                SARA
          (realizing)
Oh... this is weird, isn't it? Do
you feel weird talking about this?

                LINDSAY
Well, yeah. Kind of.

                SARA
Are you okay with us?

                (CONTINUED)

CONTINUED: (3)

> LINDSAY
> Yeah, sure. Why would I care?

> SARA
> Cool.

Lindsay forces a smile.

> SARA (CONT'D)
> Hey, you want to go shopping
> sometime?

> LINDSAY
> Uh, yeah... maybe.

We can see that Lindsay desperately wants to get away from
this girl as they keep walking. Sara looks oblivious.

> CUT TO:

INT. AUDIO VISUAL ROOM - DAY

Sam, Bill, Neal and Gordon are working in the A/V room. Neal
is putting films back in their cases, Sam's cleaning a
projector lens and Bill's filing catalogues.

> NEAL
> Okay, my worst day was when I had
> to show "Night and Fog," "Signal
> 30" <u>and</u> a VD film all right after
> lunch.

> BILL
> I got kinda woozy when I had to
> show that girls' "time of the
> month" movie.

> SAM
> They wouldn't even let me into
> class to show that one. They said
> the girls would be embarrassed.

> GORDON
> That's because I heard you get to
> see a girl's boobs in it.

> NEAL
> You don't. Trust me. I've watched
> it five times.

Mr. Fleck enters.

> (CONTINUED)

CONTINUED:

> MR. FLECK
> All right, fellas, our happy little
> A/V family is going to get a new
> addition.

> BILL
> Oh, are you pregnant?

> MR. FLECK
> No, Daniel Desario is going to be
> joining us here in A/V for the rest
> of the year.

Silence. The geeks exchange looks.

> GORDON
> Why?

> MR. FLECK
> Oh, I guess he's been having a
> little trouble and Mr. Rosso
> thought a stay in A/V might be a
> good attitude adjustment for him.

> NEAL
> Wait a minute. You're saying that
> they're putting him in A/V as
> punishment?

Just then, Daniel comes in. He looks like this is the last
place in the world he wants to be.

> MR. FLECK
> And speaking of the devil, here he
> is now. Welcome to the audio visual
> department, Mr. Desario.

> DANIEL
> (in Hell)
> Thanks.

Daniel looks around the room, brow furrowed.

The geeks all exchange looks.

> SAM
> Hey, Daniel. How's it going?

> DANIEL
> Great.

(CONTINUED)

CONTINUED: (2)

> GORDON
> Do you know how to fix projectors?

> DANIEL
> No.

> GORDON
> We can show you how.

> DANIEL
> Great.

And with this, Daniel plops down in a chair and sulks. The geeks all exchange worried looks.

CUT TO:

INT. MR. CASPER'S CLASSROOM - DAY

Lindsay, Kim and Nick are in class. MR. CASPER stands in front of the class with a very goofy look on his face. He's excited about something. He stares at the class for a beat.

Lindsay exchanges a look with Kim. What the hell's wrong with the guy?

> MR. CASPER
> I have an announcement that is
> going to make someone in this room
> very, very happy.

> KIM
> You're quitting?

The class LAUGHS. Mr. Casper gives a good natured smile.

> MR. CASPER
> No, Ms. Kelly. One of our top
> students has just received a very
> big honor.
> (to Kim)
> And what a surprise. It's not you.

Kim rolls her eyes.

> MR. CASPER
> Every year, the University of
> Michigan picks from the top one
> percent of all students in the
> state to take part in an Academic
> Summit. And it seems that our very
> own Lindsay Weir has been selected.

(CONTINUED)

CONTINUED:

Lindsay's eyes go wide as the entire class turns and looks at her. She's embarrassed and thrown.

                    LINDSAY
          What's an Academic Summit?

                    MR. CASPER
          Oh, Ms. Weir, you are in for a
          treat. It's a teenage think tank,
          if you will. Two glorious weeks on
          the U of M campus reading,
          debating, matching wits with the
          best and brightest
          students in Michigan. You'll be
          ranked daily, there'll be
          competitions, rivalries, intense
          meetings of the minds. Oh, you are
          one lucky girl.

Lindsay looks around the room at everyone staring like she's the biggest loser in the world. She looks at Mr. Casper, who gives her a big goofy smile.

                  MR. CASPER (CONT'D)
          Well, what do you have to say about
          that?

                    LINDSAY
          Um...I'm one lucky girl?

Lindsay looks completely thrown and not at all happy.

                  END OF ACT ONE

                  ACT TWO

FADE IN:

INT. ROSSO'S OFFICE - DAY

Lindsay is sitting in front of Rosso's desk. She doesn't look happy.

                    ROSSO
          See, here's the weird thing.
          Usually students are happy about
          getting selected to be in the
          Academic Summit.

                    LINDSAY
          Why did they pick me? I didn't even
          sign up for it.

                                       (CONTINUED)

CONTINUED:

>   ROSSO
>   I submitted all our top students. I
>   do every year.

>   LINDSAY
>   But how can I be in the top one
>   percent? I don't study that much.
>   Are kids in Michigan schools <u>that</u>
>   stupid?

>   ROSSO
>   No, you're just that smart.

Lindsay sinks down in her chair and lets out an impatient
sigh. Rosso studies her.

>   ROSSO (CONT'D)
>   You know what I think? I think
>   you're feeling a little out of
>   sorts.

>   LINDSAY
>   Gee, really?

He takes her sarcasm and smiles knowingly. Then he nods.

>   ROSSO
>   "Maybe you're tired and broken/Your
>   tongue is twisted with words half-
>   spoken and thoughts unclear."

Lindsay gives him a strange look, knowing that he's just
recited something to her. He continues, acting it out.

>   ROSSO (CONT'D)
>   "What do you want me to do, to do
>   for you to see you through?"
>   (stands)
>   "A box of rain will ease the pain
>   and love will see you through."

He sits on the front of his desk and gives Lindsay a look
that says "now do you feel better?"

>   LINDSAY
>   Mr. Rosso, why are you talking like
>   that?

>   ROSSO
>   I'm just quoting the Dead. I know
>   it always makes <u>me</u> feel better.

(CONTINUED)

CONTINUED: (2)

>   LINDSAY
> Quoting the who?

>   ROSSO
> Not "The Who."
>   (chuckles at his joke)
> The Grateful Dead. I would think
> you'd be a fan.

>   LINDSAY
> I never really thought about them.

>   ROSSO
> You oughta check 'em out. You'd dig
> them. When I was in college, I
> always put their album "American
> Beauty" on whenever I was
> stressing. It always helped.

Mr. Rosso smiles and goes to his file desk. Slides open the
bottom door. Inside are a bunch of albums. He pulls out a
copy of "American Beauty." Hands it to Lindsay.

>   ROSSO
> You know what? I'm gonna loan it to
> you. Put it on while you're
> studying for finals and soon you'll
> be rarin' to go to that Academic
> Summit.

Lindsay takes the album from him. She looks confused. He just
gives her a knowing smile.

>   CUT TO:

INT. AUDIO VISUAL ROOM - DAY

Daniel is sitting, looking bored. The geeks are standing off
to the side as Mr. Fleck is walking around the room showing
Daniel all the features of the A/V room.

>   MR. FLECK
> ...Now over here is where we keep
> the film catalogues. Thanks to
> Bill, these have all been filed in
> alphabetical order according to the
> name of the rental companies. Once
> you've used one, make sure you put
> it back in its proper place. Either
> that or suffer the wrath of Bill.

Daniel looks over at Bill. Bill looks terror-stricken.

>   (CONTINUED)

CONTINUED:

> BILL
> You can mess them up. I don't care.

> NEAL
> (nervous)
> He loves filing.

> MR. FLECK
> Now; let me tell you all about the
> filmstrips.

> DANIEL
> (getting up)
> Hey, you know what, man? I'm gonna
> take off. Just tell Rosso I was
> here and I did something, okay?

> MR. FLECK
> Sorry, can't do that, friend. I'm
> in charge of you.

> DANIEL
> C'mon. Help me out, man.

> MR. FLECK
> Afraid I can't. Rosso's orders.

Daniel stares at Mr. Fleck for a second, then heads for the
door.

> MR. FLECK
> You walk out that door and I
> guarantee I'll get you slapped in
> summer school. I've seen your
> transcript. It'd be the easiest
> thing I ever did.

Daniel stops and turns back. The geeks look at Daniel, then
at Mr. Fleck. They can't believe what's happening in their
A/V room. Daniel and Mr. Fleck have a stare down. Then...

> DANIEL
> All right. I'm all yours.

Daniel walks in and plops down in a chair, full of "screw
you" attitude. He puts his feet up on Mr. Fleck's desk
defiantly.

> MR. FLECK
> Lucky me.

(CONTINUED)

CONTINUED: (2)

The geeks just stare at Daniel in horror. Their haven has now been officially invaded.

                                                    CUT TO:

INT. CAFETERIA - DAY

Lindsay is walking through the cafeteria with her hot lunch tray looking for the freaks. She has the Grateful Dead album tucked under her arm. MR. LACOVARA, who's the day's lunch monitor, walks past.

                    MR. LACOVARA
            Lindsay, I understand
            congratulations are in order.
            Welcome to the one percent club. I
            was one back in 1956. And look what
            it did for me.

He chuckles goofily and holds out his arms to say "ta da." Lindsay forces a smile.

                    LINDSAY
            Thank you.

Mr. Lacovara backs away as he gives Lindsay a "you're welcome" nod. Right as he turns around, he collides with a student carrying a hot lunch tray. CRASH! The tray smashes to the floor. All the students CLAP and WHISTLE.

                    MR. LACOVARA
                (to student)
            Oh, my goodness. I'm so sorry.
                (to lunchroom)
            It was my fault. I'm the clumsy
            Claude.

Lindsay watches this and looks even more depressed. Just then she hears...

                    VICTOR
            Hey. "American Beauty." Great
            album.

Lindsay looks over to see a small table with a freaky but friendly looking couple in tie-dye shirts, VICTOR and LAURIE.

                    LINDSAY
            Oh...yeah. I've heard.

                    LAURIE
            You a Head?

                                            (CONTINUED)

CONTINUED:

                    LINDSAY
          What?

Laurie points to the Grateful Dead album under Lindsay's arm.

                    LAURIE
          Are you a Deadhead?

                    LINDSAY
          Oh... uh, no, not really. Somebody
          gave me this album to listen to.

                    VICTOR
          Oh, man, if you've never heard it
          before then you're in for a treat.
          It's like the best album ever.

                    LINDSAY
          Really? Is it that good?

                    LAURIE
          Hey, I wish I'd never heard it just
          so I could hear it for the first
          time again.

Lindsay gives them a strange look, unsure. They just give her
big happy smiles.
ANGLE ON: THE FREAK TABLE

Ken is sitting with Nick and Sara, who are snuggling. Ken's
wearing a ski vest. Nick's chair keeps bumping into Ken's.

                    KEN
          Uh, Nick? Could you move? You're
          like on top of me, man.

                    SARA
               (playfully)
          Nick likes to be on top.

Sara and Nick giggle. Ken looks like he wants to vomit. Sara
turns to Ken.

                    SARA
          That's such a cool vest, Kenny.

                    KEN
               (in disbelief)
          Kenny?

                                        (CONTINUED)

CONTINUED: (2)

> SARA
> I'm gonna call you Kenny from now
> on. Hey, you want to come over to
> Nick's after school? We're gonna
> practice some dance moves.

> KEN
> I don't think so.

> SARA
> C'mon, it'll be fun.

> NICK
> Ken doesn't dance.

> SARA
> That's just 'cause you don't know
> how. I taught Nick how to do the
> Hustle in less than an hour. But
> you'd probably learn even faster
> 'cause you'd have both of us
> coaching you.

Ken looks at Nick, weirded out.

> KEN
> Um, no.

> SARA
> Okay. Your loss. You guys need
> anything? 'Cause I'm gonna go get
> another milk.

Ken shakes his head "no." Sara turns to Nick.

> SARA (CONT'D)
> Okay. I'll be right back, baby.

> NICK
> I'll be here.

They kiss each other good-bye, then Sara takes off. Nick
watches her go.

> KEN
> All right, Nick. I give up. When
> does Allen Funt come boogie-ing
> out?

> NICK
> Huh?

(CONTINUED)

CONTINUED: (3)

> KEN
> That girl is so annoying.

> NICK
> No, she's not. She's just got a
> bubbly personality.

> KEN
> Well, can you pop her bubble soon?
> 'cause I can't take her anymore. I
> want to jump off a cliff.

> NICK
> (pissed)
> You know what, man? That's not
> cool. She's my girlfriend.

> KEN
> Nick, she's turned you into some
> disco zombie. Do I need to remind
> you that you used to hate disco?

> NICK
> Yeah, I know but I didn't really
> give it a chance. I mean, it's not
> that bad.
> (off Ken's look)
> It's not. I mean, what's the
> difference between disco and
> Zeppelin, really? You know, they
> both have heavy drums and bass. You
> know that Foxy song, "Hot Number?"
> It kinda rocks.

> KEN
> No, I don't know it, thank God. But
> I can guarantee it sucks.

> NICK
> You know what sucks? You do. I've
> been trying to get a decent
> girlfriend forever and now that
> I've got one, you're being a total
> jerk. Everybody was happy for you
> when you got Amy, you know.
> (ALTERNATE)
> Just because Amy broke up with you,
> don't take it out on me.

(CONTINUED)

CONTINUED: (4)

>   KEN
> Nick, you're just dating Sara to
> make Lindsay jealous. And it's not
> working. Admit it.

>   NICK
> You know what, man? Screw you.
> Thanks for all the support.

Nick sits up and storms away just as Lindsay arrives at the table.

>   LINDSAY
> What was that all about?

>   KEN
> Lindsay, could you do me a favor
> and start dating Nick again? 'Cause
> I don't think I can take much more
> of this.

ANGLE ON: THE GEEK TABLE

The geeks and Gordon are eating their lunches, depressed.

>   NEAL
> This is terrible. That Daniel guy's
> gonna ruin the only place we like
> in the school.

>   BILL
> Why did Mr. Rosso do this to us?
> It's so unfair to make us end our
> year like this.

>   GORDON
> I bet that Daniel guy's high on
> drugs. If we get him mad, he might
> freak out and smash up the A/V
> room.

>   SAM
> No, he won't. He's not a bad guy.
> He's friends with my sister. I've
> talked to him before.

>   NEAL
> Sam, he got you a porno. I
> wouldn't exactly say you've got a
> meaningful relationship going with
> the guy.

(CONTINUED)

CONTINUED: (5)

> SAM
> Well, none of us really know him
> that well.

> NEAL
> All I know is, he's mean to Mr.
> Fleck. So what we have to do is get
> Daniel assigned to go show movies
> everyday. That way he'll be out of
> our hair. It's our only chance to
> get him out of there. Agreed?

They shake their heads yes. Sam looks at Neal, displeased.

                                        CUT TO:

INT. LINDSAY'S BEDROOM - DAY

Lindsay is in her bedroom standing by her stereo. She takes
the Grateful Dead album out of its dust sleeve and puts it on
the turntable. She puts the needle on the album.

MUSIC UP: THE GRATEFUL DEAD'S "BOX OF RAIN"

As the music starts, Lindsay stares at the turntable for a
second. Not particularly impressed. She walks over and sits
on her bed. Takes off her shoes and lies back.

She heaves a long and heavy SIGH. As the lyrics of the song
begin, Lindsay stares at the ceiling, listening.

IN A SERIES OF CUTS, we see Lindsay begin to enjoy the song.
She gets up and plays the song again.

Lindsay picks up the album cover. Puts the song on again. As
she reads the back of the album cover, she starts to sway to
the music a bit. Puts the song on again.

She puts the album onto her bed and begins to really start
moving around her room to the music.

As the song goes into its guitar solo, Lindsay seems to get
swept up in a wave of euphoria as she starts to dance and
spin around her room.

                                        CUT TO:

INT. WEIR DINING ROOM - NIGHT

The Weirs are around the dinner table eating. Harold and Jean
both look happy. Lindsay looks strangely happy, too.

                                        (CONTINUED)

CONTINUED:

>   JEAN
>   Our daughter in the top one
>   percent. Like my grandpa used to
>   say, "If I was wearing a vest, all
>   the buttons would pop."

Sam gives Jean a strange look, not getting the comment.

>   HAROLD
>   I certainly owe you an apology,
>   Lindsay. Here I didn't think you
>   were applying yourself and now,
>   look. You must be absolutely
>   thrilled.

>   LINDSAY
>   (very casual)
>   Yeah, but I don't know. I'm not
>   sure if I really want to go. I
>   mean, what's the point?

Silence. Harold looks at her like she's nuts.

>   HAROLD
>   Are you wacky?

>   SAM
>   (laughs)
>   Wacky?

>   HAROLD
>   Can it. Lindsay, you're going to
>   that Summit. This isn't even up for
>   debate.

>   LINDSAY
>   Dad, I didn't say I'm not going. It
>   just sounds kinda... dumb.

>   HAROLD
>   Dumb? To spend two weeks with the
>   intellectual elite of your peers?
>   Yeah, that sounds mighty dumb.

>   JEAN
>   Honey, this is the opportunity of a
>   lifetime. And think of all the
>   people you'll meet.

>   LINDSAY
>   I know, mom, it's just--

(CONTINUED)

CONTINUED: (2)

> HAROLD
> "It's just" nothing. I can't
> believe we're even having this
> discussion. This is your key to the
> best schools in the world. Harvard,
> Yale, Princeton. Don't blow this,
> Lindsay.

> LINDSAY
> I didn't say I wasn't going. God,
> can we even have a normal
> discussion about something?

> HAROLD
> When it's something like this, no.

Lindsay goes back to her food, no longer happy.

CUT TO:

INT. MR. CASPER'S CLASSROOM - DAY

MR. CASPER is in front of the class. Lindsay, Kim and Nick
are in their desks among all the other students.

> MR. CASPER
> Well, everyone, the last week of
> school can mean only one thing. And
> that's that today is movie day.

The class reacts positively.

> MR. CASPER (CONT'D)
> But just so we're not completely
> wasting time, we'll be watching the
> 1968 Franco Zeffirelli version of
> Shakespeare's "Romeo and Juliet."

The class GROANS.

> MR. CASPER (CONT'D)
> Before you judge, you should know
> that this film actually contains a
> few seconds... of nudity.

The class is happy again. Mr. Casper looks at his watch.

> MR. CASPER (CONT'D)
> Now, if one of the astute members
> of our A/V squad would get his butt
> in here, we could get this show on--

(CONTINUED)

CONTINUED: (3)

KNOCK KNOCK. Mr. Casper makes a big production out of going to the door. When he opens it, an unenthusiastic Daniel is standing there with a projector on an A/V cart.

>   DANIEL
>   I'm here to show your movie.

Kim hears Daniel's voice, as do Lindsay and Nick. They look over, see him. Daniel sees them and his face fills with dread. He didn't know this was their class.

>   FADE OUT.

                          END OF ACT TWO

                            ACT THREE

FADE IN:

INT. CLASSROOM - DAY

Lindsay, Nick and Kim are staring at Daniel standing in the doorway with his A/V cart. They try not to laugh.

>   MR. CASPER
>   Glad you could make it. I was
>   starting to think I'd have to act
>   the film out myself.

Daniel wheels the cart in and sees the freaks. He makes a face that shows he didn't know this was their class. He looks embarrassed but covers by trying to act cool as he starts to wheel the cart to the back of the room.

>   NICK
>   (pretending to cough)
>   Geek.

Nick, Lindsay and Kim stifle laughter. Daniel gives Nick a "you're dead" smile. As he walks past Nick, he elbows him in the head. Nick grabs his head and laughs.

>   MR. CASPER
>   (as Daniel sets up
>   projector)
>   Now, this version of "Romeo and
>   Juliet" is unique in that it's the
>   first time a film had chosen to let
>   actual teenage actors portray the
>   two star-crossed lovers.

>   (CONTINUED)

CONTINUED:

Daniel plugs in the projector, then tries to set it up. He
can't seem to get the arms of the projector up.

He tugs on it, jiggling the cart and causing the take-up reel
to CRASH to the floor. Mr. Casper flinches. The freaks stifle
more laughter.

>
                    MR. CASPER (CONT'D)
>   Do you need a hand, sir?

>   DANIEL
>   I think I can handle it.

Daniel looks at the freaks, then around at the class staring
at him. Daniel gets unnerved. He goes back to tugging on the
projector arm NOISILY.

>   MR. CASPER
>   The version made before Mr.
>   Zeffirelli's masterpiece starred
>   two actors well into their
>   thirties, which caused the film to
>   feel artificial and--
>   (distracted by Daniel)
>   Could somebody show Mr. DeMille how
>   to set up that projector, please?

The class LAUGHS. A VERY NERDY KID stands up and pushes the
release button on the projector. He then raises the projector
arm. Daniel looks humiliated. The kid goes to do the other
one.

>   DANIEL
>   I got it, man. I got it. I'm not
>   stupid.

Daniel goes back to setting up the projector as Mr. Casper
makes an "oh, you're not?" face to the class. They giggle.

>   DISSOLVE TO:

INT. MR. CASPER'S CLASSROOM - MINUTES LATER

Daniel is still struggling with the projector, feeding film
through it. The class is now all turned around in their desks
and staring at him. Mr. Casper is sitting on his desk, arms
folded.

>   (CONTINUED)

CONTINUED:

>   MR. CASPER
> Any chance that we'll be ready in
> the near future?

>   DANIEL
> I got it, man. Just cool it.

Mr. Casper makes a mocking turning-a-key-to-lock-his-lips
motion to the class. They LAUGH.

>   DANIEL (CONT'D)
> Okay. It's ready.

>   MR. CASPER
> Saints be praised.

Daniel switches the projector on. CHICKA-CHICKA-CHICKA-
CHICKA. The film starts grinding through the projector,
causing the image on the screen to jump up and down.

Daniel jumps up and starts fooling with the film. He doesn't
turn the projector off. The class starts to SNICKER. Daniel
hears this and starts to get frustrated.

>   DANIEL
>   (loudly to himself)
> C'mon, ya stupid thing. What the
> hell?

Daniel hits the projector a couple of times, doing absolutely
nothing. Mr. Casper rolls his eyes.

>   MR. CASPER
> Excuse me, Muhammad Ali, but
> instead of hitting it, you might
> want to make your film loop a
> little bigger.

>   DANIEL
> My what?

The nerdy student gets up again and turns off the machine. He
fiddles with the film for a second, then turns the projector
back on. The film goes through it perfectly.

The class CLAPS. Daniel looks around at them, embarrassed and
upset. He looks over at Kim, who is too embarrassed to look
at him. He then plops down in a desk next to the projector.
SIGHS.

>   DISSOLVE TO:

INT. MR. CASPER'S CLASSROOM - THE END OF CLASS

NOTE: IF BEHIND SCHEDULE, THIS SCENE CAN BE CUT

The film is running. We HEAR a stringy score. Some girls are sniffling. Daniel looks bored beyond belief. Mr. Casper looks at the clock and starts to head back to Daniel.

> MR. CASPER
> (whispering to Daniel)
> We should probably stop here and
> start it again tomorr-- Oh my God!

Daniel jumps, as does the whole class. He turns and looks down. A mountain of film is on the floor behind the projector. Daniel forgot to hook up the take-up reel. He looks beyond embarrassed.

The light switches on. The class sees all the film and bursts out into LAUGHTER.

Nick and Lindsay start to laugh but stop themselves when they see Daniel. Kim just shakes her head, embarrassed too.

> CUT TO:

INT. AUDIO VISUAL ROOM - DAY

BLAM! Daniel crashes the projector cart through the door. He shoves it across the room, where it bangs into a shelf. The geeks jump, as does Mr. Fleck.

> MR. FLECK
> Mr. Desario, that's the school's
> equipment.

> DANIEL
> Yeah, then let the school run it.

> MR. FLECK
> Things not go well?

> DANIEL
> You know what, man? Let your little
> boys run your projectors for you
> from now on because I ain't doing
> it anymore!

Daniel walks out of the room and slams the door behind him. The geeks exchange a stunned look.

> (CONTINUED)

CONTINUED:

>   NEAL
> Well, that didn't work.

                                                    CUT TO:

INT. CAFETERIA - DAY

Lindsay is sitting with Victor and Laurie, the Deadheads, at
their table.

>   LINDSAY
> So, you guys just drive around and
> follow the Dead everywhere?

>   VICTOR
> Yeah, tons of people do. It's
> really great. You meet so many cool
> people.

>   LINDSAY
> Are their concerts that different?
> I mean, doesn't it get boring?

>   VICTOR
> No, that's the cool thing about it.
> The shows are never the same, even
> if they play the same songs.

>   LAURIE
> Yeah, it's like nothing you've ever
> experienced. Once, we saw them in
> New Jersey and right in the middle
> of the show, it started raining.
> Suddenly, everybody goes running
> down into the pit and starts
> dancing in the mud. And then the
> sun comes out and there's a rainbow
> over the stage. I started crying.
> It was beautiful.

>   LINDSAY
> But isn't it just all about getting
> high? I mean, isn't that why
> everybody's into it?

>   VICTOR
> No, getting high's part of it for a
> lot of people but the whole thing
> is about having a good time
> together, as one. Nobody's judging
> you if you don't get high. The
> Dead's not about that.
>   (MORE)

                                                    (CONTINUED)

CONTINUED:
                    VICTOR (CONT'D)
          It's just about being connected,
          about being together and free.
          There's nothing better, I'm telling
          you.

                    LINDSAY
          That sounds wild.

                    LAURIE
          Yeah, we're driving down to Texas
          once school's out to follow the
          tour up to Colorado. Nine shows in
          a week and a half. I can't wait.

Lindsay nods, a little jealous.

                    VICTOR
          What are you doing this summer?

                    LINDSAY
          Oh, I got into this Academic Summit
          thing at U of M. It's kinda goofy.

                    LAURIE
          Sounds cool.

                    LINDSAY
          I guess. I don't know. It beats
          working at my dad's store.

                    VICTOR
          Hey, man, you gotta do what you
          gotta do.

Victor and Laurie laugh. Lindsay smiles, embarrassed.

                                        CUT TO:

INT. NICK'S BASEMENT - DAY

MUSIC UP: DYNASTY'S "I DON'T WANT TO BE A FREAK"

Nick and Sara are practicing their disco dancing in Nick's
basement. Nick's moves have improved since we last saw him.

                    SARA
          C'mon. You promised me.

                    NICK
          I don't know. I'm just a little
          freaked out about it. I'm not good
          at contests.

                                    (CONTINUED)

CONTINUED:

                    SARA
          Nick, you're a great dancer. You're
          <u>really</u> good. I'm not just saying
          that.

This sinks in on Nick. He confidently spins Sara. He's
enjoying himself.

                    NICK
          You know, it's weird. I always used
          to think disco sucked. But I guess
          deep down I was destined for it or
          something. You know?

                    SARA
          Yeah, totally.

                    NICK
          Sometimes you end up being good at
          the thing that you hate. Like
          Lindsay. She hates math, but she
          was the head of the Mathletes.

Sara forces a smile, suddenly preoccupied.

                    SARA
          Let's take a break.

                    NICK
          Okay.

They sit on Nick's couch.

                    SARA
          Nick? Do you still like Lindsay?
          It's okay if you do. I just want to
          know.

                    NICK
          No.

Sara smiles, relieved.

                    NICK
          But I'm always gonna love her. I
          mean, I'm not "in love" with her
          anymore, but I still care about
          her.

Sara's smile fades a bit. Nick puts his arm around her.

                                        (CONTINUED)

CONTINUED: (2)

> NICK
> I really like you, Sara.

Sara waits for Nick to say more, but he doesn't. He just leans in and kisses her. Sara melts.

> SARA
> I've had a crush on you since sixth grade.

> NICK
> Really?

> SARA
> Remember we were both in Mr. Duer's social studies class?

> NICK
> Oh, yeah.

> SARA
> I always sat behind you, even though you were so tall I couldn't see the board.
> (in awe, vulnerable)
> I just can't believe you like me.

Sara is truly smitten. She hugs Nick tightly. OFF Nick, feeling a bit confused...

> CUT TO:

INT. UNDER THE STAIRS - DAY

Kim and Daniel are hanging out. Daniel's upset and has been on a tirade. Kim looks at the end of her rope.

> DANIEL
> God, I can't believe I've gotta go to A/V again today. It's so stupid. Rosso's such a fascist. And that Mr. Fleck guy's a total loser.

> KIM
> Well, nobody asked you to pull the fire alarm, Daniel.

> DANIEL
> What, I was supposed to flunk a test?

> (CONTINUED)

CONTINUED:

> KIM
> Well, you should have studied.

> DANIEL
> But I suck at math.

> KIM
> (an irritated sigh)
> What do you want me to say?

> DANIEL
> I don't know. You're my girlfriend.
> You're supposed to help me. I
> listen to all your stupid problems.

> KIM
> You know what, Daniel? Why don't
> you go tell it to the fire alarm?

She storms away, leaving a stunned Daniel.

CUT TO:

INT. SCHOOL HALLWAY - DAY

Sam, Neal and Bill come down the stairs and head down the
hallway.

> BILL
> I want my new Dungeons and Dragons
> character to be called Gorthon.

> NEAL
> Why "Gorthon?"

> BILL
> 'Cause it sounds cool. "I am
> Gorthon the thief. Surrender your
> jewels, princess."

> NEAL
> Bill, don't be a thief. You always
> get killed trying to steal jewels.
> (to Sam)
> So, Sam, is Logan the Huge going to
> be making an appearance?

> SAM
> I told you guys, I don't want to
> play.

(CONTINUED)

CONTINUED:

> NEAL
> Why. You too cool for us all of a
> sudden?
> > (ALTERNATE)
> Why? You're too cool for us now
> that you broke up with Cindy.

> SAM
> No, I don't know. It's just...it's
> a geeky game. What's the point? We
> just sit around doing dumb voices.

> NEAL
> The point is, you used to like
> doing it.

> SAM
> Yeah, I know.
> > (then)
> I left my science book in the A/V
> room. I'll see you guys later.

A depressed and distracted Sam goes into the A/V room as Neal
and Bill exchange a look and head off.

CUT TO:

INT. AUDIO VISUAL ROOM - CONTINUOUS

Sam enters the room. It's empty. He looks around, then goes
to a shelf and grabs his science book. He hears a NOISE in
the equipment room. Sam walks over and peeks inside the
cracked open door.

INT. INSIDE THE EQUIPMENT ROOM - CONTINUOUS

Daniel is standing by a projector with a service manual in
his hand. He's reading the manual and looking at all the
parts of the projector, trying to figure it out.

Sam looks surprised. He watches Daniel for a minute, then
quietly backs away and leaves the A/V room.

CUT TO:

INT. SCHOOL HALLWAY - DAY

Lindsay walks up to Kim, who's heading down the hall. Lindsay
looks depressed.

> KIM
> What's eating you?

(CONTINUED)

584

CONTINUED:

> LINDSAY
> Oh, nothing. I just wish I didn't
> have to go to this Academic Summit.
> It just feels like I'm going right
> back to school.

> KIM
> Life's tough.

> LINDSAY
> What's that supposed to mean?

> KIM
> It means you've been moping around
> ever since you got into that stupid
> thing. Quit complaining about it.
> At least you get to get out of this
> town for a while.

> LINDSAY
> Kim, it's summer vacation. You can
> go out of town, too. You can go
> anywhere you want.

> KIM
> No, I can't, Lindsay. I don't have
> any money. Besides, Daniel never
> wants to go anywhere.

> LINDSAY
> So, go without him. Kim, you don't
> have to stay here, you know.

> KIM
> That's easy for you to say. 'Cause
> you get to leave. I don't.

Kim heads up the stairs, leaving Lindsay behind. Lindsay
watches after her, surprised.

                                                    CUT TO:

INT. AUDIO VISUAL ROOM - DAY

Daniel is sitting in a chair on the opposite side of the
room. He is staring at the floor, lost in thought, running a
small piece of film through his fingers. Sam is filing
catalogues on the other side of the room. The rest of the
geeks are sitting around the A/V room having a great time.

                                                (CONTINUED)

CONTINUED:

                         HARRIS
          Gentlemen, tonight will be our best
          D&D campaign ever. Let me just say
          two words -- ancient Babylonia.

                         NEAL
          Oh, no, don't do a Babylonian
          adventure. It's no fun if I have
          to pretend my character's wearing
          sandals.

                         GORDON
                (looking through book)
          Hey, did you guys see the drawing
          of the goddess Ishtar in here?
          Hubba hubba.

                         BILL
          You should look at the goddess of
          vice. You can see her butt.

                         NEAL
          Ooo, a drawing of a butt. How
          exciting.

                         HARRIS
          Well, I hope you guys are prepared
          to avoid the Dancing Sword.

                         DANIEL (O.C.)
          What's a Dancing Sword?

Sam looks over, surprised. The geeks all look up at Daniel,
who's staring at them, interested. They look nervous.

                         BILL
          Well... um...

                         HARRIS
          It's a sword that can fight without
          you holding it.

                         DANIEL
          So you can just send your sword in
          to battle for you and stay home?
          That's kinda stupid.

Sam sees that Daniel's interested and steps forward.

                                              (CONTINUED)

CONTINUED: (2)

> SAM
> No, you've gotta be at least three
> inches away from it whenever it's
> fighting. That way you can fight
> two guys at once.

Daniel thinks about this a second, nodding. He stares at the
geeks in such a way that they can't tell if he thinks they're
crazy or not. Then...

> DANIEL
> (serious)
> Oh. That's pretty cool.

> HARRIS
> Hey, Daniel, we're all playing D&D
> tonight. You wanna come?

Neal, Bill and Gordon look at Harris like he's nuts. Daniel's
a little surprised at the offer.

> DANIEL
> Why?

> HARRIS
> Because I think you'd like it. We
> could show you how to play.

> DANIEL
> (after a beat)
> Nah, I can't do something like
> that.

> NEAL
> Yeah, you wouldn't enjoy it. It's
> really boring.

Sam hears this and steps forward.

> SAM
> No, it isn't, Neal. You love it.
> (to Daniel)
> We just sit around and crack jokes
> and eat junk food all night and
> pretend to fight dragons and save
> princesses and stuff. It's pretty
> fun.

> NEAL
> Yeah, and the best part is you get
> to be somebody you can't be in real
> life.

(CONTINUED)

CONTINUED: (3)

> BILL
> Like Neal gets to pretend he's a
> handsome, funny stud.

Bill laughs as Neal gives him a look. Daniel stares at them.

> DANIEL
> (after a beat)
> Okay. Cool. I'll play.

> NEAL
> Really?

> DANIEL
> Yeah. Just don't expect me to be
> good at it or anything.

> HARRIS
> You can't be any worse than Bill.

> BILL
> Hey!

> HARRIS
> So, Sam, are you in?

> SAM
> Yeah, I guess.

> BILL
> (busting him)
> I thought you were busy... Logan
> the Huge.

Sam gives Bill a look as the geeks look semi-impressed with
themselves.

> FADE OUT.

<u>END OF ACT THREE</u>

<u>ACT FOUR</u>

FADE IN:

INT. BOWLING ALLEY - NIGHT

Lindsay and Ken enter the bowling alley. Ken's on a mission.

> LINDSAY
> Ken, we shouldn't be here. Let Nick
> do what he wants.

(CONTINUED)

CONTINUED:

                    KEN
I can't do that. The poor guy's
brain washed. I can't let him dance
in this stupid contest. It's
against everything we stand for.

                  LINDSAY
Well, I'm not going to stop him.

                    KEN
Just talk to him. At least tell him
he doesn't have a chance with you
so he'll break up with Sara.

                  LINDSAY
I don't think that's gonna work.

                                    CUT TO:

INT. DISCOTHEQUE - NIGHT

DISCO MUSIC.

Nick and Sara are standing off to the side of the dance
floor. The disco is not at all crowded.

                  NICK
Man, I'm nervous.

                  SARA
Don't be nervous. Just go out there
and do all your sexy moves.
        (pulls him close)
Remember, you're the best dancer in
here. Now, get out there and shake
your groove thing.

She gives him a stern but loving smile. Nick looks at her,
uncertain.

                KEN (O.S.)
        (loudly)
Hey, Nick!

Nick looks over. His face falls.

NICK'S POV: Lindsay and Ken are standing in the doorway. Ken
sees Nick and makes a beeline over to him. Lindsay follows.

                                    (CONTINUED)

CONTINUED: (2)

> NICK
> Oh, no.

CUT TO:

INT. WEIR DINING ROOM - NIGHT

Daniel is sitting at the Weir's dining room table, along with Harris, Gordon, Sam, Bill and Neal. They are all set up to play Dungeons and Dragons. They have dice in front of them along with pads of paper. Harris sits behind a "screen," which is a foot high folded piece of cardboard which hides his dice and books. There is junk food and pop on the table.

> HARRIS
> (to Daniel)
> Okay, first you need to create a
> character. Roll your dice to find
> your ability scores.

> DANIEL
> What's that?

> SAM
> They tell you if you're strong or
> smart and if you're good with
> weapons or not.

> DANIEL
> (to Harris)
> What's your character? Like some
> super smart guy?

> HARRIS
> I don't have a character. I'm the
> Dungeon Master. I control the game
> and act out all the characters
> you'll encounter.

> DANIEL
> So, that means you're in charge?

> HARRIS
> You got it, bub.

> GORDON
> And watch out for him, Daniel. He's
> sneaky.

(CONTINUED)

CONTINUED:

                    BILL
          Yeah, he thinks that being a
          Dungeon Master is a license to mess
          with our heads.

                    HARRIS
          Oh, I'm sorry. I guess I should let
          you encounter kittens and grandmas
          so as not to upset you.

                    SAM
          C'mon, Daniel. Roll the dice. Let's
          see what your character's going to
          be.

                    DANIEL
          All right. Here goes nothing.

Daniel scoops up the dice and shakes them.

                                        CUT TO:

INT. DISCOTHEQUE - NIGHT

Ken and Lindsay walk up to Nick and Sara.

                    SARA
          Lindsay and Kenny showed up to
          cheer you on. That's so great. Hey,
          guys.

                    KEN
             (walking up to them)
          Nick, Lindsay has something she
          wants to say to you.

                    LINDSAY
          No, I don't.

                    KEN
          Yes, you do.

                    LINDSAY
          Ken! Stop it. Nick, I'm sorry about
          this. It's just that Ken--

Just then, the music goes down.

                    DEEJAY
             (over the loudspeaker)
          Hey, everybody, check it out.
                    (MORE)

                                   (CONTINUED)

CONTINUED:
                    DEEJAY (CONT'D)
          It's our opinionated little rock
          and roller friend.

Ken looks around.

                    KEN
          Who's he talking about?

                    LINDSAY
          I think he's talking about you.

Lindsay points. They look up at the deejay booth. The DEEJAY
is indeed looking right at Ken. He continues to talk to Ken
over the loudspeaker.

                    DEEJAY
          Hey, man, aren't you one of the
          guys who's always yelling into here
          that disco sucks?

Ken looks completely uncomfortable as the patrons all turn
and look at him.

                    DEEJAY
          What's the matter, man? You can
          only communicate by yelling into
          doors and running away? Is that
          what rock and roll teaches you?

                    KEN
               (calling back)
          Uh, no, man. It teaches me that
          disco sucks.

The crowd reacts. Lindsay looks mortified. Sara does, too.

                    NICK
          Ken, don't.

                    KEN
          What, man? The guy asked me a
          question.

                    DEEJAY
          Yeah? Well, you know what, man?
          Rock and roll sucks. You hear the
          Rolling Stones "Miss You" album?
          They've gone disco. They're willing
          to admit that rock is dead. Why
          can't you?

Nick hears this and looks embarrassed. Lindsay doesn't know
what to do.

                                        (CONTINUED)

CONTINUED: (2)

> KEN
> Me? This place is empty. Disco is
> dead, man. Give it up. Why don't
> you go back to selling shirts at
> the mall?

Just then, a BOUNCER comes over to Ken.

> BOUNCER
> All right, man. Let's go.

> NICK
> Oh, great. Way to go, Ken.

> DEEJAY
> Disco ain't dead, man! Disco's
> alive! You know it. The whole
> world knows it! And Ms. Gloria
> Gaynor knows it too.

MUSIC UP: GLORIA GAYNOR'S "I WILL SURVIVE"

The crowd cheers weakly for the deejay. As the bouncer pulls
Ken away past Lindsay...

> KEN
> (to Lindsay)
> Where the hell's Daniel when you
> need him?

                                                              CUT TO:

INT. WEIR DINING ROOM - NIGHT

Daniel is staring at the geeks as they sit around the table.

> DANIEL
> Wait a minute? I've gotta be a
> <u>dwarf</u>? Why can't I be a fighter?

> SAM
> Dwarves <u>are</u> fighters. They're
> really good at it.

> DANIEL
> (to Neal)
> Are you a dwarf?

> NEAL
> (insulted)
> No, I'm Kragenmore the Destroyer.

                                                        (CONTINUED)

CONTINUED:

                         DANIEL
          Well, I don't wanna be a dwarf. I
          wanna be some huge guy.

                         HARRIS
          Dwarves can do a lot of things that
          huge guys can't do.

                         GORDON
          It's true. Take it from me.

                         SAM
          Daniel, dwarves are really tough.
          And they're good at finding jewels.

                         DANIEL
          Yeah? Really?
              (thinks a beat)
          Okay. I'll be a dwarf. But my name
          is Carlos.

                         BILL
          Carlos the dwarf?

                         DANIEL
              (tough)
          Yeah. You got a problem with that,
          Gorthon?

                         BILL
          No, not at all.

Daniel breaks into a smile as the geeks crack up. Bill sighs
relief.

                                             CUT TO:

INT. BOWLING ALLEY - NIGHT

Nick and Lindsay follow as Ken is carted out of the bowling
alley by the bouncer.

                         NICK
              (calling after)
          You know what, man? Thanks a lot.
          Thanks for embarrassing me. Now
          I've gotta go in there and dance in
          front of those people.

                                           (CONTINUED)

CONTINUED:

> KEN
> Gee, Nick, best of luck. I mean it.
> Give me a call when you get over
> your Saturday Night Fever.

Nick and Lindsay stop as the bouncer takes Ken to the door.
Before he puts him outside, the bouncer leans in to Ken.

> BOUNCER
> Hey, I agree with you, man. This
> place sucks. And you're right.
> They're closing the disco next week
> and bringin' in Foxy Boxing. Come
> back and check it out. Rock and
> roll.

Ken gives him an "oh, you hate disco too" smile as the
bouncer closes the door on him. Nick starts heading back to
the disco, upset. Lindsay follows.

> NICK
> What's wrong with that guy? Why's
> he gotta give me such a hard time
> about this?

> LINDSAY
> He's just confused. Ken's got it in
> his head that you're doing all this
> stuff to... I don't know. To get me
> back.

Nick stops at the snack counter. He sits and turns to
Lindsay.

> NICK
> That's so not true.

> LINDSAY
> I know. I told him that but he
> wouldn't listen.

> NICK
> I'm with Sara now, you know? I'm
> not some idiot. You told me to move
> on and I did.

> LINDSAY
> I know. I think it's great.

(CONTINUED)

CONTINUED: (2)

>   NICK
>   Yeah. Well, it is. Sara's the best.
>   She's really opened me up to new
>   things. And she loves me, you know?
>   I mean, that's important.

>   LINDSAY
>   It is. I'm really happy for you,
>   Nick.

Nick looks at Lindsay, studying her. She gives him a sincere
smile. He suddenly sounds like a guy trying to convince
himself of something.

>   NICK
>   Yeah, well, you should be. You know
>   what? I'm not even smoking pot
>   anymore. It's like I don't even
>   want to now. I've like completely
>   cleaned myself up.

>   LINDSAY
>   (surprised by this)
>   God, Nick. That's so great. I knew
>   something was different. You just
>   seem like you're having more fun
>   than you ever did with me.

>   NICK
>   Well, you know...I am.

>   LINDSAY
>   That's great, Nick.

They look at each other a beat. Then...

>   LINDSAY (CONT'D)
>   Well, I'm gonna get going. I've got
>   a lot of reading to do for the
>   Academic Summit. And I should start
>   studying for finals.

>   NICK
>   Yeah. I'm gonna do that, too. After
>   I win the dance contest.

>   LINDSAY
>   Good luck.

Lindsay gives him a smile and heads for the door. As Nick
watches her go, his face starts to fall. We can see in his
eyes that he's still completely in love with Lindsay.

                                              (CONTINUED)

CONTINUED: (3)

MUSIC UP: HEATWAVE'S "GROOVE LINE"

> DEEJAY (O.C.)
> All right, everybody. We're gonna
> shake some groove things 'cause
> it's time for the disco contest.
> Let's bring up our first contestant
> of the night, Mr. Nick Andopolis!

Nick hears this as he's staring after Lindsay. Sara comes out and gets him.

> SARA
> Nick, you're up. C'mon, baby. It's
> time to boogie oogie oogie.

Nick turns and looks at Sara. She gives him a big smile. He looks at her strangely, nods and heads into the disco.

                                                    CUT TO:

INT. DISCOTHEQUE - CONTINUOUS

Nick makes the long walk through the disco to the dance floor. Sara walks with him, looking proud. As Nick walks, he looks like he's getting madder and madder. He glances back toward the door a couple of times.

INTERCUT WITH:

INT. BOWLING ALLEY - CONTINUOUS

Lindsay is walking out of the bowling alley. As she walks, she seems a little sad. However, her face slowly gets a tiny smile, as if she were thinking that she had just done the right thing.

                                                 CUT BACK TO:

INT. DISCOTHEQUE - CONTINUOUS

Finally, Nick gets to the dance floor and starts dancing. However, it's an angry dance. His face is dead serious as he does his moves. It's obvious that he's choreographed his dance but it's still very simple.

His anger makes him seem like a much better dancer. However, it's still not that impressive of a routine. People watch fairly impassively, except for Sara, who claps and cheers.

                                                  (CONTINUED)

54.

CONTINUED:

Nick continues to dance, in his own world, looking like he's trying to get back at Lindsay with his moves.

                                              CUT TO:

INT. WEIR DINING ROOM - NIGHT

Sam, Neal, Bill and Daniel are all listening to Harris intently.

                    HARRIS
          You enter a dark cave. You can hear
          the scurrying of rats' nails on the
          dampened stone.

                    BILL
          Eww, gross. I hate rats.

                    NEAL
          Exactly how <u>damp</u> is it in here?
          Because Kragenmore's just getting
          over the flu...

                    DANIEL
          Awww. Wanna borrow Carlos' coat?

                    NEAL
          Sorry, I think it's too small.

                    HARRIS
          A fierce gust of wind blows out
          your torches just as a large
          boulder crashes down behind you,
          sealing off your only exit.

                    GORDON
          Oh, great. Thanks for making us
          come in here, Gorthon.

                    BILL
          Hey, I wasn't gonna go to the
          bathroom outside.

                    HARRIS
          You consult your map and see that
          the cave leads only to the Pit of
          Eternal Doom.

The geeks look at each other. What do they do? Then...

                                         (CONTINUED)

CONTINUED: (2)

> DANIEL
> How can we read the map if it's
> dark in here?

> HARRIS
> It's not completely dark.

> DANIEL
> Then that means there's a hole in
> the cave somewhere. And I'm betting
> that Carlos is small enough to
> climb through it.

> HARRIS
> It's possible. Roll your dice and
> find out.

The geeks look at Daniel, impressed, as Danie[
roll.

> NEAL
> Good thinking, Daniel.

> DANIEL
> (pleased with himself)
> Thanks, man.

Daniel picks up his dice to roll as the gee[

NOTE: WE'LL ALSO SHOOT RANDOM D&D AS EACH P[
DICE TO SEE IF THEY CAN ACCOMPLISH SOMETHIN
REACTING TO EACH ROLL AND HAVING A GREAT, A
CAN BE INTERCUT IN MUSIC MONTAGE WITH NICK

INT. DISCOTHEQUE - NIGHT

Nick is still dancing.

> DEE JAY
> All right, Mr. Andopolis, it's
> for you to clear the floor and
> way for the next competitor. L[
> and gentlemen, I'd like you al
> put your hands together for th
> magical disco stylings of...Eu

Nick exits the floor. Sara runs up to h[

CONTINUED:

> SARA
> You were great, Nick. You were so
> great. You're gonna win for sure.

Nick forces a smile as EUGENE, an odd guy dressed in a disco
suit and fedora hat, takes the floor. Nick watches him.

Eugene starts to dance but after a few seconds, he throws his
hand out the side. A black cane suddenly appears. It's one of
those magic store appearing canes. The crowd reacts.

> NICK
> Hey, they didn't say you could do
> magic.

Eugene starts dancing and begins pulling colored silks out of
his sleeve. The crowd seems to enjoy this and APPLAUDS. Even
Sara seems to enjoy it as Eugene pulls out another silk.

> SARA
> Wow, that's pretty cool.

Eugene continues to dance and do the cut-and-restored rope
trick as Nick stares in disbelief.

CUT TO:

INT. WEIR DINING ROOM - NIGHT

The geeks are all laughing and having a great time. Daniel
stands up and talks to Harris in some strange voice.

> DANIEL
> Greetings, Princess, it is I,
> Carlos the dwarf. The dragon has
> been slain and you are now free to
> rule your kingdom again. That is,
> once you pay me five hundred
> rubies!

The geeks crack up. Daniel looks around at them proudly as
Harris closes his Dungeon Masters Guide.

> HARRIS
> Congratulations, Daniel. You just
> finished your first D&D campaign.

The geeks all APPLAUD for him. Daniel looks beyond happy.

> DANIEL
> Hey, we should do this again
> tomorrow night.

(CONTINUED)

CONTINUED:

          SAM
Sure.

          BILL
I would, except Harris killed me
again.

          DANIEL
You can kick his ass tomorrow
night, Bill. Just leave it to
Carlos. Hey, I'm gonna grab a pop.
You want anything?

The geeks shake their heads "no." Daniel smiles and heads
into the kitchen, looking happy. The geeks all lean in to pow-
wow.

          GORDON
Wow, he's a pretty cool guy.

          BILL
Does him wanting to play with us
again mean that he's turning into a
geek...or that we're turning into
cool guys?

They think about this a second. Then...

          SAM
I'm not sure, but I'm gonna go for
us being cool guys.

          NEAL
I'll buy that.

The geeks all look at each other and feel a lot better about
themselves.

                        CUT TO:

EXT. BUS STATION - DAY

Jean, Harold and Sam are walking Lindsay out to her bus.
Harold is carrying her suitcase.

          JEAN
You sure you don't want us to drive
you to U of M? We don't mind.

          LINDSAY
No, Mom, that's okay. I'd kinda
like to do this.
          (MORE)

                      (CONTINUED)

CONTINUED:

> LINDSAY (CONT'D)
> You know, so I can get my head
> together before I get there.

> JEAN
> Oh, okay. I understand.

They stop in front of the waiting bus. Jean hugs Lindsay.

> JEAN (CONT'D)
> Oh, honey, we're so proud of you.
> You go and have a great time.

> HAROLD
> Yeah, go and make the Weirs proud.
> Be smarter than all those other
> kids.

> JEAN
> (giggling)
> Oh, Harold, really.

> SAM
> Have a good time, Lindsay. I'll
> miss you.

> LINDSAY
> Thanks, Sam. But I'll only be gone
> for a couple of weeks. You'll never
> even know I'm gone.

Lindsay gives Sam a kiss on the cheek. Just then, Neal and
Bill run up.

> NEAL
> Lindsay! Wait! I've got something
> for you.
> (hands her a box)
> It's chocolates. Something sweet
> for your trip.

> BILL
> Hey, we always give my grandma
> chocolates when we put her on a
> bus. That and we pin her name and
> address on her coat in case she
> gets lost.

> LINDSAY
> Thanks, Neal. That's nice of you.

Lindsay gives Neal a kiss on the cheek. Neal smiles. Then
Lindsay gives Bill a kiss on the cheek too.

(CONTINUED)

CONTINUED: (2)

>   NEAL
>   Hey, he didn't get you anything.

>   LINDSAY
>   That's just for coming down.

>   BILL
>   Wow, that didn't cost me a cent.

Lindsay laughs and picks up her suitcase. She turns and
smiles at her family.

>   LINDSAY
>   I'll see you guys soon.

>   HAROLD
>   Okay, honey. We'll see you.

MUSIC UP: THE GRATEFUL DEAD'S "BROKEDOWN PALACE" (MUSIC WILL
PLAY THROUGH TO END OF SHOW)

Lindsay nods and starts to get on the bus. She stops and
turns back to her parents. She looks slightly troubled.

>   LINDSAY
>   Mom?

>   JEAN
>   Yes, sweetie?

>   LINDSAY
>   (after a beat)
>   I'll see you soon.

>   JEAN
>   Okay, honey.

>   LINDSAY
>   Okay. Love you.

Lindsay gets on the bus as Harold, Jean, Sam, Neal and Bill
wave goodbye.

>   CUT TO:

INT. BUS - CONTINUOUS

Lindsay gets on the bus and finds a seat. She looks around.
The bus is pretty empty. She looks out the window again.

>   (CONTINUED)

60.

CONTINUED:

LINDSAY'S POV: Everybody waves to her. Lindsay waves back, looking a little troubled. She SIGHS as the bus starts to move.

DISSOLVE TO:

INT. BUS - DAY

Later on. Lindsay is sitting on the bus, lost in thought. The BUS DRIVER calls out.

> BUS DRIVER
> All right, everybody. Lunch stop.

CUT TO:

EXT. ANOTHER BUS STATION - DAY

The bus pulls up to a station. A few people get off. Then Lindsay steps off, carrying her suitcase. She looks around. Sees something and smiles.

LINDSAY'S POV: Kim is leaning against a car, arms folded. She breaks into a smile.

Lindsay laughs and starts to head over. As she approaches, we see that behind Kim are Victor and Laurie, the Deadheads.

They are standing next to a VW Microbus that has Grateful Dead symbols painted on it.

Lindsay walks up to Kim. Kim gives her a hug. Victor takes Lindsay's suitcase and puts it in the van.

They all jump into the van. It starts up, then drops into gear.

The VW Microbus pulls out onto the road and heads off.

FADE OUT.

<u>END OF SHOW</u>

FREAKS AND GEEKS.

Scrapbook

At school, it was probably the ostracizing of a kid nicknamed "Groucho" because of his thick eyebrows and resemblance to said Groucho. A popular kid, Sam LaBonia, said he saw Groucho beating off in the showers freshmen year and the kid's high school career was ruined. I knew it wasn't true but the kid could not walk down the halls without being mocked for his entire four years.

*Nr.1
calls
that*

Or.

17) Geeks take No-Doze and go bananas.

Sam Weir is 13 and what we currently refer to as a "geek." He's not a nerd in the classical Hollywood sense -- he doesn't wear glasses with tape in the middle or snort when he laughs. He's not even into computer programming. He's just part of the group in school that didn't really fall into any category.

He and his friends are all a little backwards and immature. They're obsessed with things like Monty Python, Warner Brothers cartoons and *Star Wars*. They work on the school plays and in the Audio/Visual room.

They think about girls from time to time, but only as mysterious and sometimes scary creatures. The thought of sex overwhelms them -- the concept of being exposed both physically and emotionally in front of a female other than their mothers is far too terrifying to even consider. Imagining themselves on a date that ends with a kiss on the lips is about the most that they can handle without having their minds blown.

7. WHAT KIND OF MAN READS PLAYBOY?
After carefully studying Playboy, Neal decides that he IS the Man who reads Playboy. Of course, the only thing that is missing is a mustache -- so he grows one and with comes a whole new and DANGEROUS Neal.

9) SAM HAS INCESSANT BONERS.

Bill Haverchuck - a mentally slow tall guy, Bill is another of Sam's core entourage and a guy no one can figure out. He's seems like he should be in special ed and there's been times that the school has tried to place him there, but he and his mom refuse to go along with it. So, Bill gets bad grades but he tries as best he can.

Bill is an only child and a TV junkie, spending most of his hours in front of the set. He's a science fiction and comedy fan like the other geeks but, then again, he's a fan of everything. There's constantly arguments going on because Bill thinks that "Silver Spoons" and "Different Strokes" are the two funniest shows on TV.

Bill's also given to excessive daydreaming and is just this side of being a pathological liar. He believes everything that everybody tells him and is constantly passing on bad information. If there's one source for every untrue rumor in the school, it's Bill. He's also one of those guys who you never know if he's serious or not. Lots of what he says can either be taken as him being dumb and not understanding what you're saying or else he's just giving you shit. He does both, so there's no way to even tell (he's constantly getting almost beaten up by both jocks and freaks because of this). Bill's problems in class and in life are due to the fact that he probably has Attention Deficit D

Retarded guy bumps into cool guy in cafeteria. ❦ "Watch where you're going, you retard!" "I'm not a retard! He's a retard." Points at really retarded guy. Constant battle against people thinking he's retarded, even though he's in special ed. He's just big and slow.

Neal Schweiber - One of Sam's entourage, Neal is strangely self-confident for being a rather odd looking guy. He's got an underbite and a fleshy face that makes him look like a cartoon bulldog. His hair is thick and he's constantly running his hands through it in class when he's deep in thought, causing it to stick straight up in the air when he removes his hand. This is the cause of much hilarity, both among the geeks and the other students, jocks and all, who have classes with Neal.

Neal is very smart and is usually the top student in his classes, especially science. However, intelligence seems to be in his genes. His father, **Jost**, immigrated from Germany with his wife, **Berta**, soon after they were married. Jost is a surgeon and Berta is a medical researcher. Jost works as the head surgeon at one of Detroit's main hospitals and Berta works for a local drug company doing testing on animals (this will pit her against Lindsay in an episode, in which Lindsay will try to champion the cause of animal rights and basically turn Neal's mother into a pariah to many in the school).

(handwritten diagonal note:)

R. Daniel has sex with quarterback? illfated the causing ...

Daniel Krantz - One of Lindsay's best friends, Daniel was her gateway to the freaks. It was Daniel whom Lindsay met the day she walked up in front of the 7-11 and asked to try a cigarette. He's one half of the school's "mature" couple, his girlfriend being Kim Kelly. They're the couple that everyone in school knows is sexually activ[e]

Daniel lives on his own, having split from his parents recently. His parents, C[...] and **Eugenia**, are bona fide trailer trash and are so into drugs and alcohol that they d[o] even notice that Daniel's gone. They live on welfare and will most likely end up dead soon. Daniel loves them but has, for his own self-preservation, given up on them completely. Occasionally, he brings them groceries or pizza but he gets so depressed [by the] way they live that keeps his visits few and far between.

Daniel works as a pizza delivery guy, a job he loves because it's another way [for] him to meet women. It's also a great job because he gets to eat all the [...] In fact, pizza is about all Daniel eats -- pizza and Hostess SnoBalls. T[his may lead to] him being fat later in life but for now, he's a good looking guy wh[...] keeps him looking fit.

Daniel is a guy with literally no ambition. He knows th[at ...] what he wants to do with his life but he just can't get that excite[d ...] spends all his time and energy fixing and souping up his rusty c[ar ...] that he might have some kind of mechanic job in his future. But once again, [...] excites him. He just likes to hang out, smoke pot, do the occasional drug and watch [...] he has any dream, it's to move to Hawaii and do nothing but smoke pot all day and e[njoy] the nice weather.

Daniel's also a bit of a cat and he really wants to have sex with everything aro[und] him. It's not a malicious act for him -- he just can't help himself. He knows he's att[ractive] and he's supremely confident and so he literally can't help but hit on every female in [...] school including teachers. This drives Kim crazy and they have an understanding th[at ...]

Lindsay Weir is a modern day, female Holden Ca[ulfield]. She's 16 and has just gone through a major change[...] been a devoted student. She was easily on her way to being [a...] model girl, believing in God, believing in her future and bel[ieving in her] place.

Then her grandmother died -- a vibrant woman who[...] It challenged Lindsay['s belief in] everything. It sent h[er into a] Plath-reading malaise[...]

(partial right margin list:)

- Intim[...]
with princip[...]
- Mean nicknam[...]
- Principal's office se[...]
- Janitors! Hall monitor[...]
- When teachers are ma[...]
you put his wife down[...]

ething to do with cars. In all actuality, he'll probably end up working on an assembly
like his father used to.

Kim Kelly - a tough, angry freak girl. She's the leader of a small group of tough
, that also includes **Karen Scarfolli** and **Sue Caralich**. They are in many ways
es like Alan White and his group, except that Kim has the possibility to be much more
gerous. The product of an abusive home, Kim keeps her family life to herself and
ead channels her negative energy into the confrontation and verbal abuse of anybody she
siders old (which is anybody over 30).

Kim's father, **Arlo**, is an alcoholic who has physically abused her in the past. Not
ally but through beatings and other forms of physical punishment. Arlo is a frustrated
. Frustrated by his life, frustrated by his career, frustrated by his family. He had
ms of being a stock car racer that vanished the minute he knocked up his then girlfriend
now wife, **Cookie**. Vowing to do the right thing -- getting married, getting a job,
ing his dreams aside -- he's regretted every minute of it. However, he's too much of a
s to leave them and too much of a mess to actually be a good father.

And so, Arlo drinks. He has a job at an auto parts store (he bounces from job to job
always gets fired for insubordination) but hasn't really gotten any kind of a promotion
ears. He's too irresponsible and bad with the customers to be a manager and so he's
ty much relegated to running the stockroom. Being around people who know about
is the only joy he gets out of life and so the auto parts store is the only place that he's
remotely happy at. All tolled, Arlo's a guy
ver left his family.

Cookie, Kim's mother, is an immature
hering. She works part time as a hair dress
paying job doesn't provide. Cookie's alw
ossible task of keeping Arlo happy and so
ling them to their rooms whenever Arlo d
fear that Arlo may leave her and so will do
y is that Arlo would probably like her mu
ing on him hand and foot).

Kim has an older brother, **Chip**, wh
in the house has taken its toll on him.
time. He keeps a room in the house bu
re Chip goes but it's a pretty good bet t

- aduf who get kids

ssessing they teach fudery in an
nglish class. "Liberal" teacher
t me to discipline - admissive

ade lord beast the shit out of

Cold open - under bleachers
intro (geeks reference geeks?)
Act I - meet geeks in cafeteria, meet freaks on
smoking patio, one of
Lindsay's old friends asks
her why she's gone over.

Football couple - You just
seem so distant! I need
to know that you're committed
to me. Teen soap type talk
Ends with kiss.
Freaks - a discussion
about the existence of
God as they pass a joint
Geeks - acting out WB
cartoons
Lindsay comes over and gets
Sam, says mom and dad
want them home for dinner.

RANDOM IDEAS BASED ON A FEW EMOTIONS:
RAGE

- Bill wants to beat the shit out of Sam after Sam befriends a girl Bill likes
- Daniel gets in a fist fight with Mr. Kowchevski
- Lindsay keys Mr. Rosso's car
- Ken and Nick get into a fist fight over Lindsay
- Neal tries to beat up Mr. Fredricks
- The freaks beat the shit out of Alan

- Millie gets mad at Lindsay and plants a gun on her
- Daniel sets the auto shop on fire
- Lindsay and Sam start to hate each other
- Neal tries to burn the school down
- Nick destroys his drums when he realizes he's not good
- The freaks vandalize Ken's neighbors after they call the cops on a freak
- Sam tries to fight Daniel after Daniel sleeps with the drama teacher
- Neal wants to kill Bill when Bill won't stop touching Neal's hair

POSSIBLE REVELATIONS
- Daniel has a one year old son
- Ken's gay
- Sam's adopted
- Bill's dad is a Hell's Angel
- Millie's being molested by her father

...the most embarrasin
in high school. My frien
messages. I started being
my pants and the chair I
accident by spilling diet
that I had a 'medical con
wore a Harvard sweatshir

LUST
- Ken becomes obsessed with Lindsay and stalks her
- Bill becomes addicted to masturbation
- Millie tries to get Daniel to take her virginity
- Mr. Rosso falls in love with Lindsay
- Sam finds Mr. Kowchevski screwing a lunch lady
- Bill becomes obsessed with the cheerleaders
- Ms. Noble gets drunk and tries to seduce Sam
- Millie tutors Ken and Ken tries to sleep with her
- Nick gets high with Kim and they have sex
- Kim helps Bill lose his virginity

JEALOUSY
- Neal becomes jealous of Sam's happy parents
- Bill falls in love with Kim and wants to fight Daniel
- Ken wants Nick's drums
- Harold Weir becomes jealous of Daniel's looks and youth
- Jean becomes jealous of Sam's relationship with Ms. Noble

FRUSTRATION
- Bill hates being told he's stupid and wants to drop out
- Bill terrorizes Millie because she makes him feel stupid in class
- Neal starts being mean to girls because they laugh at his size
- Sam gets fed up with Alan and starts terrorizing him
- Nick gets mad at school band for not letting him join, so he smash
equipment
- Ken gets suspended from auto shop and goes on a drug binge

Sam -

Overall look: Sam looks like a kid who cares about how he l
dresses more for comfort and his fashion sense is limited to
wearing and then trying to approximate their look. He think
in his clothes (everything looks fine to him from head-on in
that what he can't see doesn't really hang well). He's not so
poorly made clothes.

Shirts: Pullover Velour V-neck shirts with collar (a little bagg
knit pullover with zipper V-neck and collar (white stripe on e
terrycloth pullover with 2 or 3 button V-neck and collar (sho
than rest of shirt, with a stripe on each

the fact that the class was right after lunch and we were crashing fro
was the class was just boring as hell.

17)   What's the dumbest thing you ever did in high sc
I did a drawing of Rob Kraft, this cool guy I had a crush on who w
Then I submitted it to the school literary magazine. It was publish
thought I was a desperate, crazy stalker and never talked to me ag

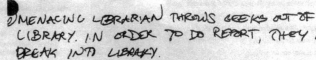

2 MENACING LIBRARIAN THROWS GEEKS OUT OF
LIBRARY. IN ORDER TO DO REPORT, THEY MUST
BREAK INTO LIBRARY.

The arrival of Dawn - One day, a new student arrives at McKinley. It is Dawn, a very fat girl. She walks down the hall quite confidently, carrying herself as if she were proud of the fact that she was obese. We see people laughing behind her back and a few make jokes to her face but it doesn't really seem to phase her. In fact, whenever somebody makes fun of her, she picks their one most obvious flaw and makes fun of *them*. This usually shuts down all her critics. In drama class, as Sam is painting some scenery, Dawn walks in and informs Ms. Noble that she wants to join the drama club as a costumer. She's funny and full of life. Sam jokes around with her a bit and the two hit it off immediately. Throughout the day, they run into each other and never fail to make each other laugh. Sam introduces her to the geeks. Bill makes a joke about her weight (not a mean joke, just more of a dumb observation) and she immediately fires back a comment about his glasses that cracks up Sam and Neal. She is immediately okay with the geeks and they all become friends. However, she and Sam seem to have a special bond. (Dawn will be in the show throughout and will cause Sam much confusion as he realizes that Dawn is the perfect girlfriend for him, except for the fact that he can't get around the fact that she's so overweight. It becomes the source of much guilt as he realizes that he should be able to look past her excessive weight and yet he simply cannot when comes to thinking of her as a romantic interest. Dawn, however, knows that they'd make a good couple and as the season goes on, she will drop more and more hints to Sam that they should become a couple.)

The Arrival of Earl - One day, the first black kid ever to attend McKinley arrives. He's a very quiet and detached freshman named Earl. Earl has a big afro but he's on the short side and wears glasses. He's very quiet but not in a shy way. He just seems to not be aware or care about anyth... ound him. Being the only black kid, he immediately becomes the kid ... vith, for the novelty of it. He pretty much blows everyone ... ne of day. He seems to be in his own world. The geeks ... actually ... him.

13. WHO DID I WISH I WAS.

Again, only because you asked.

I wished I was Scott Turner. Scott was my age and was one of the most popular kids in the school. We never really hung out as friends but I got to know him a little my Junior year. He was super athletic, but also of a dope smoker. He wore cool hippie clothes all the time including every once in awhile a bandanna on his head -- very hip. He even wore his hair in a curly perm (remember when guys got perms?). Scott was a member of the student government and Key Club so he was attached to and well liked by everyone in the school.

All this was fine and dandy but Scott had even more than good looks, popularity, and charm -- he had a girlfriend who was a Senior that would give him a blow job in the parking lot every single day during lunch. I wanted to be Scott but knew deep down that I never would or could be him.

To all the loyal fans of *Freaks and Geeks*
who refused to forget about us.
Thanks for keeping us alive.

Pictured (left to right), back row: Dave (Gruber) Allen ("Mr. Rosso"), Jason Segel ("Nick Andopolis"), John Daley ("Sam Weir"), Seth Rogen ("Ken Miller"), Martin Starr ("Bill Haverchuck"); middle row: Busy Philipps ("Kim Kelly"), Natasha Melnick ("Cindy Sanders"), James Franco ("Daniel Desario"), Paul Feig (Creator/Co-Executive Producer), Steve Bannos ("Mr. Kowchevski"); front row: Tom Wilson ("Mr. Fredricks"), Sarah Hagan ("Millie Kentner"), Linda Cardellini ("Lindsay Weir"), Samm Levine ("Neal Schweiber"), Judd Apatow (Executive Producer), Michael Beardsley (just one of our many, many talented and hard-working background artists)

The Only Official Companion Books to *Freaks and Geeks* Available from Newmarket Press

Published for the first time in November 2004, the books feature exclusive introductions by Paul Feig and Judd Apatow and commentaries by the writers of each episode, plus never-before-published scrapbooks of behind-the-scenes photos, memos, and notes. Though only airing for 18 episodes, the DreamWorks television comedy/drama (NBC, 1999-2000) earned extraordinary acclaim and a devoted fan base. This two-volume set allows longtime fans and first-timers alike to enjoy the writing behind one of television's most poignant and funny programs about high school.

Freaks and Geeks: The Complete Scripts, Volume 1

The first volume collects the first nine shooting scripts (episodes 1-9) of the Emmy® Award–winning series, including the pilot episode directed by Jake Kasdan, and is introduced by creator Paul Feig. The book features individual commentary from the writers of each episode plus a scrapbook that reveals the writers' own high school experiences, ideas that were never developed, internal memos, and more.

624 pages • 6⅛" x 9¼" • 15 b&w photos
1-55704-645-X • $19.95 ($29.95 Can.) • Paperback

Freaks and Geeks: The Complete Scripts, Volume 2

This second volume collects the final nine teleplays (episodes 10-18) of the Emmy® Award–winning series, and is introduced by executive producer Judd Apatow. The book features individual remarks from the writers of each episode plus a scrapbook that reveals even more behind-the-scenes details, including photos, additional storyline ideas, and fascinating character descriptions.

624 pages • 6⅛" x 9¼" • 15 b&w photos
1-55704-646-8 • $19.95 ($29.95 Can.) • Paperback

Newmarket Press books are available from your local bookseller or directly from the publisher. Prices and availability are subject to change. Catalogs and information on quantity order discounts are available on request.

Newmarket Press, 18 E. 48th Street, New York, NY 10017;
phone: 212-832-3575 or 800-669-3903; fax: 212-832-3629;
e-mail: mailbox@newmarketpress.com.
www.newmarketpress.com